CHILDREN AND ASCETICISM IN
LATE ANTIQUITY

In memoriam magistrae magistrorumque meorum

Omnia mutantur, nihil interit

(Ovid, *Metamorphoses* 15.165)

Children and Asceticism in Late Antiquity

Continuity, Family Dynamics and the Rise of Christianity

VILLE VUOLANTO

University of Oslo, Norway and University of Tampere, Finland

ASHGATE

© Ville Vuolanto 2015

All rights reserved. No part of this publication may be reproduced, stored in a retrieval system or transmitted in any form or by any means, electronic, mechanical, photocopying, recording or otherwise without the prior permission of the publisher.

Ville Vuolanto has asserted his right under the Copyright, Designs and Patents Act, 1988, to be identified as the author of this work.

Published by
Ashgate Publishing Limited
Wey Court East
Union Road
Farnham
Surrey, GU9 7PT
England

Ashgate Publishing Company
110 Cherry Street
Suite 3-1
Burlington, VT 05401-3818
USA

www.ashgate.com

British Library Cataloguing in Publication Data
A catalogue record for this book is available from the British Library

The Library of Congress has cataloged the printed edition as follows:
Vuolanto, Ville.
  Children and asceticism in late antiquity : continuity, family dynamics, and the rise of Christianity / by Ville Vuolanto.
    pages cm
  Includes bibliographical references and index.
   ISBN 978-1-4724-1436-6 (hardcover) -- ISBN 978-1-4724-1437-3 (ebook) -- ISBN 978-1-4724-1438-0 (epub) 1. Asceticism--History--Early church, ca. 30-600. 2. Families--Religious life. 3. Parent and child--Religious aspects--Christianity. I. Title.
  BV5023.V86 2015
  270.2--dc23

2014036491

ISBN 9781472414366 (hbk)
ISBN 9781472414373 (ebk – PDF)
ISBN 9781472414380 (ebk – ePUB)

Printed in the United Kingdom by Henry Ling Limited,
at the Dorset Press, Dorchester, DT1 1HD

Contents

Preface		*vii*
1	Approaches and Strategies	1
2	Family, Kin and the Right Way of Living as a Christian	45
3	Ascetics and the Family of Christ: Metaphors, Family Dynamics and Continuity	69
4	Chastity as Immortality	81
5	Choosing Asceticism: Demography and Decision Making in the Domestic Sphere	95
6	Family Economy and the Profits of Asceticism	131
7	Progeny, Reputation and Memory	147
8	Children, Strategies and Continuity	177
9	Not All of Me Will Die: Conclusions	205
Bibliography		*225*
Index		*257*

Preface

The research project leading to the present book has taken many unexpected twists and turns during a decade. During all its phases, however, I have had the pleasure of being surrounded by able and encouraging teachers, colleagues and friends, contributing to my work with in-depth conversations, advice and practical help, for which I am deeply grateful.

First of all I wish to thank Päivi Setälä, without whose influence and encouragement I would never have ended up an ancient historian. Sadly, she will not read my words of thanks. This work is dedicated to her memory, and to the memory of Heikki Kotila and Juha Sihvola, peerless academic mentors.

This book would never have appeared without the influence of Marjatta Hietala, on whose support and wise advice I have always been able to count, and of Paavo Castrén, who introduced the captivating worlds of Late Antiquity to me. Antti Arjava, Judith Evans Grubbs and Ray Laurence have on many different occasions steered me forward in past years. I am deeply indebted to their support and critical guidance.

Elizabeth A. Clark, Mary Harlow, Markku Hyrkkänen, Sari Katajala-Peltomaa, Christian Krötzl, Christian Laes and Katariina Mustakallio have read the manuscript or parts of it, and their comments have been invaluable for the shaping and completion of the book. I also owe thanks to the anonymous referee for the most useful and learned suggestions. They have not only made me further define my argument with their thoughtful criticism, but have also opened up new insights for further work.

In the final phase I have been lucky to be able to work with true professionals: Michael Greenwood from Ashgate, who reliably guided me through the potential pitfalls of publishing, and Brian McNeil, who corrected my written English. Thanks are also due to the Discipline of History at the University of Tampere, and the Department of Philosophy, Classics, History of Art and Ideas (IFIKK) at the University of Oslo for financial support and an innovative working atmosphere. In a crucial phase of the process, a grant by the Finnish Cultural Foundation made it possible to continue the research work. Furthermore, Oxford University Press, Mohr Siebeck and Acta Instituti

Romani Finlandiae have kindly given me permission to partially re-use my work previously published by them (from my chapter 'Children and Memory of the Parents' in *Children, Memory and Family Identity in Roman Culture,* edited by Veronique Dasen and Thomas Spath (Oxford: Oxford University Press, 2010); from my chapter 'Choosing Asceticism: Children and Parents, Vows and Conflicts' in *Children in Late Ancient Christianity,* edited by Cornelia Horn and Robert Phenix (Tübingen: Mohr Siebeck, 2009); and from my article 'Early Christian Communities as Family Networks: Fertile Virgins and Celibate Fathers' (Rome: Institutum Romanum Finlandiae, 2010) respectively).

Lastly, I need to express my gratitude to my family, who have patiently and with love endured my long days, frequent absence and constant enthusiasm for things long past.

Oslo, 13 March 2014, on the feast day of St Eupraxia,
Ville Vuolanto

Chapter 1
Approaches and Strategies

> Does not an industrious peasant plant trees the fruit of which he will never see? Does not a great man found laws, institutions and society itself? What does the procreation of children mean, what the cares to continue our names, what the adoption of children, what the diligence in drawing up wills, what even the inscriptions on monuments and panegyrics, but that our thoughts run on the future, too?[1]

Asceticism became a widespread phenomenon in the Christian world of Late Antiquity, although it had been almost unknown to the mainstream of Greco-Roman culture. At first sight, asceticism was in opposition to traditional family life and its goals of promoting the familial line for coming generations; to remain unmarried was not an option before the rise of Christianity and there was no room for voluntary bachelors and spinsters. This shift was already noted by contemporary authors: as Gregory of Nyssa remarked, motherhood had been seen as a public duty among the Romans, something which he saw as at variance with ascetic Christian values.[2] Indeed, by the end of the fourth century CE, asceticism had found its way into the everyday lives of families and households[3] throughout the Roman world, and the whole idea of married life and family was questioned by celibate sons and daughters. Married couples took vows of abstinence and widows and widowers refused to remarry. How was it possible for this change in attitudes and behaviour to be propagated and

---

[1] Cicero, *Tusculan Disputations* 1.14.31: 'Ergo arbores seret diligens agricola, quarum aspiciet bacam ipse numquam; vir magnus leges, instituta, rem publicam non seret? quid procreatio liberorum, quid propagatio nominis, quid adoptationes filiorum, quid testamentorum diligentia, quid ipsa sepulcrorum monumenta, elogia significant nisi nos futura etiam cogitare?' Unless otherwise noted, all translations are my own.

[2] Gregory of Nyssa, *On Virginity* 19.

[3] As a working definition, by a family I mean the wife and husband (or a lone widow/widower), and other (step-) relatives who lived under the same roof. The Latin word *familia*, in turn, is here used as a synonym for a Roman household including slaves, freedmen and other possible co-resident persons. On these terms, their interrelatedness and problems of definition, see esp. S. Dixon, *The Roman Family* (Baltimore and London, 1992), pp. 1–5. On the continuance of this use of the concept of *familia* in Late Antiquity, see B. Shaw, 'The Family in Late Antiquity: The Experience of Augustine', *Past and Present* 115 (1987), pp. 11–14 and 49–50.

how did it affect actual family relationships, especially between children and their parents?

The beginning of the period covered in my study, the last quarter of the fourth century and the first half of the fifth century, belonged to the wealthy and comparatively peaceful world of Late Antiquity. However, the accumulation of external and internal crises from the 360s onward was quickly gathering pace, especially in the western part of the Roman world, culminating in the Sack of Rome in 410 by Alarik and the Visigoths. If the eastern part of the Empire was able to retain much of its economic and cultural impetus despite constant warfare, for the western Empire, the Vandals taking of Roman Africa in the 430s ushered in the beginning of the final general crisis and impoverishment. Simultaneously there was another change taking place: the Christianization of the society and culture. Christianity became the only legally accepted religion in the Roman Empire at the beginning of the 390s, but there were heated theological debates going on between different Christian groups, such as the Origenist controversies, and disputes between the 'Catholics' and groups like Donatists in North Africa, Pelagians especially in Gaul and North Italy, and Arians in the northern and eastern parts of the Roman Empire.

The different Christianities argued not only over dogma, but also over what was a proper Christian lifestyle and identity, that is, over the essential questions of social and cultural enculturation and differentiation.[4] Asceticism in particular challenged the traditional norms and practices of family life, and the proper place and worth of sexuality, marriage and family for Christian life became an issue of debate. There was a legion of minor groups with strictly dualistic and encratic overtones that highlighted the value of celibacy and shunning marriage. On the other hand, more moderate forms of asceticism gained support among the intellectuals of mainstream ecclesiastical circles in the fourth century, causing disagreements on the proper relationship between Christianity and the traditional social order. There arose an urgent need to define the limits for the 'orthodox' position. Thus, the ecclesiastical writers[5] were led to discuss and to evaluate the traditional forms of thought and practices which in the writings of their predecessors and of non-Christian authors were thought to be self-evident and not worthy of mention, let alone lengthy comment. This is shown clearly, for

---

[4]   On the construction of religious identity in Late Antiquity, see esp. I. Sandwell, *Religious Identity in Late Antiquity: Greeks, Jews and Christians in Antioch* (Cambridge, 2007).

[5]   Here, I will not use the concept of 'church fathers', as it could give an authority and status to their views which they acquired only after the period under scrutiny here. Moreover, the epithet 'father' denotes a special status in the symbolic family sphere, the development of which is scrutinized in the following chapters.

Approaches and Strategies 3

example, in the Jovinianist controversy in Rome of the 380s and 390s over the status of asceticism in the Christian way of life. For the winning side, asceticism represented a higher form of Christianity.[6] For them, the only acceptable reason for sex was to produce offspring; therefore, the discussions of the role of sex and marriage inevitably concerned the 'worth' of children for Christians and for human communities. However, these discussions were by no means begun only by the end of the fourth century and they were neither limited to the western part of the Empire nor to singular polemics.[7] This expansion of the public discourse on the families, real and imagined, even transcended the limits of mainstream Christianities.[8]

It is in these kinds of situations, in times of cultural change and the clash of values, that the former commonplaces had to be re-assessed. In this process, the dominating cultural values, discourses and structures become visible. In the context of Late Antiquity, the collision of two seemingly opposing lifestyles – the ascetic career and family life – offers a perfect case for the testing of a theoretical framework of continuity strategies and for studying the interplay of the early Christian ideology of asceticism and its practical solutions within families.

The world that appears in my study is the world of *honestiores* – not necessarily of senators and the super-rich aristocracy (although some of them will make appearances), or of the more well-off landowners, but rather those who had at least been able to rise above the masses. These elites formed the backbone of the Roman Empire and held public authority, legal privileges and a view of the universal Roman-ness of the Empire as a whole. Among them

---

[6] See P. Brown, *Through the Eye of a Needle: Wealth, the Fall of Rome, and the Making of Christianity in the West, 350–550 AD* (Princeton, 2012), esp. pp. xxv and 50–52; D. Hunter, *Marriage, Celibacy, and Heresy in Ancient Christianity: The Jovinianist Controversy* (Oxford, 2007), esp. pp. 2, 5, 11–12; K. Cooper, *The Virgin and the Bride: Idealized Womanhood in Late Antiquity* (Cambridge, MA, 1996), pp. 88–91, 114–15.

[7] See e.g. Augustine, *On Marriage and Concupiscence*, 1.4 (5); *Letters*, 130.16.29; *Enchridion* 21.78; *On the Good of Marriage*, 9 (9) and 13 (15); Jerome, *Against Jovinian*, 1.19; *Consultations of Zacchaeus and Apollonius* 3.1.13; Gregory Nazianzen, *Oration 37*, 9; with e.g. Clemens of Alexandria, *Stromata*, 2.23.137–42, 3.12.79 and 82 and discussion below in Chapter 2.

[8] See e.g. Hunter, *Marriage, Celibacy*, pp. 158–9 on Manichaeism; B. Cabouret-Laurioux, 'Parenté et stratégie familiale en Syrie a l'époque tardive: l'exemple de la famille de Libanios', in C. Badel and C. Settipani (eds), *Les stratégies familiales dans l'Antiquité tardive (IIIᵉ–VIᵉ siècle)* (Paris, 2012), pp. 321–38 on (a non-Christian) Libanius and his family in his writings. More generally on the interest on autobiographical writings and family stories in Late Antiquity, see V. Vuolanto, 'Family Relations and the Socialization of Children in the Autobiographical Narratives of Late Antiquity', in L. Brubaker and S. Tougher (eds), *Approaches to the Byzantine Family* (Aldershot, 2013), pp. 47–74.

also lived those men, deeply engaged with the Greco-Roman *paideia*, cultural heritage and urban way of life, who became the leading figures for late fourth- and early fifth-century Christianities, and who wrote the texts used in this study as my sources.[9] I concentrate on the western parts of the Empire, mainly Italy and Northern Africa, but Eastern sources especially from Roman Cappadocia and Syria, as well as texts from southern Gaul will be extensively discussed as comparative material.

The Task and Older Scholarship

This is the first book-length study to analyse the interplay of asceticism, family life and children in early Christian ideology, and also the first to scrutinise in depth the role of children in the actual family dynamics of the Roman world. By studying the family imagery and family dynamics of the elites, I am looking for new interpretations for the success of ascetic discourse and ascetic practices. However, contributing to the scholarship on asceticism of the Christian mainstream in Late Antiquity is only a secondary aim for my study: asceticism is used here as a way to study family history of the late Roman world and, more generally, strategies of continuity. Analysis of the patterns of thought in the rhetoric of asceticism and its adaptation in the actual circumstances of family life enables the study of values in connection with everyday life, and of the possible changes due to the Christianizing process of Late Antiquity.

As one of the principal tasks of this study is to scrutinize the different ways of aspiring to continuity in the late Roman world, as a starting point, and a hypothesis to be tested, I have developed a theory of continuity strategies to serve as the theoretical basis, or 'a mental tool'.[10] This theory is the main conceptual apparatus for the interpretation of the discourses and processes taking place within asceticism and family life. The focus is on family dynamism and human strategic behaviour in comparative and long-term perspectives in the context of social history, social anthropology and sociology. The importance of the different aspects of the ambition for continuity – connected to children, patrimony, reputation, commemoration and afterlife – is systematically analysed.

---

[9] For a more thorough 'setting of the scene' for the same period and people, see Brown, *Through the Eye of a Needle*, pp. 3–11.

[10] The concept is taken from E.A. Clark, *History, Theory, Text: Historians and the Linguistic Turn* (Cambridge, MA, and London, 2004), p. 185, denoting the way in which theory can be used for research process.

By the term 'asceticism', I mean a physically and mentally disciplined life, based on practices (or 'exercise', ἄσκησις) aiming to contribute to the contemplative life, the control of the passions, abstinence from physical comforts and pleasures, and the renunciation of worldly power and wealth. I am aware that this definition cannot be a universal one,[11] but it is well suited to the forms of asceticism described in the sources I have used. I am primarily interested in asceticism as a form of social behaviour and, more specifically, in those aspects of asceticism leading to celibacy and potentially to the renunciation of kinship ties. It should be noted that during the period under scrutiny, the monastic communities with specific rules were only just taking shape, and the discussions analysed in this study constituted an essential part of this very formation process. For example, especially in the western part of the Empire, by the end of the fourth century, the majority of women ascetics seem to have lived not as anchorites or coenobites, but were connected with ordinary households (home-asceticism).[12] This made the link between families and asceticism even more substantial than could be deduced from the later, or present-day, forms of Christian monasticism.

This volume has three interlinked goals: to study family ideology, the role of children and elite family dynamics in the late Roman world; to contribute to the study of Christian asceticism in Late Antiquity; and to develop a theory about continuity strategies. These issues are scrutinized by analysing the role of children during the transformation of Greco-Roman culture in the period of the rise of Christianity to its culturally dominant place during the late fourth and early fifth centuries CE. This process is approached from both ideological and social-historical perspectives: what was the place reserved for children in the emerging Christian family ideology? What was the place for children in actual family dynamics and life course? And what were the limits of children's own actions? From an ideological perspective, the focus is on Christian family

---

[11]   For the problems in making any universal definition of asceticism, see V. Wimbush and R. Valantasis, 'Introduction', in V. Wimbush and R. Valantasis (eds), *Asceticism* (New York and Oxford, 2002), pp. xix–xxxiii; and D. Martin, 'Introduction', in D. Martin and P. Miller (eds), *The Cultural Turn in Late Ancient Studies: Gender, Asceticism, and Historiography* (Durham, NC and London, 2005), pp. 14–16.

[12]   For the importance of home asceticism especially for women in the fourth-century West, see E.A. Clark, 'Ascetic Renunciation and Feminine Advancement', in E.A. Clark, *Ascetic Piety and Women's Faith: Essays on Late Ancient Christianity* (Leviston, 1986), pp. 180–85. For Egypt and the Middle East, see E. Wipszycka, 'L'ascétisme féminin dans l'Égypte de l'antiquité tardive: topoi littéraires et formes d'ascèse', in H. Melaerts and L. Mooren (eds), *Le rôle et le statut de la femme en Égypte hellénistique, romaine et byzantine* (Leuven, 2002), pp. 377–96, criticizing S. Elm for taking too much at face value the stories of women ascetics living in the desert as (semi-)anachorets.

6   *Children and Asceticism in Late Antiquity*

rhetoric: it will be shown that evading death and striving for continuity through family life were conceived as basic components of a good life in the late Roman world. The social-historical part of the study deals with family-level adaptations of the ideals: how did asceticism fit into the elite culture and mentality, and how was it put into practice at the family level in the lives of children? These processes are informative in showing how the late Roman elite families functioned and what the role of children was in the contemporary culture.

To tackle these questions, it is necessary to combine discussions of different research fields: research on early Christian asceticism, on the Roman family and childhood, and on more modern family and continuity strategies must be integrated with studies of Late Antiquity.

In the past 30 years early Christian asceticism, and especially women ascetics, have received much attention in scholarly work. Most recently, the research has concentrated on questions of body and gender, and the secular, political and spiritual power of the ascetics, whereas the older social historical questions on the impact of ascetic women in the process of the Christianization of the late Roman world have been left aside.[13] Searching for the origins or motivation for asceticism, which was once a common approach in studies, has lately been of less interest to scholars too.[14] My aim, however, is to take the issues of gender,

---

[13]   See e.g. V. Burrus, *Saving Shame: Martyrs, Saints, and Other Abject Subjects* (Philadelphia, 2008); C. Schroeder, *Monastic Bodies: Discipline and Salvation in Shenoute of Atripe* (Philadelphia, 2007); Hunter, *Marriage, Celibacy*; K. Cooper, *The Fall of the Roman Household* (Cambridge, 2007); C. Rapp, *Holy Bishops in Late Antiquity: The Nature of Christian Leadership in an Age of Transition* (Berkeley, CA, 2005); papers in D. Martin and P.C. Miller (eds), *The Cultural Turn in Late Ancient Studies: Gender, Asceticism, and Historiography* (Durham, NC and London, 2005) with R. Finn, *Asceticism in the Graeco-Roman World* (Cambridge and New York, 2009) and P. Rousseau, 'The Historiography of Asceticism: Current Achievements and Future Opportunities', in C. Straw and R. Lim (eds), *The Past Before Us: The Challenge of Historiographies of Late Antiquity* (Turnhout, 2005), pp. 89–101. For the earlier, vast body of literature on Christianization, women and asceticism, see e.g. S. Elm, *Virgins of God: The Making of Asceticism in Late Antiquity* (Oxford, 1994); Cooper, *The Virgin and the Bride*; and E. Castelli, 'Gender, Theory, and the Rise of Christianity: A Response to Rodney Stark', *Journal of Early Christian Studies* 6(2) (1998), pp. 227–57, all with further references.

[14]   Indeed, according to Elizabeth Clark, searching for the origin of Christian asceticism has proved not to be productive (E.A. Clark, *Reading Renunciation: Asceticism and Scripture in Early Christianity* (Princeton, 1999), pp. 18–27, esp. p. 18. On the explanation of the origins of the Christian asceticism in general, see R. Uro, 'Explaining Early Christian Asceticism: Methodological Considerations', in A. Mustakallio, H. Leppä and H. Räisänen (eds), *Lux Humana, Lux Aeterna: Essays on Biblical and Related Themes in Honour of Lars Aejmelaeus* (Helsinki and Göttingen, 2005), pp. 458–74. For a general theory of the social function of asceticism, also outside of Christianity, see R. Valantasis, 'A Theory of the Social

rhetoric and relations of power back to the questions of motivation. The difference from the previous research is that I have no intention of searching for the origin (of the cultural idea) of Christian asceticism. What interests me is how the benefits of the unmarried state were propagated to the individual would-be ascetics and their relatives, and how these arguments were accepted in family contexts. What kind of reasons and what kind of motivation led individuals and their relatives to take the ascetic vow seriously?

In dealing with questions of shared values, collective ethos and worldview – in a word, mentality[15] – the discourses are a part of the reality in which people live. The culturally dominant discourses neither precondition actual choices of the people, in some way reflecting their mentality, nor do they constitute a separate sphere of life on their own without any connection to the actual family-level behaviour. To avoid the temptation of drawing conclusions which go to extremes in either direction, it is necessary not to concentrate only on the family rhetoric of asceticism, but to pay attention also to the interaction of asceticism and actual family life. For what goals was asceticism (and the ideas and discourse on asceticism) used in the context of family life? What kind of influence did asceticism have in the family dynamics and in the individual patterns of thought and action? The problem here is that we have to study what actually took place in families through these same rhetorical texts that propagate the ascetic ideals and lifestyles. Thus, it is both useful and necessary to ask how discourses of filial submission and hierarchy, gender, resistance and sainthood evolve when the genres of literature change from letter-writing to the first panegyric accounts of a future saint's life and finally to full-blown hagiographies.

In some studies the relationship between asceticism and family has already been taken into consideration. These studies include most notably Peter Brown's *Body and Society*, many studies by Elizabeth Clark, and an article by Michael Verdon on kinship and female asceticism.[16] More recently, research by Michelle Salzman on the *nobilitas* and *honor* of the Christianizing aristocracy, by Kate Cooper on the relationships between the aristocratic household and asceticism,

---

Function of Asceticism' in V.L. Wimbush and R. Valantasis (eds), *Asceticism* (Oxford and New York, 2002), pp. 544–52 and its criticism in Martin, 'Introduction', pp. 14–15.

[15] For the concept of mentality – or *mentalité* – in general and the *mentalité* of the late Roman aristocracy in particular, see further M. Salzman, 'Elite Realities and *Mentalités*: The Making of a Western Christian Aristocracy', *Arethusa* 33 (2000), pp. 349–55 and 362.

[16] P. Brown, *Body and Society: Men, Women and Sexual Renunciation in Early Christianity* (New York, 1988); M. Verdon, 'Virgins and Widows: European Kinship and Early Christianity', *Man* 23(3) (1988), pp. 488–505; for Elizabeth Clark, see e.g. *Ascetic Piety and Women's Faith* and 'Antifamilial Tendencies in Ancient Christianity', *Journal of the History of Sexuality* 5 (1995), pp. 356–80.

by Rebecca Krawiec on family discourses and biological kinship in monastic communities, by Andrew Jacobs on *pietas* and asceticism, and by Caroline Schroeder on children in the monastic discourse have all taken up the interplay between asceticism and family discourse.[17]

Although the study of the late ancient period has become a flourishing field of research since the 1970s and has become increasingly popular in recent years,[18] the discussion of the history of family and children in Late Antiquity has only recently started to gain ground, especially from the social-historical viewpoint. The pioneering historians in the study of the family in Late Antiquity are Evelyne Patlagean and Brent Shaw.[19] However, there has been surprisingly little further work on families. In the context of research on Roman law, attention was already being paid to the family issues of Late Antiquity over half a century ago, but it was only in the early 1990s that this interest led to more far-reaching and contextualized studies of late Roman families, especially by Judith Evans Grubbs, Antti Arjava, and Joëlle Beaucamp.[20] Other studies that pay attention to

---

[17] M. Salzman, 'Competing Claims to *Nobilitas* in the Western Empire of the Fourth and Fifth Centuries', *Journal of Early Christian Studies* 9(3) (2001), pp. 359–85 and *The Making of a Christian Aristocracy: Social and Religious Change in the Western Roman Empire* (Cambridge, MA, and London, 2002); R. Krawiec, *Shenoute and the Women of White Monastery: Egyptian Monasticism in Late Antiquity* (Oxford and New York, 2002), pp. 133–74 and '"From the Womb of the Church": Monastic Families', *Journal of Early Christian Studies* 11(3) (2003), pp. 283–307; K. Cooper, 'The Household and the Desert: Monastic and Biological Communities in the Lives of Melania the Younger', in A. Mulder-Bakker and J. Wogan-Browne (eds), *Household, Women, and Christianities* (Turnhout, 2005), pp. 11–35 and Cooper, *The Fall*; A. Jacobs, 'Let Him Guard *Pietas*: Early Christian Exegesis and the Ascetic Family', *Journal of Early Christian Studies* 11(3) (2003), pp. 265–81; C. Schroeder, 'Queer Eye for the Ascetic Guy? Homoeroticism, Children, and the Making of Monks in Late Antique Egypt', *Journal of the American Academy of Religion* 77 (2009), pp. 333–47 and 'Child Sacrifice in Egyptian Monastic Culture: From Familial Renunciation to Jephthah's Lost Daughter', *Journal of Early Christian Studies* 20 (2012), pp. 269–302.

[18] See e.g. the recent companions and handbooks such as P. Rousseau (ed.), *A Companion to Late Antiquity* (Oxford, 2009); and S.F. Johnson, *The Oxford Handbook of Late Antiquity* (Oxford and New York, 2012).

[19] E. Patlagean, 'L'enfant et son avenir dans la famille byzantine (IVe–XIIe siècles)', *Annales de démographie historique* (1973), pp. 85–93 and *Pauvreté économique et pauvreté sociale à Byzance 4ᵉ–7ᵉ siècles* (Paris, 1977), esp. pp. 128–45; Shaw, 'The Family' (it is curious that in this seminal paper there is nothing on the interplay between asceticism and the family).

[20] See esp. J. Beaucamp, *Le statut de la femme à Byzance (4ᵉ–7ᵉ siècle)*, vols I–II (Paris, 1990, 1992); A. Arjava, *Women and Law in Late Antiquity* (Oxford, 1996), esp. pp. 157–72 and 'Paternal Power in Late Antiquity', *Journal of Roman Studies* 88 (1998), pp. 147–65; for Judith Evans Grubbs, see e.g. '"Pagan" and "Christian" Marriage: The State of the Question', *Journal of Early Christian Studies* 2(3) (1994), pp. 361–412; *Law and Family*

Approaches and Strategies   9

particular aspects of the family, and which have also proved useful for the present research, include Raymond van Dam's book on the families of the 'Cappadocian Fathers', Gillian Clark's book on women in Late Antiquity and Jens-Uwe Krause's monograph on widows and orphans in early Christianity. The conclusions drawn by Geoffrey Nathan in his book on the impact of Christianity on the families of Late Antiquity – still the only book-length study that aims to build an overall view of late Roman family life – form the central point of comparison to my present study, even if family dynamics is not his main interest in the book.[21]

In all these studies the role of asceticism in actual family-level behaviour has occasionally been taken up, but it has not been at the core of the analysis. In view of the recent interest in the Roman family and in Late Antiquity on the one hand, and of the huge body of literature on asceticism on the other hand, this is somewhat surprising. Nathan, for example, even explicitly states that the analysis of the discussions on asceticism would be beside the point in studying families in Late Antiquity.[22] However, the interest in families and childhood is growing among church historians: a collection of papers edited by Halvor Moxnes and a monograph by John Hellerman have analysed the prominence of family metaphors in early Christian discourse, concentrating on the first two centuries of the Christian era, whereas Denise K. Buell's study of the family rhetoric of Clement of Alexandria deals with the same naturalizing effects of family vocabulary that are my primary interest in the first two chapters of the present study.[23] During the last few decades, the contributions of David L. Osiek and

---

in Late Antiquity: The Emperor Constantine's Marriage Legislation, 2nd edn (Oxford, 1999); 'Promoting *Pietas* through Roman Law', in B. Rawson (ed.), *A Companion to Families in the Greek and Roman Worlds* (Oxford and New York, 2011), pp. 377–92; 'The Dynamics of Infant Abandonment: Motives, Attitudes and (Unintended) Consequences', in K. Mustakallio and C. Laes (eds), *The Dark Side of Childhood in Late Antiquity and the Middle Ages* (Oxford, 2011), pp. 21–36. For a synthesis of the juristic view of (also) the late Roman family, see C. Fayer, *La familia romana: Aspetti giuridici ed antiquari*, 3 vols (Rome, 1994, 2005, 2005).

[21]   R. van Dam, *Families and Friends in Late Roman Cappadocia* (Philadelphia, 2003); G. Clark, *Women in Late Antiquity: Pagan and Christian Lifestyles* (Oxford, 1993), esp. pp. 94–105; J.-U. Krause, *Witwen und Waisen im frühen Christentum. Witwen und Waisen im Römischen Reich 4* (Stuttgart, 1995), esp. pp. 74–92; G. Nathan, *The Family in Late Antiquity: The Rise of Christianity and the Endurance of Tradition* (London and New York, 2000) esp. pp. 120–32. See also C. Badel, 'Introduction. Que sont les stratégies devenues?', in Badel and Settipani (eds), *Les stratégies familiales*, pp. x–xi on Nathan's perspective to family.

[22]   Nathan, *The Family*, p. 132.

[23]   H. Moxnes (ed.), *Constructing Early Christian Families: Family as Social Reality and Metaphor* (London and New York, 1997), which, in spite of the subtitle, has very little to say about the social reality; J. Hellerman, *The Ancient Church as Family* (Minneapolis, 2001); D.K. Buell, *Making Christians: Clement of Alexandria and the Rhetoric of Legitimacy*

10   *Children and Asceticism in Late Antiquity*

Carolyn Balch have done much to contextualize the social history of first- and second-century Christian families, and in 2005, Odd Magne Bakke published a provocative book on the positive effect of early Christianity on attitudes towards children.[24] However, except for Bakke, these studies do not consider the period in which I am interested – the fourth and fifth centuries CE.

Moreover, except for the pioneering works by Patlagean and Shaw, the previous research has seldom contributed to the discussion of social dynamism inside the families and during the life course of an individual – an important aspect in the studies of earlier Roman family history as written, in particular, by Richard Saller and Mireille Corbier.[25] Scholars of both the ancient world and early Christianity have been interested mainly in ideals of family and childhood in society and the possible impact of the rise of Christianity; however, these fields have seldom been in communication with each other and the viewpoint of the studies has tended to be parent-oriented instead of focusing on children. Moreover, it was only the 2009 volume by Cornelia Horn and John Martens on childhood and children in early Christianity that tried to integrate the scholarship of early Christian studies and Roman family history into a new synthesis. Many collections of articles that include contributions which tackle the role of children in the family dynamics of Late Antiquity have appeared or

---

(Princeton, NJ, 1998). See also R. Aasgaard, *'My Beloved Brothers and Sisters': Christian Siblingship in Paul* (London and New York, 2004).

[24]   C. Osiek, 'The Family and Early Christianity: "Family Values" Revisited', *Catholic Biblical Quarterly* 58 (1996), pp. 1–24; C. Osiek and D. Balch, *Families in the New Testament World: Households and House Churches* (Louisville, KY, 1997); D. Balch and C. Osiek (eds), *Early Christian Families in Context: An Interdisciplinary Dialogue* (Grand Rapids, 2003); O.M. Bakke, *When Children Became People: The Birth of Childhood in Early Christianity* (Minneapolis, 2005).

[25]   See esp. R. Saller, *Patriarchy, Property and Death in the Roman Family*, 2nd edn (Cambridge, 1997), synthesizing and developing further the earlier work of Saller (and Brent Shaw) on demography and family dynamism (see Saller, *Patriarchy*, pp. xi and 241 (for bibliography) and, for example, M. Corbier, 'Divorce and Adoption as Roman Familial Strategies', in B. Rawson (ed.), *Marriage, Divorce and Children in Ancient Rome* (Oxford, 1991), pp. 47–78 and 'Introduction. Adoptés et nourris', in M. Corbier (ed.), *Adoption et fosterage* (Paris, 2000), pp. 5–41). For a laudable synthesis of this kind of approach, see M. Harlow and R. Laurence, *Growing Up and Growing Old in Ancient Rome: A Life Course Approach* (London and New York, 2002). See, however, K. Cooper, 'Closely Watched Households: Visibility, Exposure and Private Power in the Roman *Domus*', *Past and Present* 197 (2007), pp. 3–33 on authority and power in the Roman *domus*, and Evans Grubbs, 'The Dynamics' on child abandonment and family dynamics and Vuolanto, 'Family Relations', pp. 47–74 on children and family dynamics.

will shortly be published,[26] but there are only a handful of recent studies that investigate the interplay of children and asceticism as an integral part of family dynamics – and none of these discusses their findings in the broader context of family history.[27]

From the point of view of continuity strategies, my approach can be interpreted as combining three separate currents of scholarship. First, there are studies using concepts such as 'marriage strategies' or 'family strategies' to denote families and kin groups acting to defend and enhance their economic or social status by using the family members, connections and labour efficiently. This approach has been prominent in family studies since the 1970s and had been utilized in research dealing with societies as diverse as Ancient Greece and the modern United States. However, the problems inherent in this approach have made it necessary for me to develop new conceptual tools to analyse the dynamism of families.[28] Second, there are the more theoretical philosophical, sociological and psychological studies of the strategies of (symbolic) immortality

---

[26]   C. Horn and J. Martens, *'Let the Little Children Come to Me': Childhood and Children in Early Christianity* (Washington DC, 2009). For the *status quaestionis* in the study of early Christian and (late) Roman childhood, see esp. M. Harlow, R. Laurence and V. Vuolanto, 'Past, Present and Future in the Study of Roman Childhood', in S. Crawford and G. Shepherd (eds), *Approaches to Childhood in the Past* (Oxford, 2007), pp. 5–14; and E. Southon, M. Harlow and C. Callow, 'The Family in the Late Antique West (AD 400–700): A Historiographical Review', in Brubaker and Tougher (eds), *Approaches*, pp. 109–30. For the article collections, see esp. C. Horn and R. Phenix (eds), *Children in Late Ancient Christianity* (Tübingen, 2009); A. Papaconstantinou and A.-M. Talbot (eds), *Becoming Byzantine: Children and Childhood in Byzantium* (Washington DC, 2009); Badel and Settipani (eds), *Les stratégies familiales*; L. Brubaker and S. Tougher (eds), *Approaches to the Byzantine Family* (Aldershot, 2013); C. Laes, K. Mustakallio and V. Vuolanto (eds), *Children and Family in Late Antiquity: Life, Death and Interaction* (Leuven, 2015). See also the relevant chapters in J. Evans Grubbs, T. Parkin and R. Bell (eds), *The Oxford Handbook of Childhood and Education in the Classical World* (Oxford and New York, 2013), esp. pp. 559–643.

[27]   B. Caseau, 'Stratégies parentales concernant les enfants au sein de la famille: le choix de la virginité consacrée', in Badel and Settipani (eds), *Les stratégies familiales*, pp. 247–64; C. Schroeder, 'Children in Early Egyptian Monasticism', in Horn and Phenix (eds), *Children in Late Ancient Christianity*, pp. 317–38; V. Vuolanto, 'Choosing Asceticism: Children and Parents, Vows and Conflicts', in Horn and Phenix (eds), *Children in Late Ancient Christianity*, pp. 255–91; V. Vuolanto, 'Children and Asceticism: Strategies of Continuity in the Late Fourth and Early Fifth Centuries', in K. Mustakallio, J. Hanska, H.-L. Sainio and V. Vuolanto (eds), *Hoping for Continuity: Childhood, Education and Death in Antiquity and the Middle Ages* (Rome, 2005), pp. 119–32.

[28]   See e.g. T. Hareven, 'The History of the Family and the Complexity of Social Change', *American Historical Review* 96(1) (1991), pp. 115–19; R.J. Emigh, 'Theorizing Strategies: Households and Markets in Fifteenth-Century Tuscany', *History of the Family 6*

developed in order to understand human cultural responses when facing death.[29] Third, there are some scattered remarks on the importance of the notions of continuity and (this-worldly) immortality in Late Antiquity; however, this theme has as yet received only one article-length discussion, by Ton van Eijk.[30] This research field will be more thoroughly scrutinized below, with the discussion of the theoretical background of the study and the concepts of family strategies and symbolic immortality.

Taken as a whole, therefore, in relation to older scholarship, my aim is to introduce three elements for the family history of Late Antiquity: the approach taking a dynamic view of family as a field of interaction and decision making; the discussion of the role and function of children in families and society in Late Antiquity; and the theoretical background of continuity strategies. All of these aspects are also relevant to our understanding of the prominence and relative popularity of ascetic discourse and asceticism in early Christian culture.

Structure of the Study and the Sources Used

The three themes of the study – early Christian asceticism, late Roman family history and the theory of continuity strategies – have led to a structure for this volume in which the present chapter is quite multifaceted. We begin by introducing the sources; this is followed by the theoretical and methodological starting points. The main part of the chapter discusses 'continuity' both in (earlier) Roman culture and ideology, and in the earlier studies in family dynamics. At the end of the chapter, a model of 'continuity strategies' is introduced, which connects the ideological continuity discourses with the role of 'actual children' in individual and family strategies.

(2001), pp. 495–517; and P. Viazzo and K. Lynch, 'Anthropology, Family History, and the Concept of Strategy', *International Review for Social History* 47 (2002), esp. pp. 423–5.

[29] See esp. R. Lifton, 'The Sense of Immortality: On Death and the Continuity of Life', in H. Feifel (ed.), *New Meanings of Death* (New York, 1977), pp. 273–90, Z. Bauman, *Mortality, Immortality and Other Life Strategies* (Stanford, 1992), and S. Scheffler, *Death and the Afterlife* (Oxford, 2013).

[30] T. Van Eijk, 'Marriage and Virginity, Death and Immortality', in J. Fontaine and C. Kannengiesser (eds), *Epektasis. Mélanges patristiques offerts au Cardinal Jean Daniélou* (Paris, 1972), pp. 209–35. See also S. Nicosia, 'Altre vie per l'immortalità nella cultura greca', in S. Beta and F. Focaroli (eds), *Vecchiaia, giuventù, immortalità: fra natura e cultura: Le maschere della persona: identità e alterità di un essere sociale* (Fiesole, 2009), pp. 50–69; C. Edwards, *Death in Ancient Rome* (New Haven and London, 2007), pp. 207–20; and Verdon, 'Virgins and Widows', pp. 498–500.

In the subsequent seven main chapters, the different ways of constructing and contributing to the strategies of continuity are analysed in the light of the theoretical background outlined. These chapters can be divided into two parts. The first part, Chapters 2–4, deals with family ideology and continuity in the ascetical discourses of the late fourth and early fifth centuries. The right Christian lifestyle and the disposition towards married life became major issues in contemporary theological debates, shaping and defining what we now call Catholic Christianity. The idea of a Christian family was not at all clear-cut: the family was both cherished and abandoned as the basic structure for society and for Christian communities by different theologians and Christian groups. In this part of the book the focus is on rhetoric and on the construction of the idea of personal and family continuity on which the ecclesiastical writers of Late Antiquity built.

Chapter 2 presents the ideological role of children in Christian families of Late Antiquity. It starts with an analysis of the requirement for 'hating the parents'; this is followed by a discussion of the (un)importance of family wealth and *patria* in the Christian discourse. The chapter ends with a study of the interplay of ascetic ideology and the traditional ideas of family obligations that were crystallized in the Roman notion of *pietas* in the elite Christian family ideology. How should Christian children behave and respond to the requirements of both their family background and Christian (ascetic) ideology? Chapter 3 shows how the ideological discrepancies and the current ideas of family life affected the disputes about asceticism, and how reconciliation was sought through the family terminology and metaphors. By constructing the Christian Church as the new family, with ascetics as its privileged members, the ecclesiastical writers pointed out the superiority of the new lifestyle in fulfilling the needs of family groups and individuals. Simultaneously, they lay bare the prevalent attitudes and expectations connected with the biological family and with children as the ultimate source of continuity for individuals. The family metaphors not only serve as convenient tools to argue for the ascetic Christian ideology, but also reflect the function of children as conveyors of continuity and immortality in late Roman culture. Death, continuity, asceticism and children are inevitably interwoven in the new Christian discourse. This is the theme for Chapter 4, which concludes the first part of the book.

The second part of the study, Chapters 5–8, deals with the main themes of the propagation of asceticism and its adaptation at the family level. The preceding chapters depicted the ideological structure used in the propagation of asceticism, culminating in the idea of evading death and striving for continuity as the most basic human need. In what now follows, the idea of continuity is deconstructed to analyse how asceticism was seen as being compatible with the different forms of continuity and, subsequently, how asceticism actually fitted into the elite culture and mentality, and how it was put into practice on the family level to contribute to the needs of family members.

Chapter 5 introduces the framework in which Christian families of Late Antiquity discussed the future of their children, and the contexts in which the children themselves lived their lives. This includes, most importantly, the demographic issues and interfamilial relationships, especially between parents and children. By comparing 'real-life' examples of entering ascetic Christianity and hagiographic accounts of what was viewed to be the desired mode of conduct, this chapter studies the possibilities of independent action by children and parents. Here the authority of the parents and the differing experiences of girls and boys reaching marriageable age are the central issues dealt with. The function of the subsequent chapters is to clarify the motives that led parents to give, or not to give, their children to asceticism.[31] These chapters have the concept of the family life course as their background. Chapter 6 discusses the use of asceticism as a strategy for the surplus of children and the role of asceticism in the strategies for inheritance and dowry, or in gaining some other sorts of economic profit. The theme corresponds to what has been called family strategies in older studies on family history. Chapter 7 continues to ponder motives for parents in donating their children to the ascetic lifestyle, addressing the question of how family traditions and memory were perpetuated through asceticism to acquire familial and spiritual nobility and continuity. Chapter 8, the last chapter in this part, brings together the parallel blessings of having children and giving them to asceticism. By analysing both ideological statements of the many troubles of bringing up children and asceticism as freedom, and the actual family dynamics which indicate that elite families did not opt exclusively for children or asceticism but tried to merge these requirements, this chapter discusses what children were for in late Roman society.

The final chapter, Chapter 9, concentrates on the three most central issues of the book: the interplay between the family discourses of Late Antiquity and Christian/Roman identities; the rise of asceticism influencing family dynamics in Late Antiquity and what difference Christianity made in the history of children and childhood; and, lastly, on a more general level, how strategies for continuity functioned in Late Antiquity. In the epilogue, the model of continuity strategies is tentatively used as a tool for analysing the claimed change in the continuity strategies brought about by the shift from pre-modern to modern and postmodern world.

---

[31] The structure of these chapters follows the scheme presented in Figure 1, p. 41.

The chronological and geographical limits of the study have a threefold structure. The core of the study is the analysis of the texts by the western ecclesiastical writers from Italy and Northern Africa in the half-century between c. 375 CE and 425 CE. The authors in question, Ambrose of Milan, Jerome, Augustine of Hippo and Paulinus of Nola, formed a network of mutual contacts and influences during this period. These texts are supplemented by other contemporary works, both Eastern and Western, especially by Athanasius of Alexandria, Basil of Caesarea, Gregory of Nyssa, Gregory Nazianzen, John Chrysostom, John Cassian and Sulpicius Severus, and by the imperial legislation and canons of the ecclesiastical councils of the day. The third class of sources, used for purposes of comparison, consists of Christian hagiographies of the fourth and fifth centuries.[32]

I have concentrated on the writings of the side which ultimately emerged as the winner in the ecclesiastical struggles of the fourth and fifth centuries, the Nicaeans, who called themselves Catholics and Orthodox, that is, representatives of the 'universal' and 'right-praising' church. This is due to the fact that the epistolary material is available almost exclusively from the Nicaean authors. Views of other groups, however, are also presented to show what kind of alternative viewpoints on asceticism and family life were adopted in the contemporary cultural contexts. Even more importantly, the Nicaeans themselves used these groups and their views as tools for highlighting their own differing positions. It is true that these writers constituted a kind of special generation ('the golden age' of patristic literature) among ecclesiastical writers, with their intense networking, their need to construct the 'new orthodoxy'[33] amid the ecclesiastical struggles, and with their renown and influence among later generations. Still, my intention is to show that the basic cultural values and discourses in their writings, dealing with the different ways of aspiring for continuity, are by no means specific only to them or to their contemporary world.

The sources of the study can be divided into five groups according to literary genre. The most significant of these consists of letters by the already-mentioned core of western authors.[34] The letters are dated between the mid-370s and the mid-420s. These have been systematically read and references to family relationships in relation to asceticism have been analysed. Special attention is

---

[32]   I have not included texts written later, even if they claim to deal with people and happenings of this earlier era – it is more than probable that the texts tell more about their time of writing than about the time of their protagonists.

[33]   A concept borrowed from Hunter, *Marriage, Celibacy*, p. 5, albeit for a narrower sense on the interpretation of the (superior) place of asceticism in Christianity.

[34]   *Letters* of Ambrose of Milan, Jerome, Paulinus of Nola and Augustine of Hippo.

16   *Children and Asceticism in Late Antiquity*

paid to cases dealing with asceticism in connection with family relationships, even if the letters also provide information on ideas, attitudes, values and fears linked to particular individuals and circumstances. Even if the focus of the letters is undeniably elitist and their approach is overtly rhetorical, in many cases it is possible to single out the underlying family structure, the principal actors, and the reasons for conflict and possible reconciliation.

The second group consists of Western and Eastern texts and treatises on virginity and widowhood, propagating the practice and value of the individually and voluntarily chosen unmarried life.[35] Only a little information on actual cases can be reliably extracted from these stories; however, the values and presuppositions are apparent, and are contextualized in their contemporary society in a way that enables the scholar to find out at least what the authors in question assumed to be relevant for their own society.[36] Third, I have used the hagiographic accounts of the fourth and fifth centuries, Eastern and Western, connected to both fictitious and otherwise known individuals. These accounts vary from eulogies after the death of important ascetic figures (such as the obituary of Paula the Elder by Jerome – in fact, a letter) to the remote and formularized accounts even hundreds of years after the death of the actual (or supposed) saint, such as the *Life and Miracles of Thecla*. The great biographical collections of the early fifth century – the anonymous *History of the Monks in Egypt*, the *Lausiac History* by Palladius and the

---

[35]   In the early Christian usage, the words for virgins (*virgo*, παρθένος) and virginity denoted both male and female celibates. The texts systematically scrutinised include: *On Virgins* (*De Virginibus*), *On Virginity* (*De Virginitate*), *Exhortation to Virginity* (*Exhortatio Virginitatis*), *The Consecration of a Virgin* (*De Institutione Virginis*) and *On Widows* (*De Viduis*) by Ambrose of Milan; *Against Helvidius* (*Adversus Helvidium*) by Jerome; *On the Good of Marriage* (*De Bono Coniugali*), *On the Good of Widowhood* (*De Bono Viduitatis*), *On the Care of the Dead* (*De Cura pro Mortuis Gerenda*), *On Marriage and Concupiscence* (*De Nuptiis et Concupiscentia*), *On Holy Virginity* (*De Sancta Virginitate*) and *On Continence* (*De Continentia*) by Augustine; the anonymous *On the Fall of a Consecrated Virgin* (*De Lapsu Virginis Consecratae*); *To the Church* (*Ad Ecclesiam*) by Salvian; *An Anonymous Homily on Virginity* (published in D. Amand De Mendieta and M.-C. Moons, 'Une curieuse homélie grecque inédite sur la virginité addressée aux pères de famille', *Revue Bénédictine* 63 (1953), pp. 18–69 and 211–38); *On Virginity* (*De Virginitate*) and *Against the Opponents of Monastic Life* (*Adversus Oppugnatores Vitae Monasticae*) by John Chrysostom; *On Virginity* (*De Virginitate*) by Gregory of Nyssa; *On Virginity* by 'Pseudo-Athanasius'; and *Sermon 7* (*Homilia 7, De Virginibus*) by Eusebius of Emesa.

[36]   For a similar approach, see Shaw, 'The Family', esp. pp. 5–7, on Augustine, with A. Jacobs and R. Krawiec, 'Fathers Know Best? Christian Families in the Age of Asceticism', *Journal of Early Christian Studies* 11(3) (2003), esp. p. 261.

Religious History by Theodoret of Cyrrhus – are also systematically analysed.[37] In some cases even these sources may offer glimpses of actual circumstances.[38] These sources are especially interesting when they occasionally present clashes between the claimed values and actual described behaviour, and when they use various rhetorical devices to reconcile them.

The fourth group consists of more miscellaneous texts from other contemporary sources such as the *Confessions* and the *City of God* by Augustine, *Carmina* by Paulinus of Nola, the autobiographical *Carmina* by Gregory Nazianzen, *On the Priesthood* by John Chrysostom, and letters by other Western and Eastern authors. The last group consists of the normative material: canons of local synods and church councils, the imperial Roman legislation of Late Antiquity and the earliest monastic rules. They provide material particularly through their references to the (supposed) conflicts inside families caused by the ascetic urges.[39]

It is a difficult task to access the actual cases and patterns of social interaction, as there is little information left at the grassroots level of negotiations and confrontations. The ancient literature was created by elite men, to whom the family was not the centre of interest when they acted in public life – and it was as a part of this public activity that 'the classical literature' was produced. Families, and especially children, were seldom issues as such. They occur in the texts mostly to give support to the author's rhetoric, with the aim of convincing the audience. During Late Antiquity, the situation changed with the rise of Christianity: the new writing elite, bishops doing pastoral work by preaching and through admonitory letters, became more interested in the everyday doings and morals of the people. Glimpses of family life and attitudes to it are offered by retracing the evolution of the discourses of asceticism through the different literary genres, as the discourse on asceticism further intensified the need to take an explicit stand

---

[37] Jerome, *Letter* 108 (404 CE); *Life and Miracles of Thecla* (mid-fifth century CE); *History of the Monks in Egypt* (c. 400 CE; its near-contemporary free translation into Latin by Rufinus, *Historia monachorum*, is also extant); Palladius, *The Lausiac History* (c. 420 CE); Theodoret of Cyrrhus, *Religious History* (c. 444 CE). See also especially *Life of Macrina* by Gregory of Nyssa (early 380s CE) and *Life of Melania the Younger* by Gerontius (mid-400s CE; both Latin and Greek versions are extant).

[38] Even if, naturally, we have no means of checking the reliability of the information given. See e.g. the above-mentioned letter on Paula the Elder (Jerome, *Letter* 108); Theodoret of Cyrrhus, *Religious History* 9.15; 13.3; 13.16–18 (Theodoret on himself); Gregory of Nyssa, *Life of Macrina* (Gregory on his sister Macrina).

[39] For the legislative and normative material as a source material for the ancient social history, see e.g. Arjava, *Women and Law*, pp. 10–18; and Saller, *Patriarchy*, pp. 156–9; see also more generally D. Johnston, *Roman Law in Context* (Cambridge, 1999), pp. 17–29.

with regard to the dominant family values and practices.[40] The viewpoint taken in the present study is therefore mostly concerned with the senatorial aristocracy and local secular elites, the curial families. Indeed, the ecclesiastical writers of the fourth and early fifth centuries had their background in these groups. Thus, my study mostly concerns those people and groups that shared the elite mentality and 'status culture', based on their common educational background and values.[41] There are only occasional references to the mentality and behaviour patterns of the ordinary people, and not much more on the 'sub-elites'[42] such as the clergy.

The question of how far any single genre of source materials is representative of late Roman culture and its discourses makes a comparative approach inevitable. Here, the indubitable heterogeneity of the material as a whole serves as an advantage, since if the sources – normative and descriptive, Italian and Cappadocian, legendary and epistolary – give a consonant view in all their differences of genre, of their place of composition and of the status of their producers and audiences, the case for their representative character is strong.

Discourses and Theories: Family Strategies and Symbolic Immortality

Any text is rooted in the historically determined conventions of writing and its relations to other texts. All the sources for the present study form part of highly rhetorical genres and literary traditions. Only the recognition of the different figures of language and of the specific textual features of the genre in question makes it possible to proceed to an understanding of the cultural context and intentions[43] in the creation of the text. Failure to recognize rhetorical figures such as *topoi*[44] may mean that the interpretation of the texts, and thus the

---

[40] See also Shaw, 'The Family', p. 4, although he does not identify the discourse on asceticism as a cause for the intensification of the family speech and the widening 'hiatus between the concept of family and its actual practice' in Late Antiquity.

[41] On the shared elite cultural background and *mentalité* for the Western elites, see Salzman, *Elite Realities*, esp. pp. 353–5, 362. On the background of the bishops in Late Antiquity, see Rapp, *Holy Bishops*, pp. 173–95.

[42] On the sub-elites of Late Antiquity and the Church, see P. Brown, 'The Study of Elites in Late Antiquity', *Arethusa* 33 (2000), pp. 339–42.

[43] As far as this is possible: a *crux historicorum* is that the study of intentions and historical interpretations based on intentions are inevitable for historians, even if no certainty on these can be achieved. See also Clark, *History, Theory, Text*, p. 140.

[44] By *topoi* I mean structurally similar or formulaic textual elements and narrative archetypes, aiming at mediating a meaning anchored in the shared cultural conventions of the authors and their addressees.

understanding of the social realities, are distorted. A de-rhetorizing reading of the textual strategies and discursive practices, that is, the identification of the different layers of the text with their respective traditions and cultural contexts, makes it possible to ask what these features of textual level can tell us about ideological and social circumstances of the late Roman world.

For the present study, the analysis of the discourses is only one phase in the analysis of the texts, serving as a strategy for approaching texts with the aim of shifting the viewpoint from texts to contexts and meaning. It is a question of the analysis of the discourses (as a tool) rather than a discourse analysis (as an approach). Therefore, 'discourse' is not understood here in the Foucaultian sense as an overall approach for working out the dominant discourses and thus the structures of power, although the idea of discourses as cultural, historically defined practices and conventions which construct modes of thought with their own logic, strategy and reason also holds true here. Instead, I use here the concept of discourse as 'a set of words beyond the level of the sentence',[45] as a complex message (in comparison to simple signs) that serves a communicative function; that is, as a practice producing cultural meanings in communication.

Discourse, therefore, is a certain way of writing about a certain thing. A discourse can be identified as such by the repetition of certain expressions and practices of explanation. It is thus a network of overlapping but non-continuous concepts; in this respect it comes close to the ideas of language games and family resemblance. The identification of these discourses, or games, is essential both in defining concepts and expressions and in understanding meanings. The analysis of discourses is a process of 'describing' the game with its rules, actors and playground (that is, its traditions, intentions and concepts). A single text is structured by multiple discourses, which have to be broken down for analysis.

Understanding the textual structure and immediate contexts of individual sources – that is, to practise source criticism – is not enough for an historian aiming at understanding what was going on, that is, identifying the contexts to which the texts were attached in the contemporary discourses. Therefore, the tools for the texts must include devices for further classification of the material. This classification depends on the selected contexts and viewpoints, and is thus closely linked to the theoretical standpoint of the researcher.

The work of creating a meaningful context for the present study process led to the framework of continuity strategies. At the beginning of the research process, the concept of 'family strategy' seemed to be the most useful starting point, often understood as explicit decisions made by families (or kin-groups)

---

[45]   R. Barthes, 'The Discourse of History', *Comparative Criticism* 3 (1981), p. 7.

20   *Children and Asceticism in Late Antiquity*

to achieve survival or economic and social power and privileges for the family and kin. The concept is widely used in scrutinizing the dynamism of families by modern family historians, although it seldom appears in research into ancient family history. From the historian's standpoint, it is useful to distinguish three – even if partly overlapping – trends in the previous research: the study of the peasant economy; the study of the economic strategies of the working class; and the study of kin strategies.[46]

However, the lack of precision in the use of the word 'strategy' posed a problem. Not only is the very concept of strategy often left undefined and untheorized, but concepts like family (or *famille*) and kinship (or *parenté*) are also used quite indiscriminately.[47] It is necessary to make clear whose strategies we are dealing with here. Should a single act by a single actor be understood as forming a strategy, and is it a strategy of a particular individual or a particular family? Are the different strategies the result of deliberate and explicit policies? Is it justified to refer to any observed behavioural pattern as a strategy in the absence of accurate knowledge of the motivation behind individual choices that lead to such practices?

It is crucial to be aware of the function that the concept has in the conceptual field. In particular, one must ask if the 'strategy' in this connection is an analytical tool for describing (the sources of) the empirical reality or if it is a

---

[46]   For the prominence of the 'family strategy' concept in the family history and the problems inherent in it, see e.g. Hareven, 'The History of the Family', pp. 115–19 (family strategies as one of the five major lines of study in family history); P. Moen and E. Wethington, 'The Concept of Family Adaptive Strategies', *Annual Review of Sociology* 18 (1992), pp. 233–51; R.J. Emigh, 'Theorizing Strategies: Households and Markets in Fifteenth-Century Tuscany', *History of the Family* 6 (2001): 495–517; M. van der Linden, 'Introduction' and 'Conclusion' in J. Kok (ed.), *Rebellious Families: Household Strategies and Collective Action in the Nineteenth and Twentieth Centuries* (Oxford and New York, 2002), pp. 1–23 and 230–42; Viazzo and Lynch, *Anthropology*, esp. pp. 423–5; T. Engelen, J. Kok and R. Paping, 'The Family Strategies Concept: An Evaluation of Four Empirical Case Studies', *History of the Family* 9 (2004), pp. 239–51.

[47]   For Giovanni Levi, for example, who made extensive use of the concept of (family) strategies in his studies, the 'family' is not, in fact, a domestic or familial unit, but a kin group (see e.g. *Inheriting Power: The Story of an Exorcist* (Chicago and London, 1988), esp. pp. 145–57 and 'Family and Kin – A Few Thoughts', *Journal of Family History* 15(4) (1990), pp. 568–9). For ancient studies, see the articles in J. Andreau and H. Bruhns (eds), *Parenté et stratégies familiales dans l'antiquité romaine* (Rome, 1990) and Badel and Settipani (eds), *Les stratégies familiales*, and especially the introduction of the first mentioned: Andreau and Bruhns, *Parenté et stratégies familiales*, pp. viii–xiv, xx–xxi. Mireille Corbier has addressed this ambiguity in 'Épigraphie et parenté', in Y. Le Bohec and Y. Roman (eds), *Épigraphie et histoire: acquis et problèmes* (Lyon, 1998), pp. 101 and 103.

synthetic concept for putting together and understanding the phenomena in focus. In much of the older research the difference between these two ways of understanding strategies is not made clear.[48] The first option is to understand the concept of 'strategy' as a tool for describing the actual decision making in individual lives and family groups. In this approach there is an assumption that strategies are a part of the reality in which family members act, and strategies are seen as results of the more or less explicit (long-term) bargaining of the family members. The focus is on the particular individual families and their members: strategies are to be found (if at all) in the particular families under scrutiny.[49] The other option for understanding family strategies is to perceive the concept as a tool for understanding the patterns of behaviour on the individual and the family level. For this 'synthetic' view, strategies are a part of the reality not of families, but of scholars: family strategy is in reality a metaphor used by the family historian in the endeavour to find explanations for the actions in focus and to transmit this understanding to the audience. The strategies observable for the scholar are the patterned end results of individual agency and short-term tactics, or 'selections from the culture which the family offers': the behaviour examined appears as a goal-oriented pattern of action, a strategy, in the eyes of the observer, the scholar.[50] This latter view is adopted in the present study:

---

[48] See also L. Tilly, 'Beyond Family Strategies, What?', *Historical Methods* 20(3) (1987), p. 124, who distinguishes between the family members' version ('principles that inform bargained interdependent decisions') and the social historians' version ('principles which lie behind predictable, interdependent behaviour in which one outcome is regularly favoured over another') of the strategies, with Viazzo and Lynch, *Anthropology*, pp. 429–36, esp. p. 432. Strategies are also to be distinguished from the singular and random choices, or short-term 'tactics' of an individual (see D. Smith, 'Family Strategy: More than a Metaphor?', *Historical Methods* 20(3) (1987), p. 118; and Viazzo and Lynch, *Anthropology*, esp. pp. 441 and 451).

[49] This kind of view would lead to definitions of family strategies as 'une conduit partagée par la majorité des membres de la famille sur une longue durée, une voire plusieurs générations' (Badel, 'Introduction', p. ix). But how can the 'majority' be defined here (if two 'patriarchs', a man and his grandson, would be doing far-reaching choices for the future of the whole family group without consulting the others, would this be called a 'strategy')? And if strategic plans of these patriarchs (e.g. trying to rise from the local to the imperial aristocracy) fail, would this failure be undone these actions as strategies proper, as the end result is not actually visible for the modern scholar? On the other hand, what if individual short-term choices ('tactics') would later be integrated to form a seemingly long-term familial politics ('strategy')? We have to conclude that the scholars, in their interpretations, cannot be dependent of the original assumed intentions (about which we have only little, and only unreliable, information) of the actors.

[50] Synthetic concepts bring 'extra' meaning to the text, to shift the narration from description to explanation and from past to present. Every synthetic expression involved in

22   *Children and Asceticism in Late Antiquity*

strategies are to be understood primarily as analytical constructs for the use of the scholar and, as such, are not necessarily visible to the contemporary actors.

But how can a strategy be implicit or unconscious? Common-sense logic would require that a 'strategy' refers to a conscious choice on the basis of some pre-discussed principles. In particular, Pierre Bourdieu's claim that strategies are neither completely conscious nor unconscious has aroused confusion and criticism.[51] However, there are studies showing the existence of implicit strategies. The scholar cannot trust that the individuals one studies have accurate knowledge of the motivation and reasons for their own action, even less that they accurately describe these motivations. As the strategies are embedded in the regular aspects of the cultural repertoire, they are of low visibility both for the actors themselves and for the scholar.[52] Esther Goody has used a concept of 'culturally stable strategy' to denote a phenomenon in which effective solutions recognized in the community become institutionalized as the 'right' thing to do. These processes occur over time and are difficult to perceive in action. Thus, the 'culturally stable strategy' emerges in the process of a practice which, little by little, assumes a more normative character, while simultaneously becoming invisible to contemporary observers.[53]

---

the formation of new meanings and new understanding is by nature metaphoric. See e.g. P. Ricoeur, *Interpretation Theory: Discourse and the Surplus of Meaning* (Fort Worth, 1976), esp. pp. 52–3, 66–8; and Hayden White and Georg Iggers in E. Domańska, *Encounters: Philosophy of History after Postmodernism* (Charlottesville and London, 1998), pp. 24 and 106. Quote from D. Bertaux and P. Thompson, 'Introduction', in D. Bertaux and P. Thompson (eds), *Between Generations: Family Models, Myths, and Memories* (Oxford, 1993), p. 2.

[51] P. Bourdieu, 'Les stratégies matrimoniales dans le système de reproduction', *Annales (ESC)* 27(4–5) (1972), pp. 1105–6, 1124, stressing the cultural and normative aspects of the actual decision making. See also P. Bourdieu, *The Logic of Practice* (Cambridge, 1990), p. 53. For critical discussion, see Diane Wolf, 'Daughters, Decisions and Domination: An Empirical and Conceptual Critique of Household Strategies', *Development and Change* 21 (1990), p. 55; and Viazzo and Lynch, 'Anthropology', pp. 432–41, 448–51. See also Smith, *Family Strategy*, p. 119, who misleadingly claims that strategy is regarded as a set of social or normative rules by Bourdieu, and Emigh, 'Theorizing Strategies', p. 498, who refers to the works published in 1979 and 1989 as forming a framework 'applied' by Bourdieu in 1972. A sketch of the extremes (labelled as a structural approach and a rational choice approach) is also provided in Moen and Wethington, 'The Concept', pp. 234, 243–5.

[52] This is a logical sequel to the synthetic view adopted. See also P. Bourdieu, *Outline of a Theory of Practice* (Cambridge, 1977), pp. 18–22. However, Wolf, 'Daughters' has criticized the family strategies approach especially because the interviewees did not identify their behaviour as strategies.

[53] E. Goody, 'Sharing and Transferring Components of Parenthood: The West African Case', in Corbier (ed.), *Adoption et fosterage*, pp. 369, 381–2. For an example, see H. Forbes, 'Of Grandfathers and Grand Theories: The Hierarchised Ordering of Responses to Hazard

Approaches and Strategies 23

But what makes an observed pattern of behaviour 'a strategy' instead of 'a structure'? A strategy is a means to an end. There have to be future-oriented intentions. Thus, only if a goal can be identified can a behaviour pattern be seen as forming a part of a strategy. The problem is that scholars have to reconstruct the original aims of the actors on the basis of the behaviour, with little actual knowledge of the intentions and motivation of the actors.[54] In this interpretative work the basic assumptions of the scholar, the problem setting and the theoretical framework chosen are the decisive factors. Thus, even if this practical situation makes the research more challenging, this would not make the approach, which assumes the existence of strategic action, fallacious. Still it would be true that this intentionality would also need a certain margin of liberty for choice and genuinely alternative ways of responding to certain life situations.[55]

In the older research, considerations of inheritance and wealth have been seen as the most essential features in strategies of families and households. Possible economic strategies may include migration, savings and investment for lean times, cutting down expenses and acquiring outside sources of income such as having recourse to the money, housing, tools and services of relatives, friends, networks and patrons, or support from one's children in old age. For this line of research, a family (or household) strategy is 'a shorthand for the application of (culturally specific) perceptions of practical (subsistence) demands of daily life'.[56] For this approach, the problems faced by households are immediate economic problems. In some studies there is even a tendency to perceive the strategies as conscious patterns of actions based on cost-benefit calculations.[57]

---

in a Greek Rural Community', in P. Halstead and J. O'Shea (eds), *Bad Year Economics: Cultural Responses to Risk and Uncertainty*, 2nd edn (Cambridge, 1995), pp. 87–97.

[54]   On this critique, see Viazzo and Lynch, 'Anthropology', pp. 436–50; and Smith, 'Family Strategy'.

[55]   See also Badel, 'Introduction', pp. viii–ix.

[56]   L. Tilly and J. Scott, *Women, Work, and Family*, 2nd edn (New York, 1987), p. 7. See also C. Cox, *Household Interests: Property, Marriage Strategies and Family Dynamics in Ancient Athens* (Princeton, 1997); Forbes, 'Of Grandfathers'; Tilly, *Beyond Family Strategies*; T. Hareven, *Family Time and Industrial Time: The Relationship between the Family and Work in a New England Industrial Community* (Cambridge, 1982), pp. 189–217 with R. Rudolph, 'The European Family and Economy: Central Themes and Issues', *Journal of Family History* 17(2) (1992), pp. 119–38 and other 'Chayanovists' (see Emigh, 'Theorizing Strategies', p. 500).

[57]   Van der Linden, 'Introduction', pp. 3–4, 6; van der Linden, 'Conclusion', pp. 230–34; T. Brück, *Coping with Peace: Post-War Household Strategies in Northern Mozambique* (Oxford, 2001); see also Moen and Wethington, 'The Concept', pp. 244–5 and Wolf, 'Daughters', pp. 60, 64–5.

24 *Children and Asceticism in Late Antiquity*

More rarely, strategies have been seen not so much as means of immediate survival, but more as a source of future maintenance and improvement in the economic and social status of the family, aiming at the continuity of the families in the unpredictable future. Thus, considerations of inheritance are seen as essential; in pre-industrial societies especially, this implies a special emphasis on landed wealth and its retention.[58] Yet the economy is not separable from its social contexts and cultural values in shaping the strategies. Pierre Bourdieu has stressed the aim of transferring power and privileges by strategies of social reproduction in order to preserve the economic and social status of the family in a certain social hierarchy, and to ensure the biological continuity of the line and the reproduction of the labour force. He defines the strategies for reproduction as 'the sum total of the strategies through which individuals or groups objectively tend to reproduce the relations of production' by conserving or expanding the material and symbolic capital. Giovanni Levi, using the concept of strategies in much the same way, defines strategies as aiming at the 'transmission of social skills, occupations, activities, and roles' for the (material) survival of the kin. The centre of interest is on a network of relatives aiming for the continuity of wealth, power and privileges.[59] If the studies consider immaterial factors at all, whether cultural or social, these are mostly seen as outside interference, imposing limits and constraints on the possible behaviour models available for contributing to the ultimate goals of the strategies: survival, welfare, preservation of the patrimony and (economic) security.[60]

---

[58] See e.g. L. Feller, 'Introduction. Enrichissement, accumulation et circulation des bien', P. Freedman, 'North-American Historiography of the Peasant Land Market' and C. Dyer, 'The Peasant Landmarket in Medieval England', all in L. Feller and C. Wickham (eds), *Le marché de la terre au Moyen Âge* (Rome, 2005) with Rudolph, 'The European Family'.

[59] Bourdieu, 'Les stratégies', pp. 1106, 1124–5; Bourdieu, *Outline*, p. 70; Levi, *Inheriting Power*, esp. pp. xiv–xvii, 36–49, 145–55.

[60] Brück, *Coping with Peace*, pp. 20–22; van der Linden, 'Conclusion', pp. 232–3; M. Baud, 'Patriarchy and Changing Family Strategies: Class and Gender in the Dominican Republic', *History of the Family* 2(4) (1997), pp. 355–6; Moen and Wethington, 'The Concept', pp. 235, 237–8, 245–8; Rudolph, *The European Family*; and Hareven, 'The History of the Family', p. 117. For Levi, the primary aim is to understand the 'irrational' elements in social action and economic transactions (Levi, 'Family and Kin', p. 569). See also Jack Goody, who identifies security (in old age; on patrimony; for the afterlife) as the ultimate aim of inheritance strategies. However, Goody concentrates on the material side of heirship and he himself defines the goals of strategies differently elsewhere (see J. Goody, *Production and Reproduction: A Comparative Study of the Domestic Domain* (Cambridge, 1976), pp. 86–7, 97; *The European Family* (Oxford and Malden, MA, 2000), p. 10). See also Emigh, 'Theorizing Strategies', pp. 498–9, 512–13 on the preservation of patrimony as the

If the focus of a study is to understand economic behaviour, and the question is material survival, focusing on economic aspects is naturally justified. To this end, reducing the family to a production unit can be an efficient and fruitful strategy for research. However, even the basic question of what part is played by the non-economic aims in overall family strategies has scarcely been studied. Therefore, the study of family strategies has in some statements been limited to the upper levels of society and to modern times, the logic being that people living on a subsistence level have had no options or choices to make: they could not have any strategies.[61] Furthermore, the emotional ties between the individuals have not been taken into consideration.[62] People strove for continuity of their property and privileges – but what about their memory and reputation, cultural values or identities, their afterlife? It is taken as self-evident that people would want their property (and privileges) to end up in the right hands after their death, but how can this desire be understood in purely economic terms?

The starting point in my present study is that both material and non-material aims are inevitably intertwined in any strategies: the family economy approach is not sufficient to explain the behaviour patterns of families as a whole and of their individual members, and economic strategies cannot be treated in isolation. Indeed, the other constituents of the Ancient Greek concept of economics, ἡ οἰκονομία, as management of a web of relations constituting a household or a family,[63] has to be taken into consideration for a more balanced analysis of the family dynamics and 'economies'. Moreover, the idea that wealth, power and privileges (whether acquired directly by economic strategies, or indirectly by the accumulation of symbolic heritage or immaterial legacy) would constitute the nucleus around which the strategies would inevitably turn has to be widened by including the aims of security and continuity. Social and cultural factors not

---

assumed goal of studies on pre-industrial family strategies. Emigh also mentions security as a possible goal.

[61] See e.g. Viazzo and Lynch, 'Anthropology', pp. 430–31 on Natalie Zemon Davis. However, L. Fontaine and J. Schlumbohm ('Introduction', in L. Fontaine et J. Schlumbohm (eds), *Household Strategies for Survival, 1600–2000: Fission, Faction and Cooperation* (Cambridge, 2001), p. 9) claim that strategies (and also non-material strategies) can be found even in concentration camps.

[62] See, however, Engelen, Kok and Paping, 'The Family Strategies', p. 249. Of the scholars cited above, only Giovanni Levi mentions emotions, and even he sees them as a means towards understanding the economic rationale behind the actions; Levi, 'Family and Kin', pp. 568–9.

[63] According to Aristotle, for example, ὁ οἶκος is built up by relationships between individuals: husband and wife, parents and children, master and slave (Aristotle, *Politics* 1254 b2–6, 1259 a37–1260 a14, 1278 b32–37).

only play a role in limiting the boundaries of action and 'accepted' behaviour for achieving fundamentally material goals, they also affect these goals.

Therefore, the concept of 'continuity strategies' supplants here 'family strategies' as a guiding theoretical frame of reference. Inevitably, any theories which guide the process of interpretation include underlying assumptions about what is considered to be 'normal' human behaviour. For the present study, it is possible to point out three basic assumptions behind the concept of continuity strategies, following the general idea of human nature conceptually divided into three basic spheres, involving biological, social and psychological viewpoints. First, I acknowledge the drives for reproduction and survival as basic biological human traits, and already as such contributing to an individual person's pursuit of continuity. Second, the behaviour of an individual also depends on interdependency, affection and solidarity towards the persons on whom continuity is dependent. It is another question altogether as to whether 'altruism' is in fact to be reduced to ingrained cultural norms or to the need for continuity, not to mention the reduction of all these factors to biology and evolutionary processes. These questions are far beyond the scope of the present study and, in any case, even if these background constituents are conceptually separate, they are inevitably interwoven in social practices.

Third, instead of economic security, I have identified the pursuit of immortality – or, more exactly, the individual pursuit of a sense of continuity – as the ultimate goal of the continuity strategies and as the best path to understanding both the argumentation of the ecclesiastical writers and the patterned behaviour featured in the sources. The most important background principle for continuity strategies is the idea of symbolic immortality. This concept is derived from the work of Robert J. Lifton, who sees the pursuit of the sense of symbolic immortality as a driving force which leads an individual to seek different ways to transcend death.[64]

As distinct from the sparse existing scholarship on symbolic immortality, I aim to highlight the nature of continuity strategies as culturally conditioned

---

[64] R. Lifton, 'The Sense of Immortality: On Death and the Continuity of Life', in H. Feifel (ed.), *New Meanings of Death* (New York, 1977); R. Lifton, *The Broken Connection: On Death and the Continuity of Life*, 3rd edn (Washington DC, 1996), esp. pp. 13–35 with L. Vigilant and J. Williamson, 'Symbolic Immortality and Social Theory: The Relevance of an Underutilized Concept', in C. Bryant (ed.), *The Handbook of Thanatology, Vol. 1, The Presence of Death* (Thousand Oaks, CA, 2003). Lifton proposes five major modes for an individual to achieve immortality: natural (continuity as a part of the natural world); creative (continuity by creative acts, and in passing of the values, skills and knowledge); transcendental (continuity in religious imagery); biological (continuity in children and in institutions carrying collective social identity); and the experiential mode (as the sense of personal continuity already achieved).

and discursively structured. Moreover, the psychological or sociological models presented do not pay attention to issues of property, which constitute essential parts of my continuity strategies approach, whereas he philosophical and psychological theories present the basic constituents and drives for continuity common to all human cultures. Thus, they do not fit as such into the analysis of culturally embedded forms of behaviour – what makes the issue interesting from the historian's point of view are the changing forms which the strategies for continuity take.[65] On the other hand, Zygmund Bauman's theory identifies the aspiration to immortality specifically with modern and postmodern worlds. His starting point is that the risk of death is the foundation of culture, as 'human culture is a gigantic ongoing effort to give meaning to human life'; thus, the efforts to transcend death are at the very core of culture and society.[66] As his standpoint is modernity, he affirms that everything 'pre-modern' is one and the same: culture dominated by religions, and thus a timeless world without any problem about solving the meaning of life. After all, Christian beliefs guarantee immortality and therefore there was no task for survival for an individual, as in modernity.[67] I will return to these Bauman's claims in the *Conclusions*, as my study challenges his views on continuity and how the way of life was perceived in pre-modern societies.

---

[65]   See e.g. Lifton, *The Broken Connection*, pp. 17–18. See also E. Shneidman, 'The Postself', in J.B. Williamson and E.S. Shneidman (eds), *Death: Current Perspectives*, 4th edn (Mountain View, CA, 1995), using the concept of 'postself'; D. Unruh, 'Death and Personal History: Strategies of Identity Preservation', *Social Problems* 30(3) (1983), pp. 340–45, 349, introducing the idea of strategies for identity preservation; for a philosophical approach, see Scheffler, *Death and Afterlife* with the list by Arnold Toynbee of the various ways for human beings to reconcile themselves with death in A. Toynbee, 'Traditional Attitudes Towards Death', in A. Toynbee et al., *Man's Concern with Death* (London, 1968). On property as a central constituent for the sense of symbolic immortality, see S. Kan, *Symbolic Immortality: The Tlingit Potlatch of the Nineteenth Century* (Washington DC, 1989).

[66]   Bauman, *Mortality, Immortality*, pp. 8 and 31; for the different means for aiming immortality, see pp. 24–33, 51–87. Bauman's principal claim is that modern strategies for immortality consist mostly of the deconstruction of death, crystallized in death management by medicalization. On the other hand, this strategy is destined to fail, since the ultimate death remains inevitable. In response to this, Bauman sketches an emerging postmodern strategy for immortality, immortality deconstructed as self-representation – but not producing a renown that continues into the future, instead of the fame of the moment. There is only 'now', as he claims (Bauman, *Mortality, Immortality*, pp. 129–60 and 166–99).

[67]   Bauman, *Mortality, Immortality*, pp. 91–2.

Continuity and Roman Culture

The identification of the sense of continuity as the goal for strategies is not, however, only due to the theoretical literature. Even if continuity strategies in the Roman Empire have not previously been an object of study *per se*, and the use of the concept of family or household strategies has been limited among ancient historians, various strategies have been referred to in research. These studies serve as the basis for the theory of continuity strategies with systematically formed subcategories to describe the possible strategic means of pursuing continuity. These subcategories, in turn, make it possible to analyse the possible changes in discourses and practices.[68]

A starting point for the categorization of strategic means is provided by Peter Garnsey, according to whom the strategies for ensuring the security and everyday subsistence of the non-elite can be categorized into three groups: production strategies, demographic adaptive mechanisms and social economic relationships. Production strategies include dispersal of landholding, storage and diversification of product. The particular demographic adaptive strategies that Garnsey mentions include the age at marriage, intervals between births, contraception, abortion, exposure of the newborn and infanticide. The social and economic relationships, in turn, include market exchange and reciprocal exchange of goods among equals, social networks with solidarity between kinsmen, neighbours and friends, and relationships of patronage.[69] In the ancient contexts there were seldom opportunities to live without relations with one's family and kin. In contrast, the prevalence of strategies outside the family sphere in the modern world should also be noted: acquiring a proper education, an occupation, even changing occupations 'in the open labour market' and ending up as a retiree supported by a regular pension are individual strategies dependent on the community and society as a whole rather than on families. However, migration, with the local labour markets, should be added

---

[68] Since the lists by Z. Bauman, R. Lifton, A. Toynbee and others of the different 'constituents of continuity' are not based on any particular material that is systematically scrutinized, these can help only marginally here in directing the attention to certain features in the ancient sources.

[69] P. Garnsey, *Famine and Food Supply in the Greco-Roman World: Responses to Risk and Crisis* (Cambridge, 1989), pp. 43–68. On a more general level, in most societies there are in use 'an array of different strategies in a hierarchy of responses, which are equated with both the scale of the producing and consuming units (individual, households, villages, state) and with the magnitude of the resource failure encountered' (P. Halstead and J. O'Shea, 'Introduction. Cultural Responses to Risk and Uncertainty', in Halstead and O'Shea (eds), *Bad Year Economics*, p. 4.

Approaches and Strategies 29

to Garnsey's list, even if its importance in the ancient contexts is difficult to assess.[70]

Especially for the wealthier in society, there were a variety of further strategies available to maintain and enhance social prestige, political sway and the survival of the family line. Indeed, in ancient studies, the concept of 'strategies' in a sociological or anthropological sense is most often used in the context of the alliance politics of the aristocratic families of Athens and Rome. The stress has mostly been on political and economic motives and factors. These strategies were not directed only towards the future; the continuity of lineage in the past was part of the power strategies of the highest elite, sometimes taking the form of fictive genealogies and *exempla* taken from the (imagined) heritage of the ancestry. This mode of study is pervasive in the monumental collection of papers edited by Jean Andreau and Hinnerk Bruhns, and by its 'sequel' collection edited by Christophe Badel and Christian Settipani on kinship and family strategies.[71] During the 1990s, this approach was especially prominent in the studies by Mireille Corbier and Cheryl Ann Cox.[72]

Instead of studying (in-)family dynamics, interest has been focused on the social and political power and machinations of the kin groups, in which the strategies for networks of friendship, patronage and alliance play the prominent role. Roman aristocracies had a range of strategies designed for 'regulating the circulation of women and wealth, the formation of alliances between families and between individuals, and the definition of legitimacy in the context of political power'. For this, forming of social networks by marriages, remarriages, divorces, adoption and public donations are seen as

---

[70] For migration as a modern family strategy, see e.g. van der Linden, 'Introduction', p. 7. On migration for work and survival in Ancient Rome, see C. Holleran, 'Migration and the Urban Economy of Rome', in C. Holleran and A. Pudsey (eds), *Demography and the Graeco-Roman World: New Insights and Approaches* (Cambridge, 2011) with K. Killgrove, 'Migration and Mobility in Imperial Rome', PhD dissertation (University of North Carolina, 2010).

[71] Andreau and Bruhns (eds), *Parenté*; Badel and Settipani, *Les strategies familiales*. For the retrospective genealogy, see esp. M. Dondin-Payre, 'La stratégie symbolique de la parenté sous la République et l'empire romains', in Andreau and Bruhns (eds), *Parenté*, pp. 53–76; and M. Grant, *Greek and Roman Historians. Information and Misinformation* (London and New York, 2000), p. 65.

[72] Cox, *Household Interests*, esp. xix (elite marriage strategies concerning political and material consolidation), pp. 62–7, 216–29; M. Corbier, 'Les Comportements familiaux de l'aristocratie romaine (IIe siècle av. J.-C. – IIIe siècle ap. J.-C.), in Andreau and Bruhns (eds), *Parenté*, esp. 225–6 and 244–5; Corbier, 'Divorce and Adoption', pp. 47–9; 62–8, 73–4; Corbier, 'Introduction', pp. 11–16.

the main strategic means.[73] These strategies sought success for the kin group in order to acquire and retain power and privileges while simultaneously safeguarding survival of the line and continuity of the name, honour and *domus* without dispersing the patrimony among too many heirs.

The principal instrument for these strategies for *fama* and *nobilitas* was marriage: 'However large the family groups for which, and within which, strategies are planned, and whatever the purpose served by such strategies, they all (except adoption) involve marriage relations.'[74] The decisive place of marriage in the strategies already implies that divorces and remarriages were also important vehicles for strategic ends.[75] Naturally marriage played a crucial role in all levels of society on a more general sense: parents expected their progeny to marry, to establish the succession and survival of the family and its name in the future. Marriage formed the basis of biological and social reproduction.

However, on level of survival and advancement, the most important strategy for achieving political success, honour and status for oneself or one's children was wealth itself. Property was 'a primary concern in the maintenance of the family standing or the acquisition of higher status', and in this public munificence played a major part.[76] There are also instances of public generosity and seeking after communal honour and remembrance among the non-elite, although advancement in the political sphere does not appear in this group. On the other hand, to seek benefits from munificence and patronage served

---

[73]   Quote from Corbier, 'Divorce and Adoption', p. 77. See also Andreau and Bruhns, 'Introduction', pp. x–xi; J. Gardner, *Family and Familia in Roman Law and Life* (Oxford, 1998), pp. 136–43; Badel, 'Introduction', pp. xii–xvii.

[74]   J. Crook, '"His and Hers": What Degree of Financial Responsibility Did Husband and Wife Have for the Matrimonial Home and Their Life in Common, in a Roman Marriage?', in Andreau and Bruhns (eds), *Parenté*, p. 153; on elite marriage strategies, see the individual contributions in Andreau and Bruhns (eds), *Parenté* (esp. Bénabou; Burnand; Copet-Rougier; Corbier; Humbert; Jacques; Massa-Pairault; Moreau; Mossé; and Rémy); and Badel and Settipani, *Les stratégies familiales* (esp. Pietri; Freu; Mathisen; Joye; and Cabouret-Laurioux) with Corbier, 'Divorce and Adoption', pp. 62–3; Corbier, 'Épigraphie et parenté', pp. 103–4, 118–23; Harlow and Laurence, *Growing Up*, pp. 93–103; Cox, *Household Interests*, esp. pp. 62–4, 128. K. Hopkins, 'Seven Missing Papers', in Andreau and Bruhns (eds), *Parenté*, p. 625 warns against assuming that the family was subordinated to the politics.

[75]   Corbier, 'Divorce and Adoption'; Dondin-Payre, 'La stratégie', p. 53; and Andreau and Bruhns, 'Introduction', p. xx.

[76]   P. Garnsey and R. Saller, *The Roman Empire: Economy, Society and Culture* (London, 1996), pp. 112–23; Saller, *Patriarchy*, p. 229 (quote). On public munificence in this context, see e.g. Gardner, *Family*, pp. 137–8.

as a survival strategy for the poor.[77] The continuity of patrimony was primarily ensured by inheritance strategies. Roman law provided for many sophisticated options for structuring the material succession.[78] *Fideicommissum* and *usufructus* were particularly suitable for ensuring that patrimony ended up with the right inheritors: when the child was still a minor, the administration of the property was given to a guardian without ownership.[79] Strategic emancipation of family members was another, although probably less popular, option for following a strategy and playing favourites in the succession.[80]

Since Roman law could have been used to validate many customary patterns of behaviour, it cannot itself explain any one particular pattern.[81] However, testaments were the main means by which individuals tried to continue their influence even after death. Testaments themselves were not only made for financial security in one's old age, for doing 'the right thing' for others or for fulfilling the expectations of the surviving relatives and the community as a whole. The testators also sought 'security in the foreknowledge that one's family would continue after one's death ... and security in the feeling that one would be remembered after one's death', thus ultimately aiming at this-worldly immortality.[82] The continuance of name, patrimony and self in the memories of the survivors is a central motivation in the considerations of succession in Roman culture. In fact, the pursuit of continuity has been seen as one of the most prominent features in Roman culture: 'The consideration of perpetuating the line seems always to have retained great importance for the Romans.'[83] Much depended on the existence and survival of progeny.

---

[77]   See V. Vuolanto, 'Male and Female Euergetism in Late Antiquity. A Study on Italian and Adriatic Church Floor Mosaics', in P. Setälä et al., *Women, Power and Property in Roman Empire* (Rome, 2002), pp. 245–302 on the late antique church floor donations by non-elite persons. On patronage as a survival strategy, see Garnsey, *Famine*, pp. 266–8.

[78]   Gardner, *Family*, pp. 103–4, mentioning wills, dowries, emancipation children and adoption. See further pp. 105–40, 190–204, 274–7, with Saller, *Patriarchy*, esp. pp. 160–62, 171–7 and Dixon, 'The Circulation', pp. 226–7. See also J. Rowlandson and R. Takahashi, 'Brother–Sister Marriage and Inheritance Strategies in Greco-Roman Egypt', *Journal of Roman Studies* 99 (2009), 104–39.

[79]   Saller, *Patriarchy*, pp. 171–6; and J. Hillner, 'Domus, Family, and Inheritance: The Senatorial Family House in Late Antique Rome', *Journal of Roman Studies* 93 (2003), p. 134 for Late Antique Rome.

[80]   Gardner, *Family*, pp. 103–4, 112–13; Saller, *Patriarchy*, p. 175.

[81]   Saller, *Patriarchy*, p. 180.

[82]   E. Champlin, *Final Judgments: Duty and Emotion in Roman Wills 200 B.C.–A.D. 250* (Berkeley, 1991), pp. 21–2, 25. Champlin notes here in passing the resemblance of this idea to that of Jack Goody, *Production and Reproduction*, p. 87 of people seeking security.

[83]   Gardner, *Family*, p. 202.

In the absence of natural children, alternative strategies were developed. Whereas adoption proper in the Roman context contributed mostly to the aristocratic alliance strategies for creating networks of friendship and links between the families,[84] different ways of custodial arrangements were used to form relations of quasi-kinship to ensure an easier old age and the continuity of the family name and property after death. This happened most often through different modes of fostering, or 'quasi-adoption', permanent relocation of children (which, for the most part, were not juridically binding adoptions according to Roman law). These applied to foundlings, but the most favoured of the home-born slaves (*vernae*) could also be informally adopted. Some children were given or even pawned to other households.[85] Suzanne Dixon has also pointed out that the socially inferior position of the *alumni* would have contributed to their usefulness as guarantors of security in old age, and also to the continuity of traditions such as family cult, or memory of the ancestors.[86] On the other hand, 'slaves and freedmen formed an active part of the *familia* and in both economic and psychological terms could serve as an alternative strategy to children and 'family''[87] for those who could afford it.

The wealth at one's disposal effectively limited the options for adopting means of continuity. For the non-elite, the above-mentioned legal strategies for patrimony and inheritance were of less importance. The reason for this is not only the relative lack of property, but also ignorance of the legal devices. In the transmission of wealth, the arrangements used were usually not official in nature, even if they were intended to be binding on the local community in

---

[84]   Corbier, 'Divorce and Adoption', pp. 63–76; J. Gardner, 'Status, Sentiment and Strategy in Roman Adoption', in Corbier (ed.), *Adoption et fosterage*, pp. 71–5; Gardner, *Family*, pp. 136–40, 190–204; C. Badel, 'L'adoption: un modèle dépassé?', in Badel and Settipani, *Les stratégies familiales*, pp. 81–108. See also J. North, 'Family Strategy and Priesthood in the Late Republic', in Andreau and Bruhns (eds), *Parenté*, pp. 527–43 on a family adoption strategy to get a son into a priestly *collegium*.

[85]   S. Dixon, 'The Circulation of Children in Roman Society', in Corbier (ed.), *Adoption et fosterage*, pp. 226–7 (support in old age). On quasi-adoption, see Dixon, 'The Circulation', pp. 223–4; Hanne S. Nielsen, 'Quasi-kin, Quasi-adoption and the Roman Family', in Corbier (ed.), *Adoption et fosterage*, pp. 249–62; and Badel, 'L'adoption', pp. 89–100. See also B. Rawson, *Children and Childhood in Roman Italy* (Oxford, 2003), p. 352 and Corbier, 'Épigraphie et parenté', pp. 134–6. For the pawning and giving away of children, see V. Vuolanto, 'Selling a Freeborn Child: Rhetoric and Social Realities in the Late Roman World', *Ancient Society* 33 (2003), pp. 192–5.

[86]   Dixon, 'The Circulation', p. 223.

[87]   A. Wallace-Hadrill, 'Houses and Households: Sampling Pompeii and Herculaneum', in B. Rawson (ed.), *Marriage, Divorce and Children in Ancient Rome* (Oxford, 1991), p. 227; see also Dixon, *The Roman Family*, pp. 113–14.

question. Most often, these took some form of quasi-*fideicommissum*, quasi-*tutela* or quasi-adoption.[88] Despite the formal legal prohibitions, for example, there were attempts by husbands to leave the guardianship and property management of their minor children to their mothers. They were seen to be the most reliable in safeguarding the patrimony for the next generation, even if legally they belonged to another *familia*. Indeed, even Roman legislation yielded in certain limits to acknowledge the strong role mothers had in the lives of their children: magistrates were obliged to obey the will of the mother in nominating guardians, the mother had the duty to oversee guardians in their management, and mothers often did act as (unofficial) guardians and advisors for their children. Mothers' guardianship was institutionalized in the late fourth century CE, even if only on condition that the mother did not remarry. This, together with changes in the second-century inheritance legislation, securing the succession rights between mothers and children, highlights the legal intentions to strengthen the links between the mothers and children for the preservation of the property inside the (maternal) family line.[89] In the widest sense, the legal Roman *familia* itself can be seen as a means to an end, a mechanism to promote the welfare and contentment of families of whatever composition,[90] that is, a means to pursue continuity.

Except for immediate survival and social advancement for the self or for one's progeny, the considerations of old age were of paramount importance. Outside the elite, the only possibility of ensuring at least relative security was to rely on one's relatives, and more specifically on the relatives who were under a special moral obligation to oneself: one's own children. As Keith Bradley has pointed out, the sorrow of the parent after the death of a child also included sorrow over the loss of material security in old age. Progeny were expected to give both food and succour, economic and moral support. Control of and investment in labour

---

[88]   See e.g. for adoption, Gardner, *Family*, pp. 190–99; and C. Kotsifou, 'Papyrological Perspectives on Orphans in the World of Late Ancient Christianity', in Horn and Phenix (eds), *Children in Late Ancient Christianity*, pp. 347–8; for *fideicommissum* and *usufructus*, see V. Vuolanto, 'Women and the Property of Fatherless Children in the Roman Empire', in P. Setälä et al., *Women, Power and Property in the Roman Empire* (Rome, 2002), pp. 227–9 with Saller, *Patriarchy*, pp. 174–5; on making wills by the 'lesser people', see Champlin, *Final Judgements*, pp. 55–9.

[89]   Vuolanto, 'Women and the Property', esp. pp. 229, 240–43; Beaucamp, *Le statut de la femme, vol. I*, pp. 314–19 and 325–37. For the inheritance legislation and its intentions, see T. McGinn, 'Roman Children and the Law', in Evans Grubbs, Parkin and Bell, *The Oxford Handbook*, pp. 346–7.

[90]   Gardner, *Family*, p. 279.

and education for the children brought a return in the form of support for the parents in old age.[91]

Children were not only vehicles for carrying on the memory, even the physical likeness, and traditions of already deceased family members in Roman ideology, thus maintaining or even enhancing family status and honour,[92] but already the very idea that a child would outlive a parent resulted in solace and a sense of personal continuity. Children surviving into adulthood would mean material and emotional support for the parents and continuity both for themselves and for earlier generations.[93] Indeed, Cicero even derived the etymology of the word *superstitio* from those who spent whole days praying and sacrificing to ensure that their children would survive them (*superstites essent*).[94] For the individual, this-worldly continuity, especially to have progeny, was of primary importance.

However, there were conflicts between the various strategic aims. For example, seen only from the point of view of strategies of reproduction aiming for the biological continuance of the self, it would be advantageous to maximize the number of children: to marry early, to find a young and fertile mate, not to remain a widow or widower. However, to have a family without means to provide for it would not be profitable in attempting to achieve continuity, and even if there were means, splitting up patrimony among too many heirs would not promote the honour of the family.[95] Moreover, for women, this strategy could be perilous in times of high puerperium mortality.[96] Regardless of social

---

[91] K. Bradley, 'Child Labor in the Roman World', in K. Bradley, *Discovering the Roman Family: Studies in Roman Social History* (Oxford, 1991), pp. 117–18; T. Parkin, *Old Age in the Roman World: A Cultural and Social History* (Baltimore and London, 2003), pp. 205–26; see also C. Laes, 'High Hopes, Bitter Grief: Children in Latin Literary Inscriptions', in G. Partoens et al. (eds), *Virtutis Imago. Idealisation and Transformation of an Ancient Ideal* (Leuven, 2004): esp. pp. 50–51.

[92] C. Baroin, 'Ancestors as Models: Memory and the Construction of Gentilician Identity' and V. Dasen, 'Wax and Plaster Memories: Children in Elite and Non-Elite Strategies', both in V. Dasen and T. Späth (eds), *Children, Memory, and Family Identity in Roman Culture* (Oxford, 2010), pp. 19–48 and 109–45.

[93] See e.g. Dio Cassius, 56.3.1–5: a person who has children lives on in them and their successors; see Dixon, *The Roman Family*, pp. 109–11, 115; and Rawson, *Children*, esp. p. 225.

[94] Cicero, *On the Nature of the Gods*, 2.28.72 (45/44 BCE): 'nam qui totos dies precabantur et immolabant, ut sibi sui liberi superstites essent, superstitiosi sunt appellati'.

[95] On this, see Saller, *Patriarchy*, pp. 161; Corbier, 'Les Comportements familiaux', pp. 229; Andreau and Bruhns, 'Introduction', p. xx.

[96] Indeed, older women seem to have remained widows rather than remarrying. See R. Bagnall and B. Frier, *The Demography of Roman Egypt* (Cambridge, 1994), pp. 126–7.

standing, high infant mortality often ruined parents' hopes for posthumous continuity and immortality by means of their children.[97]

Any categorizations of strategies should not obscure the fact that an effective means would contribute to multiple strategic ends simultaneously. This can be illustrated by referring to a number of possible profits for the relocation of children (child labour, apprenticeship and different modes of care arrangements): these would cut down the expenses of upkeep, extend and re-affirm the existing relationships of kinship and patronage, and rationalize the division of inheritance.[98] Adoption, on the other hand, was a useful strategy not only for short-term political motives, to (re)structure posterity and the order of succession or to gain continuity for the patrimony, but also for the continuity of the family itself, its traditions, name and cult of the family. For Cicero, legitimate reasons for adoption included the transmission of inheritance, name, wealth and rites (*hereditas nominis pecuniae sacrorum*). The concern for the name is also evident in the practice known as 'testamentary adoption': taking the name of the testator was the prerequisite for inheriting.[99] These reasons were also relevant in the lower scale of society, as the unofficial adoption agreements show. In a system which legally saw women as 'a beginning and end of her *familia*', it would be meaningless for women to be adopted and to adopt, if we do not take into account also the need for a sense of emotional security and continuity. And, indeed, women adopted progeny. The continuity of family property itself was a matter of sentiment, also affecting testaments and their bequests.[100]

---

[97] See e.g. Dixon, *The Roman Family*, pp. 111–12, 115. On infant and childhood mortality, see T. Parkin, 'Life Cycle', in M. Harlow and R. Laurence (eds), *A Cultural History of Childhood and Family in Antiquity* (Oxford, 2010), pp. 97–114, 199–201.

[98] Vuolanto, 'Selling a Freeborn Child', esp. pp. 189–97, 203–6 (selling, pawning and apprenticeship of children); Bradley, 'Child Labour', esp. pp. 117–18 (child labour, apprenticeship); Dixon, 'The Circulation', esp. pp. 222–7 (apprenticeship, exposure and quasi-adoption of children, alumni). On child exposure, see also Evans Grubbs, 'The Dynamics'.

[99] Cicero, *On His House*, 13.35 with Corbier, 'Divorce and Adoption', pp. 63–4, 69; Dixon, 'The Circulation', p. 223; Corbier, 'Introduction', pp. 13–16; Gardner, *Family*, pp. 129–30, 141–3; Champlin, *Final Judgements*, p. 26. There are, however, only a few known cases of adoption and of testamentary adoption, and almost all come from the senatorial elites (O. Salomies, 'Names and Adoption in Ancient Rome', in Corbier (ed.), *Adoption et fosterage*, pp. 145–7; Gardner, *Family*, pp. 133–45).

[100] Champlin, *Final Judgements*, p. 178; Gardner, *Family*, pp. 155–65; and J. Gardner, 'Status, Sentiment and Strategy in Roman Adoption', in Corbier (ed.), *Adoption et fosterage*, esp. pp. 64–7, 77–8; Badel, 'L'adoption', pp. 89–100; for some reason Christophe Badel argues for not using the concept 'strategy' for the lower social scale adoptions as, according to him, these aimed merely at the survival of the people in question, and thus the actors would have had no choice (thus, 'tactics' would be a better word). However, not only there

As the discussion of the functions of adoption also shows, the strategies were not restricted to economic or material considerations, but included ideas like remembrance, and continuity of the cult and name. In particular, the continuity of one's name was a key way of living on in one's descendants. The cases of 'testamentary adoptions' present only one way in which this becomes evident. Nor is continuity of the name a concern only for the elite; parents from other levels of society also expected their successors to perpetuate the family name in the future.[101] This can be seen with particular clarity in the clauses in testaments and funerary monuments which specify that the property in question, whether patrimony or tomb, should not leave the name, or *ne de nomine exeat*, as the formula often ran.[102] Whether a condition for the institution of an heir or for property left as a *fideicommissum*, the central aim is the transmission of the name. From this perspective, it is not surprising that even if the immediate family was by far the most frequent beneficiary in testaments, freedmen, carrying on the name, were preferred over more remote kin. Beyond the nuclear family, only siblings and their children were normally of importance. In this respect, there was a prevalence of name over blood.[103]

On a more general level, the desire for continuity of the name is visible in all uses of inscriptions and, as such, it was not restricted to the elites, nor did it cease among the Christians. The tombs themselves, situated close to the road and city walls, with the names of the deceased clearly marked, provided a useful and well-exploited vehicle for preserving the name and the memory of an individual – even in perpetuity, as the common formula *memoriae aeternae* implied. Moreover, it was specified in many cases that tombs and their inscriptions were set up because of the explicit will of the deceased, and they included formulae prohibiting them from going to the heir, since that would have jeopardized the survival of the name of the original proprietor of the tomb. On the other hand, the frequent use of clauses giving the right to use tombs for the *libertis libertabusque posterisque eorum* ('to freedmen and freedwomen and their posterity') contributed both to

---

were other options available (e.g. sending their children to work outside of homes or pawning them), but more importantly, it would be difficult to see what would have coerced the adopter to act. What would have been the essential difference here with the more elite sort of adopters?

[101] Cf. e.g. Harlow and Laurence, *Growing Up*, pp. 92–5; Laes, 'High Hopes', esp. p. 51.

[102] Saller, *Patriarchy*, pp. 169–70; Champlin, *Final Judgements*, 26 and 177–9. On the importance of honour associated with the name among the aristocracy, see Saller, *Patriarchy*, pp. 79–80.

[103] Saller, *Patriarchy*, pp. 168–71, 178–80, 230–31; Champlin, *Final Judgements*, pp. 129–30.

the continuity of the memory of the name (since it was shared with the former master) and the continuity of the upkeep of the tomb.[104]

Epitaphs, however, were passive aids to the memory of the survivors, whereas funerals, ongoing rituals and annual feasts at the tomb were more active ways of commemorating the departed. These were the duty of the immediate relatives, especially of the children. In the absence of blood relatives, freedmen, friends, burial clubs and the like would carry out the commemoration and would thus produce a kind of posterity for oneself.[105] Not surprisingly, in many testaments there are detailed instructions for the upkeep of tombs, prohibitions against their alienation and instructions for regular cultic acts. The favouring of the closest relatives in the testaments had little to do with the continuance of the family property or family cult in terms of religious fervour or altruism. The intent of the more specific family settlements recorded on tombs and in inscriptions was essentially the same: to keep in the family the property on which the testator's tomb was situated, and thus to keep the name and memory of the deceased alive among family members.[106]

One aspect of becoming immortal is through one's fame and reputation in society at large. This idea was cherished by the Roman elite. Reputation was sought in the offices held and in the deeds carried out in one's lifetime, the *res gestae*, the memory of which survived in family traditions, such as funeral speeches, ancestral busts and genealogies, and in a more general and public way in panegyric literature and biographies, and sometimes in the inscriptions celebrating triumphs and victories.[107] Literature was also a way to make the writer himself immortal. As Horace claims: *exegi monumentum aere perennius*. The *topos* of an author writing for posterity, looking for merit and thanks only from them, is a commonplace in Roman literature.[108] Even for the Roman

---

[104] See e.g. Champlin, *Final Judgements*, pp. 174–9.

[105] Rawson, *Children*, pp. 225–6; Harlow and Laurence, *Growing Up*, pp. 140–41; Dixon, *The Roman Family*, pp. 108–15; Laes, 'High Hopes', p. 49.

[106] Champlin, *Final Judgements*, pp. 25–7, 161–8, 175–82.

[107] On family measures, see: Dondin-Payre, 'La stratégie'; Corbier, 'Épigraphie et parenté', pp. 124–31; Grant, *Greek and Roman*, pp. 65–6; on history writing, see: A. Woodman, *Rhetoric in Classical Historiography: Four Studies* (London and Sydney, 1988), pp. 41–4, 95–6 with e.g. Cicero, *For Rabirius* 29: 'neque quisquam nostrum in rei publicae periculis cum laude ac virtute versatur quin spe posteritatis fructuque ducatur'; Cicero, *Letters to Friends* 5.12.1: 'neque enim me solum commemoratio posteritatis ad spem quandam immortalitatis rapit'. See also Laes, 'High Hopes', esp. pp. 51–2.

[108] Horace, *Odes* 3.30; See also e.g. Lucian, *How to Write History*, 61; Livy, *History of Rome*, praef. 3; Ovid, *Letters from the Black Sea* 2.6.30–36, 4.8.45–51; Tertullian, *On the Testimony of the Soul* 4.10.

Stoics, for whom any form of pursuing immortality would in principle be a sign of irrationality, the posthumous *fama* due to virtue alone was worth aiming for as a way of survival for an individual.[109] The desire for immortality was seen as a perennial force in the human being, as can also be seen in the *post mortem* punishments nowadays called *damnatio memoriae*.[110]

The desire for the perpetuation of one's reputation is also evident in public munificence, such as the funding of food distribution and alimentary programmes, games and buildings. In this kind of virtuous behaviour of contributing to the community, commemoration was achieved simultaneously on two different levels: first, in the act itself and, second, in the inscriptions proclaiming the donation. Only in the Christian tradition in the fifth century did anonymous donors emerge, a phenomenon unknown to the earlier Greek or Latin traditions.[111] Often, the acts of benefaction resulted from testamentary foundations. In these contexts, the aim of achieving immortality for the founder was often explicitly articulated: for the average Roman testator, personal immortality was survival in the memory of others.[112] The donations were intended to perpetuate the memory of the individual in a community as a magnanimous benefactor.

During the late Republic and the Principate, the beliefs in an afterlife, centred on the immortality of the soul, were neither widespread nor strong. Nevertheless, the emphasis on burial was a major factor in Roman culture. Funeral banquets with offerings of food and wine might have had vague ideas of a transcendental soul behind them, but proper burial, preferably in the vicinity of one's ancestors and performed meticulously with traditional rites, was seen

---

[109] Seneca, *Letters to Lucilius* 79.19: 'Si quod est pretium virtutis ex fama, nec hoc interit.' Cicero, *Stoic Paradoxes* 2.18: 'Mors terribilis iis, quorum cum vita omnia extinguuntur, non iis, quorum laus emori non potest', with e.g. Cicero, *For Archias*, 11.26–7. For a similar idea in the Hellenistic Jewish tradition, see *Wisdom of the Salomo* 4, esp. 4.1.

[110] See especially Cicero, *Tusculan Disputations*, 1.14.31 (the motto of this chapter) with Cicero, *Cato the Elder on Old Age* 23.82: 'Sed nescio quo modo animus erigens se posteritatem ita semper prospiciebat, quasi, cum excessisset e vita, tum denique victurus esset. Quod quidem ni ita se haberet, ut animi inmortales essent, haud optimi cuiusque animus maxime ad immortalitatis gloriam niteretur' and Tertullian, *On the Testimony of the Soul* 4.9–10. On the *damnatio memoriae* (a modern concept used to cover many inter-related punishments), see C. Hedrick, *History and Silence: The Purge and Rehabilitation of Memory in Late Antiquity* (Austin, 2000) with K. Mustakallio, *Death and Disgrace: Capital Penalties with Post Mortem Sanctions in Early Roman Historiography* (Helsinki, 1994).

[111] Champlin, *Final Judgements*, p. 166; for the earliest anonymous donor known to me, see Vuolanto, 'Male and Female Euergetism', p. 280, case 133 (early fifth century).

[112] Champlin, *Final Judgements*, pp. 25–7, 155–68; see, however, the cases mentioned in Rawson, *Children*, pp. 360–61.

Approaches and Strategies   39

to contribute to the rest of the dead among the *manes* in the underworld. A proper burial was needed for immortality, either for immortality in this world in commemoration by the survivors or for peace in the afterlife. Thus, burial was regarded as a major constituent of the virtue of *pietas*, a virtue by which personal relations and behaviour were assessed, especially in the family sphere.[113] For this, the importance of progeny was paramount. Children were not only necessary for comfort and livelihood in old age or for commemoration after death, but also as a guarantee of a proper burial at death.[114]

Gain and continuity not only concerned the deceased. It was common to put the name of the erector of the tomb at the top of the inscription, before the deceased themselves. In particular, among those, who lacked other means of propagating the family name and achievements, the commemoration of the dead was important for escaping anonymity and leaving a lasting record of one's life. Monuments are for the preservation of the memory, as the imperial jurist Ulpian stated.[115] Nor were the family banquets beside the tombs only for the spirits of the dead. It may have been that the dead were present and took some solace from the offerings, but it was of primary importance to perpetuate the memory of the dead relatives on earth.[116]

For the Romans, both among elite and non-elite persons, immortality was primarily a state of being remembered: 'For the Roman testator personal immortality was survival in the memory of others.'[117] Ancestry and rituals played an important part in the system of family memory and ideologies. They were not only part of the immortality of the deceased, but might also contribute to the advancement strategies of the surviving family members and relatives, since they

---

[113] See Saller, *Patriarchy*, pp. 105–14 with E. Rebillard, *The Care of the Dead in Late Antiquity* (Ithaca and London, 2009), pp. 90–91 for burial and *pietas*. Other principal Roman virtues were *virtus, honos, fides, gravitas* and *humanitas*, linked to each other by the example of the forefathers, *mos maiorum*.

[114] Nathan, *The Family*, p. 26; D. Kyle, *Spectacles of Death in Ancient Rome* (London and New York, 1998), pp. 128–33; Champlin, *Final Judgements*, pp. 180–82.

[115] *Digesta* 11.7.2.6 (Ulpian): 'Monumentum est, quod memoriae servandae gratia existat.' See e.g. J. MacWilliam, 'Children among the Dead: The Influence of Urban Life on the Commemoration of Children on Tombstone Inscriptions', in S. Dixon (ed.), *Childhood, Class and Kin in the Roman World* (London and New York, 2001), pp. 85–90.

[116] H. Kotila, *Memoria mortuorum. Commemoration of the Departed in Augustine* (Rome, 1992), pp. 30–38; Champlin, *Final Judgements*, pp. 180–84. On the belief in the afterlife in Antiquity, see M. Beard, J. North and S. Price, *Religions of Rome, Vol 1. A History* (Cambridge, 1999), pp. 289–91.

[117] Champlin, *Final Judgements*, pp. 25–7, 180–82 (quote p. 26) with Edwards, *Death*, pp. 13–18 and Nathan, *The Family*, p. 26.

40 *Children and Asceticism in Late Antiquity*

connected the living with the dead, their deeds and social networks. The most important monument was not the physical tomb, but the invisible monument consisting of the cult and commemoration, leading to the preservation of the memory of the deceased as an individual.[118] In the desire for immortality and the setting up of monuments, the importance of family, or more specifically of children, was understood to be paramount.

Continuity Strategies and Other Tools

To draw together the results of the discussion presented above, I have composed a framework for the continuity strategies, presented here as Figure 1. This serves as the guiding principle for analysis in subsequent chapters in order to allow us to understand what was going on in the discourse on asceticism and children. Indeed, understanding means the translation of past 'texts' into present language:[119] the concept that interprets is the concept of the interpreter. Thus, any historical understanding beyond the bare chronicle of events is a construction (not merely a reconstruction) of the past, and by its very nature theoretical. Theories serve not as laws, but as guidelines or explanatory hypotheses for understanding the phenomena in question. They are tested, not proved – and if the explanatory hypotheses 'survive all attempts at disproof based on substantial evidence, we have done well'.[120]

For the purposes of analysis and conceptualization, the strategic actions of an individual for continuity are divided into strategies directed towards survival in the period of an individual's lifetime (both in the sense of immediate survival and in consideration of old age) and economic and social advancement (for power and privileges), and into the strategies for symbolic immortality, aiming at achieving a sense of continuity beyond death. However, no strict distinction can be made between the strategies for survival and advancement during one's lifetime and for continuity after death. For example, public generosity and beneficence aimed not only for immediate gain and increase of social capital, but also for continuity as reputation and commemoration after death.

---

[118] On the interaction of memorizing, individualization and the desire of evading death (especially in Greek thought), see also S. Humphreys, *The Family, Women and Death: Comparative Studies* (Ann Arbor, 1993), p. 174.

[119] Cf. e.g. H.-G. Gadamer, *Truth and Method* (London, 1985), p. 497.

[120] R. Bagnall, *Reading Papyri, Writing Ancient History* (London and New York, 1995), p. 101.

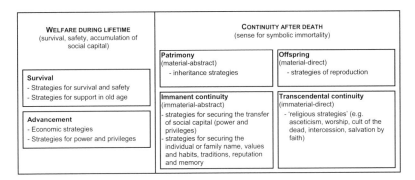

Figure 1

CONTINUITY STRATEGIES

The continuity strategies themselves may take place, or be understood to take place, in different contexts: in the family sphere, in kinship or friendship networks, in the context of local or wider communities (like such 'imagined communities' as nation states) and, finally, even in the context of human kind, nature or the cosmos as a whole. It should be noted that the strategies or their contexts do not need to be real (that is, tangible) as their relevance is in the experience of an individual.

On the other hand, to achieve after death continuity, the transfer of inheritance and immaterial legacies to the next generation had to be secured.

On the economic level, there was a constant tension between everyday consumption of economic resources for survival and attaining power and privileges, and the need for the family members to maintain and transfer the property to future generations: the relative importance of the two is situational and culture-specific. However, it is clear that they are built on each other. To take a simple example: without the means to provide a livelihood for the family, spouse and offspring, it is pointless to make an investment for the progeny and the possible continuity thereof.

The different ways in which the individual aims for continuity after death are classified into four categories with the help of the variable pairs material-immaterial and concrete-abstract. The first mentioned dichotomy denotes the essence of the vehicle for continuity. Therefore, by material constituents I mean the physical 'objects' the person leaves behind on death (land, property, monuments), as well as children and those personal groups in which the individual had participated in life (family, kin and other, even imagined, communities). In turn, immaterial continuity consists of name, memory, traditions and values, and spiritual progeny (such as pupils or converts) that is, various 'extensions of existence'[121] of the immanent realm on the one hand and the personal transcendental continuity on the other hand.

---

[121] To use the concept of Champlin, *Final Judgements*, p. 25.

The concrete-abstract dichotomy, in turn, concerns the way in which these vehicles are transmitted in order to achieve continuity: it distinguishes the concrete biological continuity of the self as continuity 'of the same blood' and the religious continuity aiming at the concrete immortality of the personal self in the transcendental realm from the abstract ways of personal continuity in the succession of name, values, memory or spiritual offspring. This category of abstract continuity can also be called 'collective afterlife',[122] as these constituents of immortality depend on the continuity of the community as a whole to carry on the individual.

In total, there emerge four categories for after-death continuity: strategies for reproduction, inheritance strategies, strategies for transcendental continuity, and strategies for commemoration and socialization.[123] The manner in which a particular community and its members assess the relative importance of these different modes of continuity is inevitably culture-bound.

Turning to families, one of the core problems in the study of family strategies has been the interplay between the individuals and their social frame of reference. The families are not unchangeable coherent blocks, but consist of persons with individual aims and ambitions, both short-term and long-term. Those willing to stress the usefulness of the family strategy approach have emphasized the 'moral economy' or 'collective ethos' as a notion of shared interests, guiding the behaviour of individual family members. Ultimately, custom, mutual need and shared experience override personal autonomy. Since the processes of 'contention, bargaining, negotiation and domination as well as consensus' take place inside the family, the result appears to the scholar as a family strategy.[124] In this way, the compromises and conflicts between individuals could fit and hide inside the strategies. However, critics have pointed out that families are no altruistic havens of solidarity in a stormy sea of self-interest,[125] and the bargaining positions of the different members of the family are not equal. Thus, a distinction

---

[122] See Scheffler, *Death and the Afterlife*, pp. 68–73.

[123] See also Corbier, 'Divorce and Adoption', p. 47 for the behaviour of aristocracies aiming at 'biological reproduction, transmission and extension of patrimony, diversification and expansion of symbolic capital'; Dixon, 'The Circulation', p. 227: individuals aiming at a pleasant old age, the maintenance of cult, status, family holdings, profession and name after death; Harlow and Laurence, *Growing Up*, pp. 94–5: Romans aiming at the procreation of legitimate children, the perpetuation of the family name, and the preservation of family property, wealth and status.

[124] Tilly and Scott, *Women, Work and Family*, p. 9 (quote) with Wolf, 'Daughters', pp. 60–64.

[125] Baud, 'Patriarchy', esp. pp. 366, 371–3; Wolf, 'Daughters', esp. pp. 43–4, 66–7. See also Viazzo and Lynch, 'Anthropology', pp. 449–50.

should be made between the strategies of the family (as a whole) and strategies in the context of the family. Family strategies are therefore strategies of those people who make the decisions and whose goals are being pursued. Family itself can be seen as a strategy for its members.[126] If there is a family strategy to be found, it is the sum total of the individual strategies of the familial power-holders that are carried out by the families. From this perspective, family strategies can be defined as implicit, recurrent patterns of familial behaviour resulting from the individual strategies of continuity at the family level.

Thus, even if a single decision may be based on the explicit reasoning of the power-holders in a family and forms a part of their individual strategies, the strategies are understood here as intellectual tools for analysing values, modes of thought and patterned behaviour in a society on a more general level. These are not necessarily obvious to the actors themselves, who do not need to know that their particular choices would be informed by certain culturally embedded continuity strategies.

The viewpoint I have adopted here for the framework of continuity strategies takes the strategies *for* family as its starting point: a family is an object of decision making rather than a decision-making unit. From this individualistic viewpoint, these are different strategies taking place in various spheres of living – family strategies in the familial sphere. Indeed, the strategies for continuity could be classified according to the particular environment or carrier thought to ascertain the personal continuity. There are strategies for families, for kin, for friendship and neighbourhood networks, for the local community and for 'imagined communities' (such as religious movements, nations and class) and, at its most extreme, the ideas of humankind as a whole, immanently or transcendentally understood nature, or the godhead or other supernatural powers.

The approach of the present study is essentially qualitative. Quantitative aspects are occasionally included in order to illustrate the scale of the relative frequencies of the phenomena in question, but they should be seen as indicative and preliminary material for closer textual analysis. For this reason, the analysis in this study is comparative in nature and is dependent on many dichotomies that must be compared with each other. Particular attention is paid to the

---

[126] See also Baud, 'Patriarchy', p. 372 with Hareven, *Family Time*, p. 370: 'the family provided its members with continuity, a resource to draw upon'. Cf. Emigh, 'Theorizing Strategies', p. 497; and Fontaine and Schlumbohm, 'Introduction', p. 7 who claim that an individualistic standpoint makes it impossible to analyse the transactions between households and the 'outside world'. However, to take into account the power structures in families hardly prevents the scholar from contextualizing the outcome as a strategy for families in their social and cultural contexts.

attitudes and prejudices in familial behaviour to be found in treatises propagating virginity and in the early hagiographic *vitae*, as they are compared to the actual cases found particularly in epistolary material. A special problem emerges in estimating the relative frequency of quarrels and disagreements relating to asceticism compared to cases in which everything has gone smoothly: most of the cases are known especially because of these real or alleged disagreements. However, it is possible to compare cases involving different kinds of families: are there differences in relation to asceticism within a family group when the person active in propagating ascetic values and practices is a *paterfamilias* or a husband, a mother or a wife, a son, a daughter or a more distant relative? Are there differences in behavioural patterns when one or both parents have died?

Moreover, it is possible to compare ideals and practices, and pay attention not only to the explicit argumentation and choices, but also to the non-reflected assumptions and the culturally embedded needs and mentalities in searching for the reasons for choosing an ascetic lifestyle for oneself or for one's relatives. Thus, 'the unspoken, unreflected assumptions of the author are sought, which, since they are precisely not "named" by the author, must be garnered from the broader culture'.[127] The traditional values referred to by the sources are compared to the emerging Christian ethos as more explicitly construed by the ecclesiastical writers who propagate asceticism. Special attention is paid to the comparison of the activities of men and women as well as to the authors' differing perceptions of masculinity and femininity. A further point of comparison is between the Eastern and Western elites; although my emphasis lies in the western part of the Empire, this helps to decipher which attitudes and practices were shared, and which were conditioned by more local practices and habits.

---

[127] As Dale B. Martin sketches the new way of doing history of Late Antiquity after the 'cultural turn' (Martin, 'Introduction', p. 17).

Chapter 2

Family, Kin and the Right Way of Living as a Christian

> Whoever comes to me and does not hate father and mother, wife and children, brothers and sisters, yes, and even life itself, cannot be my disciple.[1]
>
> But if you desire to be perfect, leave your country and your kin with Abraham, and go where you do not know.[2]

For early Christians, the Bible was the ideological source for assessing family life. In the Gospels, negative references to the biological family were used to emphasize the importance of suppressing the 'old' social connections to follow Christ. Simultaneously, this contributed to the need to undermine family loyalties, which were the carrier of the traditional cultic acts and religious thinking. The most radical expression of these needs is the demand that a disciple should not bother to bury his father, but to 'leave the dead to bury their own dead'.[3] As such, this kind of expression would have been unheard-of in the context of contemporary Mediterranean culture.[4] Moreover, for the apostle Paul, marriage is indeed an existing option (in this he opposes the most radical contemporary ascetic claims), but, as such, is only a second-rate option – again, a deviation from the Greco-Roman or Jewish cultures.[5] This certainly was not a promising start for a suspect, potentially extremist sect, and did not augur well for its chances of becoming a dominant religion. Re-definitions were needed

---

[1]   Luke 14:26. All Bible translations are from the *New Revised Standard Version*.

[2]   Jerome, *Letters*, 125.20 (to Rusticus): 'Aut si perfecta desideras, exi cum Abraham de patria et de cognatione tua, et perge quo nescis.'

[3]   Matthew 8:21–2. For the other examples of the 'anti-family' trends in the synoptic gospels, see e.g. Mark 3:31–5; Matthew 12:46–50; Matthew 19:28–9; Luke 8:19–21, with J. Barclay, 'The Family as the Bearer of Religion in Judaism and Early Christianity', in Moxnes (ed.), *Constructing*, esp. p. 74.

[4]   On the importance of proper burial and the responsibility of the children in the Greco-Roman world, see Kyle, *Spectacles of Death*, pp. 128–30, 246–54; Kotila, *Memoria mortuorum*, pp. 28–32 and 79–81.

[5]   Verdon, 'Virgins and Widows', p. 492; H. Moxnes, 'What is Family? Problems in Constructing Early Christian Families', in Moxnes (ed.), *Constructing*, esp. 38; Barclay, 'The Family', p. 75.

both for the Christian concept of abandoning the family and for the traditional Roman idea of familial *pietas*. In this chapter, as well in the two following ones, I will study the writers of the texts, their ideas, presuppositions and rhetoric of persuasion. The question of how far these views represent the general mentality of the late Roman elites and the assessment of the influence of such discourse on actual family level practices are left to subsequent chapters.

Hating the Family, Loving the Desert

The emotional attachment to parents was seen as the paragon of this-worldly ties. For many fourth- and fifth-century ecclesiastical writers, the words of Jesus in reply to Peter's question about the disciples' reward served as the basic text concerning kinship ties and the following of Christ:

> Truly, I say to you, in the new world, when the Son of man shall sit on his glorious throne, you who have followed me will also sit on twelve thrones, judging the twelve tribes of Israel. And every one who has left houses or brothers or sisters or father or mother or children or lands, for my name's sake, will receive a hundredfold, and inherit eternal life.[6]

Although the ecclesiastical authors were somewhat cautious about attaching unique spiritual gains to virginity, the underlying ethos is clear enough: for Ambrose, for example, to care for a maiden's virginity is to safeguard her passing through life to eternity. In fact, according to him, 'the Scriptures have brought to light many women, but it has given the palm of salvation only to the virgins'.[7] Augustine claims that marriage is to continence as health is to immortality; freedom from sexuality is 'both angelic exercise here and continues forever'. In another passage Augustine claims that it is wrong to hold that continence is not necessary to attain the kingdom of heaven. There is a special heavenly prize in store for holy virgins. If a girl promised by her mother to virginity would choose otherwise, she would not necessarily thereby lose the kingdom of God, but she

---

[6] Matthew 19:28–9.
[7] Ambrose, *The Consecration of a Virgin*, 17.107: 'ut transeat vitam, ad illa aeterna pertranseat'; Ambrose, *Exhortation to Virginity*, 5.28: 'Multas feminas Scriptura divina in lucem evexit, palmam tamen publicae salutis solis virginibus dedit.'

Family, Kin and the Right Way of Living as a Christian 47

would lose the high place and special rewards there.[8] A married wife can be accepted into heaven, but her bliss is not perfect.

The situation is somewhat changed if the woman is widowed and then takes a vow of chastity. Jerome, for example, promises that the dead Blesilla is exalted in triumph in heaven and reigns with Christ, since she had overcome the Devil by her asceticism in her widowhood. Similarly, Paula the Elder had gained an inheritance in heaven since she had left her family and family wealth for widowed chastity.[9] The ascetic women, especially the virgins, were the spiritual nobility with special privileges in the world to come. Therefore, Christians taking their vocation seriously should not honour their parents over God, but should leave their 'father, mother, siblings, lands and homes' for asceticism. Christians should hate their kin. Taking the Christian message seriously required – at least symbolically – a rejection of the old dependencies, duties and loyalties:

> Should your little nephew hang on your neck, should your mother, with her hair dishevelled and garments rent, show you the breasts with which she suckled you, should your father lie on the threshold, trample him under your foot and go your way.[10]

Love of God should prevail over all other bonds, and love of spiritual kindred should be preferred to relatives in flesh: blessedness comes not through just and holy relatives, but by obeying and following their teaching and conduct, as Augustine recalled.[11]

These attitudes are most pronounced in the earliest monastic rules from the eastern part of the Empire. They were strict in insisting that those admitted to the religious communities should forget their earthly kinship ties. In his rule, Basil of Caesarea prohibited members of monastic communities from visiting or caring for their relatives. Even talking to relatives or other outsiders was strictly

---

[8]   Augustine, *On the Good of Widowhood*, 8: 'Non ergo duo mala sunt connubium et fornicatio, quorum alterum peius, sed duo bona sunt connubium et continentia, quorum alterum est melius'; Augustine, *On Holy Virginity*, 13, 22–7, esp. 25; Augustine, *Letters*, 3*.1 (420s CE?). See also e.g. Eusebius of Emesa, *Sermons*, 7.5, 14 and 24: who remains a virgin will embrace the resurrection as a bride of Christ.

[9]   Jerome, *Letters*, 22.30 (on Blesilla); Jerome, *Letters*, 108.6 and 33 (on Paula).

[10]   Jerome, *Letters*, 14.2: 'Licet parvulus ex collo pendeat nepos, licet sparso crine et scissis vestibus ubera quibus nutrierat mater ostendat, licet in limine pater iaceat, per calcatum perge patrem.'

[11]   Augustine, *On Holy Virginity*, 3. See also e.g. *Anonymous Homily on Virginity* 112–17; Pseudo-Athanasius, *On Virginity*, 2; Jerome, *Letters*, 120.1; Paulinus of Nola, *Letters*, 25.7–8; Basil, *Longer Rules*, 12; Ambrose, *Commentary on Psalm 118*, 15.

controlled. Basil gives a double explanation for these principles: first, contacts with people living in the world turn the minds of the monks to earthly things, their 'hearts returning to Egypt'; and, second, the relatives of the members of the brotherhood should be treated as relatives to all the brethren.[12] In the so-called *Canons of Athanasius* it is laid down that the virgins should not be left alone with their relatives. They are not to attend the burials of their closest relatives alone, but are to be attended by the mother of the ascetic community.[13]

Even harsh treatment of the kin and the family of origin is proposed in the many exemplary tales in the hagiography and anecdotes on the desert fathers. Asceticism and chastity are repeatedly referred to as prerequisites for salvation. The total rejection of the family is depicted as one of the greatest tests on the path to perfection: all who desire to be saved should renounce their parents and all earthly things.[14] Pachomius was said to have tested prospective monks to see whether they could renounce their parents, and to have forbidden any contact between the brothers and their kin. In the case of his successor as monastic leader, Theodore, his mother had asked a bishop to intervene so that she would be allowed to see her son. When the mother arrived at the monastery, Pachomios asked Theodore if he was willing to go to meet her, but he replied: 'If I go out and meet her, will I not be found inferior before the Lord as a result of transgressing his commandment that is written in the gospel?' The mother was only able to see her son by climbing up onto the roof of a house and waiting for Theodore to come out of the monastery to work.[15]

Fittingly, one of the first temptations by which Antony the Great – the paragon of ascetic virtue – was tested was that the Devil made him remember his family status and possessions, and the duties due to his sister.[16] When John Cassian interpreted the story of Antony to a Western audience, he even claimed that Antony was initially inspired expressly by the requirement of the Gospels to hate one's family – for Athanasius, the important passage was the

---

[12] Basil, *Longer Rules*, 32 ('Ἐστράφησαν ταῖς καρδίαις αὐτῶν εἰς Αἴγυπτον', citing Num 14:4); see also Basil, *Longer Rules*, 8.2 and Basil of Caesarea, *Shorter Rules*, 107, 188 and 189, citing Matthew 12:48: 'Who is my mother, and who are my brothers?'

[13] *Canons of Pseudo-Athanasius* 92 and 101. On the rules of the Pachomian communities with similar overtones, see S. Elm, 'Gregory's Women: Creating a Philosopher's Family', in J. Børtnes and T. Hägg (eds), *Gregory of Nazianzus: Images and Reflections* (Copenhagen, 2006), pp. 293–4.

[14] Pseudo-Athanasius, *On Virginity*, 2.

[15] *Life of Pachomius* (Bohairic version), 37 (trans. J.E. Goehring). The later Greek version has Pachomius test both prospective monks and their parents (*Life of Pachomius* (first Greek version), 24).

[16] Athanasius, *Life of Antony*, 5(4).

call to perfection and eunuchdom.[17] In fact, according to Evagrius Ponticus, the demon of sadness manifests itself principally by reminding the ascetic of his former life, home and parents.[18] To illustrate this message, he told a story about a monk, who, when told about the death of his father, said to his informant: 'Stop your blasphemies. My father is immortal'.[19] God the father is the real father of a Christian.[20]

John Cassian tells of an extreme case that illustrates the proper disposition towards one's closest kin in his *Institutions*: Patermutus had entered a monastery together with his eight-year-old son. In order to test the father, the little boy was purposely neglected and exposed to blows and slaps, and it was ensured that the father knew it. One day, the superior of the monastery pretended that the crying of the child annoyed him, and told the father to throw him into the river. The father did this, not knowing that the boy would be rescued a little way down the river. According to Cassian, after this, the man's faith and devotion were confirmed by a revelation to the superior.[21]

The association between salvation, asceticism and contempt for kin, especially progeny, was close. Sulpicius Severus pointed out the need for ascetics to divorce themselves from family relationships by telling the story of an adolescent from Asia Minor, who as a military tribune in Egypt visited the desert often and met hermits there. When he 'accepted the word of salvation' from Abba John, he left his wife and a small child for the desert. However, after having achieved great virtue, 'suddenly a thought came to him, inspired by the Devil, that it would be better for him to return to his country to save his only son and his entire household including his wife'. Consequently, the monastic community was

---

[17]   John Cassian, *Conferences*, 3.4 and Athanasius, *Life of Antony*, 2.3–4; I owe the observation to Jacobs, 'Let Him Guard', p. 277.

[18]   Evagrius Ponticus, *Praktikos*, 10. See also ibid., 12 (on the demon of *acedia*), with Evagrius Ponticus, *Antirrhetikos* 2.49 and 6.7.

[19]   Evagrius Ponticus, *Praktikos*, 95: Ἐμηνύθη τινὶ τῶν μοναχῶν θάνατος τοῦ πατρός· ὁ δὲ πρὸς τὸν ἀπαγγείλαντα, παῦσαι, φησί, βλασφημῶν· ὁ γὰρ ἐμὸς πατὴρ ἀθάνατός ἐστιν'; Palladius assimilates this monk to Evagrius himself: Palladius, *The Lausiac History*, 38.13. See also Socrates, *Ecclesiastical History*, 4.23.

[20]   For the development of the idea of the fatherhood of God, see P. Widdicombe, *The Fatherhood of God from Origen to Athanasius* (Oxford, 1994). He stresses the fatherhood of God as a mere abstract formulation to reinforce the power relationship, a point refuted by van Dam, *Families and Friends*, pp. 76–7, who points to the actual experiences of fatherhood behind the notion.

[21]   John Cassian, *Institutions*, 4.27.2–3; on this case, see S. Knuuttila, *Emotions in Ancient and Medieval Philosophy* (Oxford, 2004), p. 148. A similar case with different protagonists is found in *Apophthegmata patrum*, Sisoes 10.

forced to hold the man in chains and pray for him for two years to prevent him from returning to the world.[22]

Not surprisingly, the most decisive and extreme arguments for anti-familial action can be found in the monastic literature and in the biographies of the ascetic saints, but even in the more pastoral type of contemporary literature, the message was clear enough: only virgins can be more or less certain of their salvation, since they were ready to reject their nearest kin. In general, however, to grant only a secondary place to earthly relations, and especially to family ties, should be the ideal for all Christians.

Family Wealth and the Heavenly Inheritance

In connection to the contempt for kin, the rejection of riches was a key requirement for the perfection of saintly Christians in the fourth- and fifth-century writings. Not only was it important to use wealth well in general but, very specifically, it was also essential to be able to handle the family property righteously. Tertullian had asked: 'Shall the servant of God, who has disinherited himself from the world, yearn after heirs?'[23] As an ascetic virtue, charity had an important place in connection with chastity. Inheritance and being an heir are the themes to which the ecclesiastical writers most frequently refer in their discourse on asceticism and family. Again and again the writers urge their audiences to give away their patrimony and family possessions to the poor in order to accrue the inheritance in heaven, in connection with the family of Christ.[24]

Especially in hagiographic biographies, it was a *sine qua non* to mark the break with the world by the abandonment of family wealth and giving away property as alms. In many cases, the contempt for kin and patrimony is brought up only in a laconic note that the ascetic in question had left his or her family behind

---

[22] Sulpicius Severus, *Dialogues*, 1.22: 'cum interim subiit eum cogitatio iniecta per diabolum, quod rectius esset ut rediret ad patriam filiumque unicum ac domum totam cum uxore salvaret'.

[23] Tertullian, *An Exhortation to Chastity*, 12.3: 'Sed posteritatem recogitant Christiani, quibus crastinum non est; heredes dei servus desiderabit, qui semetipsum de saeculo exhereditavit?'

[24] For development of the discourse on wealth, poor and the 'treasure in heaven' in the Western Christianity, and its relationship with the traditional Roman thinking, see Brown, *Through the Eye of a Needle*, pp. 69–90.

Family, Kin and the Right Way of Living as a Christian 51

and disposed of the property.[25] However, narratives concerning the donations by the two Melanias provide the most striking examples. Palladius tells that Melania the Elder 'persevered so much in hospitality, that she possessed not a span of land', leaving nothing for her son. When she returned to visit Rome, her propagation of ascetic values consisted of the idea of chastity, both for married couples and for virgins, and of the disposal of property. She herself, leaving Rome for the second time, 'sold all her remaining goods'. Having got rid of her possessions, she died in Jerusalem.[26] When Melania the Younger, in turn, made her husband choose chastity in marriage, her first action was to donate her silk dresses to altars and then to give away much of her property, a process for which Palladius gives a minutely detailed list. After that, there is but a simple sentence on her ascetic lifestyle.[27] In this, the account of Gerontius about Melania the Younger is not dissimilar, as the liquidation of her and her husband's enormous wealth receives due attention, and is considered as the core of their asceticism, overshadowing even her married chastity.[28] Both the Melanias are described as having exchanged their inherited family wealth for a spiritual inheritance.

What the writers usually highlighted was not only the fact of the donation, or its great worth, but its fate as patrimony dispensed to the poor and thus lost to the family. According to Athanasius, for Antony the Great, the first action of his ascetic career was to give away his familial possessions.[29] For Palladius, the very virtue of a noble couple, Verus and Bosporia, was that they defrauded their children by letting them think that they would receive their inheritance undiminished, but, in reality, they spent the patrimony on the poor and on building churches. Only one married daughter out of four sons and two daughters received anything and kept some of the patrimony for the family.[30] In the story of Paesius and Isaias, Palladius further exemplifies the connection between patrimony, almsgiving and salvation: when their father, a merchant,

---

[25]   Some examples: Ambrose, *Letters*, 27.2, Jerome, *Letters*, 58 (both on Paulinus and Therasia); Augustine, *Letters*, 130.3 (Proba); Jerome, *Letters*, 127.1, 4 and 14 (Marcella); Paulinus of Nola, *Letters*, 5.6 (Sulpicius Severus). On hagiography, see e.g. Athanasius, *Life of Antony*, 2; Palladius, *The Lausiac History*, 16.1–2 (Paesius and Isaias); Pseudo-Athanasius, *Life of Syncletica*, 12; Theodoret of Cyrrhus, *Religious History*, 30.1 (Domnina); Mark the Deacon, *Life of Porphyry*, 6.

[26]   Palladius, *The Lausiac History*, 54.2, 5–6.

[27]   Palladius, *The Lausiac History*, 61.2–5 for the property, 61.6 for the ascetic *praxis*.

[28]   Gerontius, *Life of Melania* (Greek), 9.15–19. On the authorship of this *Life*, see D. Gorce, *Gerontius, Life of Melania (Greek). Texte grec, introduction, traduction et notes* (Paris, 1962), pp. 54–6, 60–62 with Cooper, 'The Household and the Desert', p. 14.

[29]   Athanasius, *Life of Antony*, 2.

[30]   Palladius, *The Lausiac History*, 66.1.

52 *Children and Asceticism in Late Antiquity*

died, they started to think that if they adopted the merchant's career, they would have to die and leave their labour to others. However, if they embraced the monastic life, they would make a profitable use of their patrimony and would not lose their souls.[31]

Highlighting the need to despise the wealth of the family was by no means limited to hagiography. For Jerome, Pammachius and Paulinus of Nola were model examples of the right state of mind: the sign of their status in the family of Christ was that they gave away their property to the poor and the obscure.[32] For Paulinus of Nola, the contempt for inherited family property was of special importance as he praises both Sulpicius Severus for his resolution to refuse the burdens of his inheritance, and Aper and Amanda, who divested themselves of their ancestral estates and their revenues. Paulinus also assures Pammachius that his great efforts in almsgiving will ensure him the possession of heaven; since this was done for his deceased wife Paulina, she too enjoys the fruits and the honour due to his deeds.[33]

The beginning of Jerome's obituary for Paula the Elder is typical in its building on the dichotomy between earthly and heavenly inheritances. He shows Paula despising first her lineage, then her patrimony and cares about leaving an inheritance for her children, and lastly attaching herself and her children to both the spiritual family tradition of asceticism and the inheritance in heaven.[34] Distribution of inherited wealth to the poor would bring freedom and a place in heaven with Christ. Proba, a rich aristocratic widow, was exemplary in this: she sold her possessions when even priests and monks took the opportunity after the Sack of Rome of buying estates cheaply.[35] Jerome also gives other examples of such a virtue: Lucinus was to be praised, since he did not follow 'the judgment of the blood', but closed his ears to the protests of the relatives and dispersed his patrimony to the poor.[36]

In any case, perishable possessions are far surpassed by the heavenly rewards due to the combined virtues of charity and chastity. Losing one's inheritance for asceticism is like a loan to Christ, who would pay it back, partly in this world and

---

[31] Ibid., 16.1–2 and 1.4.

[32] Jerome, *Letters*, 118.5.

[33] Paulinus of Nola, *Letters*, 5.6 (on Sulpicius Severus); 39, esp. 1–2 (on Aper and Amandus); 13.11–17, 27–8 (on Pammachius).

[34] Jerome, *Letters*, 108.2–6, 26, 31.

[35] Jerome, *Letters*, 130.7 and 14.

[36] Jerome, *Letters*, 75.4: 'Lucinus noster laude sit dignus, qui clausit aurem, ne audiret iudicium sanguinis, et omnem substantiam suam dispersit.' See also Jerome, *Letters*, 14.6 ('si perfectus es, cur bona paterna desideras?'), 118, 125.20.

partly in the world to come as everlasting life. Virgins are, as members of Christ's *familia*, 'co-heirs with him in the heavenly inheritance'.[37] For widows, a chaste life in Christ is the true comfort in the midst of worldly cares and uncertainty. It promises happiness and true riches in the next world, since heavenly treasure would not be accumulated only by alms to the needy, but would also be safely deposited and protected.[38] 'Who is your heir?' asks Jerome of Furia, a rich and childless widowed lady, and answers his own question: Christ. 'The father will be saddened but Christ will rejoice. The family mourns, but the angels bring forth their joy. Let the father do what he wishes with his property.'[39] Indeed, the idea of ascetics making the poor their heirs was established as a literary *topos* by the beginning of the fifth century.[40]

The religious state of mind and the actual moral character of an ascetic were revealed in the considerations concerning patrimony and the future transfer of inheritance. Caring for the paternal inheritance and the safeguarding of its passing down the family line signified an erroneous consideration of personal continuity on earth, neglecting the heavenly inheritance and the plight of the poor.[41] Even if the ecclesiastical writers disapproved of the attention paid to inheritances, its value for the elites was well understood and even used in argumentation. To have a succession and to be able to transfer inheritance was seen as a value in itself.[42] For example, when Ambrose was fighting against the practice of taking concubines, he reminded the audience that the children of these unions were not legitimate heirs. Even if these men are not 'moved by *pudor*', they should at least consider the future transfer of their property. Moreover, when he protests against imperial legislation on the privileges of the clergy which required them to give up their property in order to gain exemption from municipal duties and services, he evokes emotions by referring

---

[37] Ambrose, *On Virgins*, 1.11.64; Augustine, *On Holy Virginity*, 5: 'sunt illi in caelesti hereditate coheredes'; Ambrose, *Letters*, 27.2.

[38] Ambrose, *On Widows*, 9.53–8; Augustine, *Letters*, 130.1 and 30 (412 CE); and Augustine, *On the Good of Widowhood*, 21 (26), with Ambrose, *On Widows*, 11.67.

[39] Jerome, *Letters*, 54.4 (395 CE): 'Quem habebis heredem? ... Contristabitur pater sed laetabitur Christus. Lugebit familia sed angeli gratulabuntur. Faciat pater quod vult de substantia sua.'

[40] See e.g. Gregory Nazianzen, *Oration 7*, 20; Ambrose, *On the Death of his Brother Satyrus*, 2.13; Jerome, *Letters*, 66.5; Jerome, *Letters*, 127.14.

[41] Augustine, *Exposition on the Psalms*, 48.1.14; see also John Chrysostom, *Against the Opponents of Monastic Life*, 3.16.

[42] See also Hillner, 'Domus' on the importance of the aristocratic *domus* as a sign of continuity for the owners and their families.

to 'paternal and ancestral property'.[43] The same ideas also abound, albeit with irony, in a speech imagined by John Chrysostom which depicts the extreme grief of a father on hearing that his son has opted for the ascetic lifestyle: he is thinking of burning the house, fields and animals, as all his hopes of continuity for the ancestral lineage and accumulated patrimony are now gone.[44]

The Late Antique ascetic discourse on family wealth and inheritance shows the culturally prominent place it played in elite thinking of the period. For ascetically minded Christian writers, the need to transmit patrimony undiminished to the following generations was one of the central ways in which the attachment to what they saw as wrong traditional values was revealed. For them, contempt for family wealth was a prerequisite for belonging to another lineage, that of the family of Christ. Children were needed to carry on the family property, but in the Christian family, with the accrued heavenly inheritance, biological offspring were no longer needed for this kind of continuity.

Patria and the Heavenly Jerusalem

The requirement to leave behind kin and family wealth when striving for the perfect life is often accompanied by a requirement to leave behind one's place of origin, *patria*, home and children for the land of promise. Chaste Christians have no earthly *patriae*, but their place of origin and final rest is the heavenly Jerusalem.[45] In his memorial for his mother Monica, Augustine highlights her virtue by quoting her answer to the friends who asked whether she fears leaving her body so far from home: 'nothing is far from God'. Monica and her husband Patricius will be Augustine's fellow citizens in the eternal Jerusalem. The home of a Christian is in the city of God.[46] Similarly, Paulinus of Nola describes how his vocation had torn him from his native land and kin, making heaven his true

---

[43] Ambrose, *On Abraham*, 1.3.19 with Evans Grubbs, *Law and Family*, pp. 313–14; Ambrose, *Letters*, 73.13.

[44] John Chrysostom, *Against the Opponents of Monastic Life*, 2.2, 3.1. For further references to this function of children in Chrysostom, see B. Leyerle, 'Appealing to Children', *Journal of Early Christian Studies* 5(2) (1997), p. 263.

[45] See e.g. Pseudo-Athanasius, *On Virginity*, 24 (320–400 CE); Mark the Deacon, *Life of Porphyry*, 4. Augustine approvingly refers to Plotinus, who urges the real philosophers to escape the worldly life to the real *patria*: 'there is the Father, and there is everything' (Augustine, *City of God*, 9.17: 'Fugiendum est igitur ad carissimam patriam, et ibi pater, et ibi omnia').

[46] Augustine, *Confessions*, 9.11.28 (c. 400 CE): 'Nihil, inquit, longe est Deo' and ibid., 9.13.37. For burial as a symbol of attachment to family life and earthly values, see e.g. Jerome, *Letters*, 38.5; 39.4; 22.21.

Family, Kin and the Right Way of Living as a Christian 55

home and *patria*. He also attributed the same destiny to Melania the Elder, who by abandoning the worldly life became exiled from her fellow citizens, but, simultaneously, a citizen among the saints.[47] In the funeral oration for his sister Gorgonia, Gregory Nazianzen describes her as being loyal to the heavenly Jerusalem and its citizenship. The father of Gorgonia and Gregory, in turn, is pictured as 'the Abraham of our days', leaving his home and kin for the Promised Land.[48] Many hagiographical texts describe the protagonists' estrangement from their family and *patria*, often followed by an actual departure from their home and native country to embrace the ascetic life.[49]

Jerome frequently raises the image of ascetics leaving behind their relatives and native land. Bonosus had left his family and enrolled his name for citizenship of the new, heavenly city; Rusticus is to follow Abraham into exile from his country and kindred; Heliodorus should flee from his paternal home and come back only after he has acquired citizenship of his true country, the heavenly Jerusalem. A monk or a virgin cannot be perfect at home.[50] Likewise, one of the key themes of the obituary of Paula the Elder by Jerome was the confrontation between earthly kinship ties and the urge to live a truly Christian life: Paula deserted her *patria* (Rome), her *domus* and her *familia* (children, brothers, kin) by leaving for Jerusalem, which is for Jerome not only a place in Palestine but also a symbol of her dedication to strive for a heavenly heritage.[51]

However, Jerome had by no means forgotten his *patria*. Alaric's sack of Rome in 410 CE was a shock to him, and the importance of the city of Rome as the centre and symbol of the whole *orbis Romanus* is shown by his subsequent letters.[52] Moreover, although he urged men to leave their homes for the ascetic life, he stressed the need for virgin daughters to stay enclosed in their parental homes and to remain obedient to their parents. He complains to Rusticus that there are some virgins who leave their home and kin, and 'under the pretext of *pietas* seek suspect companions': they 'hate their family and are not touched by their affection'. However, Jerome urges Rusticus himself to leave his homeland

---

[47] Paulinus of Nola, *Letters*, 11.2, 14, 29.10. See also Ambrose, *Letters*, 27.1 on Paulinus of Nola leaving his home, country and kin.

[48] Gregory Nazianzen, *Oration 8*, 6 (369–74 CE). See also John Chrysostom, *Letters to Theodore*, 1.13 and 16 and John Chrysostom, *Homilies on Ephesians*, 21.4.

[49] See e.g. *Life of Caesarius of Arles*, 1.4; Hilarius of Arles, *Life of Honoratus*, 12; Mark the Deacon, *Life of Porphyry*, 6; Theodoret of Cyrrhus, *Religious History*, 8.1 (on Aphrahat).

[50] Jerome, *Letters*, 3.4 (to Bonosus); 125.11 and 20 (to Rusticus): 'si perfecta desideras, exi cum Abraham de patria et de cognatione tua, et perge quo nescis'; Jerome, *Letters*, 14.2 and 7 (to Heliodorus). See also Jerome, *Letters*, 22.1; 30; 54.2–3.

[51] Jerome, *Letters*, 108, esp. 2, 6 and 33.

[52] Jerome, *Letters*, 126.2; 127.12; 128.4; 130, esp. 3 and 6.

56   *Children and Asceticism in Late Antiquity*

and relatives. Similarly, although he advises Eustochium to leave her paternal home, she was requested not to leave her house or to have visitors there.[53]

Other authors also highlighted the positive points about female virgins living with their parents, isolated from the rest of the society. Even if the parental home was seen as the paragon of old values and attachment to the earthly realm and family obligations, it nevertheless signified the virtues of obedience, chastity and dutifulness. Thus, in reality, the relationships between the ascetics and their families and relatives often continued and remained close.[54]

These contradictory ideas can be reconciled by understanding that the requirement for leaving home and fatherland was a symbol of disengagement from the earthly bonds rather than an actual prompting to action. This is connected with the practicalities due to gender: whereas a monk cannot stay at home, or in his *patria*, and a widow is praised if she is able to leave her dearest kin, a female virgin is virtuous if she stays with her relatives, secluded in her parents' home. The alternative, often referred to in contemporary depictions, would have been to take refuge in an ascetic home community often led by an older (widowed) female relative.[55] In these early phases of asceticism, when the monastic life was not always a *de facto* option, home was seen as a safe bastion in the battle against earthly passions.

The frequent references to the idea of *patria* in connection with the duties towards family and attachment to kin show its importance for the ecclesiastical writers of the time in the construction of individual identities. Being a member of a family meant sharing a common identity as an inhabitant of a certain place and as an owner of certain estates or plots of land. Breaking with the emotionally charged place of origin meant leaving behind not only the local community, friends, land, household and the *domus* itself, but also the home

---

[53]   Jerome, *Letters*, 125.6 to Rusticus: 'Sunt, quae oderunt suos, et non suorum palpantur affectu'; 'sub nominibus pietatis quaerentium suspecta consortia'; 20: 'Aut si perfecta desideras, exi cum Abraham de patria et de cognatione tua, et perge quo nescis'. Eustochium: Jerome, *Letters*, 22.1 vs Jerome, *Letters*, 22.16–17. On the necessity of seclusion and staying at home, see also Jerome, *Letters*, 22.16; 22.25; 24.4; 117 with G. Cloke, *'This Female Man of God': Women and Spiritual Power in the Patristic Age, AD 350–450* (London and New York,), pp. 65–7.

[54]   E.g. Eusebius of Emesa, *Sermons*, 7.22; Ambrose, *On Virgins*, 1.7.32; Ambrose, *The Consecration of a Virgin*, 1.1 and 17.107; Gregory of Nyssa, *Life of Macrina*, 5 and 10; John Chrysostom, *Regulares feminae*, 7; *Canons of Pseudo-Athanasius* 98, with Nathan, *The Family*, pp. 81–2. On the frequent relationships between the ascetics and their biological kin, see R. Krawiec, '"From the Womb of the Church": Monastic Families', *Journal of Early Christian Studies* 11(3) (2003), pp. 295–6 with further references.

[55]   For documentation of this kind of communities, see Krause, *Witwen und Waisen*, pp. 75–7.

and family nucleus. All hope of family support was to be abandoned; all hope of the transfer of the family heritage, whether biological, economic or social, was to be exchanged for spiritual continuity in the context of Christian asceticism.

Right and Wrong Asceticism

In the early third-century Act of Thomas, chastity is shown as a passport to immortality: earthly marriage and spiritual marriage with Christ are depicted with the help of pairs of opposites: greediness and avidity in earthly marriage, and light and immortality in incorruptible spiritual marriage; the transitory human bridegroom, and Jesus the true and immortal bridegroom; bridal gifts that fade and grow old, and living words that never fade away; communion of destruction, and life eternal.[56] The text reflects the radical distinction made between material and spiritual worlds among some Syrian Christians. Marriage is likened to sin and is strictly separated from a lifestyle that leads to heavenly bliss. Indeed, the second- and third-century ecclesiastical writers claimed that many groups had made asceticism, and celibacy in particular, the prerequisite for salvation; marriage is fornication, introduced by the Devil or an evil demiurge.[57] In Manichaeism, the radical dualism between the Darkness, represented as material substance in this world, and Divine light, in this world mixed with the material, led to strict asceticism. The Elect, God's chosen, were required to abstain from any activity that contributed to the mixing of Light with material substance. To attain salvation, they had to follow a special diet, fast regularly and refuse to marry. The Hearers had to live a virtuous life in order to be reborn and to aspire to joining the body of the Elect. Marriage was not only a second-rate option but also a direct reason for the failure to attain salvation.[58]

This kind of anti-familial thinking survived inside Christianity despite the attacks against it by authors who were later identified as representing mainstream Christianity. The decisions of the Council of Gangra against the excesses of

---

[56]   *Acts of Thomas*, 12 and 124.

[57]   See e.g. Brown, *Body and Society*, pp. 103–21; and R. Uro, 'Ascetism and Anti-familial Language in the *Gospel of Thomas*', in Moxnes (ed.), *Constructing*, pp. 216–34, with Clemens of Alexandria, *Stromata*, 3.3.12, 3.3.22; 3.4.45; 3.4.49; 3.12.80–14.95; 3.17.102–4; Eusebius of Caesarea, *Ecclesiastical History*, 4.29 and Epiphanius, *Panarion*, 45.2; 46.2–3; 47.1.7; 47.9.

[58]   For Manichean attitudes against marriage, see M. Browder, 'Coptic Manichaean *Kephalaia of the Teacher*', in V. Wimbush (ed.), *Ascetic Behavior in Greco-Roman Antiquity: A Sourcebook* (Minneapolis, 1990), pp. 187–212.

58   *Children and Asceticism in Late Antiquity*

the Eustathians, who were said to loathe marriage and deny the possibility of salvation for housewives, show the persistence of the extremist trends in the mid-300s CE.[59] In enumerating the heretics, Augustine mentions among them Tatians, *Adamiani, Apostolici, Abeloitae* and Manichaeans as those who despise marriage. He claims that at least the latter two were active as contemporary groups in the region of Hippo, albeit that the *Abeloitae* were a dying sect.[60]

The connection between the ascetic teachings and groups held to be extremist, even heretical, caused problems for the ecclesiastical writers who aimed to erect distinctions between the 'pagan' lifestyle and the Christian ethos. Those fourth- and fifth-century writers who identified themselves as Catholics needed to be careful not to become associated with those who rejected marriage and family life as impure. They were at pains to distinguish their views from those of the Manichaeans, Marcion and other dualistic groups, and maintained that although they put virginity above marriage, they do not condemn marriage – if the desire for children is the sole reason for intercourse. Marriage is good, but pure and reasonable celibacy is better.[61] Athanasius, for example, had been careful to point out that Antony the Great had nothing to do with Manichaeans or other heretics despite his strict adherence to asceticism.[62]

When John Cassian tells a story about the marriage of the future Abba Theonas, he has his hero reproach his wife, who is not willing to live in celibacy with him. According to Theonas, salvation is obtained and Hell evaded only through chaste marriage. This would imply that salvation is not possible in normal married life, and Theonas indeed ended up leaving his wife. Later in the text, John defends himself: he is by no means condemning marriage, but only relating how the conversion of Theonas really took place. He has no opinion to

---

[59]   *Council of Gangra, Canon* 1, 14 and *Introductory Letter*, 1 (early 340s CE?). On the dating, see A. Silvas, *The Asketikon of St Basil the Great* (Oxford, 2005), pp. 59 and 486, with Socrates, *Ecclesiastical History*, 2.43 on Eustathius. See Elm, *Virgins*, pp. 106–11 and Silvas, *The Asketikon*, pp. 19–20, 56–60 on the Council of Gangra and Eustathius. More generally on heresy, asceticism and family in the Eastern part of the Empire, see Patlagean, *Pauvreté économique*, pp. 130–44.

[60]   Augustine, *On Heresies*, 25 (Tatian and Encratites); 31 (*Adamiani*); 40 (*Apostolici*); 46.13 (Manicheans); 87 (*Abeloitae*). Apostolici were still extant in the fourth century, but seem no longer to have existed by the times of Augustine (Epiphanius, *Panarion*, 61.1–2). For an attack on the Manichean theology of marriage, see Augustine, *On Continence*, 9.22–12.26.

[61]   See e.g. Gregory Nazianzen, *Oration 37*, 9–10; Augustine, *On Marriage and Concupiscence*, esp. 1.4(5); Augustine, *On the Good of Marriage*, esp. 1.8.13(15); John Chrysostom, *On Virginity*, 1–10; John Chrysostom, *Against the Opponents of Monastic Life*, 3.15; Jerome, *Against Jovinian*, 2 and 8.

[62]   Athanasius, *Life of Antony*, 68.

voice about whether the ideas and acts of Theonas were justified. In conclusion, however, he refers to the future of Theonas as a clear sign of God's approval of his deeds.[63]

John was typical in his use of careful wording to evade any accusation of heresy. Claims about the superiority of virginity were often accompanied by disclaimers pointing out that the author in question does not want to deny the worth of earthly marriage. As Ambrose of Milan wrote: 'I am not discouraging marriage, but enlarging upon the benefits of virginity ... The former is not reproved, and the latter is praised.' The marriage bond is not to be eschewed as sinful, but rather avoided as being a burden. Moreover, he condemns those who are inclined to resist or censure marriage.[64] For Augustine, who was suspected of Manichaeism because of his opinions on celibacy and his past as a Manichaean Hearer, 'marriage and fornication are not two evils, of which the second is worse, but marriage and continence are two goods of which the second is better'. He puts virginity firmly above marriage, but is careful not to condemn the latter and he impugns those who did so.[65] Thus, the extremist views opened up a possibility for other propagators of virginity to depict themselves as representing the moderate opinions.

As the caution of the authors hints, asceticism was by no means universally acclaimed in mainstream Christian communities. This is well illustrated by the Jovinianist controversy in the 380s and 390s. According to Jovinian, virgins, widows and married Christians have equal merit, but Jerome attacked these views by claiming that 'if it is good not to touch a woman, it is bad to touch one: for there is no opposite to goodness but badness. But if it be bad and the evil is pardoned, the reason for the concession is to prevent worse evil'. He also recalled the words of St Peter that marriage hinders praying; since St Paul tells Christians to pray always, Jerome comes to the conclusion that marriage is inevitably noxious.[66] Many interpreted these words to mean that Jerome had

---

[63]   John Cassian, *Conferences*, 21.9–10. See also Vitricius of Rouen, *The Praise of Saints*, 3.

[64]   Ambrose, *On Virgins*, 1.6.24: 'Non ego quidem dissuadeo matrimonium, sed virginitatis attexo beneficium ... Illa non reprehenditur, ista laudatur', translated by H. de Romestin et al. (Nicene and Post-Nicene Fathers, ser. II, vol. 10), with e.g. Ambrose, *Letter Outside the Collection* 14.62 and 15.3; Ambrose, *On Widows*, 13.81. Jerome, *Letters*, 22.2; Gregory of Nyssa, *On Virginity*; John Chrysostom, *Against the Opponents of Monastic Life*, 3.15.

[65]   Augustine, *On the Good of Marriage*, 8: 'Non ergo duo mala sunt connubium et fornicatio, quorum alterum peius, sed duo bona sunt connubium et continentia, quorum alterum est melius', with Augustine, *On Holy Virginity*, 13 and 30; Augustine, *On the Good of Widowhood*, 4; Augustine, *Letters*, 151.8 and 157.4.37.

[66]   Jerome, *Against Jovinian*, 1.7: 'Si bonum est mulierem non tangere [1 Cor 7:1 – words of the Corinthians, not Paul's own words], malum est ergo tangere, nihil enim bono contrarium est, nisi malum; si autem malum est, et ignoscitur, ideo conceditur, ne malo quid

60 *Children and Asceticism in Late Antiquity*

condemned marriage as an option for true Christians. Even his friends held that these statements were too extreme: Pammachius went so far as to try to remove copies of the tract from circulation. Jerome was forced to write apologist letters to deny the accusations that he had condemned marriage and to take back some of his words.[67]

Jovinian was not the only one to criticize the excessive praise for the virgins and widows. Earlier on, Jerome had argued against a layman, Helvidius, who insisted that Mary lost her virginity after giving birth to Jesus, since the Gospels mention his brothers and sisters, and because of a similar kind of argumentation, Bonosus, Bishop of Sardica, was condemned by Pope Siricius. The best-known case is that of Vigilantius. Jerome complains:

> Shameful to relate, there are bishops who are said to be associated with [Vigilantius] ... who ordain only deacons that have been previously married; who credit no celibate with chastity ... and, unless the candidates for ordination appear before them with pregnant wives, and infants wailing in the arms of their mothers, they do not administer to them Christ's mysteries.[68]

Nor were the ascetic ideas always enthusiastically received in the East. An early treatise by John Chrysostom is directed particularly against such Christian opponents of the monastic life in Antioch. Not all praised asceticism as the superior way of living as a Christian.[69]

---

deterius fiat.' Translated by W.H. Fremantle et al. (Nicene and Post-Nicene Fathers, ser. II, vol. 6). See also Jerome, *Against Jovinian*, 1.12; Siricius, *Letters*, 7.4–5; and Augustine, *On Heresies*, 82. On the Jovinianist controversy, ecclesiastical authority and the construction social hierarchies, see D. Hunter, 'Rereading the Jovinianist Controversy: Asceticism and Clerical Authority in Late Ancient Christianity', *Journal of Medieval and Early Modern Studies* 33(3) (2003), pp. 454–70 with Hunter, *Marriage, Celibacy*, esp. pp. 241–2.

[67] Jerome, *Letters*, 48, esp. 2 and the detailed re-interpretation of *Against Jovinian* in Jerome, *Letters*, 49, esp. 3–5, 14 (both addressed to Pammachius in 393 CE). See also Jerome, *Letters*, 50, esp. 3 and 5 and epist. 54.2–3. On the reception of *Adversus Jovinianum*, see Hunter, *Marriage, Celibacy*, pp. 244–59.

[68] Jerome, *Against Vigilantius*, 2: 'Pro nefas episcopos sui dicitur sceleris habere consortes, si tamen episcopi nominandi sunt qui non ordinant diaconos, nisi prius uxores duxerint, nulli caelibum credentes pudicitiam, immo ostendentes quam sancte vivant, qui male de omnibus suspicantur, et nisi praegnantes uxores viderint clericorum infantesque in ulnis matrum vagientes, Christi sacramenta non tribuunt.' See also Jerome, *Letters*, 109.2.

[69] John Chrysostom, *Against the Opponents of Monastic Life*, 3 and esp. 1.2. Further on Vigilantius and situation in Gaul, see D. Hunter, 'Vigilantius of Calagurris and Victricius of Rouen: Ascetics, Relics and Clerics in Late Roman Gaul', *Journal of Early Christian Studies* 7(3) (1999), pp. 401–30; and Hunter, *Marriage, Celibacy*, pp. 258–9. On the criticism of

In taking up these disagreements about the proper place of asceticism and marriage in Christianity, I am interested in the use of asceticism, not so much as a source for social power, but as a discourse forming hierarchies of distinction, informing us about culturally shared values and mentalities. The prominence of the mental images of kinship, home, patrimony and place of origin in these discussions shows how deeply the traditional lifestyle and values were anchored in these themes. More specifically, asceticism was identified by the most prominent ecclesiastical writers of Late Antiquity as the embodiment of the distinctively Christian way of living. Therefore, even if the choice for asceticism was made by only a minority of Christians, the discussion of asceticism and continuity in the context of the family was very much at the heart of the discourse on the right Christian praxis.

Asceticism and *Pietas*

Ascetic ideals flourished in the world of families. The challenge for the ecclesiastical writers who highlighted asceticism as the perfection of the Christian life was to conceptualize asceticism in a way that would reconcile it with the traditional (elite) ideas of the good life. In order to achieve this, the Roman virtue of *pietas* had to be re-defined. *Pietas* was one of the main constituents of the Roman traditional ethos, incorporating ideas of duty and compassion towards relatives, patrons and gods. In the family context, Richard Saller has defined *pietas* as 'a reciprocal devotion to family members'.[70] At first sight, this Roman concept was directly antithetical to the biblical anti-familial tradition and the discussions it inspired among the Late Antique Christian writers. However, in the Pastoral Epistles of the New Testament, a more positive attitude towards the family can already be seen. As in the Roman ethos, the way a man manages his household reveals his real moral character; the community leader (*episkopos*) should 'manage his own household well, keeping his children submissive and respectful in every way; for if a man does not know how to manage his own household, how can he care for God's Church?'[71]

---

ascetic ideals, see also Sandwell, *Religious Identity*, 253 and 256 (East) and Hunter, *Marriage, Celibacy*, pp. 53–63 (West).

[70]   Saller, *Patriarchy*, pp. 105–14 esp. 110 and 131 with Evans Grubbs, 'Promoting *Pietas*' for the relevance of *pietas* in Late Antique legislation.

[71]   1 Timothy 3:4–5, with 1 Timothy 5:8: 'If any one does not provide for his relatives, and especially for his own family, he has disowned the faith and is worse than an unbeliever'; and further Barclay, 'The Family', pp. 76–8.

For a teaching to be comprehensible to the growing audience, its precepts had to be interpreted according to the lines set by the dominant values. Since there was an urge to depict Christianity as the very embodiment and fulfilment of *romanitas*, there was a double challenge to Christian preachers and apologists: to translate the Christian message to the language of Roman *pietas*, and to reconcile the positive and negative statements in the Christian tradition about marriage and familial relationships. If the family was the basis of everyday life for a Christian, how was it possible to propagate the need to set aside familial duties in order to live a perfect Christian life? Should parents be honoured (Eph. 6:1–3) or hated (Luke 14:26)? The divine nature of the Scriptures made it impossible that there could be mutually contradictory requirements for a truly Christian lifestyle. As an anonymous fifth-century writer wrote, Jesus seems to impose family disloyalty (*impietas*) as a condition for Christian perfection; however, as he noted, 'nothing hard, nothing improper (*impium*), nothing contradictory is commanded by God'.[72]

Lactantius gave a straightforward, but in practice insufficient reply to this challenge in his reinterpretation of the concept. According to him: '*Pietas* is nothing else than the recognition of God as a parent.'[73] A century later, Augustine defined *pietas* as worship of God, but admitted that the word is also used of dutifulness to parents. In another context, he claims that it was virtuous in the times of the Old Testament to have many children, but 'now surely no one who is made perfect in *pietas* seeks to have sons, save after a spiritual sense; but then it was the work of *pietas* itself to beget sons carnally'.[74] *Pietas* is still linked with familial duty, but the meaning is shifted to the spiritual realm and to duty towards God. These statements represent the first steps in the process of transformation of *pietas* from a virtue with predominantly interpersonal and familial connotations to a virtue describing the relationship between a believer and God.

---

[72] Pseudo-Hilary of Poitiers, *Commentary of the Psalm* 118, 15.3 (fifth century CE): 'Verum nihil a deo durum, nihil impium, nihil contrarium anterioribus praeceptis iubetur.'

[73] Lactantius, *Divine Institutes* 3.9: 'Pietas autem nihil aliut quam dei parentis agnitio.' For Lactatius and *pietas*, see C. Blandine, 'Analyse du sens et discours chrétien chez les auteurs latins du IVe siècle', in M. Baratin and C. Moussy (eds), *Conceptions latines du sens et de la signification, Actes du Colloque de Linguistique latine du Centre Alfred Ernout (CNRS/Paris IV)* (Paris, 1999), esp. pp. 245–8.

[74] Augustine, *City of God*, 10.1: 'Pietas quoque proprie dei cultus intellegi solet, quam Graeci εὐσέβειαν vocant. Haec tamen et erga parentes officiose haberi dicitur'; Augustine, *On the Good of Marriage* 17(19): 'Nunc quippe nullus pietate perfectus filios habere nisi spiritaliter quaerit; tunc vero ipsius pietatis erat operatio etiam carnaliter filios propagare'. See also Augustine of Hippo, *Enchridion*, 2.

Family, Kin and the Right Way of Living as a Christian 63

Although Lactantius and Augustine did not imply that an act of *pietas* excluded the biological parents or other relatives, some writers went further and required disregard for family and lineage. According to Hilary of Arles, his predecessor in the see of Arles, Honoratus, was the subject of an attempt by his father to alienate him from the ascetic urge, since the father grew troubled over his son's lack of 'earthly sense of familial duty' (*terrena pietas*) towards the family.[75] Honoratus possessed the traditional virtues of an aristocrat, but his *pietas* was directed not towards the earthly family, but instead the heavenly realm. Similarly, Paulinus of Nola praises Sulpicius Severus, who rejected his patrimony and put his 'heavenly Father before his earthly one'.[76] The earthly loyalties towards one's parents and family line should be changed to *pietas* towards God the Father and fellow Christians.

Such views, making familial and religious *pietas* mutually incompatible, were, however, limited to the hagiographic accounts among the writers linked with mainstream Christianity. The pastoral teaching and letters were more moderate. Here, in order to explain the discrepancies between hating and loving, the ecclesiastical writers used different strategies of exegetical analysis, especially by using the parallel texts in the Bible and referring to the need for contextualization in the interpretation.[77] Hating is required only when parents try to make the child love them more than God and try to hinder their children's pursuit of perfection by dissuading a child from following Christ to martyrdom or asceticism. *Pietas* is a Christian value indeed, but it had to be directed towards the new family and kin, the family of God, which is the true source of safety. This kind of argumentation had a long history, and by the fourth century it had become a commonplace. Ambrose crystallizes the argument: '*Religio* takes precedence over familial duties.' *Religio* here does not mean only the right religion as we would understand it (that is, Christianity versus other religious practices), but also more generally the right relationship between family members and God.[78] However, not even in the situation of parental opposition

---

[75]   Hilarius of Arles, *Life of Honoratus*, 6.1.

[76]   Paulinus of Nola, *Letters*, 5.6: 'caelestem patrem anteverteras terreno parenti ... patrimonii derelicto Christum secutus'.

[77]   For the exegetical strategies, see also Jacobs, 'Let Him Guard', esp. pp. 270–71.

[78]   Ambrose, *Commentary on Luke*, 7.146: 'Religio enim praestat pietatis officiis', with e.g. Ambrose, *Commentary on Psalm 118*, 15–17; Jerome, *Letters*, 54.3; John Chrysostom, *Homilies on Ephesians*, 21.1; John Chrysostom, *Homilies on Matteus*, 35.1; Pseudo-Hilary of Poitiers, *Commentary of the Psalm* 118, 15.3; *Anonymous Homily on Virginity*, 112. See also Jacobs, 'Let Him Guard', p. 272, although he emphasizes maybe too strongly the Christian–non-Christian antagonism for the fourth-century context.

is *pietas* to be forgotten, as Ambrose shows in his comments on Jesus' rejection of the messenger who tells him that his mother and brothers are standing outside:

> He who will later enjoin upon others that anyone who does not leave behind his father and mother is himself the first to submit to this regulation – not by refusing the obedience that springs from filial dutifulness towards his mother [*maternae ... pietatis*], as it is [God's] command that one who does not honour mother and father will be put to death – but because he knows that he is under a greater obligation to the mysteries of the Father than to the affections due to mother.[79]

The passage makes it clear that for Ambrose, 'the ethical teacher' (*moralis magister*) would not neglect traditional virtues like *pietas*, but the family of Christ, bound together by the mysteries of God the Father, is to be preferred to earthly kinship ties. This theme is also present in other writings of Ambrose. For example, he praises his friend Eusebius of Bologna on his parental *pietas*, which led Eusebius to marry off his sons and send them away from the paternal home. In the case of his daughter Ambrosia, Eusebius had 'advanced even further'. Traditional *pietas* is described as a virtue, but it was perfected only outside the traditional limits of paternal *pietas*, in dedicating a child to asceticism.[80] Family *pietas* is a positive and necessary quality in virtuous virgins and widows, but it should be overcome, if need be, in order to become perfect: 'Maiden, overcome your filial devotion [*pietas*] first. If you overcome your home, you overcome the world.'[81] Jerome, in turn, faces the discrepancy over *pietas*, for example, in explaining the behaviour of Paula the Elder as she sails for the Holy Land. As she left her weeping children in the quay, he claims that there is indeed nothing more cruel than parents separated from their children – it is even against the law of nature. However, in so doing, Paula 'overcame her *pietas* for her children by

---

[79]   Ambrose, *Commentary on Luke*, 6.36: 'Praescripturus enim ceteris quoniam qui non reliquerit patrem et matrem suam non est filio dei dignus, sententiae huic primus ipse se subicit, non quo maternae refutet pietatis obsequia ipsius enim praeceptum est: qui non honorauerit patrem et matrem morte morietur sed quia paternis se mysteriis amplius quam maternis affectibus debere cognoscat.'

[80]   Ambrose, *The Consecration of a Virgin*, 1.1: 'caeteros enim instituis ut emittas domo, atque alienis copules, istam semper tecum habebis; in caeteris quoque paternae uteris pietatis necessitudine: in hac ultra patrem procedis, votoque et studio progrederis, ut placeat Deo'.

[81]   Ambrose, *On Virgins*, 1.11.63: 'Vince prius, puella, pietatem. Si vincis domum, vincis et saeculum', with Ambrose, *On Widows*, 2.7; Ambrose, *Letters*, 38; and John Chrysostom, *Against the Opponents of Monastic Life*, 2.9 for the traditional *pietas* as virtue.

her *pietas* for God'.[82] A similar hierarchy is revealed in Jerome's frequent use of the biblical motif of leaving the father unburied in order to follow Christ: 'The father is not to be buried; it is a form of *pietas* to be undutiful [*impius*] because of the Lord.' Traditionally *pietas* revealed itself particularly in taking care of the burials of one's nearest kin.[83]

A rather elaborate way of arguing for the relevance of *pietas* is offered by Salvian when he protests against the traditional idea of bequeathing the family wealth to children as the highest form of *pietas*. If the children have *pietas* towards their parents, they will wish that their parents should not perish, and thus they will accept their decision of giving the property away. Salvian reminds parents that *pietas* binds them too: it would be an act of impiety not to bequeath property to unfortunate relatives, loyal brothers, faithful spouses, destitute kinsmen and their relatives who are in want, and to those who are dedicated to God. Giving to the nearest and dearest relatives is not wrong – quite the opposite – and children should be loved above anything else (*super omnia*), but the subordination of the soul to the interests of the continuity of the family wealth goes against *pietas*, rather than against only considerations of charity.[84]

Indeed, Christians should hate not the persons themselves, but the earthly and thus transitory relationships between the persons that impede proper devotion to the spiritual life. The ecclesiastical writers claimed that the required hatred was extremely hard or even impossible to fulfil, and therefore served as the ultimate test for the right state of one's soul as part of the spiritual struggle for perfection in Christ. It is not a question of actually hating one's parents or relatives, but of prioritizing the family of Christ, and the best way to do this was to opt for the virginal life.[85]

Augustine goes even further. When the mother of Laetus tries to convince him to give up ascetic life in a monastic community by reminding him of the agonies of childrearing, her nourishing of him, the pains of childbirth and of carrying him 10 months in her womb, Augustine urges Laetus to leave these arguments aside. Even if these arguments are justified, she is wrong to consider it

---

[82]   Jerome, *Letters*, 108.6: 'pietatem in filios pietate in Deum superans', with Jerome, *Letters*, 39.6: 'grandis in suos pietas inpietas in Deum est.'

[83]   Jerome, *Letters*, 38.5: 'sepultura non datur patri et pietatis genus est inpium esse pro Domino', with e.g. Jerome, *Letters*, 39.4, 54.2–3. *Pietas* in burial: Augustine, *City of God*, 1.13; Augustine, *On the Care of the Dead*, 3(5); and Augustine, *Sermons*, 172.2 (3).

[84]   Salvian, *To the Church*, 1.4.9–10; 3.3.12–3.4.18. See also Palladius, *The Lausiac History*, 6.3, Augustine, *Exposition on the Psalms*, 131.19; and Augustine, *Sermons*, 9.20 with further references in Shaw, 'The Family', 20.

[85]   John Chrysostom, *On Virginity*, 73.3–4; Jerome, *Against the Pelagians* 2.15 with Jacobs, 'Let Him Guard', pp. 275–7. See also Ambrose, *Commentary on Luke*, 10.22–5.

'of greater value that she bore you from her own womb than that she was born, along with you, from the womb of the Church'. Laetus should hate that part of his mother, which refers to the earthly and carnal bonds she employs in trying to prevent him from achieving spiritual progress.[86] More generally, 'whoever wishes to practise here and now the life of that kingdom should not hate those persons, but those personal relationships by which this life, which is fleeting, is supported, a life agitated by being born and dying'. According to Augustine, *terrena coniugia*, with its double reference to all personal ties in general and to the marriage bond in particular, is to be avoided because it only causes death and dying. This link between marriage, giving birth and dying can be broken by one's devotion to the other reality and hating one's nearest and dearest kin. In the eternal kingdom, there are no such temporal relationships; all Jesus' disciples are called brothers.[87] It is not that the monastic family is necessarily superior to the natural one,[88] but that *pietas* requires that on some occasions the familial *pietas* be put in second place after *pietas* for God. Augustine is not advising anybody to despise familial bonds. A son should 'pay his familial duty [*pietas*] in all cases; it has its place when higher things do not call', and Laetus should specifically take care of the future financial wellbeing of his household.[89] A good son is loyal to his biological family.

Only on specific occasions – as when a parent tries to obstruct the ascetic urge – should *pietas* be subdued: 'Thus, love your father, but not over your God. Love your mother, but not over the church ... Love your wife, love your children according to God's will.' However, the need for proper *pietas* is certainly valid for ascetics too, and the need for surpassing its requirements was also required for non-ascetic Christians if need be.[90] The value of *pietas* for Augustine can also

---

[86] Augustine, *Letters*, 243.3–7: 'ne quod ex utero suo te genuit, pluris pendat, quam quod ex utero Ecclesiae genita est tecum', with Augustine, *Retractions*, 1.19.5. For Augustine's letter to Laetus, see the superb analysis by Krawiec, 'From the Womb', pp. 289–92.

[87] Augustine, *On the Sermon on the Mount*, 1.15.40: 'Oportet ergo ut quisquis illius regni vitam iam hic meditari voluerit, oderit non ipsos homines sed istas necessitudines temporales, quibus ista quae transitura est vita fulcitur, quae nascendo et moriendo peragitur.' Translation by Jacobs, 'Let Him Guard', pp. 274–5 with slight modification. See also the next paragraph: a good Christian cherishes in a woman what is human in her, but hates what is wife – that is, sexual union.

[88] Cf. C. Harrison, *Augustine: Christian Truth and Fractured Humanity* (Oxford, 2002), p. 173.

[89] Augustine, *Letters*, 243.3–4: 'Servet potius ubique pietatem: habeant haec locum ubi maiora non vocant', with Shaw, 'The Family', p. 21 and Krawiec, 'From the Womb', pp. 289–90.

[90] Augustine, *Sermons*, 344.2: 'Ama ergo patrem, sed noli super Deum tuum. Ama matrem tuam, sed noli super Ecclesiam, quae te genuit ad vitam aeternam ... Ama uxorem,

be seen in his exhortation to Proba to be an example to the other members of the household (both relatives and members of her religious community), since he links prayer and the spiritual life to the proper management of the Christian household by using *pietas* as the binding element: 'the more dutifully [*pie*] you conduct your household, the more fervently should all of you persevere in prayer, not engaging yourselves with worldly affairs, except inasmuch as *pietas* demands'.[91]

In all, for the late fourth- and early fifth-century Christian writers, *pietas* was considered a truly Christian virtue, defining family life and family relationships. The cultural ideal of familial piety became a central model for Christian writers who were willing to describe Christians as true Romans, exceeding in their virtues the heroes of Roman history and mythology. In this rhetoric, one of the main targets was *pius Aeneas*, in whose figure *pietas* as familial devotion and duty was exemplified in the Roman imperial culture.[92] Only heretics act without respect for the traditional familial values: asceticism should not be used as an excuse to neglect the children. As Ambrose wrote: 'That fathers love their children is a natural law; that spouses love each other, a divine law; that brothers love each other, a natural privilege.' Acting against these precepts would be unnatural – and impious.[93]

The ascetic and monastic lifestyles developed in dialogue with family values and practices of everyday life in households. This transformed not only family ideals, metaphors and practices, but also asceticism and discourses on it were shaped through this interplay. Moreover, the debate of the 'orthodox fathers' against Manichaeism and other such groups (which emphasized the sinfulness

---

ama filios secundum Deum.' Cf. Jacobs, 'Let Him Guard', p. 278, who claims that familial hatred is required only in extraordinary circumstances, as in the form of ascetic rejection, but for 'the mass of Christians, the norm is *pietas*'.

[91] Augustine, *Letters*, 130.16.30: 'Quanto enim magis domum vestram pie tractatis, tanto impensius orationibus instare debetis, rerum praesentium non occupatae negotiis, nisi quae flagitat causa pietatis.'

[92] See e.g. Lactantius, *Divine Institutes*, 5.10.5–9; Augustine, *City of God*, 10.21 with M. Lafferty, 'Augustine, the Aeneid, and the Roman Family', in K. Mustakallio et al. (eds), *Hoping for Continuity: Childhood, Education and Death in Antiquity and the Middle Ages* (Rome, 2005), pp. 105–18; Rawson, *Children*, pp. 32–4; Saller, *Patriarchy*, pp. 105–6. On the reciprocal duties of parents and children in the early Christian discourse, see also Osiek and Balch, *Families*, pp. 163–7.

[93] *Council of Gangra, Canon* 15; Ambrose of Milan, *Commentary on Psalm 118*, 15–17: 'Amare patribus filios lex naturae est, maritis coniuges lex divina est ... Diligere fratribus fratres naturae praerogativa est' with Ambrosius of Milan, *On the Duties of the Clergy*, 1.27.127 and 1.30.150; John Chrysostom, *Homilies on Ephesians*, 21, esp. 1.

of sex or even marriage) required them to take a more positive approach to family life. The reconciliation of the biblical passages, and the need to keep a distance from the extremist anti-familial rhetoric, ensured that the family language was deeply rooted in early Christian usage. In the context of mainstream Christianity the ultimate value of *pietas* is not called into question; the requirement for commitment to the heavenly family was not directed against familial *pietas* or 'natural' emotions and the connection between the various family members.

There was, however, an in-built tension as *pietas* required a dutiful attitude towards both earthly and heavenly families. In traditional usage, *pietas* towards other members of the household was at the same time an indication of one's disposition towards the *patria* and towards the rule of the gods, but in the Christian rhetoric, different modes of *pietas* were separated from each other to build up a hierarchy. Yet the need to break the old family loyalties was spelled out in the traditional language. The requirements of *pietas* were to be kept when the ultimate loyalty and the source for identity was shifted to the family of Christ. As long as family members followed the requirements of the godly lifestyle, *pietas* towards the family of God and *pietas* towards one's earthly family go hand in hand, and even support each other. Asceticism would not be an antithesis to family *pietas*; it would perfect it. In this way, seemingly paradoxical passages of the Scripture were reconciled, and family values and concepts were adopted for Christian use.

Chapter 3

Ascetics and the Family of Christ: Metaphors, Family Dynamics and Continuity

We believe that the Jerusalem above is our city and our mother. We call God our father. We will live here wisely, in order that we might have eternal life.[1]

This chapter scrutinizes how the ascetic lifestyle was reconciled with traditional Roman values by embedding the family terminology in the ascetic Christian rhetoric. Paradoxically, the ecclesiastical writers argued that asceticism was in line with Roman family values and was a superior way of contributing to the same ultimate needs as family life. Here they took advantage of the metaphors drawn from family life – marriage, fertility and the continuity of the lineage – which referred to functions that biological families were understood to have. These discussions also reveal the prevalent attitudes and expectations connected with the biological family and children.

Fathers and Mothers of the Church

In the earliest known Christian writings, the Epistles of Paul, family metaphors abound. The apostle seeks to convince his readers that Christians should live with each other as a family. For this, he uses terms of kinship extensively; in particular the idea of the Christian community as a brotherhood, the father-children metaphor and the idea of a heavenly inheritance are used in a number of passages.[2] By the beginning of the third century, this use of familial language had been widely adopted by Christian communities and, indeed, became one

---

[1] Pseudo-Athanasius, *Life of Syncletica*, 90: 'Τὴν ἄνω Ἰερουσαλὴμ ἡγησώμεθα ἑαυτῶν πόλιν τε καὶ μητέρα· πατέρα δὲ τὸν Θεὸν καλέσωμεν ἑαυτῶν.'

[2] Paul as father in 1 Cor 4:14–17 and 1 Thess 2:11–12; Cf. the many references to his 'brothers and sisters', e.g. 1 Cor 1:26, 2 Cor 8:1; Rom 8:12–17; Gal 1:11; 1 Thess 2:17 and Phil 4:1. For further analysis of Pauline family metaphors, see Hellerman, *The Ancient Church*, pp. 92–126 and 213–25; and papers in Moxnes (ed.), *Constructing*, Part II, on pp. 103–97.

of their identity markers. The first Christian communities were defined as cohesive families consisting of brothers and sisters led by a spiritual father. The concepts of paternity and spiritual authority were closely interwoven.[3] In theory, the unity of Christian communities was guaranteed by the ideals of spiritual brotherhood and mutual charity. Even non-Christians such as Lucian noted the self-identification of the early Christian communities as brotherhoods.[4]

Although Apostle Paul frequently adopted a position as father towards the new Christian communities, claiming, for example, that in Christ they had been begotten (ἐγέννησα) by him through the Gospel, he more often used the vocabulary of siblingship to portray his relationship towards the recipients of his letters.[5] The apostolic way of 'paternalistic' address seems not to have been self-evidently used by all later church leaders[6] – still in the early fourth-century versions of *Life of Pachomius*, it was necessary to explain that Pachomius 'deserves to be called a father because our Father who is in heaven dwells in him'. However, the identification of the spiritual leader as a father is a commonplace in the later versions of the *Life* and in contemporary Egyptian papyri from the mid-fourth century.[7] By the early fifth century, it was usual in both East and West to refer to spiritual and ecclesiastical leaders as fathers. The bishops addressed their congregation as their children, and were correspondingly described and addressed as fathers:[8]

---

[3]   See Buell, *Making Christians*, esp. 51–4, 107 and 180–82 with Hellerman, *The Ancient Church*, pp. 127–67.

[4]   For the charity and familial rhetoric, see Hellerman, *The Ancient Church*, esp. pp. 221–5; Lucian, *The Death of Peregrinus*, 13. Still, as Reidar Aasgaard rightly points out, Hellerman is quite too eager to see these ideological statements as reflecting socal reality (Aasgaard, *'My Beloved Brothers and Sisters'*, pp. 17–18). Hellerman stresses the role of God as the father, not studying the use of paternal metaphors for Church leadership.

[5]   1 Cor 4:14–17; for siblingship (and the rhetoric of paternity) in Paul, see Aasgaard, *'My Beloved Brothers and Sisters'*, pp. 262–303.

[6]   Even if, for example, Clement of Alexandria uses this metaphor: Buell, *Making Christians*, 51–4.

[7]   *Life of Pachomius* (Sahidic version), frg. 1.3 (early fourth century CE, translated by J.E. Goehring) – compare with e.g. *Life of Pachomius* (Bohairic version), 32 (mid-fourth century CE). See also *The London Papyri* VI, 1923–29 (mid-fourth century CE with letters to 'father apa Paphnutios' – mentioned e.g. in 6.1924 and 6.1928: the word *apa*, or *abba*, had lost its association with fatherhood, becoming a mere honorific, at least in the mind of these writers).

[8]   In the West, in his first letter to Eustochium in the early 380s, Jerome assumes that the monastic use of the word 'father' needs explanation: Jerome, *Letters*, 22.33, 35. Later, no explanations are given. For some of the less formulaic cases, see e.g. Jerome, *Letters*, 52.7; 60.7 (396 CE); 91 (400 CE); Augustine, *Letters*, 150 (413 CE).

The apostles were sent as fathers. In place of the apostles, sons are born to you, that is, bishops are appointed. From what source have they been born, the bishops who are spread throughout the world today? The Church itself calls them fathers; she herself has given birth to them and has established them on the seats of the fathers.[9]

The fatherhood of Church leaders seems to have developed quickly into an abstract honorific, with minimal links to actual parenthood. For present purposes, it is, however, important to study cases in which fatherhood is noted in less formulaic contexts, and the parental roles attached to these 'ascetic fathers' are still visible. For example, according to Hilary of Arles, when Honoratus and his brother Venantius planned to go abroad, 'their entire homeland felt that it was losing fathers in these young men'. Likewise, on the death of Simeon the Stylite, his disciplines allegedly cried to him: 'Our father, you have left us like orphans … you filled for us the place of family and siblings and father.'[10] Paulinus of Nola asks Alypius if he was ordained for the priesthood by 'our father Ambrose' and, if so, they would share the 'same father in God'. In this connection he refers to the Church as 'the mother of the sons of God, who accepts with rejoicing those who renounce their lineage of flesh and blood' and enter into the regal and sacerdotal stock.[11]

More specifically, a bishop – especially a celibate bishop – would be a father for his clergy, that is, for his spiritual sons. This is highlighted notably in the rhetoric of Ambrose of Milan. This exclusive family inside the Church was completed by the daughters, as a special parental relationship was formed between a bishop and a virgin whom he had consecrated. As head of a family consisting of virtuous family members, a bishop was able to attach their holiness to himself. Moreover, by identifying himself as the father of the clergy and of the

---

[9]   Augustine, *Exposition on the Psalms*, 44.32: 'Patres missi sunt Apostoli, pro Apostolis filii nati sunt tibi, constituti sunt episcopi. Hodie enim episcopi, qui sunt per totum mundum, unde nati sunt? Ipsa Ecclesia patres illos appellat, ipsa illos genuit, et ipsa illos constituit in sedibus partum.' Translation from David Hunter, 'The Virgin, the Bride and the Church: Reading Psalm 45 in Ambrose, Jerome and Augustine', *Church History* 69(2) (2000), p. 301.

[10]   Hilarius of Arles, *Life of Honoratus*, 11.2: 'Amittere enim se omnis patria in iuvenibus illis patres sentiebat'; Jacob of Serug, *Homily on Simeon the Stylite*, 664 (trans. S.A. Harvey) with Sulpicius Severus, *Letters*, 3.9; *History of the Monks in Egypt*, 1.44; 10.2; 26; Theodoret of Cyrrhus, *Religious History*, 17.10.

[11]   Paulinus of Nola, *Letters*, 3.4: 'vocatus a Domino, quibus exordiis segregatus ab utero matris tuae, ad matrem filiorum Dei prole laetantem, abiurata carnis et sanguinis stirpe, transieris, et in genus regale et sacerdotale, sis translatus … patre nostro Ambrosio'. See also Paulinus of Nola, *Letters*, 17.4 on Martin of Tours and Clarus as living on in Sulpicius Severus, who was their spiritual child.

virgins, he becomes a virtuous *paterfamilias*, showing his capacity for dealing with public affairs through his conduct in the 'private' sphere.[12] Another strategy for highlighting the paternal role of a bishop was used by Gregory Nazianzen: in referring to his father's non-Catholic past, conversion to Christianity and eventual episcopacy at Nazianzos, Gregory compares his parents to Abraham and Sarah. Beyond all his aspirations, Gregory the Elder became the father of many nations, with his wife Nonna spiritually giving birth to them.[13] Other spiritual teachers, monks, priests and Church officials – as well as bishops – were also understood to be fathers for the laypeople. Jerome, for example, routinely referred to his younger correspondents as his daughters and sons.[14] With the bishop identified as a father, it is not surprising to find the relationship between diocese and bishop compared to that of husband and wife – thus, a bishop who exchanges his see for another is an adulterer.[15]

The fatherhood of a bishop or even of an ordinary priest is also reflected in the belief that if he did not already practise asceticism, he should renounce sexual relations with his wife after his consecration, although this official line was not unanimously supported and there was local opposition to this principle. The Council of Nicaea, for example, could not agree on the proposal that sexual relations between the higher clergy and their wives should be forbidden.[16] Yet, at the end of the fourth century, the idea was actively spread both by the leading ecclesiastical notables and by local synods, especially in the western parts of the Empire.[17] In the East, it seems there were still no stricter rules even for bishops in the early fourth century, although the requirement for abstaining from intercourse was gaining increasingly support. There appears to have been much

---

[12] See Ambrose, *On the Duties of the Clergy*, 1–2; 1.7.23–24; 3.22.138 on clergy, and Ambrose, *The Consecration of a Virgin*, 1.1 and 17.107 with Hunter, 'The Virgin', pp. 288–90 and Hunter, 'Rereading', p. 461 on the veiling of virgins as a source of paternity and authority for a bishop.

[13] Gregory Nazianzen, *Oration 8*, 4.

[14] For sons, see e.g. in Jerome, *Letters*, 62.2; 68.1; 71.1; 118.1; 125.1; for daughters, see e.g. in Jerome, *Letters*, 22.26 and 38; 54.6; 75.5; 123.17.

[15] Athanasius, *The Second Apology*, 1.6; See also Jerome, *Letters*, 69.5.

[16] See Socrates, *Ecclesiastical History*, 1.11 on Bishop Paphnutius torpedoing the resolution. The story as such is somewhat suspect, as the opinions supposedly expressed by Paphnutius are identical to those of Socrates himself and the 'liberal side' of the early fifth-century discussants (see Socrates, *Ecclesiastical History*, 5.22). For the resistance in Southern Gaul and Northern Italy, see Hunter, *Marriage, Celibacy*, pp. 214–24.

[17] Siricius, *Letters*, 5 and 10.5–6; Ambrosius, *On the Duties of the Clergy*, 1.50.248–249; *Council of Carthage (390 CE), Canon 2*; *Council of Carthage (419 CE), Canon 4, 25 (28)* and 70 (73); Innocentius, *Letters* 2.9; Jerome, *Against Vigilantius*, 2 with Hunter, 'Vigilantius of Calagurris', esp. pp. 429–30 and Hunter, *Marriage, Celibacy*, pp. 214–24.

Ascetics and the Family of Christ   73

local variation, but no eastern local synods decreed that those already married should abstain from sexual relations with their wives once they had been ordained.[18] Even if the propagators of clerical celibacy backed their argument with references to the ritual purity needed for performing priestly duties and for the moral qualities required to give a good example for the laity,[19] there also appeared a tendency to mould the ecclesiastical hierarchy into a family. Here it is not necessary to enter further into discussion on clerical celibacy, a wide topic in its own right, but simply to point out the way that ecclesiastical networks at every level of the Church hierarchy, from the ordinary parishes to the close-knit ascetic communities and from friendship relationships to episcopal entourages, were being shaped on the example of the family.[20] The bishop was to be the father with *patria potestas*, and the members of this family would ideally be cut out from the influence of their earthly families.

Fatherhood entails obligations and, indeed, the earliest ecclesiastical rules concerning asceticism stressed the need to put these precepts into practice. It is the duty of the bishops and monastic communities to take paternal care of the poor and children who had lost their parents, and thus become 'fathers of the orphans'. Both these children and those given by their parents to be brought up by the community 'should be reared with all piety as children belonging to the entire community'. The so-called *Canons of Athanasius* even decreed that rich women without virgin daughters should 'adopt' a maid, caring for her as a daughter, and bringing her up as a virgin.[21] It is hard to find early cases of this kind of parenting; still, at least the ascetic communities founded by Augustine in North African Hippo and Macrina at Cappadocian Annesi took care of poor children and orphans. In the case of the community of Macrina, there were also foundlings picked up from the road.[22] The parenthood of ecclesiastical leaders

---

[18]   See *Council of Ancyra, Canon* 10; *Council of Neocesarea, Canon* 7; *The Apostolic Constitutions* (8, *Canons* 5 and 50) even forbade bishops and priests to put away their wives, but new marriages were not allowed after ordination. See also *Council of Gangra, Canon* 4 and *Introductory Letter* 11–12; Socrates, *Ecclesiastical History*, 5.22; Epiphanius, *Panarion*, 49; John Chrysostom, *Homilies on First Timothy*, 10, esp. 1; Synesius, *Letters*, 105; Jerome, *Against Vigilantius*, 2.

[19]   Hunter, *Marriage, Celibacy*, pp. 215–24.

[20]   On the ascetic communities, see also Krawiec, 'From the Womb', pp. 300–306; and Elm, *Virgins*, pp. 374–5 (her conclusions. She stresses quite unnecessarily the transformation and the ruptures with the 'traditional' families).

[21]   Basil of Caesarea, *Longer Rules*, 15.1: 'ὀρφανῶν πατέρας'; '... ἐκτρέφεσθαι μὲν αὐτὰ ἐν πάσῃ εὐσεβείᾳ ὡς κοινὰ τέκνα τῆς ἀδελφότητος'; *Canons of Pseudo-Athanasius* 16, 56, 80, 104 (Arabic text), with Ambrose, *On the Duties of the Clergy*, 2.15.71.

[22]   Augustine, *Letters*, 20*, esp. 2 and 32; Gregory of Nyssa, *Life of Macrina*, 26.

was not always entirely of a spiritual nature, and this further strengthened their claim to a parental role and authority.

Just as the male spiritual leader was called father, a female leader had the honorary title of mother. Superiors of the female monastic communities were already referred to as 'mothers' in the fourth century both in the East and in the West. Jerome, for example, points out that virtuous Christians should honour all respectable widows as mothers, and virgins as sisters. Indeed, he depicts the ascetic community of Aventine ladies as a family, led by the widowed Albina the Elder. She is not only called the mother of the community members, but is referred to as 'our common mother'.[23] Later, he reproaches some older women he claims to know, who first seek to make their young freedmen their spiritual children 'by the false name of mother', and then slip into a marital relationship.[24] Although it is left unclear whether the reason for the criticism was the abandonment of chastity or the assumption of spiritual leadership by a woman, this passage illustrates well the fact that this kind of motherhood was a status worth aspiring to, a way of acquiring spiritual successors and authority in the community.

A bishop, as the embodiment of the teachings of the Church, could also assume feminine traits: Paulinus of Nola depicts himself as an infant urging Augustine to nurse him with his breasts of faith. In the next sentence, Paulinus refers to Augustine as his brother in episcopacy and as a father in understanding, even if younger in years. In another instance, Paulinus recommends a certain Licentius (whom he calls his son) to accept Augustine as his father, mother and wet-nurse.[25] The precedent allowing these texts to describe a Christian teacher as a nurse had already been set in the imagery of Paul.[26] What is important here is that the family metaphors contributed to building up both hierarchies of authority and an intimate network of identity by referring simultaneously to a variety of concepts, all with connotations of the family.

---

[23] See e.g. *Life of Pachomius* (first Greek version) 32; Gregory of Nyssa, *Life of Macrina*, 26: 'μητέρα αὐτὴν καὶ τροφὸν ἀνακαλοῦσαι'. For the 'mothers' of the female communities under Shenoute, see Krawiec, *Shenoute*, 77–9; Jerome: *Letters*, 32: 'Albinam, communem matrem valere cupio'; 45.4; 60.10; with 7.6. See also e.g. Augustine, *Letters*, 211.4 and 15; Gerontius, *Life of Melania* (Greek), 37, 41, 58, 62 and 66.

[24] Jerome, *Letters*, 125.6: 'per ficta matrum nomina'.

[25] Augustine, *Letters*, 25.3: 'Atque ideo ut infantem adhuc verbo Dei et spiritali aetate lactentem, educa verbis tuis, uberibus fidei, sapientiae, caritatis inhiantem'; Augustine, *Letters*, 32.4; see also 109.1, in which Severus is drinking the milk of Augustine.

[26] See e.g. 1 Thess 2:7, with B.R. Gaventa, *Our Mother Saint Paul* (Louisville, 2007), pp. 17–62.

The ecclesiastical offices gained prestige and honour through their connection to the ascetic virtues. As Claudia Rapp has shown, the ascetic authority of the leaders of the local churches was 'a focal point at the intersection between spiritual and pragmatic authority' in forming the ecclesiastical leadership and power networks within Christian communities.[27] In this, chastity, especially of the holy bishops who led their dioceses as fathers, was not only an important symbol and example, but also served to divest the Church and its ministers of the need to contribute towards the continuity of biological families. Moreover, the familial *pietas* and the loyalty of the clergy were directed towards the family of Christ, the Church, as the imagery of the Roman *familia* was consciously used to embed the ascetic way of life and ascetic communities in the classical ideals.

Indeed, every time an ecclesiastical teacher is mentioned as a mother or father, the idea of spiritual lineage and continuity is present. It was a way of weaving oneself into the texture of history. As Copres, an Egyptian ascetic, was reported to have humbly said: 'There is nothing wonderful about my own achievements, my children, when they are compared with the rule of life which our fathers followed.'[28] The narrator is transmitting the legacy from the fathers to his children. It is not by accident that those ecclesiastical writers who also supply the material for the present study are currently often called 'the fathers of the church'.

The Church as the Mother, the Ascetics as the Family

With the development of ecclesiology, the idea of the Church as mother, often more specifically as a virgin mother, begins to appear during the second century.[29] The identification was well established and frequently used by all the main authors analysed for the present study. Ambrose, for example, refers to Isaiah's praises of a barren woman rejoicing as she now has children without the pangs of birth. By this he eulogizes the Church, which on Easter Sunday 'gives birth to many sons and daughters', thereby referring to baptisms and to virgins

---

[27] Rapp, *Holy Bishops*, esp. pp.16–18 (quote), 137–53.

[28] *History of the Monks in Egypt*, 10.2: 'Οὐδὲν γάρ ... θαυμαστόν, ὦ τέκνα, τὸ ἐμὸν ἔργον πρός τὸ τῶν πατέρων ἡμῶν πολίτευμα'.

[29] For the earlier accounts, see e.g. Cyprian, *On the Unity of the Church*, 6: 'Habere iam non potest Deum patrem, qui ecclesiam non habet matrem'; Eusebius of Caesarea, *Ecclesiastical History*, 5.2.7 and 5.1.45: 'τῇ παρθένῳ μητρί'; and Buell, *Making Christians*, pp. 115–16, 161–3 on Clement of Alexandria, with Hellerman, *The Ancient Church*, pp. 152–7; J. Plumpe, 'Ecclesia Mater', *Transactions of the American Philological Association* 70 (1939), pp. 536–51.

76   *Children and Asceticism in Late Antiquity*

taking the veil. The Church is indeed 'fertile in giving birth, in chastity a virgin, in offspring a mother'.[30] As the Virgin Mary was both the mother of Jesus and a virgin, at the end of the fourth century, an idea developed of parallelism between the Church and the Virgin Mary.[31] For Augustine, who was particularly keen on this motherhood metaphor, Mary was the *typus* not only of the Church but also of individual virgins. Augustine states that if virgins do the will of God, 'they are together with Mary mothers of Christ' – like all pious souls.[32] He further elaborates that 'you are secure if you have God as your father and his church as your mother', as she is 'gentle for some, severe for others; an enemy to none, but mother for all'. The Church is both a virgin and the mother of the members of Christ.[33] The Church, and especially virgins, comprises a family network founded upon the example given by the Virgin Mary, with Christ as the nucleus.

The representation of the Church as the true mother incorporated the view of the Church as giving birth to its members and as taking care of their (spiritual) needs. In the texts under scrutiny, the essential family nature of the Christian Church and the mutual solidarity of the Christian communities are pointed out repeatedly. In connection with the common parenthood for all believers, the evoking of sibling terminology also brought with it the ideas of equality and solidarity. The ideal Christian community is a fraternity (*consortio fraternitatis*) built up by the family of faith (*domesticos fidei*), characterized by mutual help and almsgiving. For example, Augustine's parents, Monica and Patricius, are his spiritual brothers in the context of the mother church.[34] Indeed, all holy men

---

[30]   Ambrose of Milan, *Exhortation to Virginity*, 7.42: 'Dominus sterilem et parientem facit: sed altera in tristitia parit, altera in sterilitate laetatur. Habet enim filios sine partus dolore [cf. Is. 54:1]'; 'Uno ergo die sine aliquo dolore multos filios et filias solet Ecclesia parturire'; Ambrose, *On Virgins*, 1.6.31: 'Si sancta ecclesia immaculata coitu, fecunda partu, virgo est caritate, mater est prole'. See also e.g. Ambrose, *On Virgins*, 1.9.49; Jerome, *Letters*, 52.6; Augustine, *Letters*, 24.4; Paulinus of Nola, *Letters*, 39.5; Augustine, *On Holy Virginity*, 36(37).

[31]   Ambrose, *Commentary on Luke*, 2.7 with Hunter, 'Rereading', p. 460 on this idea in Ephrem the Syrian.

[32]   Augustine of Hippo, *Enchridion*, 10.34; Augustine, *On Holy Virginity*, 5–6: 'Et ipsae cum Maria matres Christi sunt, si Patris eius faciunt voluntatem ... Item mater eius est omnis anima pia, faciens voluntatem Patris eius fecundissima caritate' (cf. Matthew 12:48).

[33]   Augustine, *Answer to Petilian*, 3.9.10: 'qualescumque nos simus, securi estis, qui Deum Patrem et eius ecclesiam matrem habetis'; Augustine, *The First Catechetical Instruction*, 15.23: 'aliis blanda, aliis severa, nulli inimica, omnibus mater', with Augustine, *Sermons*, 22.10 and 188.4; Augustine, *Letters*, 93.2.6 and 93.13.53; Augustine, *On Holy Virginity*, 7; Augustine, *On the Good of Widowhood*, 10(13); Augustine of Hippo, *Enchridion* 9.29 and 10.34.

[34]   Jerome, *Letters*, 120.1, citing Gal 6:10; Augustine, *Confessions*, 9.13.37, with Lafferty, 'Augustine', p. 118.

and holy women, as co-heirs of the heavenly inheritance, were brothers and sisters.[35]

Although it is never explicitly denied, the equal status of all Christians as children of God is not particularly highlighted in the texts that propagate asceticism. Even for Augustine, who stressed the nature of the Church as a virgin mother of Christians and the wife of Christ, and even points out that all newborn Christians were God's children,[36] the ascetically minded members of the Church constitute the core of the family of Christ. In indicating to Laetus the benefits of leaving his mother to embrace the ascetic Christian community, Augustine emphasizes that the kinship ties are not broken, but expanded, not only for the ascetic, but also for the original family. In the household of God, the mother of Laetus will be loved with a universal love, as God is her father and the Church her mother. Thus, if she becomes a sister in Christ, she will simultaneously be a sister for Laetus, for Augustine and 'for all, who have the heavenly inheritance, and God as their father, and Christ as their brother'. This sisterhood is no longer private and bound to death, but forms a universal and eternal tie between all Christians. The understanding of this unity of the heavenly family leads to contempt for death.[37]

Two points merit special attention here: first, both Laetus and his mother were already Christians, but Augustine depicts entering into an ascetic community as the real step to becoming a part of Christ's family. In a private letter, Augustine can take the role of the teacher of asceticism instead of stressing ecclesiastical integrity and Christian equality.[38] Second, Augustine expressly combines asceticism, belonging to the household of God, and contempt for death. Just as membership of a worldly family means a promise of both inheritance and succession stretching beyond an individual death, belonging to the family of Christ is a promise of heavenly immortality.

Thus, a vow of chastity was interpreted as forming a special family relationship between all ascetics in general, and between the members of a single ascetic community in particular. Not surprisingly, references to sibling relationships abound, particularly in the ascetic discourse. Members of the

---

[35]   Augustine, *On Holy Virginity*, 3 and 5, referring to Gal 4:6–7.

[36]   Augustine, *On Marriage and Concupiscence*, 1.4 (5); Augustine, *Enchridion* 10.33.

[37]   Augustine, *Letters*, 243.3–4: 'Quod autem soror in Christo est, et tibi est et mihi, et omnibus quibus una coelestis haereditas, et pater Deus, et frater Christus.'

[38]   See also Augustine, *Letters*, 130.16.31, and compare Augustine's 'correctness' in equating the bride of Christ only with the Church in his theological tractates, and giving other Christians too the possibility of becoming 'mothers of the Christ' (above, and Hunter, 'The Virgin', pp. 296–302).

monastic communities were brothers and sisters to each other, and the individual fellow-bishop, fellow-priest and fellow-ascetic were addressed or referred to as one's brothers or sisters.[39] A monastic community would also assume the role of a mother: in an idealistic description of the coenobitic communities by Jerome, their lifestyle is characterized both by the pervasiveness of prayer and by the universal caring attitude. The fathers of the community take care of all the needs of the members, and if a monk falls ill, he is nursed so that he will 'not even miss his mother's kindness'.[40] Even more elaborate kinship relations were developed: Paulinus of Nola held that as his friend Sulpicius Severus had renounced his family and patrimony after his wife had died, he 'won as [his] mother forever the holy mother-in-law [i.e. Bassula, mother of his deceased wife] who is nobler than any parent', as they share the same ascetic lifestyle. Moreover, since Sulpicius had exchanged parents, brothers and friends for Paulinus as his spiritual relative, there is a special spiritual relationship even between Paulinus and Bassula, who is referred to as both 'our mother' and 'our sister' in his letters.[41] Thus, not only monastic communities but also looser ascetic networks developed conceptually into enlarged families.

The heavenly Jerusalem was seen as the ideal type for the Church on earth, and therefore also as the caring mother, especially of virgins. Indeed, the ascetically minded Christians formed the real, uncorrupted household of God already in this world.[42] Taking the ascetic vow would make a Christian a distinguished member of the family of Christ, reshaping the earthly (family) relationships, turning husband and wife into sister and brother, or even two

---

[39] E.g. Augustine, *Letters*, 211.4, 6, 9–14; Jerome, *Letters*, 32 and 108.2; John Chrysostom, *Letters to Theodore*, 2.1; Basil of Caesarea, *Longer Rules*, 32.1. Addressing: Paulinus of Nola, *Letters*, 11.3–4, Augustine, *Letters*, 254; Jerome, Letters, 60.10; *History of the Monks in Egypt*, 2.12.

[40] Jerome, *Letters*, 22.35: 'nec matris quaerat affectum'.

[41] Paulinus of Nola, *Letters*, 5.6: 'merito socrum sanctam omni liberaliorem parente in matrem sortitus aeternam'; 5.19; 31.1; 11.3 with Sulpicius Severus, *Letters*, 3.1. See also R. Alciati, 'And the Villa Became a Monastery: Sulpicius Severus' Community of Primuliacum', in H. Dey and E. Fentress (eds), *Western Monasticism Ante Litteram. The Spaces of Monastic Observance in Late Antiquity and the Early Middle Ages* (Turnhout, 2011), pp. 85–98 for the monastic communities of Sulpicius Severus, and of Paulinus of Nola and Therasia as enlarged families.

[42] Ambrose, *On Virgins*, 1.1.4 and 1.9.49; Jerome, *Letters*, 22.24; Pseudo-Athanasius, *Life of Syncletica*, 90; Augustine, *Exposition on the Psalms*, 26.2.18; *On the Good of Marriage*, 16 (18).

brothers. The ascetic calling could even make servants the brothers and sisters of their (former) owner.[43]

Thus, the ideas of universal kinship between all Christians and the special distinction due to ascetic practices were combined, highlighting both the intimacy and nearness to the Godhead and the parental power resulting from ascetic practices. It was possible not only to refer to the ideologically proper spiritual merits of the Christian ascetics, but also to bring out the hierarchies of position and age. A telling example is the polite address of Salvian to his former student Salonius, now a bishop: 'master and most blessed pupil, father, and son, pupil by instruction, son by affection, and father by rank and honour'.[44] Family language was a fine tool for forming distinctions of status and authority. In addition, by using the language of the family, ecclesiastical authors established a net of spiritual kinship relations between members of the *familia Christi*, referring to the profits of equality, closeness, fruitfulness and inheritance, and thus evoking ideas of belonging and continuity.

The Nuclear Family of God: Authority, Values and Identity

As the traditional Roman family vocabulary infiltrated Christianity, the value-loaded family metaphors provided a powerful toolkit for skilful orators. On the other hand, asceticism was at the outset the very negation of family life. Since it was potentially anti-familial, asceticism was easily seen as opposing the traditional value system – an argument willingly exploited in contemporary reactions (both Christian and non-Christian) to the ascetic forms of Christianity. It was therefore important to transfer the positively laden concepts of family language and their connotations (of authority, caring and continuity) to the use of the ascetic discourse. In order for this shift to work, it was crucial to show not only that the concepts fitted the new rhetoric, but also that they responded to the same functions and needs as they did in their original contexts.

The parental roles attached to ecclesiastical authorities and Christian teachers served many purposes inside the communities of believers. These roles were, naturally, a basis for the claim to the legitimacy of power, backed up by the need

---

[43]   Jerome, *Letters*, 108.2 and 118.4; Jerome, *Letters*, 75.2 (wife as a brother); Jerome, Letters, 71.3 and 7 (sister as a man); Paulinus of Nola, *Letters*, 18.5; Jerome, *Life of Malchus* 6.7–9 and 10.3; Augustine, *On the Sermon on the Mount* 1.15.42; Constantius, *Life of Germanus of Auxerre*, 2; Palladius, *The Lausiac History*, 8.2; Salvian, *Letters*, 4.9.

[44]   Salvian, *Letters*, 9.1: 'Domino ac beatissimo discipulo, patri, filio, per institutionem discipulo, per amorem filio, per honorem patri.'

for filial obedience and *pietas*. It would not do justice to the ecclesiastical writers, however, to suggest that the use of family rhetoric – or ascetic rhetoric – derived solely from this need to establish patriarchal power structures in the Christian communities, or to claim that they consciously tried to reconcile ideas like asceticism and fertility, which 'originally' would indeed have been contradictory, simply in order to evade disputes and back up their authority.[45] The imposition of meanings does not occur outside the world of social interaction of 'real' people, ecclesiastical writers included. The processes of negotiating meanings inevitably reflect contemporary ideas about the relationships between the practices that are held to be of primary importance. Not surprisingly, following Christ for salvation, interpreting the Bible for information about the right praxis, and family values linking these processes to the traditional Greco-Roman thinking, emerge as such things.

The fundamental nature of Christian communities constructed as *familiae Christi* was (ideally) manifested in mutual charity between all the members, whether living or dead. Features and values traditionally attributed to family relations, like that of *pietas*, were attached to the Church and the spiritual communion of the faithful. Within this wider household of God, the community of Christian ascetics was a special family, its members assuming the roles of the different members of the biological family. Not only were the close-knit ascetic communities shaped on the example of the family, but ascetics and ascetic communities formed a networking core for the household of Christ, a kind of nuclear family inside the extended family that consisted of all Christians and the Church as a whole.

As symbolic and spiritual kinship were constructed as a basis for the new Christian identity, the familial language became not only useful but also inescapable in propagating the Christian lifestyle and, even more pointedly, asceticism. The parental functions of the ascetics and the clergy played a role in the inner economy of the family of Christ, with the connotations of *pietas*, solidarity and support. The familial roles were used to construct a distinctive identity for Christian communities, a social network which would transcend the limits of any earthly *familia*.

---

[45] As Andrew Jacobs notes: 'We should not imagine that the Fathers, somehow against their own (ascetic) will, found themselves compelled by the power of family values to tote a "profamily" banner.' Jacobs, 'Let Him Guard', pp. 279–80. Cf. e.g. Brown, *Body and Society*, p. 345 on Ambrose's motivation for the promotion of asceticism.

Chapter 4
Chastity as Immortality

Rejoice, you childless one, you who bear no children, burst into song and shout, you who endure no birth pangs; for the children of the desolate woman are more numerous than the children of the one who is married.[1]

The family metaphors dealt with so far in this volume were mostly concerned with defining the place of ascetics in the new family of Christ, that is, with building up a community of belonging. However, the ascetic community could not be a competitive alternative to the biological family or kin group network without offspring and continuity. The would-be ascetics had roles to play as individual members of their original families, especially as potential parents. Fertility in all its aspects was a crucial concern in pre-modern society. The fertility of the soil sustained society as a whole, and the lives of the peasants and their families depended directly on the crops. The fertility of women, in turn, ensured the future of families. Writers who promoted asceticism had the difficult task of arguing that the unmarried lifestyle was compatible with the values attached to fertility and having children. How would chastity contribute to fertility, fruitfulness and continuity?

Wise Bridesmaids and Wives of Christ

In the ascetic discourse, the wise bridesmaids (ἀι παρθένοι) with burning lamps waiting for the bridegroom in Matthew 25:1–13, as well as the bride in the *Song of Songs*, were soon assimilated to the ascetic virgins. One of the first cases, if not the very first, in which this connection was made is in the *Acts of Thomas*, written at the beginning of the third century, which aims to highlight chastity as a means for attaining salvation.[2] This theme and its interpretation was widely adopted by the late fourth- and early fifth-century writers who propagate asceticism

---

[1] Gal 4:27 (see Isa 54:1).

[2] *Acts of Thomas*, 12 and 124 and *Acts of Paul and Thecla* esp. 6, 12 and 16 with Van Eijk, 'Marriage and Virginity', p. 212. For the earlier interpretation, see Eph 5:25–32; 2 Cor 11:1–2; John 3:29; Rev 19:7–9 and 21:9, with e.g. Clemens of Alexandria, *Stromata*, 3.4.49 and Tertullian, *An Exhortation to Chastity*, 5. For Origen, the bride stood for both the

82   *Children and Asceticism in Late Antiquity*

in mainstream Christianity: the relationship between the virgin and Christ is referred to as a betrothal, virgins preserving their purity while waiting for their bridegroom. The actual marriage occurs only in heaven, after the Judgement, when the virgin moves into the heavenly bridal chamber of her husband. This 'new' interpretation is expressed in numerous texts. Through her divine spouse, a virgin will obtain not only eternal life, but also special heavenly rewards over and above those earned by other Christians.[3]

Ambrose represents a kind of turning point in this tradition in the West. He identifies the bride of the *Song of Songs* as the Church in his *On the Mysteries* – in line with the more traditional interpretation – but in his *Exhortation to Virginity*, she is understood to be a type of chaste virgin, a bride hastening to her groom, Christ.[4] Christ is the bridegroom not only for the Church or for virgins in general, but the bridegroom for every single virgin – even, in some contexts, for male virgins.[5] Some of the texts stress even more pointedly the nature of the union as a marriage. Jerome pointed out that as a virgin, Eustochium had Christ as her husband, patriarchs as brothers, Israel as father – and the Lord as the closest relative. Paulinus of Nola, in turn, urged his audience: 'Let us kiss him whose kiss is chastity. Let us have intercourse with him, to wed whom is virginity.'[6]

Church and an individual soul (E.A. Clark, 'The Uses of the *Song of Songs*: Origen and the Later Latin fathers', in Clark, *Ascetic Piety*, pp. 389–99).

    [3]   E.g. *Anonymous Homily on Virginity*, 44 and 56–7; Pseudo-Athanasius, *On Virginity*, 2 and 24; *Canons of Pseudo-Athanasius*, 97–8 (Arabic text); Eusebius of Emesa, *Sermons*, 7.14 and 24; Gregory of Nyssa, *On Virginity*, 3.8; John Chrysostom, *To a Young Widow*, 3; Pseudo-Athanasius, *Life of Syncletica*, 8 and 92. See Clark, 'The Uses', pp. 402–10 on the exegesis of *the Song of Songs*; and Hunter, 'The Virgin', on the exegesis of *Psalm 45* in the fourth-century West.

    [4]   Ambrose of Milan, *On the Mysteries*, 7.35–41 with Ambrose, *On Virgins*, 1.6.31 (c. 377 CE) vs. Ambrose, *Exhortation to Virginity*, 5.28–9 (early 390s CE) with Ambrose, *The Consecration of a Virgin*, 17.107 (early 390s CE) and *On Virgins*, 2.2.16; Jerome, *Letters*, 22.41 and 39.7–8; Augustine, *On the Good of Widowhood*, 19 (24). See Hunter, 'The Virgin', pp. 285–90 on the 'bridal exegesis' of Ambrose.

    [5]   Paulinus of Nola, *Letters*, 41.1 with M. Kuefler, *The Manly Eunuch: Masculinity, Gender Ambiguity, and Christian Ideology in Late Antiquity* (Chicago, 2001), pp. 139–43, who stresses the significance of male bridehood, but his argumentation rests on relatively weak ground because of the paucity of actual contemporary references.

    [6]   Jerome, *Letters*, 22.18, 24–5; Paulinus of Nola, *Letters*, 23.42: 'Illum osculemur, quem osculari castitas est. Illi copulemur, cui nupsisse virginitas est.' See also Vitricius of Rouen, *The Praise of Saints*, 13; *On the Fall of a Consecrated Virgin*, 5.21; Mark the Deacon, *Life of Porphyry*, 101; Gregory of Nyssa, *On Virginity*, 16.2. In Augustine, *On Holy Virginity*, 55 (54) and in John Chrysostom, *Regulares feminae*, 7 and 9, Christ is a lover.

This promise was not only for virgins, but also for widows. The widows vowed to continence were not, however, brides; they were already established as wives of Christ. Tertullian had depicted a dedicated widow as one wedded to God, belonging to the angelic family and a sharer of the immortal blessings.[7] In the period under scrutiny, Jerome is most eager, but not alone, in calling attention to the eternal profits of widowhood. He seeks support from the Psalms for his claim that the reward for the chastity of the widow is that the King desires her beauty: Christ is not only a fiancé, but her lord and husband. Palladius even calls the elite widow Olympias the wife of the Word of Truth.[8] The identification of an ascetic as a bride or wife of Christ does not appear to depend on the status of the writer,[9] but it seems that a more concrete and carnal metaphor of an actual, 'consummated' marriage suited the widows, who took Christ as their second husband, better than the virgins. The discourse on virgins centres on their purity and eternal bodily integrity.

Whether widow or virgin, the common point was to indicate the unique intimacy between Christ and the ascetic. Whether it was seen as a betrothal or as an actual marriage, the taking of the vow was in every aspect compared and likened to a marriage contract: it implied leaving the family of origin, shifting loyalty to the family of the bridegroom and partaking of the (future) joys of marriage. A bond was formed between the ascetic and Christ, which was seen as equally binding and unbreakable as the marriage bond. Nor would offspring be lacking in such a union.

Fertile Virgins, Fruitful Ascetics

Although a place in Heaven and intimacy with Christ are things for which one must wait, other fruits of asceticism are to be attained in this world. The idea that asceticism offers a foretaste of the heavenly life was common. Among men, the unmarried were seen as angels receiving 'sevenfold more' in the present time and immortal life in the world to come.[10] The exact nature of these earthly

---

[7]   Tertullian, *An Exhortation to Chastity*, 13; Tertullian, *To His Wife*, 1.4. See also Brown, *Body and Society*, p. 171 (on Origen).

[8]   Jerome, *Letters*, 54.3, with e.g. Jerome, *Letters*, 108.6 and 33; 22.30; Palladius, *The Lausiac History*, 56 (c. 420 AD: 'σύμβιος τοῦ λόγου τῆς ἀληθείας'). See also John Chrysostom, *To a Young Widow*, 3 and 7; and Gerontius, *Life of Melania* (Greek), 65.

[9]   Cf. Hunter, 'The Virgin', pp. 291–2.

[10]   Ambrose, *On Virgins*, 1.11.64: 'Nemo est qui reliquerit domum aut parentes aut fratres aut uxorem aut filios propter regnum dei et non recipiat septies tantum in hoc

84 *Children and Asceticism in Late Antiquity*

gains is often left rather vague, with one exception: the most usual way in which ecclesiastical writers emphasized the profits due to chastity was, paradoxically, to highlight the fertility of the ascetics. Virginity is a fertile state, bound to yield plentiful fruit and abundant offspring both in the world to come and in this world: 'Virgins are fruitlessly barren in flesh but fruitfully chaste in spirit.' The young women should imitate the examples given both by the Church, itself a virgin having more children than any bride, and the mythological virgins of the Christian past, like Thecla, Agnes and Pelagia, who by their example had produced noble offspring. A virgin is left without children and without the pains of childbearing, but she is abundantly fruitful.[11]

Augustine of Hippo exemplified this fruitfulness of virgins with the idea of a wealthy woman buying slaves from foreign lands to turn them into Christians. Augustine stresses that in fact this kind of lady would have given birth to more members of Christ than even the greatest fruitfulness of the womb – yet her money is nothing compared to the fruits of sacred virginity. There is no reason for the virgins of God to be sad, even if they cannot be mothers of the flesh.[12] Demetrias, for example, a young lady vowed to God, is more fertile in her virginity than in earthly marriage. She will attain more fecund happiness even for her parents than would be possible in married life with children.[13] The parents of ascetics will not lack grandchildren, since they will have the continuity of spiritual virtues and immortality as their children's offspring.[14] Gregory of Nyssa makes elaborate use of these same themes in his treatise on virginity: a virgin gives birth to immortal children through the Spirit, and virginity 'has always the offspring of devotion to rejoice in.'[15]

There are also references to the fertility of chaste widows. However, since many of the widows already had biological progeny, it is natural that this theme

---

tempore, in saeculo autem venturo vitam aeternam possidebit.' Cf. Luke 18:29–30. See also e.g. Basil of Ancyra, *On True Purity of Virginity*, 51–5; Ambrose, *Exhortation to Virginity*, 4.19; Gregory of Nyssa, *On Virginity*, 14.4; John Chrysostom, *On Virginity*, 79.2; John Chrysostom, *Against the Opponents of Monastic Life*, 3.21; Jerome, *Letters*, 65.1 and 130.4.

[11] Paulinus of Nola, *Letters*, 41; quote from 41.3: 'Virginibus secundum carnem sterilitas infecunda, secundum spiritum fructuosa castitas adest'; Ambrose, *Letters*, 7.36; Ambrose, *On Virgins*, 1.6.30–31 with Augustine, *On Holy Virginity*, 5; Ambrose, *On Virgins*, 1.10.60 and John Chrysostom, *On Virginity*, 80.2.

[12] Augustine, *On Holy Virginity*, 5–10 (9).

[13] Augustine, *Letters*, 188.1; Augustine, *Letters*, 150.

[14] John Chrysostom, *Against the Opponents of Monastic Life*, 3.16; Ambrose, *Letters*, 27.2; Methodius of Olympus, *Symposium*, 1.1.

[15] Gregory of Nyssa, *On Virginity*, 3.8: 'ἀεὶ ἐπαγάλλεται τοῖς τῆς εὐσεβείας γεννήμασι', with *On Virginity*, 13 and 19.

attracts less attention than the theme of fertile virgins (either male or female). The fruits of the widows are, moreover, pointedly of an abstract nature. Ambrose refers to the case of Naomi in the Old Testament, who had lost her husband and 'the offspring of her fruitfulness', but found support in her relatives. The progeny cannot safeguard one's old age, but 'a widow is fruitful in the offspring of virtues', and a chaste and good widowhood guarantees support for itself.[16] Augustine urges a widow to take the vow herself and not to marry off her daughter 'in order to have more numerous and more fertile virtues, not in order to have grandchildren'.[17] Grandchildren may be lacking, but the continuity of the lineage is secured.

The virginity of a daughter may become a source of actual fertility for her family and community. Ambrose makes the point that in the more densely populated (eastern) areas, there are also more virgins. Thus, the consecration of virgins does not diminish the birth rate, but in fact increases it: virginity is not to be held as injurious, especially as 'through a virgin came the salvation that was to make the Roman world more fruitful'. Similarly, Jerome praises Laeta, who in consecrating her daughter Paula to chastity 'exchanged sorrowful fertility for life-giving children'. This claim is developed further when he claims that dedicating the firstborn child to the Lord would make the mother fertile so that she would have even more children in the future.[18]

Male ascetics were also potent and had progeny. Augustine warns against thinking that a person made perfect in piety would seek to have sons. Times had changed since the days of Abraham, when it was a virtue to have many children. 'Now', he writes, 'the way is surely open to abundant spiritual offspring, wherever they have been born in the flesh.'[19] John Chrysostom, in turn, refers to his own labour pangs with spiritual children. Fertility for spiritual offspring and kinship in the context of the family of Christ make biological progeny superfluous. These

---

[16]   Ambrose, *On Widows*, 6.33–4: 'quae fructus fecunditatis amiserat'; 'fecunda sit vidua prole virtutum'.

[17]   Augustine, *Letters*, 3*.3: 'Cape propter habendas plures uberioresque virtutes, non propter nepotes.' See also Augustine, *On the Good of Widowhood*, 19 (24).

[18]   Ambrose, *On Virginity*, 7.36: 'ubi paulae virgines, ibi etiam pauciores homines; ubi virginitatis studia crebriora, ibi numerum quoque hominem esse maiorem ... per virginem salus venerit, orbem fecundatura Romanum'; Jerome, *Letters*, 107.3 and 13: 'tu lucruosam fecunditatem vitalibus liberis conmutasti. Fidens loquor, accepturam te filios, quae primum foetum domino reddidisti', with John Chrysostom, *Homilies on Ephesians*, 21.1.

[19]   Augustine, *On Marriage and Concupiscence*, 1.13(14): 'Patet quippe iam ex omnibus gentibus spiritaliter gignendorum, undecumque carnaliter nati fuerint, copia filiorum'; Augustine, *On the Good of Marriage*, 17 (19). See also Augustine, *On the Good of Marriage*, 9; *On the Good of Widowhood*, 8(11); *Confessions*, 8.11.27; *Letters*, 243.9.

children of ascetics, moreover, do not cause cares to their progenitors, and being without children has nothing to do with a lack of manliness and authority.[20]

In Paulinus of Nola's praise of Aper and Amanda, a married couple living in abstinence, various forms of fruitfulness are combined. Paulinus hopes that they and he would be able to cultivate the spiritual fertility which they owe to God. Their 'soil is fertile', since they bring forth a thirtyfold fruit for God by their continence, a sixtyfold fruit by the daily advancement in their common faith – and they promise a hundredfold fruit through their sons who are offered to God to live a chaste live. In his rhetoric, Paulinus builds upon the use made by many contemporary writers of the parable of the sower to show the blessings of virginity – although a more common understanding of the parable was that in the world to come, a thirtyfold fruit was reserved for married couples, a sixtyfold for widows and a hundredfold for virgins.[21]

The idea of the fruitfulness of ascetics also appears in hagiographic stories of ascetic fathers who increased the fruitfulness of vineyards, ended droughts and enabled barren women to give birth. In the case of Abba Or, for example, his efforts turn the barren land green; this story serves as an introduction to his vision, in which an angel announced that he 'will beget a great nation ... Those who will be saved through you will be ten myriads'. Actual fertility is combined with spiritual fatherhood. In the eyes of the faithful, the ascetics had become masters of the powers of fertility by negating their own sexuality.[22] Couples yearning for offspring tried to get in touch with the ascetics to beg them to pray to God for children, and peasants are said to have collected the sand of the desert trodden by the ascetics: by their blessing it was rendered extremely fertile.[23] Indeed, these ascetics had plenty of offspring: their pupils and followers.

---

[20] John Chrysostom, *Homilies on Penitence*, 1.1; John Chrysostom, *Against the Opponents of Monastic Life*, 3.16; Ambrose, *On the Faith*, 4.8.81(82)–82(83); Augustine, *Exposition on the Psalm* 127, esp. 2, 13 and 15. See also already Eusebius of Caesarea, *Proof of the Gospel*, 1.9.

[21] Paulinus of Nola, *Letters*, 39.1–2: 'quam fertilis terra deo sitis'; on the children of Aper and Amanda, see also Paulinus of Nola, *Letters*, 44.5–6 (against P. Walsh, *Letters of Paulinus of Nola* (Westminster, MD and London, 1967), p. 341). See e.g. Pseudo-Athanasius, *On Virginity*, 14; Ambrose, *On Virgins*, 1.10.60; Jerome, *Against Jovinian*, 3; Augustine, *On Holy Virginity*, 45 (46); John Cassian, Conferences, 21.9; see also Paulinus of Nola, *Letters*, 39.1 (the thirtyfold fruit is here reserved for married couples living in continence).

[22] *History of the Monks in Egypt*, 2.2–4: Ἔση εἰς ἔθνος μέγα καὶ πολὺν λαὸν πιστευθήσῃ· ἔσονται δὲ οἱ σωζόμενοι διὰ σοῦ μυριάδες δέκα', with Jerome, *Life of Hilarius*, 7, 17 and 22; *History of the Monks in Egypt*, 1.10; *Apophthegmata patrum*, Macarius 1.

[23] Praying for progeny e.g. in Theodoret of Cyrrhus, *Religious History*, 13.16; peasants: *History of the Monks in Egypt*, 10.26–29.

The fruitfulness of the ascetics, therefore, is revealed in the number of their heirs. When Jerome defended his choice to stay chaste and recommended virginity to others, he noted that for him it is alright if those people are willing to marry, 'who eat their bread by the sweat of their face, whose land brings forth to them thorns and thistles, and whose crops are choked with briers. My seed is fertile with hundredfold fruit'.[24] His manliness should not be in doubt. When Paulina, an elite lady, died, Jerome consoled her husband Pammachius with the thought that even if she had no children, she had both Pammachius and the blind, the mute, the poor, the crippled and the sick as her offspring and heirs: Pammachius, because he had assumed the ascetic vocation with her, and also the poor and wretched among whom he had lavishly distributed Paulina's property.[25] If there is a childless widow, she should give to the poor that which would have been her children's share; if there are children, she should make Christ their co-inheritor. To give one's inheritance to the poor is equivalent to the acquisition of biological heirs for oneself: alms produce children and grandchildren for the donator.[26] In a hagiographic treatise probably originating in the fifth-century West, the virgin Helia is presented boasting of her heavenly spouse, her silent children and painless daily childbirth giving her a multitude of spiritual children; her body is a field untouched by mortal men, but irrigated by the dew of heaven, and thus fruitful beyond imagination.[27]

This idea reflects the pervasiveness of the idea of the family wealth by itself continuing the family tradition and lineage. In all, by conventional standards, both by counting offspring and by thinking about the continuance of the patrimony, Christian chastity is the most fruitful state.

The use of the themes of kinship and fruitfulness were not limited to the Christian ascetic rhetoric in Late Antiquity. For Libanius, who remained

---

[24] Jerome, *Letters*, 22.19: 'nubat et nubatur ille qui in sudore faciei comedit panem suum, cui terra tribulos generat et spinas, cuius herba sentibus suffocatur: meum semen centena fruge fecundum est'. See also Jerome, *Against Jovinian*, 1.3 with Kuefler, *The Manly Eunuch*, pp. 201 and 204.

[25] Jerome, *Letters*, 66.5.

[26] Augustine, *Exposition on the Psalm 127*, 16; Jerome, *Letters*, 120.1: 'Igitur et tu, quia paucos non habes filios, habe plurimos'; Jerome, *Letters*, 127.14; Gregory Nazianzen, *Oration 7*, 20; Ambrose, *On the Death of His Brother Satyrus*, 2.13.

[27] See V. Burrus, '"Honor the Father": Exegesis and Authority in the Life of Saint Helia', in H.-U. Weidemann (ed.), *Asceticism and Exegesis in Early Christianity: The Reception of New Testament Texts in Ancient Ascetic Discourses* (Göttingen, 2013), pp. 453–4. The critical edition and commentary of *The Life of Saint Helia* (by Virginia Burrus and Marco Conti) was published by Oxford University Press in December 2013, unfortunately too late for me to consult it for the present study.

unmarried, his art (that is, rhetoric) was his bride, and Porphyry called the lovers of true wisdom his children.[28] The mental distance is not great between them and the figure of Honoratus, who, according to his biographer Hilary of Arles, prayed to God to give him wisdom for a wife, or Bishop Synesius, who claimed that the philosopher Hypatia had been to him a mother, a sister and a teacher.[29]

In all, fertility is best ensured through virginity since 'through it are attained the inheritance of the heavenly kingdom and the succession of heavenly rewards'.[30] Marriage is for the continuity of the human race, but after the incarnation of God, there is an abundant supply of spiritual children and there is no longer a particular need for posterity in flesh. The fertility of the ascetics renders void the need for biological children.[31] Succession by children is superseded by salvation in Christ. In theory, earthly fertility was something to be despised by Christians, yet in practice, not only did the heroes of the renunciation (that is, ascetic saints) become masters of fertility, but ecclesiastical writers used biological fertility as an important part of their argumentation that virginity is bound to yield plentiful fruit and abundant offspring. Moreover, the parental roles of the ascetics and ecclesiastical leaders signified fruitful progeny for themselves; their flock, their disciples and their followers were their children. The spiritual offspring and successors ensured the survival of both their fame and their values of life even after their biological death, ensuring them an earthly succession and a sense of continuity unrelated to biological reproduction.

Continuity and Death, Asceticism and Children

The discourse on spiritual and biological offspring and on the significance of succession reveals what ecclesiastical writers saw as central in the Christian lifestyle. Their choice of arguments also reveals their expectations of what would be the common way of thinking among their audiences. It is therefore significant that the theme of individual continuity ensured by children is repeatedly

---

[28] Libanius, *Autobiography*, 54; Porphyry, *To Marcella*, 1.

[29] Hilarius of Arles, *Life of Honoratus*, 7; Synesius, *Letters*, 16.

[30] Ambrose, *Letter Outside the Collection* 15.3: 'Bonum conigium per quod est inventa posteritas successionis humanae, sed melior virginitatis per quam regni caelestis hereditas acquisita et caelestium meritorum reperta successio.'

[31] Eusebius of Caesarea, *Proof of the Gospel*, 1.9; Ambrose, *On Paradise*, 10.47; Ambrose, *On Virgins*, 1.7.34; Augustine, *On Holy Virginity*, 9; Augustine, *On the Good of Marriage*, 9; 13 (15); 16 (18); Augustine, *On the Good of Widowhood*, 8 (11); Gregory of Nyssa, *On the Making of Man*, 17.1–2. See also Van Eijk, 'Marriage and Virginity', p. 227 on Basil of Ancyra.

mentioned, and that the ideas of immortality and salvation in Christianity were equated with the roles played by children in families. Human nature, in its mortality, requires children to diminish or alleviate the threat posed by death. Children, however, signified not only an abstract continuity for the human race, but also the propagation of kin and immortality for an individual – and this is why children are spoken of as great gifts of God.[32]

Augustine is more explicit than most of the other writers in using this theme in his writings. I shall now follow his argumentation to demonstrate how the relationships between continuity and children on the one hand, and continuity and asceticism on the other were conceptualized and linked together. Augustine explains the individual desire to be succeeded by offspring by identifying the wish to continue living and to evade death as the deepest human wish.[33] 'He had children: he is not dead', as he crystallizes with an ironical twist what he identifies as the common idea among his parishioners.[34] Augustine acknowledges the importance of lineage and memory in children on earth for the sense of immortality. However, he makes way for the Christian claim of the hope for resurrection as fulfilling this wish more perfectly, since ultimately, the succession of children is an imperfect way of ensuring this continuity: 'Whatever a father reserves for you in this life, he dies in order that you may succeed; he will make a place for your life by his death.' God is the superior father: he remains always with his children, sharing in the inheritance. There are no successors and predecessors, but life eternal.[35] Jerome refers to the same idea when he comments that in the pre-Christian era, 'the blessing of children was the only blessing', but

---

[32]   Ambrose, *Commentary on Luke*, 1.30; Ambrose of Milan, *On Paradise*, 10.47; Augustine, *On Marriage and Concupiscence*, 1.4 (5); John Chrysostom, *Homilies in Genesis*, 18.4; and Basil of Ancyra, *On True Purity of Virginity*, 54–5. For the earlier expressions of this idea, see above, pp. 30–40 with Van Eijk, 'Marriage and Virginity', pp. 209–12 and Van Dam, *Families and Friends*, 120 (for classical philosophers).

[33]   Augustine, *Sermons*, 344.4; Augustine, *City of God*, 5.14 and Augustine, *On the Good of Marriage*, 19 (22). The idea is already present in Plato, *Symposium*, 206D–207A, 208E; see also Van Eijk, 'Marriage and Virginity', pp. 209–10.

[34]   Augustine, *Exposition on the Psalm 48*, 1.14: 'Habuit filios, non est mortuus.' For an earlier evaluation of the role played by children 'in the common opinion', see Clemens of Alexandria, *Stromata*, 2.23.142 and Methodius of Olympus, *Symposium*, 2.5.

[35]   Augustine, *Sermons*, 344.2: 'Postremo quidquid tibi pater reservat in terra, decedit ut succedas, vitae tuae locum faciet morte sua. Pater autem Deus quod tibi servat, secum servat; ut haereditatem cum ipso possideas patre, nec eum decessorem quasi successor exspectes, sed inhaereas semper mansuro, semper in illo mansurus', with Augustine, *Exposition on the Psalm 26*, 2.18 and *Exposition on the Psalm 127*, 2 and 15.

90 *Children and Asceticism in Late Antiquity*

now children are not needed, since the Son of God has established a new family for himself.[36]

Augustine makes the urge for the continuation of life an argument for the need for sacrifices in order to attain unending life as a Christian. The fear of death makes people act foolishly. The unsure and painful cures of the doctors, usually with no other effect but to hasten their patients' death, for example, result from the common fear of death. If wealth, honour and security are loved, but nevertheless are sacrificed in order to prolong life in this world, is it not right to sacrifice the world to attain everlasting life, asks Augustine. His point is that wealth, honour and security, the basics of life for the Roman aristocracy, and even the continuity of life can be attained in heaven by living a chaste life. Indeed, as the human mind 'has a craving for eternity, and is moved by the shortness of the present life', it cannot resist the light and prominence (*lumen culmenque*) of the divine authority in Christianity.[37]

In his letter to Proba, Augustine even presents a hierarchically structured theory of human needs. He asks what kind of happiness a widow should pray for, for herself and her family. The first level is the wish for temporal wellbeing (*salus temporalis*) for herself and for those she loves. If this is granted, there are greater things to possess: the wish for honours and power (*honores et potestates*). This form of prayer is ideally directed at securing life itself, health, soundness of mind and body, and such provision of house and clothing as is fitting to the social circumstances.[38] Unsurprisingly, however, Augustine concludes that all these considerations of health, wealth and honours are to be cast aside in comparison with the obtaining of immortality: 'For although the body may be thought to be in health, the mind cannot be regarded as sound which does not prefer eternal to temporal things.'[39] In earthly marriage, the conditions of being born and dying are always both present. Therefore, for a Christian, the need for succession to replace the dying generation is no argument for marriage.[40]

---

[36] Jerome, *Letters*, 22.21: 'sola erat benedictio liberorum'.

[37] Augustine, *Letters*, 127.4–5; *Letters*, 137.4.16: 'Quae tandem mens avida aeternitatis, vitaeque praesentis brevitati permota, contra huius divinae auctoritatis lumen culmenque contendat?' with *City of God*, 10.29. See already Tertullian, *On the Testimony of the Soul*, 4.9 on the desire for posthumous fame as an inborn quality in everyone.

[38] This wish should ideally be directed not only to oneself but also to one's neighbours, and thus it would stretch from one's own welfare to 'the whole human family', to whom affection is due.

[39] Augustine, *Letters*, 130.5.10–7.14; quote from 130.7.14: 'quamquam fortasse corpus, animus vero nullo modo sanus existimandus est, qui non temporalibus aeterna praeponit'. Translated by J.G. Cunningham (Nicene and Post-Nicene Fathers, ser. I, vol. 1).

[40] Augustine, *Against Julian*, 6.30, with Augustine, *City of God*, 5.14 and Augustine, *On the Sermon on the Mount* 1.15.40 (394 CE).

Chastity as Immortality

For other writers, too, the theme of death is ever-present in discussions of family life. Death cuts short all the fancied blessings of marriage – some even lose their husband before the actual marriage takes place. In marriage, death is not a possibility, but a certainty. Even if children survive the parents, one of the spouses will die before the other.[41] In particular, Gregory of Nyssa often evokes this imagery: in marriage there is a continual expectation of death and this terrible uncertainty disturbs the present joy of being married and having children. The bones of the dead wear no memorial or remnant of life's bloom. More generally, the whole course of human life is aimed at ensuring continuity in this life: buildings give shelter, agriculture provides sustenance, medicine is for sustaining health, armour and fortifications shield against violent death. All thought about how we are to go on living is occasioned by the fear of dying. Marriage, in particular, is an attempt to create one's own immortality through offspring.[42]

Not only is the fear for death a result of marriage, but death itself is caused by marriage. 'Where there is death, there is marriage. If you hate the one, the other too disappears.' And conversely, as long as Adam and Eve were immortal, they had no need of posterity. Thus, the mortality of human beings makes marriage and sexuality inevitable. Marriage and intercourse are indeed instruments of ensuring succession; not succession for life, but for death, carried on by the natural instincts of humankind.[43] Thus, marriage, the very device by which the continuity of individuals in their progeny is intended to be ensured, is in the service of death and is the cause of the failure of all continuity by binding an individual on earth.

Abstinence, therefore, is a way of fleeing death. In asceticism, one receives eternal life and grasps immortality. Virginity produces life: in it, 'death is swallowed up by life', as there are no sorrows of widowhood, orphanhood or loss of children. Those who have chosen virginal life have made themselves a

---

[41]   Jerome, *Letters*, 22.2 and 15; Eusebius of Emesa, *Sermons*, 7.15; John Chrysostom, *On Virginity*, 57.6.

[42]   Gregory of Nyssa, *On Virginity*, esp. 3.3, 3.6 and 13.2–14; *On Soul and Resurrection*, 13A–16A and *On the Making of Man*, 17.1–2 (with J. Behr, 'The Rational Animal: A Rereading of Gregory of Nyssa's *De hominis opificio*', *Journal of Early Christian Studies* 7(2) (1999), pp. 240–41). See also Van Eijk, 'Marriage and Virginity', pp. 232–4 and Brown, *Body and Society*, pp. 294–303 on the triad of death, marriage and children in his thinking.

[43]   John Chrysostom, *On Virginity*, 14.6: "Ὅπου γὰρ θάνατος, ἐκεῖ γάμος· τούτου δὲ οὐκ ὄντος οὐδε αὐτὸς ἔπεται'; Gregory of Nyssa, *On Virginity*, 14.2; Augustine, *On the Sermon on the Mount* 1.15.40. The idea is present already in the Encratic literature of the late second and early third centuries CE: Van Eijk, 'Marriage and Virginity', esp. pp. 216–17 with Brown, *Body and Society*, pp. 119–20.

barrier between life and death.[44] Chaste ascetics have offspring, successors and inheritors, that is, those who continue their lineage and patrimony in the spiritual sense. They lack the cares and sorrows of marriage, especially death. Since the desire for succession in children would be the only natural and honourable reason for sexual life and marriage,[45] for Christians who seriously look forward to the heavenly afterlife, there would be no reasons for marriage.

The arguments of John Chrysostom sum up well the relationship between children, death, family lineage and personal continuity. He remarks that ever since the Fall, the major consolation against death has been the succession of children. Adam and Eve in Paradise did not need posterity, but now mortal human beings seek to make their memory immortal both through the children begotten by them and in attaching their names to various places.[46] Chrysostom is not surprised that those who do not believe in the Resurrection weep for the deaths of their children, since their survival is the only consolation for them, but he wonders why Christians, who should know how to despise all worldly things, cry for their children or grandchildren. Chrysostom complains that expressions of anxiety over this issue come constantly to his ears: people are worried about to whom they can leave their fields, houses, servants and gold.[47] Patrimony and inheritance were seen as carrying on the family and individual and, as such, they also bind the would-be ascetic to earthly family values and the wrong kind of continuity.

In all, Christians should bear in mind their eternal continuity in heaven, and count not on earthly immortality through children, in the memory of the survivors or in the continuity of the familial line and patrimony. Ambrose claims that among Christians, the maidens climb the steps of virtue, longing for death.[48]

---

[44] Pseudo-Athanasius, *On Virginity*, 2, 19 and 24 (320–400 CE); Gregory of Nyssa, *On Virginity*, 13.3–14.1, 14.4: 'κατεπόθη ἐν ἐκείνοις τὸ θνητὸν ὑπὸ τῆς ζωῆς'; Gregory Nazianzen, *Oration 37*, 9.

[45] E.g. Augustine, *On Marriage and Concupiscence*, 1.4 (5); *Letters*, 130.16.29; *Enchridion*, 21.78; Jerome, *Against Jovinian*, 1.19; Gregory Nazianzen, *Oration 37*, 9; *Consultations of Zacchaeus and Apollonius* 3.1.13. For an earlier usage of this argumentation, see e.g. Clemens of Alexandria, *Stromata*, 2.23.137–42, 3.12.79 and 82 (with Buell, *Making Christians*, pp. 37 on Clemens). Still, Augustine remarks that he had never met a couple who had intercourse only because they hope for conception (Augustine, *On the Good of Marriage*, 13 (15)).

[46] John Chrysostom, *Homilies in Genesis*, 18.4.2; John Chrysostom, *On Virginity*, 15.1.

[47] John Chrysostom, *Against the Opponents of Monastic Life*, 2.8 and 3.16; see also Gregory of Nyssa, *On Virginity*, 3.10. For the idea of Christianity as replacing children as the ultimate guarantee of continuity with the idea of personal and societal continuity, see also Brown, *Body and Society*, esp. 120–21 and 301–2.

[48] Ambrose, *Letters*, 7.36.

Thus, for those who had best internalized the Christian ethos, the longing for death can be seen as paradoxically a part of longing for survival and continuity. These people, the saints, have shed their ultimately human motivations and needs, and are able to scorn earthly continuity.

* * *

In the argumentation for the right Christian praxis, asceticism was identified as the embodiment of a distinctively Christian way of living. On the other hand, since continuity was argued to be the ultimate human aspiration and need, the late fourth- and early fifth-century ecclesiastical writers argued that fertility, and therefore the continuity of society, families and individuals, would be even better attained if ascetic practices were rooted in the culture. Whereas the traditional Greco-Roman thinking was branded as giving the primary position to offspring and family in guaranteeing continuity, the new Christian interpretation emphasized that immortality and meaningful life was best assured by ascetic practices. The argument shows the very hopes for which marriage was entered into in the first place – children signified immortality and continuity for their parents. With the advent of Christianity, this-worldly continuity in children was to be changed to transcendental continuity in Christ.

This, however, is the situation as the ecclesiastical writers wished to present it. When our view shifts from ideology to the wider spectrum of attitudes and to the family practices, the picture takes on more dimensions. The information is filtered through the various intentions of the authors, through the many layers of both conscious and unconscious presuppositions, and through rhetorical conventions. However, enough is left to examine how the theological arguments for asceticism were adopted at a family level and what the basis was for actually choosing asceticism. Did the shift from a traditional mentality to the new thinking happen in the manner propagated by the ecclesiastical writers?

Chapter 5

Choosing Asceticism: Demography and Decision Making in the Domestic Sphere

> Should your little nephew hang on your neck, should your mother, with hair dishevelled and garments rent, show you the breasts with which she suckled you, should your father lie on the threshold, trample him under your foot and go your way.[1]

The essential point in the preceding chapters was to see how ecclesiastical writers wanted to present the relationship between the family, children, and ascetic Christianity. The viewpoint was the rhetorical construction of Christian and ascetic communities as families, separate from and superior to the biological family. In the following chapters, the focus is shifted from these ideological discourses via shared attitudes and mentalities to social history. The aim is to scrutinize the patterns of choosing asceticism by the individuals themselves or by their family members, and the motivations behind such decisions. The next section introduces these themes and shifts the perspective from the history of ideas towards social history by presenting the life course framework for such decisions. Understanding the age bases of family decision-making dynamics is essential when entering the discussion of the rhetorical emphasis on the autonomy (or lack of it) of children in choosing asceticism, forms of family authority, and the gendered expectations towards teenage boys and girls in Late Antiquity. A central question here is whether or not Christianity widened the possibilities for children to make choices for themselves. On this basis it would be possible to proceed to study the actual decision-making processes in families, and finally to scrutinize the different contributory factors for embracing asceticism.

---

[1] Jerome, *Letters*, 14.2: 'Licet parvulus ex collo pendeat nepos, licet sparso crine et scissis vestibus ubera quibus nutrierat mater ostendat, licet in limine pater iaceat, per calcatum perge patrem.' The text is addressed to Heliodorus. The nephew mentioned here is Nepotian, subsequently an ascetically minded presbyter and protégé of Heliodorus (see Jerome, *Letters*, 52 and 60).

Timing Marriage, Timing the Ascetic Vow

What were the circumstances in which elite Christian families of Late Antiquity discussed the future of their children? As the previous chapters have shown, for unmarried women and men, entering into asceticism was rhetorically understood in the context of betrothal or even marriage in the family of Christ. On the other hand, the significance of marriage in elite family strategies has been shown to be of central importance among the Greco-Roman elites. Indeed, one may plausibly propose that discussions concerning asceticism took place in families at the same time as they would in any case have been discussing the future of the offspring, that is, just before a decision about marriage was to take place. Therefore, it is important to study the age of the first marriage for Greco-Roman elites and the agency of different relatives on this phase of the individual life course: how did mortality rates affect the probability of having parents or other older relatives alive when decisions about entering the ascetic life were to be made?

For the earlier Roman Empire, the common pattern was a considerable age difference between the spouses. Among members of the elite, who in general tended to marry earlier than the rest of the population, this would mean that daughters would marry in their early to mid-teens (most often, it seems, from the ages of 13 to 15), but sons only in their early or mid-20s (from 20 to 25). For sub-elites and the ordinary population, the variations due to local cultural factors seem to have been much greater, and the reliability of the available epigraphical and papyrological sources to establish an approximation of the age for the first marriage is subject to doubt. This makes it hard to indicate any specific age, but the respective ages seem to have been somewhat higher, perhaps a little under 20 years for women, and some 6 to 10 years more for men.[2] For the present study, these approximations, even with their shortcomings, give a

---

[2]   R. Saller, 'Men's Age at Marriage and its Consequences for the Roman Family', *Classical Philology* 82 (1987), pp. 12–15; B. Shaw, 'The Age of Roman Girls at Marriage: Some Reconsiderations', *Journal of Roman Studies* 77 (1987), pp. 30–46; Saller, *Patriarchy*, pp. 36–47 and 67; Bagnall and Frier, *The Demography*, with Harlow and Laurence, *Growing Up*, pp. 80–81 and 95–102. Despite methodogical problems, this basic pattern has not been seriously challenged especially as far as the investigation of the elites is concerned: W. Scheidel, 'Roman Age Structure: Evidence and Models', *Journal of Roman Studies* 91 (2001), pp. 1–26; W. Scheidel, 'Roman Funerary Commemoration and the Age at First Marriage', *Classical Philology* 102(4) (2007), pp. 389–402; A. Lelis, W. Percy and B. Verstraete, *The Age of Marriage in Ancient Rome* (Lewiston, NY: Edwin Mellen Press, 2003), pp. 91–6 with critique in J. Evans Grubbs, 'Review of *The Age of Marriage in Ancient Rome*, by A. Lelis, W. Percy, and B. Verstraete', *Mouseion* 7(1) (2007), p. 67 and M. Kuefler, 'Theodosian Code and Later Roman Marriage Law', *Journal of Family History* 32(4) (2007), p. 348.

sufficiently firm starting point, as my material deals with the upper echelons of ancient societies, the senatorial aristocracy and local elites, of which there is at least some, although necessarily anecdotal, evidence of actual ages at first marriage. The essential feature here is the age difference between the spouses: the discussions about the future of daughters of the elite started by the very beginning of puberty at the latest, but the considerations of marriage became relevant for sons only in their late teens or early 20s at the earliest.

However, a central question remains – how far do these ages at marriage hold true for the late Roman elites? Legal principles governing the age of marriage remained the same through the whole Roman Empire to Late Antiquity – a female could enter marriage at the age of 12, a male at the age of 14. There has also been scholarly discussion on the relevance of a limit put at a certain age, instead of seeing puberty as the actual lower limit more generally. Here too, both regional and individual variation must have been wide.[3]

There has been not too much recent research focusing on the age at first marriage among late Roman populations.[4] It has been speculated that the ages at first marriage should and would have changed, especially for girls, for whom the typical age for first marriage has been claimed to have risen among Christians. Melissa Aubin and Antti Arjava have noted, after considering the methodological problems inherent in analysing inscriptions which could be interpreted as pointing to that kind of change, that no actual evidence supports this conclusion.[5] In the case of sons, even less is known about their ages at marriage in the later Roman world. The situation, however, resembles that of the daughters in that neither the anecdotal narrative sources nor the inscriptions show any clear signs of change.[6]

It is, naturally, possible to see what actual ages for marriage are given in the sources used in my study, even if the evidence is scanty at best. It appears that elite parents were indeed eager to arrange early marriages for their daughters:

---

[3]   S. Treggiari, *Roman Marriage: Iusti Coniuges from the Time of Cicero to the Time of Ulpian* (Oxford, 1991), pp. 39–43, 398–403; Saller, *Patriarchy*, pp. 25–41; Evans Grubbs, *Law and Family*, pp. 140–41 with Kuefler, 'Theodosian Code', p. 348.

[4]   See M. Aubin, 'More Apparent than Real? Questioning the Difference in Marital Age between Christian and Non-Christian Women of Rome During the Third and Fourth Century', *Ancient History Bulletin* 14 (2000), pp. 1–13; and Kuefler, 'Theodosian Code', with further references.

[5]   Aubin, 'More Apparent than Real?', pp. 8–13; and Arjava, *Women and Law*, p. 33 with Kuefler, 'Theodosian Code', pp. 351–2, 362. See also B. Shaw, '"With Whom I Lived": Measuring Roman Marriage', *Ancient Society* 32 (2002), esp. pp. 225–34 with Scheidel, 'Roman Funerary Commemoration', pp. 389–402.

[6]   Arjava, *Women and Law*, p. 31; Evans Grubbs, *Law and Family*, pp. 140–41 and 154–5.

Melania the Younger married at the age of about 14, and Demetrias, likewise the daughter of a wealthy Roman aristocratic family, was about to enter into marriage also at the age of 14 when she suddenly made the decision to become a consecrated virgin. Macrina, from a local elite family from Cappadocia, was engaged at the age of 11, when her husband-to-be suddenly died. Augustine's bride, from an aristocratic background, was only 10 and thus was also underage when the engagement was agreed.[7]

For sons, there are examples of both early and rather late ages for first marriage. Melania the Younger's husband Pinian was about 17 when they married, only three years older than his bride, forming an alliance between two of the most esteemed lineages in Late Antiquity, and Paulinus of Pella was 20 when his parents married him off. On the other hand, Paulinus of Nola who belonged, like his namesake, to the senatorial aristocracy, seems to have been around 30 when he married his equally aristocratic wife Therasia. Similarly, Augustine was already 30 when he was betrothed, and he was to wait for a further two years before entering into marriage. As Paulinus of Nola's experience shows, Augustine's higher age in entering marriage should not be seen as reflecting his lower social standing, especially since he was so conspicuously marrying a bride who stood higher on the social scale.[8]

The scattered examples from the mainly Roman aristocracy of late fourth and early fifth centuries suggest that, if there was any change, it seems to have been in the opposite direction than older scholarship had expected; in other words, the ages given, especially for females, tend to cluster at the lower end of the spectrum found in the earlier Empire.[9]

---

[7]   Melania the Younger: Gerontius, *Life of Melania* (Greek), 1; Demetrias: Jerome, *Letters*, 130; Augustine, *Letters*, 150; Macrina: Gregory of Nyssa, *Life of Macrina*, 4–5; Augustine's bride: Augustine, *Confessions*, 6.15.25. See also Melania the Elder (Palladius, *The Lausiac History*, 46; Paulinus of Nola, *Letters*, 29), who must have married in her early to mid-teens, as she had three children by the age of 22, with Evans Grubbs, *Law and Family*, p. 154 (noting also e.g. two contemporary epitaphs for married elite women who died in their teens).

[8]   Gerontius, *Life of Melania* (Greek), 1; Paulinus of Pella, *Thanksgiving*, 176–86; Paulinus of Nola, *Poem* 21 esp. 398–401 with D. Trout, *Paulinus of Nola: Life, Letters, and Poems* (Berkeley, CA, 1999), p. 53; Augustine, *Confessions*, 6.15.25.

[9]   See also A. Laiou, 'Sex, Consent, and Coercion in Byzantium', in A. Laiou (ed.), *Consent and Coercion to Sex and Marriage in Ancient and Medieval Societies* (Washington DC, 1993), pp. 167–72, showing that later in the Byzantine period the marriage agreements (among the elites) were often contracted when the girls were still very young (starting from five to seven years old), and the marriage ceremony could take place before the bride had reached puberty.

Choosing Asceticism 99

In all, the ages mentioned fit well into the marriage patterns of imperial elites that have been proposed for the earlier Empire. Thus, even if evidence is scarce, my hypothesis for the following discussion is that for the ages of first marriage, there were no marked changes between early Roman families and Christian late Roman families of the fourth and fifth centuries. The elite women married most often in their early teens and men in their 20s – even if a considerable variation at the age of marriages for men still prevails.[10] In what follows, this hypothesis will be tested against the information on the discourse on asceticism: how old were the offspring whose future was being discussed?

As the above examples also show, it was before the actual marriage, at the age of betrothal and the marriage contract, that decisions concerning marriage or asceticism had to be made. In Late Antiquity, as both the legal and economic significance of betrothal increased, this necessity was further highlighted. However, a contract of betrothal was not unbreakable and it seems that the period of betrothal was usually rather short, even if there were exceptions to this, as the case of Augustine shows. Juridically, at least after the law of 380 CE, it was possible to contract a marriage even before the girl was 10 years of age.[11] Thus, in family discussions on asceticism, the elite girl was more probably around 10 years of age or little older rather than in her mid-teens.

In Late Antiquity, a marriage arranged by parents for both girls and boys was standard practice, with the head of the family (the father if he was alive) responsible for the marriage arrangements and whose consent was legally needed for the marriage.[12] Particularly among the elites, marriage constituted a contract between two families. Although the consent of the child was also needed, in principle, the possibility that a son would protest against his father's choice of a spouse seems to have been minimal, and for a daughter not to give her consent was only a hypothetical option.[13]

---

[10]   See also Kuefler, 'Theodosian Code', pp. 351–2; and J. Evans Grubbs, 'Marrying and its Documentation in Later Roman Law', in P. Reynolds and J. Witte (eds), *To Have and to Hold: Marrying and its Documentation in Western Christendom, 400–1600* (Cambridge, 2007), p. 54.

[11]   Augustine, *Confessions*, 6.15.25 with Evans Grubbs, *Law and Family*, p. 155. On betrothal in Late Antiquity, see *Codex Theodosianus* 3.5.11 with Evans Grubbs, 'Marrying', pp. 64–72 and Kuefler, 'Theodosian Code', pp. 352–3.

[12]   Kuefler, 'Theodosian Code', pp. 347–52; Nathan, *The Family*, pp. 79–82.

[13]   S. Joye, 'Filles et pères à la fin de l'Antiquité et au haut Moyen Âge. Des rapports familiaux à l'épreuve des stratégies', in Badel and Settipani, *Les stratégies familiales*, pp. 223–8; Arjava, *Women and Law*, pp. 29–37; Evans Grubbs, 'Marrying', pp. 54–63. See, however, J. Evans Grubbs, 'Parent-Child Conflict in the Roman Family: The Evidence of the Code of Justinian', in M. George (ed.), *The Roman Family in the Empire: Rome, Italy, and Beyond*

The difference of age between daughter and son in their first marriage made their situation even more pointedly different: for daughters, the decision to enter the ascetic life had to be made when they were underage children (even by Roman standards), yet for sons there was more time to make a decision. This must have had an effect on the decision-making process: it is quite reasonable to assume that a 10-year-old girl was not in a particularly strong position to get her parents to agree with her in the case of any disagreement. How many parents would have been willing to give a voice to a 10-year-old to decide her future? Accordingly, the agreement itself, and the pre-nuptial gifts for a betrothal of girls under 12, were handled differently from cases where brides were already older.[14] A young man in his twenties had a rather different point of departure in family discussions.

In other respects too, the life choices of girls were quite limited and their bargaining position was not particularly strong. Before marriage, girls were to be kept at home and were to associate only with other girls. The separation of the sexes might not have been as strict as the normative statements would imply, but still it seems that even for the 'ordinary' elite girls, the life sphere was limited to the household, where they lived under strict observation with age peers among the household slaves. It is telling that when John Chrysostom discusses the problems in protecting virgins vowed to God from all worldly influences, his starting point is the everyday experience of a father watching over his daughter: if she ever goes out, it is only at dusk; she never comes into the presence of men since her father represents her in everything; her mother, nurse and maids help him in this guardianship. Even a dedicated virgin would have more reasons (religious services, daily provisions) to leave her house, and she is more independent. Indeed, sometimes daughters remained under the strong influence of their parents even after their marriage, as the case of Melania the Younger shows.[15] As a result, 'young girls and young women spent most of their lives in the company of other women and ... they absorbed much

---

(Oxford, 2005), pp. 99–112 for some third-century legal cases with sons in dispute with their fathers.

[14]   *Codex Theodosianus* 3.5.11 (380 CE). See also Arjava, *Women and Law*, pp. 35–7.

[15]   John Chrysostom, *On the Priesthood*, 3.17; John Chrysostom, *Quales ducendae sint uxores* 7; Gerontius, *Life of Melania* (Greek), 1–6; Jerome, *Letters*, 14.3; 22.16; 107.3–4, 9–11; 128.3 with Nathan, *The Family*, pp. 81–2, 93–5 and C. Horn, 'Children's Play as Social Ritual', in V. Burrus (ed.), *Late Ancient Christianity* (Minneapolis, 2005), p. 108. For the contemporary normative view on the need of seclusion for the girls vowed to virginity, see above p. 56.

of their social behaviour and attitudes from observing and emulating adult role models'.[16]

Moreover, this situation had important consequences: first of all, the earlier the decision had to be made in the life course of the family, the more uncertainty there would have been regarding the continuity of the family lineage through other children and grandchildren. In addition, the high mortality rate led to a situation in which considerably more sons than daughters had already lost their fathers. But we lack empirical data from Antiquity that would allow us to enter into more focused argumentation, and the use of model life tables based on modern populations is needed. Despite their inevitable inaccuracies, they would help us to approximate the relative probabilities of different scenarios. Thus, one may assume that on average, around one-quarter of elite children had lost their father at 15, the age when elite girls in any case were entering into marriages, but nearly half had done so by the age of 25, when young men were about to marry. For mothers, who in turn had married earlier in life than their husbands, the corresponding estimates come down to one-fifth for girls at 15 and at least one-quarter for young men at 25.[17] Thus, the likelihood that parents (and older relatives), or at least the father, had died before the decision about marriage or an ascetic vow had to be made was much greater for sons than for daughters.

The independence of sons at a decision-making age was further highlighted by the fact that as a rule, they seem to have lived on their own during their student years and afterwards, even if they had not entered marriage.[18] As for boys the variation in entering marriage seems to have been greater, the option to defer the decision to marry or not to marry was also open even longer. An unmarried son who had reached his late 20s was not a catastrophe for the family; it was only when Augustine was around 30 that his mother finally took hold of the situation and organized a good betrothal for her son.[19] As the legal age of majority in Late Antiquity was 25 years – before that, a legal guardian (*curator*) was needed – sons who postponed their marriage to this age would have been economically independent and free to use their patrimony as they wished.[20]

---

[16] L. Alberici and M. Harlow, 'Age and Innocence: Female Transitions to Adulthood in Late Antiquity', in A. Cohen and J.B. Rutter (eds), *Constructions of Childhood in Ancient Greece and Italy* (Princeton, 2007), p. 201.

[17] These figures are relevant, naturally, only if the calculations of Saller, *Patriarchy*, pp. 48–65 (tables), 121 and 229, are also applicable to late Roman society. For the problems in using model life tables, see e.g. Scheidel, 'Roman Age Structure'.

[18] Nathan, *The Family*, p. 94.

[19] Augustine, *Confessions*, 6.15.25.

[20] Evans Grubbs, *Law and Family*, p. 141; Evans Grubbs, 'Marrying', p. 55.

Ascetics against Their Parents: Ideology of Opposition

By analysing the gendered patterns in the discourses and practices linked to the dedication of children to God, it is possible to penetrate the discourses on family dynamics and to construct a view of the space in which Late Antique children were brought up. This offers an invaluable opportunity to scrutinize early Christian family dynamics and the roles given to family life and children.

However, before entering into a discussion of children and familial disputes over asceticism, it is necessary to investigate some features of the context in which decisions over asceticism were made. First of all, institutionalized forms of asceticism in general, and the Western system of *oblatio* in particular, only developed during the fourth and fifth centuries.[21] Therefore, it is necessary to distinguish between making a vow and giving a child an ascetic upbringing. This difference can be illustrated by referring to the early lives of Gregory Nazianzen and Theodoret of Cyrrhus. Both claim that they had been vowed to God by their mothers even before their birth. Gregory interpreted himself as having redeemed this promise by receiving baptism and dedicating himself to God's service after having been nearly drowned in a stormy sea at about 20 years of age. Theodoret rejected his patrimony and began an ascetic life sometime after his parents had died, when he was in his early 20s.[22] In the case of girls in particular, the vows of dedication did not lead them to leave home, but rather to stay as part of the original families as home ascetics.[23] This holds true more commonly for the Western part of the Empire, where there are no references from the entire period under scrutiny to children being vowed to God and given away to monastic settlements to be brought up as ascetics.

The presence of children in monastic communities did not mean that these young persons were destined to become ascetics. First of all, when ascetic recruits entered the monastic life, they often took along their children who had been born to them before their vows. The opinion of children was hardly taken into account. In this early stage of monasticism, there seems to have been a strong

---

[21] M. de Jong, *In Samuel's Image: Child Oblation in the Early Medieval West* (Leiden, 1996), pp. 22–30.

[22] Gregory Nazianzen, *Oration 2*, 77; *Oration 18*, 31; Theodoret of Cyrrhus, *Religious History*, 9.4 and 13.16–18 with V. Vuolanto, 'A Self-made Living Saint? Authority and the Two Families of Theodoret of Cyrrhus', in John Ott and Trpimir Vedriš (eds), *Saintly Bishops and Bishops' Saints* (Zagreb, 2012), pp. 52–7.

[23] See also Caseau, 'Stratégies parentales', pp. 260–62, partly on a later period. See, however, Gerontius, *Life of Melania* (Greek), 65, mentioning a girl given to the monastery by her mother 'at the altar'.

sense that, if possible, a family should not be broken up. Yet it seems that not all of these children eventually became ascetics themselves.[24] There is also evidence that it soon became customary to give children to monasteries and bishops to be taken care of and educated, both in the East and in the West. In a case mentioned by Augustine, a mother, a stepfather and a young boy turned to him for help in an economically disastrous situation. Although the boy eventually ended up as a monk and bishop, he was not given to Augustine to be brought up as an ascetic, but simply to be taken care of. In another passage, we see an elite girl under the guardianship of Augustine and seemingly living in one of the monastic communities.[25] More generally, bishops and priests were supposed to take care of orphans, and both Augustine and Gregory of Nyssa referred to foundlings who were under the care of consecrated virgins. Basil of Caesarea in his monastic rules not only urged monastic communities to take in orphans and raise them, but also assumed a more general continuing presence of children in his monastic foundations.[26] However, he made it quite clear that children given to the monasteries were not to be counted as dedicated ascetics. Instead, they were in the monastery to be brought up and educated, forming a separate group

---

[24] See e.g. Paulinus of Nola, *Letters*, 39.1–2 on the sons of Eucherius and Galla at the monastic community of Lérins; on the presence of children in Lérins, see also *Regula orientalis*, 17.36 and 18.1; Palladius, *The Lausiac History*, 41.5; Paulinus of Nola, *Poem* 21.66–71 and 313–29; Salvian, *Letters*, 4.6, 12, 16–18. For hagiographical evidence, see e.g. Cassian, *Institutes*, 4.27; Callinicus, *Life of Saint Hypatius*, 18.3; *Apophthegmata patrum*, Cario 2; and *Life of Eupraxia*, 2.7–12 with Schroeder, 'Children', p. 319.

[25] Augustine, *Letters*, 20*.2 and 252–5. John Chrysostom was eager to propagate the need for parents to send their children to the monasteries to be educated: John Chrysostom, *Homilies on Ephesians*, 21.2; John Chrysostom, *Against the Opponents of Monastic Life*, 3.11 and 18. See also Cyril of Scythopolis, *The Lives of the Monks of Palestine*, The Life of Euthymius 1. For the education in early medieval monasteries, see T. Miller, *The Orphans of Byzantium: Child Welfare in the Christian Empire* (Washington DC, 2003), pp. 152–7 with N. Kalogeras, 'The Role of Parents and Kin in the Education of Byzantine Children', in K. Mustakallio et al. (eds), *Hoping for Continuity: Childhood, Education and Death in Antiquity and the Middle Ages* (Rome, 2005) for Byzantium; and A. Guerreau-Jalabert, '*Nutritus / oblatus*: parenté et circulation d'enfants au Moyen Âge', in Corbier (ed.), *Adoption et fosterage*, pp. 275–7 for early medieval Western Europe.

[26] Basil of Caesarea, *Longer Rules*, 15.1; Gregory of Nyssa, *Life of Macrina*, 26; Augustine, *Letters*, 98.6. See also *Apostolic Constitutions*, 4.1.2 and *Canons of Pseudo-Athanasius*, 56 for normative statements, with Athanasius, *Life of Antony* 1–2 (1–5) for Antony giving his orphan sister to a monastery to be brought up.

Children and Asceticism in Late Antiquity

before they took their vows, if they so desired, at the earliest when they were 16 or 17 years old.[27]

Some of the children, however, did become ascetics, leading the 'angelic life' at their parents' homes or as part of monastic communities. In scholarly studies the assumption that most frequently seems to underlie considerations regarding the motivation of the children who practised asceticism is crystallized in a quote from Peter Brown: 'many children, mostly girls now wished to remain unmarried'. In other words, it is assumed that children themselves had opted for, and even desired, celibacy, the spiritual life and ascetic practices.[28] Even in cases in which the dependent position of home ascetics and the influence of authoritative ecclesiastical figures, especially on young female virgins, have been noted,[29] scholars have referred to the vows as the result of an individual choice, and the difference between (young) virgins and (older and more independent) widows has not been made clear. In what follows, my aim is to challenge this view.

One of the most renowned examples of familial conflicts over asceticism is the story told by Ambrose of Milan of a girl who wanted to take a vow of virginity. When her relatives tried to force her into a marriage, the girl took refuge at the church altar and there defended her resolution never to marry:

> When the others were silent, one burst out somewhat roughly: 'If', he said, 'your father were alive, would he suffer you to remain unmarried?' Then she replied with more religion and more restrained piety, 'And perchance he is gone that no one may be able to hinder me'. Which answer about her father, but a prophecy concerning himself, he proved by his own speedy death. So the others, each of them fearing the same for themselves, began to assist her and not to hinder her as before; her virginity

---

[27] Basil of Caesarea, *Letters* 199.18 and Basil of Caesarea, *Longer Rules*, 15, with Caseau, 'Stratégies parentales', pp. 249–50. See also Millar, *Orphans*, pp. 114–20, who interprets these monastic foundations partly as schools for orphans and children given by parents to be educated.

[28] Brown, *Body and Society*, pp. 191 and 275 with van Dam, *Families and Friends*, pp. 115–20; Salzman, *The Making*, p. 164; Kuefler, *The Manly Eunuch*, p. 294; Cooper, *The Virgin and the Bride*, p. 86; G. Clark 'The Fathers and the Children', in D. Wood (ed.), *The Church and Childhood* (Oxford, 1994), p. 26; S. Wemple, 'Consent and Dissent to Sexual Intercourse in Germanic Societies', in Laiou (ed.), *Consent and Coercion to Sex*, pp. 241–3; J. Salisbury, *Church Fathers, Independent Virgins* (London and New York, 1991), pp. 4, 111–16 and 120–25; Beaucamp, *Le statut*, vol. II, pp. 260–61; Verdon, 'Virgins and Widows', p. 503; and J. Drijvers, 'Virginity and Asceticism in Late Roman Western Elites', in J. Blok and P. Mason (eds), *Sexual Asymmetry: Studies in Ancient Society* (Amsterdam, 1987), pp. 241–73.

[29] Brown, *Body and Society*, pp. 260 and 263; Beaucamp, *Le statut*, vol. II, pp. 303–5; Arjava, *Women and Law*, pp. 162 and 164–5.

involved not the loss of property due to her, but also received the reward of her integrity. See, you maidens, the reward of devotion, and be warned, parents, by the example of transgression.[30]

This story is to be taken with a grain of salt. In introducing the scene, Ambrose refers both to parents and relatives of the girl. This double reference appears to be a rhetorical device, since later on the audience learns that the father of the girl was dead, a crucial detail for Ambrose's argument, and the mother is never mentioned. The time and place of the event are not specified, and all the persons involved remain anonymous. This is a curious choice if Ambrose was recalling an event which he and his audience remembered. Names would have made the story more convincing, but one notices that Ambrose is claiming only that he could remember the case – he was not claiming to have been present at the event. It seems that at least the particulars of this story represent a pious invention on the part of the narrator.[31] Thus, we are left with the impression that conflict over the choosing of virginity and property issues was a topic that was relevant to Ambrose and his audience.

However, most of the ideologically laden texts of the fourth and fifth centuries depicting antagonism between children and their relatives refer rather specifically to parents engaged in the struggle with their underage children. A typical way of presenting the argument is found in an anonymous sermon on virginity from the second half of the fourth century, where it is claimed that mothers often opposed their daughters' yearning for chastity because they were anxious for their daughters, were misled by their beauty or were consumed by jealousy. The fathers, in turn, were set against the ascetic interests of their sons since they did not understand what their sons desired.[32]

The question arises as to whether these kinds of claims are any more trustworthy than the story told by Ambrose. The paradigmatic case about a

---

[30] Ambrose, *On Virgins*, 1.11.65–6: 'Silentibus caeteris unus abruptius. "Quid si, inquit, pater tuus viveret, innuptam te manere pateretur?" Tum illa maiore religione, moderatiore pietate: "Et ideo fortasse defecit, ne quis impedimentum posset afferre." Quod ille responsum de patre, de se oraculum, maturo sui probavit exitio. Ita ceteri eadem sibi quisque metuentes favere coeperunt, qui impedire quaerebant nec dispendium debitarum attulit virginitas facultatum, sed etiam emolumentum integritatis accepit. Habetis puellae devotionis praemium. Parentes, cavete offensionis exemplum.' Translated by H. de Romestin et al. (Nicene and Post-Nicene Fathers, ser. II, vol. 10), with some modification. The treatise is based on his sermons (see ibid., 1.1.1–2 and 1.2.5).

[31] This would not be the only place where Ambrose had invented a memory. See Vuolanto, *Selling a Freeborn*, p. 174.

[32] *Anonymous Homily on Virginity*, 11–13 (parents), 99 (mothers and daughters) and 110 (fathers and sons).

teenage girl in conflict with her parents concerns Melania the Younger, who earned a great name for herself among her contemporaries (and among modern scholars) through her asceticism and her renunciation of her senatorial status and wealth at the age of about 14. The principal source for her undertakings is the *Life of Melania the Younger*, written c. 450 CE by a monk in her company, Gerontius. It describes how the parents of both Melania and her husband Pinian were against their plan to retire to a life of asceticism, since the parents were afraid of public reproach. In the end, however, Publicola, a senator and the father of Melania, is the only person whom the text singles out as opposing their plan. Gerontius claims that the father repented on his deathbed for his earlier attitude and yielded to his daughter's will, reinstating her as his inheritor. By this dramatic narrative device, Gerontius both made Melania an heiress of a spectacular patrimony and was able to claim parental opposition and highlight her struggles on her way to sanctity. In an earlier account of this incident offered by Palladius, there is no reference after Melania's marriage to any struggles against her parents. Thus, when the story goes into details, the supposed protests of the parents about Melania's and Pinian's asceticism are reduced to Gerontius' claim of antagonism between father and daughter, a claim not impossible but not too well backed. After all, Palladius refers to Publicola's financial support of the ascetic cause, and when he died, not only did his daughter and son-in-law enter into chastity, but Albina the Younger too, Melania's now widowed mother, joined her daughter in the pursuit of asceticism.[33]

The idea of parental opposition was easily woven into stories about choosing asceticism. In a letter by Jerome to Eustochium, a 15-year-old elite girl, the author points out that there should be no one to prevent her desire, whether mother,

---

[33] *Gerontius, Life of Melania (Greek)*, 6–7 and 10–12; Palladius, *The Lausiac History*, 61. For Publicola's donations to the ascetic pursuits and benefactions of his mother asceticism, see *The Lausiac History*, 54.4. As Elizabeth Clark has shown, Gerontius would have been motivated by the desire to shun Publicola and present him as opposing asceticism ('Piety, Propaganda and Politics in the Life of Melania the Younger', in Clark (ed.), *Ascetic Piety*, esp. pp. 83–4). See also H. Sivan, 'On Hymens and Holiness in Late Antiquity: Opposition to Aristocratic Female Asceticism at Rome', *Jahrbuch für Antike und Christentum* 36 (1993), p. 85. For the legal aspects and its inconsistencies in the story as told by Gerontius, see Cooper, 'The Household and the Desert', pp. 21–6. Among the scholars, more often than not, the story of Gerontius about the family conflict has been taken at face value. See e.g. F. Vasileiou, 'The Death of the Father in Late Antique Christian Literature', in Brubaker and Tougher (eds), *Approaches*, pp. 76–7; M. Dietz, *Wandering Monks, Virgins, and Pilgrims: Ascetic Travel in the Mediterranean World, A.D. 300–800* (University Park, PA, 2005), p. 124; A. Giardina, 'Macrina the Saint', in A. Fraschetti, (ed.), *Roman Women*, 2nd edn (Chicago, 2001), pp. 191, 205–6; Cloke, *'This Female Man of God'*, pp. 146–7.

sister, kinswoman or brother. However, her brother was merely a little boy, and her mother and sisters were themselves devoted (or about to devote themselves) to ascetical ideals, and certainly did not oppose her resolution.[34] Much later, however, Jerome claims that Eustochium had indeed had problems with her uncle Hymetius. His resistance to the ascetic lifestyle led him to order his wife to change the dress and appearance of his niece. Nevertheless, the authority of an uncle could not prevent the resolution of the virgin or of her mother Paula.[35] Yet what this tells us is that Jerome's original request that Eustochium should oppose all the family members was directed to the 'general audience', rather than to Eustochium and her circumstances specifically. Similarly, Ambrose of Milan supposed a general opposition, projected it on to the parents and used this as an argument for children whose mother already had taken a positive stand towards asceticism.[36] Here, therefore, the reference to a resistance to ascetic vows was used in generalizing contexts, even if the actual context given pointed to the positive circumstances for the advancement of the ascetic life.

The same scheme is present when Ambrose claimed that there were widowed mothers who opposed their virgin daughters' will to consecrate themselves to the ascetic life after the girls had heard him preach.[37] Although Ambrose reproached such widows, he claimed that by their opposition, parents were testing the calling and zeal of their daughter to be steadfast in future temptations, and were willing to be overcome (*volunt vinci*) in the end:

> They resist at first because they are afraid to believe; often they are angry that one may learn to overcome [temptations]; they threaten to disinherit in order to test whether one is able not to fear temporal loss; they entice with exquisite allurements to see if one cannot be softened by the seduction of various pleasures.[38]

Ambrose further praised those girls who chose chastity on their own initiative as a warning against parents who pushed their offspring towards virginity too

---

[34] Jerome, *Letters*, 22.24 (384 CE). On asceticism in the family of Eustochium and her mother Paula, see e.g. C. Krumeich, *Hieronymus und die christlichen feminae clarissimae* (Bonn, 1993), pp. 80–101.

[35] Uncle: *Letters*, 107.5 (c. 400 CE, referring to a case in the early 380s).

[36] Ambrose, *Exhortation to Virginity*, 7.42.

[37] Ambrose, *On Virgins*, 1.10.58.

[38] Ibid., 1.11.63: 'Contradicunt parentes: sed volunt vinci. Resistunt primo, quia credere timent; indignantur frequenter, ut discas vincere, abdicationem minantur, ut temptent si potes damnum saeculi non timere; quaesitis eblandiuntur inlecebris, ut videant si variarum mollire te non queat blanditia voluptatum.' Translated by H. de Romestin et al. (Nicene and Post-Nicene Fathers, ser. II, vol. 10), with some modification.

enthusiastically.[39] This idea is echoed in an anonymous contemporary sermon devoted to a fallen virgin. According to the author of that work, the only solace for the parents in such a situation was that the girl herself had opted for virginity; the father had depicted the many difficulties of the virginal life, but she had vehemently opposed his arguments. The situation in the family was understood in much the same way as in Ambrose's texts. Although the parents were eager to point out the seriousness of the undertaking, there was no conflict over virginity as such; the parents did not resist the girl taking the vow. Indeed, the father 'counted [her] as his singular point of pride'.[40]

The idea of opposition also found its way into descriptions of actual cases in which it is hard to imagine that any disagreements on asceticism had arisen. Demetrias, another teenage girl of aristocratic background, was under the authority of her widowed mother Juliana and her grandmother Proba, who, according to Jerome, wanted her to get married. However, the girl had the courage to oppose them and express her will to dedicate herself to virginity after the wedding day had been fixed.[41] Jerome used the theme of an arranged marriage to highlight Demetrias' independence, but other ecclesiastical writers like Augustine and Pelagius, who were commenting on Demetrias' vow, did not even mention the aim of giving Demetrias in marriage – and none of the three referred to any conflict between Juliana, Proba and Demetrias. Indeed, both widows were already familiar with the ascetic ideals. Likewise, when highlighting the virtues of Paulina, the daughter of Paula the Elder and wife of Pammachius, Jerome claimed that initially she did not want to marry and thus he implied that Paula, his paragon of a holy widow, had forced her daughter to marry and lose her virginity.[42]

A more famous example of 'family opposition' is presented by Gregory of Nyssa, who writes that after his sister Macrina had lost her fiancé, she firmly objected to any further proposals of marriage on the part of her parents. Gregory stressed the will and independence of Macrina, who was 'in her twelfth year' when her husband-to-be died, but did not presume any familial conflicts beyond this point. He did not even claim that there were any actual proposals

---

[39]   Ibid., 1.11.62.

[40]   *On the Fall of a Consecrated Virgin* 4.15 and 17: 'sibi singularem gloriam computabat'.

[41]   Jerome, *Letters*, 130.4–5.

[42]   Augustine, *Letters*, 150 and 188; Augustine, *De Bono Viduitatis*, esp. 1; Pelagius, *Letter to Demetrias*, with Augustine, *Letters*, 130 esp. 30, which shows that Proba was well introduced to the ascetic ideals by the early 410s. On Demetrias and ascetic rhetoric, see further A. Jacobs, 'Writing Demetrias: Ascetic Logic in Ancient Christianity', *Church History* 69 (2000), pp. 719–48; on Paulina, see Jerome, *Letters*, 66.3.

made to her by her parents. In fact, the parents seem to have been quite content with their daughter's wish. Besides this, the later spread of ascetical ideals among family members would point in the direction of mutual agreement regarding Macrina's chastity. Indeed, it is argued that her brother's intention in writing her life would have been to construct a model for a chaste monastic life for women.[43]

Even if no conflict as such was referred to, the success of the *topos* of the insistence of daughters against their parents' will is at least partly dependent on this story, as Macrina quickly became a paradigmatic example of an independent virgin. An echo of Macrina's *exemplum* can be heard for instance in the *Life of Syncletica*: the parents 'gladly urged the young girl toward marriage', but 'the tears of her parents did not soften her, nor the exhortation of any other relative'. There was no open conflict, however, as Syncletica did not dedicate herself to virginity before she was orphaned.[44] A story even more closely resembling that of Macrina's was told by Jerome when he wrote of Marcella, with her mother Albina the Elder playing the part of Emmelia, Macrina's mother. When Marcella was widowed after a marriage of seven months, she successfully resisted her widowed mother Albina and refused another marriage. According to Jerome, no one dared to talk to her any longer about getting married. However, this struggle, if indeed it ever took place, was not concerned with asceticism as such – there are no indications of this and, moreover, Albina and Marcella later lived together as dedicated widows.[45]

The common antecedent to the foregoing cases is the story of Thecla, allegedly a colleague of the Apostle Paul, fleeing from the influence of her mother who tried to force her to marry. That narrative gained much popularity in Late Antiquity and Thecla is referred to as an exemplary virgin in many of the stories cited above: Syncletica was her true disciple; she was a forerunner to

---

[43]   Gregory of Nyssa, *Life of Macrina*, 4–5 (c. 380 CE, on events in the early 340s) with T. Hägg, *The Art of Biography in Antiquity* (Cambridge, 2012), pp. 386–7. Susanna Elm's (*Virgins*, pp. 40–47) and Raymond van Dam's (*Families and Friends*, pp. 103–7) reading of the relevant passages put little weight on their laudatory characters, leading them to emphasize Macrina's own choices. For the rhetorical construction of 'Macrina', see E.A. Clark, 'Holy Women, Holy Words: Early Christian Women, Social History, and the "Linguistic Turn"', *Journal of Early Christian Studies* 6(3) (1998), pp. 423–9.

[44]   Pseudo-Athanasius, *Life of Syncletica*, 7, 9 and 11–12.

[45]   Jerome, *Letters*, 127.2 (412 CE, on events in early 340s; Marcella must have been in her late teens; see Krumeich, *Hieronymus*, pp. 70–71, with Clark, 'Holy Women', p. 420).

110   *Children and Asceticism in Late Antiquity*

Eustochium; Macrina was the second Thecla. More generally she is mentioned as an *exemplum* for all virgins.[46]

As these cases show, in Late Antiquity a virgin needed parental opposition in order to make plausible her claim to have an exemplary and saintly character. The basic form that this opposition took was a forced marriage. This theme had become a hagiographical *topos* by the fourth century. In the fifth-century *Life of Euphrosyne of Alexandria*, for example, Euphrosyne's father tried to marry her off to a rich and powerful family, yet the girl had secretly vowed herself to God and ran away, dressed as a man, to a monastery. In his *Lausiac History*, Palladius referred to two cases in which parents were able to force a daughter into marriage: Melania the Younger and Magna.[47]

The theme of forced marriage rarely appears with sons and, when it does, it is only in hagiography. It is claimed that some, like the future Abba Ammon, were persuaded to marry. In the *Life of Malchus*, in turn, Jerome has Malchus tell how his parents tried to marry him off, his father using threats and his mother attempting to entice him with soft words, until he ran away.[48] The ages of these sons are not mentioned in these stories, but in connection with other cases of dramatic family disputes, the age is often specified as early or mid-teens, that is, the same age that we find in the stories of struggles over the virginity of a daughter. The mid-fourth-century *Life of Pachomius* relates that Theodore ran away to an anchoritic life at 14 without informing his mother; six years later, he joined the monastic settlement of Pachomius. When Theodore's mother wanted to see him, her other son, Paphnutius, followed her and joined the Pachomian *koinonia*, also against her will.[49] The future Gallic saint Martin was also described as having met fierce opposition on the part of his parents. His father in particular opposed his 'holy actions' and aspirations to lead an

---

[46]   See e.g. *Life and Miracles of Thecla*, pr., 1 and 4; *Anonymous Homily on Virginity*, 100–101; Pseudo-Athanasius, *Life of Syncletica*, 8; Jerome, *Letters*, 22.41; Gregory of Nyssa, *Life of Macrina*, 2; Ambrose, *On Virginity*, 7.40 and *On Virgins* 2.3.19–21); with M. Pesthy, 'Thecla among the Fathers of the Church', in J. Bremmer (ed.), *The Apocryphal Acts of Paul and Thecla* (Kampen, 1996), pp. 164–78.

[47]   *Life of Euphrosyne* 3 and 6; Palladius, *The Lausiac History*, 61 and 67.1. See also the fifth century (?) *Life of Saint Helia*, which is constructed on a (violent) conflict between a mother and a daughter over marriage and virginity – following the precedent of stories on Thecla (cited in Burrus, '"Honor the Fathers"', esp. pp. 447–8).

[48]   Ammon: Palladius, *The Lausiac History*, 8.1; *Historia monachorum in Aegypto* 22 and Sozomen, *Ecclesiastical History*, 1.14.1; Jerome, *Life of Malchus*, 3.1. See also Pseudo-Athanasius, *Life of Syncletica*, 5; and *Letter of Ammon*, 2 and 30.

[49]   *Life of Pachomius* (Bohairic version), 31 and 37–8. *Letter of Ammon*, 9 says that Theodore entered the monastery at the age of 13.

ascetic life in the desert. The father had his son arrested, put in chains and sent to the army at the age of 15.[50] It is claimed that Hypatius was a little older, when he ran away from his home to a monastery at 18, after his father had beaten him in mid-fifth-century Thrace.[51]

In view of the frequency with which cases concerning teenage children and parental opposition appear in ancient letters and treatises on virginity and asceticism, one notes that outside hagiography there are no cases concerning parental opposition to the choices of sons of the same age group. Such conflicts seem to have been expected to occur only later in life. Thus, Jerome expected opposition to his friend Heliodorus on the part of his family members if he were to commit himself to asceticism, although he had already been practising asceticism with Jerome in Syria. At the time, Jerome himself was about 25 years old, and Heliodorus was most probably about the same age.[52] The argument presented to the young men was not that they should marry, but that they should stay at home and take care of running the household. One such young man was Laetus, an associate member or trainee in the monastic brotherhood of Augustine, whose mother would not allow him to retire from the world; Nebridius, another friend of Augustine's with a mother afraid of being left alone in the midst of daily cares; and John Chrysostom, whose mother referred to the burdens of widowhood in running an estate when asking her then 20-year-old son to await her death before entering asceticism.[53] If the protagonists were not always 25 (the legal age for independent management of one's property), they were at least in their late teens and were thus able to transact business under their guardians' (and mothers') supervision.[54]

---

[50]   Sulpicius Severus, *Life of Saint Martin*, 2.3–2.5, with Hilarius of Arles, *Life of Honoratus*, 6 and 8 on parental opposition of Honoratus' ascetic yarnings.

[51]   Callinicus, *Life of Hypatius*, 1.2–7.

[52]   Jerome, *Letters*, 14.2: 'Licet parvulus ex collo pendeat nepos, licet sparso crine et scissis vestibus ubera quibus nutrierat mater ostendat, licet in limine pater iaceat, per calcatum perge patrem, siccis oculis ad vexillum cruces vola!'

[53]   Laetus: Augustine, *Letters*, 243; Nebridius: Augustine, *Letters*, 10.1; John Chrysostom, *On the Priesthood*, 1.2. Chrysostom in fact retired from his home in Antioch only after the death of his mother' see J. Kelly, *Golden Mouth: The Story of John Chrysostom, Ascetic, Preacher, Bishop* (Ithaca, 1998), pp. 14–16. See also the cases of Rusticus (Jerome, *Letters*, 125, esp. 6–7 and Bonosus (Jerome, *Letters*, 3.4).

[54]   For age limits and the involvement of widows in the guardianship of children (*tutela* and *cura minorum*) in Late Antiquity, see Vuolanto, 'Women and the Property', pp. 204–6, 215–18 and 230–32; and Beaucamp, *Le statut*, vol. I, pp. 320–37 with Beaucamp, *Le statut*, vol. II, pp. 329–35.

112 *Children and Asceticism in Late Antiquity*

Outside the hagiographical accounts, two cases can be found in which fathers are depicted as opposing the plans of their sons. Paulinus of Nola wanted to give the impression that Sulpicius Severus' father was against his son's plans to leave home and devote himself to the religious life after the death of his young wife.[55] In addition, when Stagirius, a rich young man and a friend of John Chrysostom, wanted to join a monastic community, his father opposed the idea. However, his mother was willing to promote his ascetic vocation and she made a deal with Stagirius to conceal from his father what he had done. Thus, the opposition of the father could not prevent the boy from entering the community, and the mother found herself in the difficult situation of acting as intermediary between the other family members.[56] Again, there are no reasons to suppose that the sons would have been less than 20 years old in these cases, but still Stagirius wanted to conceal the fact that he had rebelled against paternal authority.

In the context of these stories, parental and family opposition are presented in order to eulogize the virtue of virginity and the determination of the ascetic. This rhetoric of resistance could also have been used to refer to more general attitudes towards ascetics. In these stories the protagonists are often independent widows and senators, and accordingly we see the local community showing resistance and uneasiness when facing the ascetic lifestyle. Well known are the alleged reactions of the people at the funeral of Blesilla, the daughter of Paula, against asceticism and monks; of the senate on the withdrawal of Paulinus of Nola and his wife to an ascetic life; and of the Roman aristocracy when Melania the Elder sailed to the East with a number of her relatives, giving a frightening example of renunciation for other senatorial families.[57]

The case of Indicia depicts a young virgin who was accused of losing her virginity and then disposing of her newborn child in order to conceal this loss. It appears that the accusation was made by Renatus, a man who had once wanted to marry Indicia, but was turned down. Indicia was living in her sister and brother-in-law's household where her brother-in-law, Maximus, built a wall separating his and his wife's quarters from those of her sister, thereby breaking

---

[55] Paulinus of Nola, *Letters*, 5.5–6.

[56] John Chrysostom, *To Stagirius*, 1.1. It seems that Chrysostom used Stagirius' story in composing an *exemplum* in favour of monasticism in John Chrysostom, *Against the Opponents of the Monastic Life*, 2.10 and 3.12. See also John Chrysostom, *Letters to Theodore*, 1.17 in which a young man first enters asceticism, but later makes up his mind to return to the elite lifestyle, urged on by his kinsmen.

[57] Jerome, *Letters*, 39.6; Ambrose, *Letters*, 27.3; Palladius, *The Lausiac History*, 54.4; Jerome, *Letters*, 107.5.

the connection between the two sisters. The reaction of Maximus shows the ambivalent attitude towards virgins. On the one hand, in the context of the Church, to have a virgin living in one's household brought honour and spiritual rewards, but on the other hand, Maximus was quick to accept the accusations against her and took measures to protect his family's reputation by cutting Indicia out of their fellowship.[58] Thus, the question is not so much about the conflict between Indicia and her sister or brother-in-law, but between Indicia on the one hand and Renatus and the *a priori* suspicious community on the other. This case does not involve a minor who chooses the ascetic lifestyle, but it does reflect the mistrust of ascetics in the late Roman world. The ascetics attracted attention and their new lifestyle was questioned by those who did not share the conviction of its blessedness.[59]

In all of the stories, the objective was to highlight the independent and free decision of the children and widows in dedicating themselves to virginity. The *topos* of independence was used even in cases where there was no mention of conflict, such as when depicting the struggles of Asella.[60] In part, the authors appear to be exercising caution, so that they themselves will not be accused of scorning marriage and coercing children to assume ascetic practices. It was ideologically important to stress that it is not possible to command anybody to lead a life in virginity.[61] This argumentation also has its roots in the theological debate about virginity linked with discussions of the status of Mary as *Theotokos* and with the idea of the role played by Mary's free will in her becoming the mother of God, and remaining perpetually a virgin.[62] For the late fourth- and early fifth-century writers, it was important to make the assumption that the other family members would oppose their children heading for the angelic life.

---

[58] Ambrose, *Letters*, 56. Jerome's fictive story on the Paul of Thebes has some similar features: Paul, in the time of persecutions, withdrew to desert, but his brother-in-law betrayed him (Jerome, *Life of Paul*, 4.2).

[59] For the opposition among the Christians, see above, esp. pp. 59–60. The scorn of non-Christians towards the ascetics is shown, for example, in Libanius, *Oration 30*, 8; Salvian, *On the Goverment of God*, 8.4; Rutilius Namatianus, *De reditu suo*, 440–48.

[60] Jerome, *Letters*, 24.2.

[61] See e.g. Ambrose, *On Virgins*, 1.5.23: 'Non enim potest imperare virginitas sed optari.' On the accusations that monks and clergy compelled virgins and widows to enter a life of asceticism, see esp. Jerome, *Letters*, 39.

[62] On asceticism and debates on the perpetual virginity of Mary, see further Hunter, *Marriage, Celibacy*, pp. 171–204.

114   *Children and Asceticism in Late Antiquity*

Making the Choice of Virginity

In the previous section, the emphasis was on the rhetoric of choosing asceticism and the propagation of the desired behaviour through sermons, treatises and other idealized and normative writings. In what follows, evidence derived from historical cases is used to scrutinize the influence of parents when their children were dedicating themselves to asceticism. This makes it possible to discern in what ways parental opposition becomes visible (if indeed it does) and how the gendered patterns of discourse and practice come out in the texts. In order to assess the comparative frequency of different kinds of cases and patterns of behaviour and discourses, I have systematically examined the correspondence of Ambrose, Jerome, Augustine and Paulinus of Nola.

Within this material, one can identify 24 cases of sons or daughters embracing virginity, where the actual familial relationships and attitudes can be inferred with some certainty. In only two of these cases was the father alive and active without any mention of the mother, but even in these cases the influence of the mother cannot be excluded. In the case of Ambrosia it was not the father but the grandfather Eusebius, to whose influence Ambrose gives credit for the vow of the granddaughter. The second case concerns the presbyter Ianuarius, who leaves the inheritance to his son and daughter who are pledged to asceticism.[63]

On the other hand, there are 13 cases in which only mothers are mentioned in the context of children who enter an ascetic life. Five of these concern mothers and sons.[64] In four cases, a son was independent of his mother and was able to make decisions individually (the age of the sons in question range from late teens to about 30), although we see that the opinions of the mothers were not easily disregarded. The fifth case is of Antoninus of Fussala; his mother

---

[63]   Ambrosia: Ambrose, *The Consecration of a Virgin*, 1.1 with Ambrose, *Letters*, 26.2 and 38.1; Children of Ianuarius: Augustine, *Sermons*, 355.3. In addition to these, in Jerome, *Letters*, 130, one finds a passing reference to an anonymous presbyter with two virgin daughters used as an *exemplum* – the historicity of this story is quite suspect. Paulinus of Nola, *Poems*, 24.499–528, 589–94 mentions a son of a certain Cytherius, dedicated as a boy to God. Particulars of this case remain, however, quite obscure. See also Gregory Nazianzen, *Oration 8*, 11, mentioning a 'pair of children' dedicated to God; however, as the reference here is to an anonymous priest and teacher of Gorgonia, and nothing more is told, it is impossible to ascertain here more information, especially as both the 'dedication' and the 'child' might have been used here metaphorically (see Van Dam, *Families and Friends*, p. 212, n. 15).

[64]   Jerome, *Letters*, 125, esp. 6–7 (on Rusticus); Augustine, *Letters* 243 (on Laetus); Jerome, *Letters*, 3.4 (on Bonosus); Augustine, *Letters*, 10.1 (on Nebridius, with Augustine, *Confessions* 6.10.17 and 9.3.6); Augustine, *Letters* 20*, esp. 2 and 32 (on Antoninus).

had intended him to be admitted into the monastic community of Augustine at Hippo as a child. Here the primary reason for entering the community was not the mother's will to have her son brought up as a monk, but the need of the family to take shelter in the Church. The situation was desperate, since the boy, his mother and his stepfather were extremely poor and starving. Antoninus' biological father was still alive, but no longer had anything to do with the members of his former family.

The cases that concern daughters and their mothers display quite different relationships between a parent and her children who enter asceticism. Eustochium was consecrated as a virgin in 384 CE. During that same year, her sister Blaesilla lost her husband and took vows. Eustochium was then in her mid-teens, while Blaesilla was around 20. It is hard to believe that the opinions of their mother Paula, who had dedicated herself to widowhood shortly before, would have played no part in their decisions.[65] The same can be assumed in the case of Demetrias, with both a mother and a grandmother as ascetic widows.[66] This pattern of taking the vow of chastity after the death of one's father is also reflected in the case of Marcella, who after the death of her husband followed the example of her mother in taking the vow of chastity, and the two women formed the core of the ascetic community on the Aventine in Rome.[67] Melania the Younger and her husband Pinian, together with Melania's mother Albina (the Younger), offer an example of a chaste couple following the same pattern: they started the ascetic life immediately after Melania's father, Publicola, had died. Thus, as a case of social history, this is an instance of asceticism beginning after the death of the father, yet as hagiography, it is a case of forced marriage and parental opposition.[68] A feature that occurs repeatedly is that of the formation of ascetic communities around widowed mothers and their children who had taken a vow of chastity.[69] A final case to be mentioned is that of a widowed mother and daughter where the mother had pledged her daughter to virginity when the daughter had recovered from a serious illness. Yet, as her son had now

---

[65]   Jerome, *Letters*, 22; 39; 108 (the husband of Paula, Toxotius, had died c. 380 CE).

[66]   Augustine, *Letters*, 188; Jerome, *Letters*, 130. See also Augustine, *On the Good of Widowhood*, esp. praef., 8.11, 19.24, dedicated to the widowed Juliana, mother of Demetrias.

[67]   Jerome, *Letters*, 127.

[68]   Augustine, *Letters* 124 and 126, with Paulinus of Nola, *Poems*, 21.60–73, 281–5 and 836–44; Gerontius, *Life of Melania* (Greek), 1–2 and 6–7; and Palladius, *The Lausiac History*, 61.1.

[69]   In addition to the above-mentioned, see Augustine, *Letters*, 212: the widow Galla and her young daughter Simpliciola, consecrated to virginity, and the ascetic community of a widowed mother, two sons and two daughters referred to in Jerome, *Letters* 7, and 8.

116 *Children and Asceticism in Late Antiquity*

died, the mother wanted to revoke the promise and instead to pledge herself to perpetual chastity as a widow.[70]

In nine cases, both parents were alive and took part in the dedication of their children. In four of these, the parents are referred to collectively without any distinction being made with regard to active or passive role in their children's dedication. The parents' positive attitude towards asceticism is taken for granted. Two of the cases concern sons and two others daughters.[71] The role of the father is emphasized in the case of a North African girl who had been rebaptized by the Donatists against the will of her parents and who had assumed the 'appearance of a nun'. Yet subsequently the father wanted her to return to the Catholic communion. Given that the father is said to have used violence in order to persuade his daughter, it seems that the girl had remained at home.[72] Yet the issue at stake was not asceticism, but heresy and parental authority. In fact, Augustine, who tells the story, gives the impression that the appearance of a nun was another way of showing her opposition to her family. Her asceticism was an effect, not the cause, of the conflict.

In two other cases, those of Florentina and Paula the Younger, the parents were alive, but the mothers had been in charge of their daughters' religious education, and they asked for advice. Florentina was evidently already an older girl, given that Augustine's letter was addressed directly to her. Paula, on the other hand, had been consecrated to God before her birth. In fact, it seems that Paula's birth was understood as the response to a *votum* her parents had made. Pacatula, still an infant, was also pledged to a life of virginity by her parents. Her father had asked for advice concerning her education.[73] In pointing out Asella as an exemplary virgin, Jerome hardly mentions the parents, wanting to stress her independence. However, she had been dedicated to God following a dream (or vision) of her father. When Jerome writes about her being blessed already in the womb, this probably means that she had been vowed to God before her birth.

---

[70]   Augustine, *Letters* 3*.

[71]   Augustine, *Letters*, 111.7 (a virgin daughter captured by the barbarians); Augustine, *Letters*, 218 (on Palatinus); Augustine, *Letters*, 13* (a girl living as a dedicated virgin with her parents); Paulinus of Nola, *Letters*, 51 (on the two sons of Eucherius and Galla).

[72]   Augustine, *Letters*, 35.4: 'Nam cum ecclesiae quidam colonus filiam suam, quae apud nos fuerat catechumena, et ad illos [i.e. Donatians] seducta est invitis parentibus, ut ubi baptizata etiam sanctimonialis formam susciperet, ad communionem catholicam paterna vellet severitate revocare.'

[73]   Florentina: Augustine, *Letters*, 266; Paula the Younger: Jerome, *Letters*, 107.3: 'Paululam nostram ... quam prius Christo consecrata est quam genita, quam ante votis quam utero suscepisti.' See also Jerome, *Letters*, 108.26; Pacatula: Jerome, *Letters*, 128.

At least, however, he gives her parents credit for her dedication and consecration (when she had 'hardly passed her tenth year').[74]

In all previous cases with a reference to a fulfilled parental vow occurring at birth, the child is a girl. Moreover, the daughter of Melania the Younger and Pinian was consecrated to God at birth. When boys had been promised to God before birth, in turn, as claimed for Theodoret of Cyrrhus and Gregory Nazianzen, giving them an ascetic upbringing was not a priority.[75] Certainly, such a predominance of female figures could be a mere coincidence. Yet Theodoret of Cyrrhus' story of his own infancy hints at an alternative explanation. Before his conception, his father had asked the hermits for their intercession so that he would have a child, while his mother vowed to dedicate her future son to a life of virginity. Nevertheless, even if Theodoret was well socialized to ascetic Christianity through frequent visits to the family hermits, his parents were rather unwilling to honour their promise, and only after they had died did he take vows and retire to the desert. It was claimed that this was because his parents were too attached to him to let him go.[76] There are two things to be pointed out here: as far as the vow was concerned, the birth of a male successor may have more readily influenced the parents to forget their promise. The daughter of Melania the Younger and Pinian, for example, was pledged to virginity from birth, but if the child had been a son, he would have been destined for a worldly career, to continue the renowned lineage. Second, since the ultimate decision had to be made before a girl's marriageable age had passed, the dedication of daughters was much more binding than that of sons, whose age of making a final decision usually came after the death of their fathers and who also had more opportunities to decide for themselves because of their gender and higher age.[77]

When one compares the situations featured in the correspondence with the hagiographic presentations from late fourth- and fifth-century sources, it is

---

[74] Jerome, *Letters*, 24.2: 'Praetermitto quod in matris utero benedicitur ei antequam nascatur, quod in fiala nitentis vitri et omni speculo purioris patri virgo traditur per quietem, quod adhuc infantiae involuta pannis vix annum decimum aetetis excedens, honore futurae beatitudinis consecrator.'

[75] Gerontius, *Life of Melania* (Greek), 1 and 6. In comparison, of the seven hagiographic stories of children chosen to ascetic holiness even before their births (between the sixth and tenth centuries CE) cited by B. Caseau, none is a girl (B. Caseau, 'Childhood in Byzantine Saints' Lives', in Papaconstantinou and Talbot (eds), *Becoming Byzantine*, pp. 144–5).

[76] Theodoret of Cyrrhus, *Religious History*, 9.4 and 13.16–18, with Vuolanto, 'A Self-made Living Saint?', pp. 52–7. See also the case of Gregory Nazianzen: *Oration 2*, 77 and *Oration 18*, 31.

[77] See also Caseau, 'Stratégies parentales', esp. p. 252, with most of the examples from the later period.

118 *Children and Asceticism in Late Antiquity*

possible to correlate the prevailing ideas of ascetic sainthood with actual cases. Of the 31 cases in which comments on the role of parents in their children's asceticism can be discerned, five record only a father dedicating his son to asceticism. Four of these cases deal with sons and one with a daughter.[78] In one case, the son, albeit already 18 years old, is depicted as fleeing from home to a monastery after his father had beaten him.[79] In eight cases, both parents are mentioned as playing equally active roles. In seven of these (five dealing with sons only, one with a son and a daughter, and one with a daughter only), the parents opposed the plans of their offspring.[80] The remaining eighth case is the story of a certain Akylas, who renounced the world with his wife and five sons.[81] In nine cases, only mothers are mentioned, and only in the case of Theodore and his brother are the children male. The others concern widowed mothers and their virgin daughters. In one of these, concerning Magna, her mother had forced her to marry, but in other cases the mother had dedicated herself to chastity or otherwise reacted positively, at least in the end, to her child's yearning for an ascetic life.[82]

---

[78]   *History of the Monks in Egypt*, 1.10 (John of Lycopolis makes a noble man dedicate his newborn son); Cassian, *Institutes*, 4.27 (Patermutus enters a monastery with his eight-year-old son); Sozomen, *Ecclesiastical History*, 7.28 (Ajax dedicates two of his sons to chastity with himself); Theodoret of Cyrrhus, *Religious History*, 21.14 (a man promised to dedicate his only son to God if he lived to maturity); Sulpicius Severus, *Life of Martin*, 19.1–2 (an ex-prefect dedicated his daughter to virginity). Only in the case of Patermutus and his son is the mother explicitly mentioned as deceased.

[79]   Callinicus, *Life of Hypatius*, 1.7 and 2.3.

[80]   Gerontius, *Life of Melania* (Greek), 1–2 and 6–7, and Palladius, *The Lausiac History*, 61.1, on Melania the Younger; *History of the Monks of Egypt*, 22.1 (on Ammon persuaded to marry; in Palladius, *The Lausiac History*, 8.1, Ammon is an orphan persuaded to marry by other relatives; see also Sozomen, *Ecclesiastical History* 1.14.1); Jerome, *Life of Malchus*, 3.1; Pseudo-Athanasius, *Life of Syncletica*, 5–7 (parents tried to marry off their son, but he ran away; Syncletica refused to marry but could not enter a life of asceticism as long as her parents were alive); *Letter of Ammon*, 2 and 30 (Ammon had run away from his pagan parents to enter monastery); Sulpicius Severus, *Life of Martin* 2.1–5 (parents oppose Martin's ascetic yearnings); Hilarius of Arles, *Life of Honoratus*, 6 and 8 (parents oppose Honoratus).

[81]   Callinicus, *Life of Saint Hypatius* 18.3 (c. 450 CE?). For a later account, see e.g. *Apophthegmata Patrum* Cario 2 (c. 500 CE).

[82]   *Life of Pachomius* (Bohairic version), esp. 37–8 (on Theodore and his brother); Ambrose, *On Virgins*, 3.7.33 (on Pelagia); Palladius, *The Lausiac History*, 31.1 (Piamun living with her widowed mother) and 57.1 (Candida dedicated her daughter to virginity); Theodoret of Cyrrhus, *Religious History*, 30.1 (Domnina, a virgin living with her widowed mother); Theodoret of Cyrrhus, *Religious History*, 9.12 (a servant daughter ran away from her master to a convent with a widowed mother agreeing); Gerontius, *Life of Melania* (Greek), 65 (a girl given to the monastery of Melania by her mother); *Life of Eupraxia*,

Eight cases deal with orphans. Five of these involve only male children, one a boy and a girl, and two deal with girls (with a grandmother alive and active in one case). Usually the protagonists are depicted as entering into asceticism immediately after the death of both parents; Antony the Great himself, for example, would have started his ascetic career only after his parents had died.[83] Similar decisions were reported to have been taken by Paul of Thebes, Hilarius, Paesius and Isaias, Syncletica, and Publius.[84] It is fitting that the orphan status is frequently pointed out in hagiographic texts, since it functions as a sign of the individual's own choice in entering the ascetic life. It also offers the possibility of depicting the *topos* of the giving away of one's patrimony as alms since it created a space for a general rejection of the past, of family traditions and of family continuity.

The 24 cases featured in the correspondence mention 17 daughters and 11 sons who were dedicated to asceticism, and the 31 cases gathered from hagiographical sources mention 26 sons and 13 daughters. Thus, one finds about twice as many sons in hagiographical accounts and one-and-a-half times more daughters in actual cases. Two external factors may account for this discrepancy – the first is that male authors of hagiographical narratives were much more concerned about male sainthood and thus were writing more about males and attached greater importance to their conversions to the ascetic life. The other factor is that actual cases are drawn from epistolary exchanges which were composed for specific and concrete occasions: when girls were about to enter into a life of virginity, they were still underage and lived under their parents' strict control. Even in a later period, ascetic women were expected to stay with their parents, meeting with other people as little as possible.[85] In order to come into contact with them, written communication was necessary. Moreover, the fact that girls vowing their lives to virginity were on average much younger than

---

2.7–12 (Eupraxia entered a monastic community, her widowed mother agreeing in the end); Palladius, *The Lausiac History*, 67.1 (Magna married off by her mother).

[83] Athanasius, *Life of Antony*, 2.1–2.

[84] Jerome, *Life of Hilarius*, 6 and *Life of Paul*, 4.1; Palladius, *The Lausiac History*, 14.1–2 (Paesius and Isaias); Pseudo-Athanasius, *Life of Syncletica*, 11; Theodoret of Cyrrhus, *Religious History*, 5.1 (Publius). The other cases with orphans are Mark the Deacon, *Life of Porphyry*, 100–102 (Salaphtha, grandmother and aunt living); and Palladius, *The Lausiac History*, 8.1 (Ammon forced to marry by an uncle, even though in *History of the Monks in Egypt*, 22.1, he is forced by his parents). Moreover, for Olympias, although she was a widow when she decided to dedicate herself to chastity, Palladius highlighted her status as an orphan: Palladius, *Dialogue on the Life of John Chrysostom*, 17.134–9.

[85] For the surveillance of virgins, see Arjava, *Women and Law*, pp. 162–3; and Beaucamp, *Le statut*, vol. II, pp. 303–5.

120   *Children and Asceticism in Late Antiquity*

their male counterparts further restricted their opportunities for being shown around and consequently increased their own or their parents' need to receive advice with regard to their education.

Comparing the hagiographical cases with those in the correspondence, one overall shared feature is the relatively small number of cases that involve fathers acting alone. One cannot find actual cases of widowers who would permit their children to take up asceticism, and seldom does one find this possibility mentioned in hagiographic sources either. Of the 24 cases that are discernible in the letters, in 13 the father is known to be dead. Of the 31 stories found in hagiographies, 16 involve children whose father is deceased. To these are to be added the exemplary tale Jerome offered of a widowed mother and her virgin daughter living together, and the case of an orphan girl throwing herself down at the altar to evade marriage, as related by Ambrose.[86] Moreover, when Augustine needed to exemplify the differing fates of twins who were born under the same horoscope, the 'standard' case consisted of a married brother, travelling much and holding high office, while his twin sister was living as a holy virgin on the estate she inherited from her deceased father. In order for this argument to sound convincing to the audience, it must have depicted a situation held to be typical.[87]

In cases outside the epistolary and hagiographic accounts scrutinized above, the fathers' absence comes to the fore as well. Both Augustine and Ambrose had lost their fathers before they made their resolution to become celibate and practice asceticism. The recent death of the father and consequent widowhood of the mother are closely followed by the taking of the vow of virginity in the case of Marcellina, Ambrose's sister.[88] The same situation also applied in the case of Basil the Elder's children – Macrina seems to have started her asceticism only after her father's death, and at any rate her brothers, Basil, Gregory of Nyssa, Peter and Naucratius, began their ascetic careers when their father was already deceased.[89] In comparison, in the other cases only the fathers of

---

[86] Jerome, *Letters*, 117; and Ambrose, *On Virgins,* 1.11.65–6.

[87] Augustine, *City of God*, 5.6.

[88] See 'Marcellina I', in J. Desmulliez et al. (eds), *Prosopographie chrétienne du Bas-Empire* 2.2: *Prosopographie de l'Italie chrétienne (313–604)* (Rome, 2000), pp. 1365–7. See also John Chrysostom, *Letters to Theodore*, 17 on the young, rich and orphaned Urbanus, who chooses asceticism (for a while).

[89] On Macrina, see Gregory of Nyssa, *Life of Macrina*, 4–5: her engagement ended in c. 340 CE with the death of her betrothed. Her father Basil the Elder died in the early 340s. For the early years of her 'self-proclaimed widowhood' (rather than asceticism), see P. Rousseau, 'The Pious Household and the Virgin Chorus: Reflections on Gregory of Nyssa's Life of Macrina', *Journal of Early Christian Studies* 13 (2005), p. 174. On the children of Basil the Elder and the effect of the death of the father, see Vasileiou, 'The Death of the Father',

Choosing Asceticism 121

Gregory Nazianzen and Stagirius are mentioned as being alive when their sons started their ascetic careers and even here, in both cases, it is the influence of mothers which is decisive in the spiritual development of the boys. For Gregory, moreover, the death of his father was a relief from his 'tyranny'.[90]

A further sign of the prevalence of the idea that the absence or non-committedness of fathers would make the pro-ascetic cause more enticing is Ambrose's remark that the recent widowhood of the mother would also make the children more susceptible to exhortations to virginity. In the hagiography examined here, the mother was deceased only in the case of Patermutus as told by John Cassian.[91] There are also no cases in the hagiographic record that depict mothers and sons together, whereas one can find descriptions of a widowed mother living in continence with her daughter as a recurrent theme. This constellation was rhetorically more convincing and it corresponded to the ideals of the time. Also, more generally, the gender of the dedicated children correlates with the gender of the parent who was active: in hagiography, mothers are coupled with daughters and sons with fathers.[92] The topical nature of this figure emerges even more pointedly if one considers the fact that in the cases featured in the correspondence, this type of pairing of parents and children along the lines of gender is absent; of the 12 cases in which mothers are active without their husbands, half of them deal with sons.[93]

Another feature that appears to be conditioned by gender expectations seems to be that religious education and the taking of actual vows were expected to depend to a great extent on mothers even when the fathers were alive. Although little Pacatula's father took the initiative in asking for advice about bringing her

---

pp. 81–4 with Elm, *Virgins*, pp. 45–6, 80–81 and 87–91. Also Chrysostom and Theodoret of Cyrrhus began their asceticism only after the death of both of their parents: *Religious History*, 9.4 and 13.16–18; John Chrysostom, *On the Priesthood*, 1.2 with W. Mayer and P. Allen, *John Chrysostom* (London, 2000), pp. 5–6.

[90] Gregory Nazianzen: *Oration 7*, 9 (c. 369 CE; his father died in 374 CE), with Vasileiou, 'The Death of the Father', pp. 84–6; John Chrysostom, *On Stagirius*, 1.1.

[91] Ambrose, *On Virgins*, 1.10.57–60; and Cassian, *Institutes*, 4.27. See also Ambrose, *Exhortation to Virginity*, 3.13–4.27: widows are represented as opposing their daughters listening to Ambrose's sermons on virginity.

[92] As the only exception, see the case of Theodore and his brother (*Life of Pachomius*, (Bohairic version), 37–8).

[93] Sons: Augustine, *Letters*, 10.1 (Nebridius); Jerome, *Letters*, 125.6–7 (Rusticus); Augustine, *Letters*, 243 (Laetus); Jerome, *Letters*, 3.4 (Bonosus); Augustine, *Letters*, 20 (Antoninus of Fussala); Jerome, *Letters*, 7 (both sons and daughters). Daughters: Jerome, *Letters*, 127 (Marcella); Jerome, *Letters*, 22 and 39 (Blaesilla and Eustochium); Augustine, *Letters*, 188 and Jerome, *Letters*, 130 (Demetrias); Augustine, *Letters*, 3* (unnamed daughter); Augustine, *Letters*, 212 (Simpliciola); Augustine, *Letters*, 124 and 126 (Melania the Younger).

up in the virginal life, Jerome addresses his reply to her mother. It was she who was to take the practical measures. Similarly, in the case of Florentina, both of the parents were alive, but the mother was in charge of the virgin's religious education and had asked Augustine for advice. The same presupposition is inherent in many other texts promoting asceticism. Palladius, for example, states that a certain Candida had instructed her daughter in virginity and brought her to Christ 'as a gift of her own body'.[94]

More generally, the tendency to highlight the role of mothers is conspicuous in the autobiographical narratives of the pro-ascetic ecclesiastical writers. It was the mother who vowed Theodoret of Cyrrhus to asceticism even before his birth and brought him up in constant contact with the hermits. Similarly, Gregory Nazianzen's mother Nonna offered him to God immediately at birth. Gregory does not tire of highlighting his mother's dedication to him and her influence on his future spiritual strivings. Monica's influence on her son Augustine is well known as she tried to bring him up as a Christian, prayed for him year after year and provided him with financial support in his studies. Emmelia, the mother of Macrina, Basil and Gregory of Nyssa, is depicted in a similar manner: Emmelia took care of both the religious and the secular education of her children, praying and reciting psalms to Macrina. As in the other cases mentioned, the role of Gregory's father is minimal – he is mentioned as active only when Macrina is about to be married off by her parents.[95] In the midst of family life, women's work and authority were acknowledged as a major factor in childhood socialization and in passing down religious values to the next generation.

After the Vow: Parents and Their Ascetic Children

In his *Exhortation to Virginity*, Ambrose appealed to Juliana's four children to enter a life of virginity by referring to the vow already made by the parents on their behalf, while stressing that it was impossible to make anybody take the

---

[94] Jerome, *Letters*, 128, esp. 2 (see also *Letter*, 107 on Paula the Younger); Augustine, *Letters*, 266; Palladius, *The Lausiac History*, 57.1. See also *Canons of Pseudo-Athanasius*, 97 (Arabic text) for an exhortation to women to pledge their daughters to virginity (there is no such exhortation for men); and John Chrysostom, *Homilies on Ephesians*, 21.2.

[95] Theodoret of Cyrrhus, *Religious History*, 9.4 and 13.16–18; Grogory Nazianzen, *Poems*, 2.1.1.118–22; 424–44; 2.1.11.51–94; and *Life of Macrina*, 2–7, 11 and 13; Augustine, *Confessions*, 3.4.7–8 and 9.9–13, with Vuolanto, 'Family Relations', pp. 59–63.

actual vow of virginity without their own decision and will.[96] Nevertheless, as has been shown, it is clear that in many cases the opinion of the children was not heard at all, since the decision was taken at such an early phase of their life. Even when the decision was claimed to have been taken by the child itself, parental influence is expected to have played its part. In addition, when parents or a widowed father or mother decided to withdraw into an ascetic life, the minor children seem usually to have followed them.[97]

An important part of ascetic practice was to subdue one's will. According to the ecclesiastical writers, this should lead to an even stricter obedience to parental authority than before the vow. A female elite virgin or young widow was virtuous if she indeed stayed with her relatives, secluded in her parent's home, or at least took refuge in a community led by an older female relative. In these early phases of asceticism, the home was a place in which it was possible to live apart from the world and its perils, a safe bastion in the battle against earthly passions. Contacts with the outer world were to be reduced to a minimum and even the maid attendants should be separated from all worldly associates.[98] Thus, for a virgin living as a member of her parent's or other relative's household, both ordinary parental power and the power of spiritual guardianship were concentrated in the hands of the same people.

Since the dedication of a child was often made without, or even in spite of, the wishes of the children, it was possible that discord erupted at a later phase of living under the ascetic vow, even if there were no (overt) disagreements when the child began the ascetic life. The possible conflicts between parents and their virgin daughters became public knowledge only in very exceptional cases, and therefore they rarely reach modern scholarly attention. Jerome, however, depicts the case of an intra-familial dispute involving a dedicated widow and

---

[96] Ambrose, *Exhortation to Virginity*, 3.13, 3.17 and 8.51. There were three daughters and one son. Rather surprisingly, when Ambrose refers to the vow taken by the parents, he draws a comparison to the Old Testament Jephthah, whose daughter went to her death because of her father's careless promise (*incauta patris oblatio*).

[97] Early life decisions: see above on e.g. Paula the Younger, Pacatula, Asella, daughter of Melania the Younger and Eustochium; parental influence, see above e.g. Demetrias, Blesilla and Marcella; children retiring with their parent(s), see e.g. children of Eucherius and Galla, Apronianus and Avita, and Salvian and Palladia, with further discussion and examples in the hagiography below, p. 152.

[98] See e.g. Jerome, *Letters*, 22.16 and 25; 24.4; and 117; Ambrose, *On Virgins*, 1.7.32; Ambrose, *The Consecration of a Virgin*, 1.1; Gregory of Nyssa, *Life of Macrina*, 5 and 11; John Chrysostom, *Regulares feminae*, 7; John Chrysostom, *On the Priesthood*, 3.17 with Arjava, *Women and Law*, pp. 162–3 and Beaucamp, *Le statut*, vol. II, pp. 303–5. See also above p. 56 and p. 100.

124 *Children and Asceticism in Late Antiquity*

her virgin daughter. The details of the case as Jerome described them, with the mother and daughter being separated and taking a non-kin male advisor, are somewhat suspect. The letter in question is a declamatory elaboration that is not addressed to any specific individual, given that it features anonymous main protagonists and 'a certain brother from Gallia', on whom Jerome claimed to rely for his information on the case.[99] Still, this text is valuable, since it shows not only Jerome's presupposition that in a 'normal' situation asceticism was an intergenerational effort, but also his sharp eye in spotting the possibility for disagreements between the elderly widow and virgin daughter who was, in theory, more honoured. The letter may have been intended as a warning and advice to those mother–daughter pairs of ascetics Jerome knew too well to address directly.[100]

Nevertheless, at least in one letter a family issue concerning asceticism was brought to the fore. Augustine mentions a nun, a *sanctimonialis*, who in the middle of the night woke up a presbyter who, because of his duties, had stayed at her parents' house. According to the presbyter, the nun started to complain about her parents and continued until he got too upset and left the room, fearing damage to their reputations.[101] The presbyter's fear was justified, since later on he was indeed accused of 'fornication or some impurity' – by the *sanctimonialis* herself. It is difficult to uncover her motivation for her latter action, unless one views the case as a chance for her to escape from her vow and her parents' house. The alternative explanation would naturally be that the presbyter's story is an invention to cover his own misdeed. Even in case we would be reluctant to accept the presbyter's version, the case certainly demonstrates the narrow limits of freedom for virgin daughters living with their parents.

The parent's will to promote asceticism could shake the foundations of a child's life in other ways. Rufina's crying or the protests of Toxotius could not stop their mother, Paula, leaving for the East. Against the laws of nature, as Jerome put it, Paula's love for her children was overcome by her greater love of God. To stress the exceptional sacrifice of the mother, he added that 'nothing is more cruel than for parents to be separated from their children'. Jerome's depiction of the situation is a literary construct and its central aim is to eulogize Paula, but children were indeed left behind, as when Melania the Elder left on

---

[99] Jerome, *Letters*, 117; contemporary readers already claimed that the letter was fictitious. Jerome called these accusations blasphemous, but he offered no arguments to refute them: Jerome, *Against Vigilantius*, 3.

[100] Esp. Paula the Elder and Eustochium, and Albina the Elder and Marcella – Jerome in fact later referred to some differences of opinion (Jerome, *Letters*, 127.4).

[101] Augustine, *Letters*, 13*: 'de parentibus suis nescio quas querelas immurmurantem'.

her quest for the angelic life in the earthly Jerusalem, leaving behind her teenage son Publicola.[102] Indeed, the records of the Council of Gangra show concern for parents who do not provide for their children with proper piety, but neglect them 'under pretext of asceticism'. Such parents were liable to be anathematized. The canon was directed particularly against the Eustathians, among whom such things were thought to happen.[103]

In hagiography the theme of the abandonment of children due to asceticism often appears. The fifth-century miracle collection of St Thecla, for example, includes the story of Dionysia, who abandoned her husband, children and house, and left for the shrine of Thecla.[104] Men also left their children and wives: an anonymous rich man from Asia featured in the *Dialogues* of Sulpicius Severus is praised for suddenly leaving his wife and small child and entering the desert. In his *Conferences*, John Cassian similarly praised Theonas for leaving his wife and fleeing to a monastery after having used all his rhetorical skills to persuade his wife.[105] There is only positive value attached to leaving children behind.

Even if there is very little information concerning intra-familial discussions of asceticism, it is clear that the psychological pressure in these situations would have been tremendous. All these cases illustrate the role of adults in decisions about children's lives, who under ordinary circumstances had very little say regarding their own affairs.

Family Dynamics: Authority and Gender in the Family Nucleus

A Christian in conflict with his or her parents was a living embodiment of the fulfilment of Christ's prophecy regarding his own role in setting 'a man against his father, a daughter against her mother, and a daughter-in-law against her mother-in-law'.[106] This was simultaneously an unheard-of action and a sign of the true faith and holiness of the ascetic person in question. As the late

---

[102] Paula: Jerome, *Letters*, 108.6 (404 CE, depicting an incident in 385 CE): 'nihil crudelius est quam parentes a liberis separari'. See also Jerome, *Letters*, 45.4 (385 CE); Melania: Palladius, *The Lausiac History*, 46.1; Paulinus of Nola, *Letters*, 29.8, with K. Wilkinson, 'The Elder Melania's Missing Decade', *Journal of Late Antiquity* 5(1) (2012), pp. 180–82.

[103] *Council of Gangra, Canon* 15: 'προφάσει τῆς ἀσκήσεως ἀμελοίν'.

[104] *Life and Miracles of Thecla* 46.

[105] Sulpicius Severus, *Dialogues*, 1.22.1–2; Cassian, *Conferences*, 21.8–10. See also e.g. Palladius, *The Lausiac History*, 22.1: Paul the Simple left behind his wife and children for life in the desert when he found her with a lover.

[106] Matthew 10:35.

Roman writers' aim was to construct the image of an exemplary Christian, their interpretation of Jesus' teaching on the necessity to leave parents and kin was an important factor. It was crucial to highlight the independent and free decision of children in their dedication to a virginal life. Conflict with one or both parents was the ultimate sign of the ascetic's preferences, and indeed of holiness, since it indicated his or her choice of the family of Christ over the authority of parents and family continuity. The biographers of ascetics and saints were eager to point out that their decision to take the vow had been independent of and, if possible, against the wishes of their parents or relatives. Thus, recourse to the topic of independence had been taken even in cases in which no conflicts were indicated and where the role of the parents was decisive. In particular, the theme of forced marriage was a frequently-used literary *topos*: it was a dramatic motif that was well suited to highlight the virtue of those model Christians who, after all their struggles, nevertheless ended up being married.

However, a marriage arranged by parents was the standard practice in Late Antiquity among Christians and non-Christians alike. The choice between marrying and taking the vow of chastity clearly followed these same lines of authority. From the parents' point of view, to force a child to marry a certain spouse was not a statement against asceticism, even if later hagiographers could interpret their actions as revealing such an attitude in retrospect. By referring to a forced marriage, Paulinus of Pella, a self-proclaimed would-be ascetic, could thus highlight his Christian virtue.[107] These stories should not be interpreted as signs of actual parental opposition, still less should they be used to argue for a distinction between a pro-ascetic East and a more critical West.[108]

Nevertheless, an open conflict with parents was to be carefully avoided. If there were disagreements and parents were opposed to the resolution of the children, these were to be resolved by waiting and using tactics of evasion or even concealment. This is evident especially when the father was alive. There are no actual cases in which the opinion of a *paterfamilias* would have been openly contested. Even in the hagiographical texts of the fourth and fifth centuries this is rare – children either yielded to their parents' opinion or alternatively were depicted as running away. Yet one does find some differences between how sons and daughters handled the window of opportunity that opened in such cases. The account of how Syncletica waited for her parents to die before she began

---

[107] Paulinus of Pella, *Thanksgiving*, 176–81. I thank Judith Evans Grubbs for directing my attention to him.

[108] See also Sivan, 'On Hymens and Holiness', pp. 81–93. Cf. Brown, *Body and Society*, p. 343: 'Unlike the austere and populous families of Cappadocia, fourth-century Romans parted with their daughters with extreme reluctance'; and Nathan, *The Family*, p. 82.

her ascetic life, while her brother ran away from parental authority, exemplifies how the story's credibility required different responses from son and daughter.

Yet even for sons, who had greater freedom of choice, abrupt reactions seem to have been the exception; after all, no cases of such behaviour are known outside the hagiographical records. In this situation, it is not surprising that the death of the parents – or at least that of the father – was often the prerequisite for the child to take the vow. In cases where the father was dead, the sons had legal rights to distribute their property and withdraw to the desert if they so wished. However, a central feature of the late Roman value system that applied in families was dutiful respect for the wishes of the parents, regardless of their juridical standing vis-à-vis their children; thus, widowed mothers had a strong influence over their children. If the mother was opposed to their vow, children, even sons, seem to have waited until she had died, as the cases of the mothers of Laetus, Nebridius, Theodoret and John Chrysostom imply.

Sons had the time to wait as the normal age for first marriages for them was much higher than for daughters; as such, when sons needed to make the final decision about asceticism, the father was often already dead. Notably in hagiography a person who enters the ascetic life very frequently has the status of an orphan son. An early and most influential case of this is the life of Antony the Great as told by Athanasius. This also shows the expectation inherent in the forming of the ascetic sainthood: orphan status is a sure sign of the individual's choice in the ascetic life. No parental pressure could have affected the decision and orphan status makes it possible to depict the topical giving-away of the patrimony as alms, since it creates a space for a general rejection of the past, family traditions and family continuity.

The material on the choice of asceticism suggests that at least among the elites, the age for a first marriage for girls had remained much the same (or had become slightly earlier); the late Roman authors, sharing an elite cultural background, held it as self-evident that discussions about entering the ascetic life would have taken place when girls approached marriageable age in their early teens. The few actual cases for which we have information fit well into this schema. For boys (or rather young men), the ascetic vow was usually taken when they were in their twenties, and choosing asceticism was connected with negotiations about marriage only in some hagiographic stories (and in these cases no indication of the age of the sons is given); for them, there was no similar link between family discussions, marriage and entering the ascetic life.[109] Consequently, it is

---

[109] The case of the 30-year-old Augustine can be interpreted here as an exception, as his engagement made the decision about an ascetic lifestyle urgent, and the intervention of Monica brings the aspect of family negotiations into play (Augustine, *Confessions*, 6.12.21–6.16.26).

reasonable to assume that a considerable age difference between elite boys and girls still prevailed at the point of a first marriage.

If sons had time to wait for the final decision about asceticism, daughters did not have the same opportunity. For young, marriageable girls in their early teens, the question concerned the immediate choice between marriage and celibacy, and the family could not wait for them to grow up too much. Moreover, it was more probable with daughters than with sons that parents, especially mothers, were still alive. This situation is echoed in the presuppositions inherent in treatises and exhortations to virginity, namely that daughters faced struggles with their parents, whereas sons were probably more able to make their decision about staying unmarried without needing to take their parents' (or at their least fathers') arguments into consideration. Ecclesiastical writers needed to warn the young maidens of possible resistance, and brand it as inevitable and even sanctifying. This resistance, however, even if it were widespread (which I very much doubt),[110] did not lead to open conflicts in spite of the war cries pronounced by the propagators of asceticism against prejudiced parents. The alternatives for daughters were essentially the opposite of those for sons: leaving home for the husband's household or staying at home as a spouse of Christ. The third possibility, rebelling against the parents, would have meant running away from home, and if there were no female ascetic communities at hand – and they were not common by the turn of the fifth century, especially in the West – there would have been nowhere to go. Not surprisingly, it is only in hagiographic texts that daughters are depicted as rebelling against their parents in order to take the vow.

This is not to say that there was no unwillingness on the part of the younger generation to follow the advice of the older, but rather that children, especially daughters, had little actual means to protest before the death of their father and, to a lesser degree, that of their mother. Still, as the case of Macrina shows – if we can have any trust in the basic information given by Gregory of Nyssa – the marriages were discussed inside the families, and even if the father would have had the last word, the decision making seems to have been a process 'rather than the imposition of an arbitrary paternal will'.[111] Naturally cases involving people

---

[110] That is, the bargaining position of the daughters especially was extremely unfavourable. See also the conclusions by Joye, 'Filles et pères', esp. pp. 238–9: 'Enfermée ou enlevée, la jeune fille apparaît plus souvent comme une victime des ambitions des membres de sa propre famille que comme un ferment actif de révolte.'

[111] Quote from R. Saller, 'The Social Dynamics of Consent to Marriage and Sexual Relations: The Evidence of Roman Comedy' in Laiou (ed.), *Consent and Coercion to Sex*, 104 (concerning, naturally, a completely different time period, but his conclusions also seem to be fitting here).

other than parents, such as neighbours or relatives, were more likely to become public than disagreements inside the family nucleus.

In all, the texts other than hagiographic accounts do not generally depict disagreements inside the family. On the contrary, the ways in which these stories are told stress the common interests of the (other) family members in having a celibate ascetic in the household. Even if older widows of secure financial backing might have had some freedom for action, for most virgins, their parents made the final decisions.[112] Even after the vow, girls were kept under strict surveillance. Thus, independence and the pursuit of freedom can scarcely be seen as real reasons why underage children entered the ascetic life; older scholarship has much overstated the opportunities that children had to decide for themselves, especially in the case of young female virgins. Instead of claiming that many children wished to remain unmarried, and that this led to familial conflicts between parents and their children, it would be more to the point to stress that parents were keen to have a celibate ascetic in the household. In the following chapters I will investigate the reasons for this.

[112] See also Krause, *Witwen und Waisen*, pp. 109–10.

Chapter 6
Family Economy and the Profits of Asceticism

Many girls are brought forward [to the monasteries] by their parents, brothers and other relatives before the proper age, not because the girls would have an inner urge towards chastity, but in order to acquire provisions for themselves.[1]

Older scholarship has seen the function of asceticism in the context of families mostly as a tool in family or kin strategies aiming at the disposal of extra children, either at birth or the age of marriage. In particular, it has been claimed that poorer families would have controlled the size of the family by giving their children to ascetic vocations instead of killing or abandoning the newborn, or that better-off parents would have used asceticism as a tool for dealing with surplus children in the context of inheritance strategies. Asceticism could have also profited the ascetics themselves with more or less direct privileges in society. The aim of the present chapter is to examine critically these claims in the context of wider considerations about family economy and inheritance, looking at the factors that motivated the choice of asceticism by the individuals themselves or their family members. In other words, this chapter deals with both continuity strategies for welfare during the lifetime of individuals and with manipulations of patrimony to secure continuity after death in a more abstract sense.[2]

Surplus Children, Inheritance Strategies and Dowry

For the elites, Peter Brown evinces the difficulties in finding husbands for girls of the small early Christian communities or, at a later date, for the older widows of the Christianized elite as a possible reason for the success of asceticism. There is, however, no evidence for this in the sources, at any rate from the late third

---

[1]   Basil of Caesarea, *Letters*, 199.18: 'Πολλὰς γὰρ γονεῖς προσάγουσι καὶ ἀδελφοὶ καὶ τῶν προσηκόντων τινές πρὸ τῆς ἡλικίας, οὐκ οἴκοθεν ὁρμηθείσας πρὸς ἀγαμίαν, ἀλλά τι βιωτικὸν ἑαυτοῖς διοικούμενοι.'

[2]   See Figure 1, p. 41.

132   *Children and Asceticism in Late Antiquity*

century onwards,[3] and this theory completely fails to explain male asceticism. The only text pointing in this direction is Jerome's reproach to parents, who 'dedicate to virginity only deformed and crippled daughters for whom they can find no suitable husbands'.[4] Even for Jerome, this problem of finding husbands is restricted to a small, special group of girls. It does not apply to Christian families in general, nor does it apply in any way to widows.

What of the theory of asceticism serving as an alternative to killing or abandoning the newborn?[5] It is difficult to see the entrusting of a child to an ascetic community to be raised – which in the context of monasteries was later called *oblatio* – as primarily motivated by such considerations. First, in the West, dedicating a child to the monastic life would not have freed the parents of the oblate from the costs of upbringing.[6] More generally, children who were abandoned were newborn, whereas the children who were given to the ecclesiastical communities and authorities to be brought up and educated were already older. Most of our information is about children in their teens, but the age of three is mentioned as an extremely low age in some sources.[7]

---

[3]   Brown, *Body and Society*, esp. pp. 147 and 191. See also Drijvers, 'Virginity and Asceticism', p. 257, backing his argument with supposedly low birthrates among the Christians.

[4]   Jerome, *Letters*, 130.6: 'Solent miseri parentes, et non plenae fidei Christiani, deformes et aliquo membro debiles filias, quia dignos generos non inveniunt, virginitati tradere.'

[5]   See especially J. Boswell, '*Expositio* and *Oblatio*: The Abandonment of Children and the Ancient and Medieval Family', *American Historical Review* 89(1) (1984), pp. 10–33, with e.g. J. Boswell, *The Kindness of Strangers: The Abandonment of Children in Western Europe from Late Antiquity to the Renaissance*, 2nd edn (London, 1989), pp. 228–55; Brown, *Body and Society*, p. 261; D. Kertzer and S. Richard, 'Historical and Anthropological Perspectives on Italian Family Life', in D. Kertzer and R. Saller (eds), *The Family in Italy from Antiquity to the Present* (New Haven, 1991), p. 11; Beaucamp, *Le statut de la femme*, vol. II, pp. 303–5; Arjava, *Women and Law*, p. 166.

[6]   De Jong, *In Samuel's Image*, pp. 5 and 293–301, which concludes that there seem to be no cases in which parents have given their small children as oblates before the rise of the Benetictine monasticism in the Western Europe of the sixth century. See also Guerreau-Jalabert, '*Nutritus /oblatus*', esp. pp. 271 and 273.

[7]   For abandonment, see J. Evans Grubbs, 'Hidden in Plain Sight: *Expositi* in the Community', in V. Dasen and T. Späth (eds), *Children, Memory, and Family Identity in Roman Culture* (Oxford, 2010), pp. 293–310 and 'The Dynamics', pp. 21–36. For ascetic fosterage, most of our information is about children in their teens, but the age of three is mentioned as a credible if extreme age in some contexts. See De Jong, *In Samuel's Image*, pp. 31–54 (for sixth- and seventh-century CE Western Europe) with Theodoret of Cyrrhus, *Religious History*, 26.4–5 (Caseau, 'Stratégies parentales', p. 253 interprets this case as an oblation by parents, but the wording of Theodoret fits better if Heliodoros is understood to have been orphaned) and Cyril of Scythopolis, *The Lives of the Monks of Palestine*, Life of Euthymius 1.

Moreover, the introduction of the practice of giving children to an ascetic career seems not to have affected its alleged alternative, namely the abandonment of children, which continued without interruption through to the early medieval period. The alternative to oblation was not abandoning the child, but rather the various other modes of dislocation such as (unofficial) adoption, service and apprenticeship.[8]

As for the more wealthy families, the ideologically laden texts have directed scholarly attention to family disputes over patrimony due to asceticism. The sources which refer to a tendency that children who had entered an ascetic lifestyle were left without inheritance have been interpreted as signs of conflicts between parents and children, and, consequently, of an independent choice by the children.[9] Indeed, a fourth-century text of Eastern provenance, the *Canons of Athanasius*, refers to the tendency to disinherit children due to their celibacy, and in the later Justinian legislation one finds references to parents who disinherited their children when they chose to enter monasteries or to become members of the clergy. It is specified that it was not legal to prevent the child from choosing such a lifestyle 'or for this reason to exclude him or her from their inheritance or succession'.[10]

The accusations that parents denied their share of the family property to children who embraced the ascetic life appear in other texts too. Jerome polemically complained that fathers who prided themselves on their piety frequently 'give to their virgin daughters sums scarcely sufficient for their maintenance, and bestow the bulk of their property upon sons and daughters living in the world'. He also gives an anonymous (and as such quite suspect) example of a 'rich presbyter' who left 'two of his daughters who were professed

---

[8]   For the continuity of abandonment in the early medieval period, see Miller, *The Orphans*, pp. 148–61 (East); D. Lett, 'L'Enfant dans la chrétienté. Ve-XIIIe siècles', in D. Alexandre-Bidon and D. Lett, *Les Enfants au Moyen Age. Ve–XVe siècles*, revised edn (Paris, 1997), pp. 36–7 (West) with V. Vuolanto, 'Infant Abandonment and the Christianization of Medieval Europe', in K. Mustakallio and C. Laes (eds), *The Dark Side of Childhood in Late Antiquity and the Middle Ages* (Oxford, 2011), pp. 3–19. For abandonment vs. other modes of dislocation of children, see Vuolanto, 'Selling a Freeborn', pp. 197–202. The coupling of oblation and abandonment also is rejected by De Jong, *In Samuel's Image*, esp. p. 5.

[9]   Arjava, *Women and Law*, pp. 46 and 158–9; Clark, *Women*, pp. 52–3; Verdon, 'Virgins and Widows', pp. 494–5.

[10]   *Canons of Pseudo-Athanasius*, 102 (Arabic text); *Codex Justinianus*, 1.3.54.5: 'non liceat parentibus vel easdem personas quocumque modo abstrahere vel propter hanc tantummodo causam quasi ingratum a sua hereditate vel successione repellere'. The law also prohibits setting those living religious life aside in the event of intestacy; see also *Novellae Iustiniani*, 123.41.

virgins with a mere pittance', while the other children were given 'ample means for self-indulgence and pleasure'. Jerome also pointed out that many ascetic women had acted thus with regard to their offspring.[11] This phenomenon was seen not only in Italy and Gaul, but also in Africa. Ianuarius, a presbyter and a member of Augustine's monastic community, disinherited his son and daughter who had also embraced the ascetic life.[12]

These references to disinheriting virgin daughters or celibate sons, however, should not be taken as indications of familial conflicts over the ascetic lifestyle. First of all, the cases are almost invariably associated with people who themselves were well-acquainted with ascetic Christian ideals, such as the fathers and mothers in Jerome's accusations, or Ianuarius, who, as a monk himself, certainly had nothing against asceticism in itself. One of the ironies in Jerome's correspondence is that the only person we know by name who actually withdrew an inheritance from a child with an ascetic calling was Albina the Elder, the mother of Marcella, who later headed a female ascetic community, and whom Jerome called his spiritual mother. On Marcella's death, Jerome illustrated her ascetic zeal and obedience to Albina by telling how 'her mother, caring for her relatives and having no sons or grandchildren, wanted to give all to her brother's children' instead of making donations for the poor and giving Marcella her share. And in fact, the daughter was left without her share of the property.[13]

Reading the highly rhetorical reproaches about the transgressions of 'many parents' easily leads the scholar astray in expecting merciless struggles and obverse motives of the actors in question. However, as the example of Albina shows, disinheritances with individual goals and strategies involved can be revealed in rather trivial contexts.

The strategic aspects of refusing to pass on family wealth to celibate children are also revealed in the affirmation that Christ would not require a dowry from his brides. In addressing would-be virgins, Ambrose referred to parents who, in opposing their daughters' vows of virginity, refuse them the dotal part of their inheritance. Given

---

[11]   Jerome, *Letters*, 130.6: 'Certe qui religiosiores sibi videntur, parvo sumptu, et qui vix ad alimenta sufficiat, virginibus dato, omnem censum in utroque sexu, saecularibus liberis largiuntur ... quod nuper in hac urbe dives quidam fecit presbyter ut duas filias in proposito virginali inopes relinqueret, et aliorum ad omnem copiam filiorum luxuriae atque deliciis provideret. Fecerunt hoc multae, pro dolor, nostri propositi feminae.' Translated by W.H. Fremantle et al. (Nicene and Post-Nicene Fathers, ser. II, vol. 6). See Salvian, *To the Church*, 3.4–5 for parents leaving no share of the inheritance to children who led a religious life.

[12]   Augustine, *Sermons*, 355.3.

[13]   Jerome, *Letters*, 127.4: 'illa suum diligeret sanguinem, et absque filiis ac nepotibus, vellet in fratris liberos universa conferre, ista pauperes eligebat'. For Jerome on Albina, see e.g. Jerome, *Letters*, 32 and 45.7.

that in Roman society the dowry formed part of a daughter's paternal inheritance,[14] Ambrose re-assured virgins that remaining unmarried (and losing the dowry) did not mean disinheritance, even if the parents would argue that way at first. Parents do not need to invest in the dowry, but nor would the virgin daughter lose, as she is inheriting her share when the parents die: 'And yet have you ever heard of anyone, because of her desire for chastity, having been deprived of her lawful inheritance?'[15] In another context Ambrose even reminds parents that they need not trouble themselves with regard to the dowry of their virgin daughters.[16]

Against this background, Publicola's alleged aim of disinheriting his daughter Melania the Younger in favour of her brother, when she and her husband had announced their wish to enter the ascetic life, can be understood from a new perspective. Indeed, there is no reason to assume that Publicola's action was a threat directed against the young couple's ascetic resolution; rather, it was a practical solution to keep the family wealth in family line. However, in the narrative offered by Melania's hagiographer, her father's goal of disinheriting her became the most important piece of evidence of her parents' opposition to her asceticism.[17]

There are also sources that point directly to familial strategies behind the decisions involved when making a family member become an ascetic. Many parents quite willingly dedicated their sons and daughters to asceticism, even against the child's wishes. Basil of Caesarea, for example, claimed that some parents and other relatives handed over underage girls to monasteries regardless of their disposition in order to gain a provision for themselves. Unfortunately, Basil does not specify what kind of advantage he had in mind. It may simply have been a question of having one less mouth to feed, yet since the argument

---

[14] On the dowry as a part of the inheritance for the girls, see Janne Pölönen, 'The Division of Wealth between Men and Women in Roman Succession (c.a. 50 BC–AD 250)', in P. Setälä et al., *Women, Power and Property in Roman Empire* (Rome, 2002), esp. pp. 160–65, 179.

[15] Ambrose, *On Virgins*, 1.11.62–63, 66: 'Et tamen quam audistis aliquando propter studium integritatis legitimae factam successionis extorrem?'.

[16] Ambrose, *On Virgins*, 1.7.32: 'Virgo ... quae non dote sollicitet, non emigratione destituat, non offendat iniuria.'

[17] Gerontius, *Life of Melania* (Greek), 6–7 and 12 with above p. 106. The editors of the *Life of Melania* claim that it is improbable that Melania the Younger would have had brothers (see Gorce, *Vie de sainte Mélanie*, pp. 145 and 150; P. Laurence, *La vie latine de sainte Mélanie / Gérontius; Edition critique, traduction et commentaire* (Jerusalem, 2002), pp. 178–9 with Cooper, 'The Household and the Desert', p. 22). However, Palladius also presumes there was a brother (Palladius, *The Lausiac History*, 54.3 and 6; 61.4), and there seems to be no special reason to doubt this.

is not that the provision would be for the girls, but for the family, it is more probable that he was thinking of the avoidance of the necessity for a dowry or of the dispersal of the patrimony.[18] Similarly, we can see parents dedicating their daughters to an ascetic life, even against their wishes, behind a decision by Pope Leo I in the mid-400s to limit the irrevocability of the ascetic vow to those young women who had taken the vow of their own free will.[19] It is quite clear that free will was not always involved.

Real or supposed transgressions led to public reactions and in 458, the Western Emperor Majorian decreed that a daughter could not be compelled to a life of virginity.[20] The edict presumed that parents were not dedicating their daughters purely for religious motives, but in order to avoid the expenses of a dowry and the dispersal of patrimony after the parents' death. Thus, it was forbidden to consecrate a daughter under 40 years old to virginity. If a daughter was dedicated to virginity and, following the death of her parents, wished to abandon her vow before she was 40, she could do so, and she could not be disinherited for so doing. The reference to an age limit of 40 years is new to the Roman legislation. The idea behind this is that only a daughter of this age was considered to be independent of the aspirations and authority of her parents and thus capable of making the decision regarding the vow on her own. Such a relatively high age was chosen in order to urge parents to marry off their widowed but childless young daughters. The edict was directed at elite families: *humiliores* still had the freedom to act as they wished towards their young daughters, and noblewomen with children had already fulfilled their duty towards the family and the *res publica*. Thus, the principal aim of the edict was to safeguard the financial interests of the parties involved. On the one hand, the ascetic life cannot be used to save the part of the inheritance due to the virgin in question; on the other hand, a person willing to marry could not be denied her share of the inheritance. Moreover, young childless widows had to give their property to their near relatives if they abstained from remarrying. The continuity of the family and the financial interests of the kin group were to be carefully safeguarded.

In the case of the elite widows whose parents were dead, the ascetic vow itself seems not to have much affected the relatives. However, when Paula the Elder

---

[18] Basil of Caesarea, *Letters*, 199.18, cited above in note 1, with Beaucamp, *Le statut*, vol. II, p. 304.

[19] Leo, *Letters*, 167.15.

[20] *Novellae Maioriani*, 6, esp. pr., 3 and 5 (458 CE), with J. Evans Grubbs, 'Virgins and Widows, Show-girls and Whores: Late Roman legislation on Women and Christianity', in R. Mathisen (ed.), *Law, Society, and Authority in Late Antiquity* (Oxford, 2001), pp. 232–4.

began to spend her money on the sick and poor at Rome, her relatives reproved her. Similarly, when Melania the Elder's husband died, the relatives objected, not to her dedication to the ascetic life, but to her plans to leave for the Holy Land with the intention of establishing an ascetic community there. Although she left the greatest part of her property to her son's guardian to be looked after, she retained ultimate control.[21] Concern for the fate of the family wealth by the relatives also lay behind the legal rule that widows without children had to give half of their property to their parents or nearest kin if they persisted in remaining unmarried. Their 'lascivious freedom to live' was too great a threat to the patrimony.[22] Widows were able to act as they wished for the most part, and as long as their whims did not threaten the family wealth or reputation, the relatives did not care. Even if the patrimony was endangered, relatives had few opportunities to intervene in the decisions of an economically independent widow. This concern was not limited to widows; when Melania the Younger and Pinian were about to start their ascetic career, the brother of Pinian wanted to remove the family wealth from them before they could distribute it.[23]

In general, the fate of the family property was of central importance for any discussions about asceticism.[24] The loss of their inheritance was a real threat to young ascetics, but the dividing line was not that of religious affiliation. There were devout Christians accused of withholding their inheritance from their children because of the children's inclinations toward asceticism. Similarly, it was not only anti-ascetic Christian parents who actually disinherited their virgin daughters or celibate sons. Thus, the cases of disinheritance cannot be considered without further qualifications as evidence of familial conflicts over asceticism; rather, these stories should be seen in connection with elite family strategies. It was not an unwelcome situation to have only a limited number of children who qualified for inheritance. The practice of denying an inheritance

---

[21] Paula the Elder: Jerome, *Letters*, 108.5. Melania the Elder: Paulinus of Nola, *Letters*, 29.10. Jerome claims that she left all her property to her son in Rome (*Letters*, 39.5), but according to Palladius, she carried all her movable property with her to the East (*The Lausiac History*, 46.1). Be it as it may, Melania certainly was able to use her property at her will even later (see Palladius, *The Lausiac History*, 54.2 and 6 with Paulinus of Nola, *Letters*, 29.11 and Wilkinson, 'The Elder Melania's Missing Decade', pp. 174, 181–2).

[22] *Novellae Maioriani*, 6.5–6.6: 'lascivam vivendi eligunt libertatem'.

[23] Gerontius, *Life of Melania* (Greek), 7, 10 and 12. Like Melania the Elder, the younger Melania too was repeatedly described as giving away all her property. See also Cooper, 'The Household and the Desert', pp. 21–6.

[24] See also Sivan, 'On Hymens and Holiness', pp. 89–91, who points out that whenever there was opposition over ascetic tendencies of a (female) family member in Late Antique Rome, in fact these considered issues of property, not asceticism as such.

to an ascetic son or daughter aimed to avoid the dispersal of the inheritance among too many heirs and thus it contributed to the promotion of power and privileges of the family.[25] For the machinations for transferring the family property, asceticism offered a new tool. Since ascetics themselves did not have offspring – and it was expected that they would donate their property to the poor and to the Church – from an economic perspective, the patrimony given to ascetics was to be regarded as squandering money that could have been used for the family succession even if it yielded great spiritual rewards. Families strove to make best use of their resources.

Asceticism for Survival? Profits for the Ascetics

Asceticism may have brought material advantages not only for the families of ascetics, but, paradoxically, also to the ascetics themselves and their communities. Both Ambrose and Jerome complained in the 380s and 390s that monks and the members of clergy could no longer inherit or accept donations from women.[26] They were referring here to the edict promulgated by Valentinian I in 370 which claimed that members of clergy were visiting the homes of widows and *pupillae* and persuading them to leave their property to the Church. The edict decrees that members of the clergy and those who 'like to be called continent' should not visit the women in question, and they are not allowed to have anything 'from those women with whom they had been in contact on the pretext of religion.'[27] There seem to have been accusations of involuntary vows, excessive donations to the ecclesiastics and even sexual exploitation, not only by the clergy but also by the ascetics.

Pupillae in the edict refers to underage girls under guardianship (*tutela minorum*). In this context, the term is especially fitting to the virgin recruits, since the decision for the virgin life had to be taken before girls reached puberty,

---

[25] Augustine, *Tractates on the Gospel of John*, 2.1.13; Augustine, *Sermons*, 57.2. See further Shaw, 'The Family', pp. 25, 44 and 47 with Andreau and Bruhns, *Introduction*, p. xx.

[26] Ambrose, *Letters*, 73.14–15; Jerome, *Letters*, 52.6.

[27] *Codex Theodosianus*, 16.2.20 (370 CE): 'Ecclesiastici aut ex ecclesiasticis vel qui continentium se volunt nomine nuncupari, viduarum ac pupillarum domos non adeant, sed publicis exterminentur iudiciis, si posthac eos adfines earum vel propinqui putaverint deferendos. Censemus etiam, ut memorati nihil de eius mulieris, cui se privatim sub praetextu religionis adiunxerint, liberalitate quacumque vel extremo iudicio possint adipisci et omne in tantum inefficax sit, quod alicui horum ab his fuerit derelictum, ut nec per subiectam personam valeant aliquid vel donatione vel testamento percipere.' On this edict, see Evans Grubbs, 'Virgins and Widows', pp. 225–7.

entered marriage and ceased to be under guardianship. Moreover, traditionally, the situation of *pupillae* was seen as economically precarious and the Roman law and *mores* severely castigated those who made use of defenceless minors who were under guardianship.[28] Thus, the connection of ecclesiastics to the misappropriation of the wealth of *pupillae*, and the equally highly reproved vice of legacy hunting (or *captatio* as it was called by more classical authors)[29] was a severe moral statement. The accusation is made worse by the fact that the Church, or the bishops, had from a very early date taken care of orphans and their guardianship, and thus the relationships between Church and wards were well known and frequent. The *Canons of Athanasius*, for example, both urge the members of clergy to take care of orphans and warn them not to mix the wealth of their wards with their own.[30]

The edict did not prohibit the Church as an institution from inheriting and it is possible that the original incentive for its promulgation was more the threat which the visits of ascetically minded Christians aroused in some aristocratic families than the references to legacy hunting in particular. However, Valentinian was clearly not opposing Christian women pledging themselves to asceticism, as other legislation by him shows; rather, the interest of the legislation focused on property matters.[31] In the 390s, it seemed to be that in the big Italian cities there would have been many women willing to donate their wealth as an inheritance to the members of clergy or to monks.

The anonymous and rather general references to misappropriation by the ecclesiastical legacy hunters could be explained partly by the negative point of view – visible enough in the edict – towards excessive donations linked to the propagators of the ascetic lifestyle.[32] However, even the pro-ascetic ecclesiastical writers refer to such problems. Ambrose, in his *Duties of the Clergy*, warns clerics not to try to seek inheritances for themselves. The indication is that there are indeed persons who 'under pretence of having self-control and gravity' aim for economic gain. He cautions that those who have dedicated themselves to the

---

[28] Vuolanto, 'Women and the Property', esp. pp. 204–7.

[29] On *captatio* in the Roman empire, see Champlin, *Final Judgements*, pp. 87–102.

[30] *Canons of Pseudo-Athanasius*, 56 (Arabic text), with above p. 73.

[31] On the other legislation by Valentinian I, see Evans Grubbs, 'Virgins and Widows', p. 226; See also *Codex Theodosianus*, 16.2.27 and 28 with Evans Grubbs, 'Virgins and Widows', pp. 228–32.

[32] See also Ammianus Marcellinus, 27.3.14 (c. 390 CE) on the Bishop of Rome living in luxury, enriched by the donations of ladies: 'futuri sint ita securi ut ditentur oblationibus matronarum'.

Lord have not done so in order to collect earthly goods for their families.[33] It is shameful for a priest to seek earthly profit. Jerome claims to have heard that there were people who by services and flattery tried to gain inheritances from childless old men and women. Although Jerome does not specify who these people are, he connects this *captatio* to the vices of ecclesiastics who seek luxury. He also refers in this context to his own ability, developed during his stay at (the Church of) Rome, to appreciate the taste of exquisite dishes. Jerome directs his remarks to Nepotian, who, as a recruit under Christ's banner, should avoid like the plague those 'clerical businessmen, who had risen from poverty to wealth and from obscurity to a high position'.[34]

Jerome refers elsewhere to monks who 'add money to money and by fawning seek after the fortunes of the matrons whose purses they squeeze' and become richer than they had been when they were laymen.[35] Men are eager to make money out of their imitation asceticism. Seeking unjust profits, they make Christianity a cloak for fraud: they live as poor men, but die rich with purses well filled, and the family wealth is increased rather than diminished. There are even people who tell stories about their fights with demons to excite admiration and thus extract money from the ignorant.[36] Even if Jerome's descriptions of the actual situation have to be taken with a grain of salt, as he had his own reasons to fulminate against his fellow (ascetic) clerics in Rome,[37] these stories still make clear the potential of making a profit out of one's ecclesiastical status, without which the stories would not have been rhetorically plausible for the contemporary audience.

The inheritances left by ascetics and members of the clergy to their relatives and to the Church also caused problems. Ambrose narrates the case of a member of the clergy who left his wealth to his brother and sister. It seems that initially the idea was that the Church would have been one of the beneficiaries but the relatives of the deceased had objected. Thus, a new deal had been struck, with Ambrose as a mediator, whereby the entire property went to the brother with *fideicommissum* on behalf of the sister, and the Church agreed to withdraw

---

[33] Ambrosius of Milan, *On the Duties of the Clergy*, 3.9.58: 'hereditates continentiae atque gravitatis simulatione captatae' with 1.30.150.

[34] Jerome, *Letters*, 52.5–6: 'negotiatorem clericum, et ex inope divitem et ex ignobili gloriosum, quasi quandam pestem fuge'.

[35] Jerome, *Letters*, 60.11: 'Alii nummum addant nummo, et marsuppium suffocantes matronarum opes venentur obsequiis, sint ditiores monachi quam fuerant saeculares.'

[36] Jerome, *Letters*, 125.16 and 125.9.

[37] Hunter, *Marriage, Celibacy*, esp. pp. 208–10. See also J. Curran, 'Jerome and the Sham Christians of Rome', *Journal of Ecclesiastical History* 48 (1997), pp. 213–29.

all claims to the property.[38] Augustine was obliged to give sermons in his own defence in cases where he declined to accept inheritances for the Church. In one of these cases Ianuarius, a presbyter and a member of Augustine's monastic community, had disinherited his children, wanting to leave his wealth to the Church. He had a son and a daughter who also embraced the ascetical life. The children disputed the will, while disagreeing with each other. As his parishioners asked for an explanation why Augustine was giving up the claim for the inheritance, he referred to Ianuarius' position as someone who in fact should not have any personal property at all, lamenting the situation ('He made a will, he instituted heirs. O the pain caused by such a people') and writing of the inheritance as 'bitter fruits'. Moreover, Augustine was unwilling to enter into a legal dispute, since he worried about the image of the Church if it got involved in a quarrel about money.[39]

Even if precautions were taken, Augustine personally had to answer the accusation that his clergy and he himself were attached to 'sordid greed' (*pecuniae turpissimus appetitus*). He had to admit that indeed he 'seems not to have left riches behind, but to come to riches', as his patrimony is reckoned to be only one-twentieth of the wealth of the Church of Hippo that he was administering. He calls God to be his witness that neither he nor Alypius, his friend and fellow-bishop in Tagaste, is 'defiled by love for money' in their administration of the affairs of the church; furthermore, this management is only a burden for them.[40] Augustine's position as a bishop, exercising his office and advising people in actual circumstances, can also be seen when he warns Laetus to give away the family wealth as alms. This kind of property should be given to his mother and members of the household. Even as an ascetic seeking poverty, his duty is to provide for his family. The same attitude is apparent in Augustine's disapproving reaction to Ecdicia's giving away the family wealth to wandering monks and stripping her son of his patrimony, and in Paula the Elder's preferring her children to the poor in the distribution of her wealth. The monastic rules of Basil of Caesarea pay very precise attention to the practicalities involved in

---

[38]   Ambrose, *Letters*, 24.7.

[39]   Augustine, *Sermons*, 355.3: 'Testamentum fecit, heredes instituit. O dolor illius societatis! ... Sed Ecclesiam scripsit heredem. Nolo munera ista, non amo amaritudinis fructum ... Filia ipsius in monasterio feminarum est; filius ipsius in monasterio virorum est.' See also Augustine, *Sermons*, 356.4 and 7 on the cases of Faustinus and Heraclius the deacons, and Jerome, *Letters*, 125.10.

[40]   Augustine, *Letters*, 126.7–9: 'non divitias dimisisse, sed ad divitias videor venisse'; 'nulla nos cupiditate pecuniae in rebus ecclesiasticis sordidari'.

bequeathing the family wealth.[41] Charity is to be practised with proper rules, not forgetting family obligations, duties and traditional values, that is, the proper *pietas*.

Ecclesiastical offices combined with asceticism offered good opportunities to collect money as alms, donations and legacies for high living. Taking care of the affairs of a wealthy local church would ensure a good income for the bishop. Indeed, Jerome saw the reason behind the decision made by the Council of Nicaea – that a bishop should not be translated from one see to another – as directed against the greed that was manifested when bishops wanted to exchange poorer dioceses for richer ones. When he claims that the financial factors are decisive, Jerome reveals his own opinion and maybe also his own experience of the reasons behind such moves in his own time.[42]

The case of Antoninus, Bishop of Fussala, shows that these considerations were not only abstract threats but were also prompted by actual problems. When he was a young boy, Antoninus and his mother and stepfather had been received into the monastic settlement of Augustine in Hippo. They lacked even their daily food. Much later, some coincidences led to Antoninus' appointment as bishop of a small town while still quite young. 'The poorest of monks became a bishop', as Augustine commented. However, becoming a bishop was not enough to satisfy Antoninus, who soon started to oppress the inhabitants and extract money and various kinds of property for himself and his allies, and build a beautiful house in Fussala.[43] The case is certainly not a standard one, but rather an extreme example, and this is why we know about it. Moreover, Antoninus was not experienced enough to accept a less conspicuous and slower manner of enhancing his wealth and status. Still, the case of Antoninus shows the possibilities of social and economic ascent that were opened up for even poorer people who adopted the ascetical lifestyle.

The financial profits that accrued due to asceticism were usually of rather a more modest nature. Augustine points out that there are many people, slaves, freedmen, persons about to be freed by their masters, peasants, artisans and plebeian labourers who aim for the monastic life not because they want to

---

[41]   Augustine, *Letters*, 243.12 and 262.4–5; Jerome, *Letters*, 108.6; Basil of Caesarea, *Shorter Rules*, 92 and 94; Basil of Caesarea, *Longer Rules*, 9.

[42]   Jerome, *Letters*, 69.5, with *Council of Nikaea I, Canon* 15 (325 CE). In fact, Jerome here refers to Athanasius' first oration against the Arians (Athanasius, *The Second Apology*, 1.6), which links the changing of the see (by the Arian Eusebius) to the greatness and wealth of the cities in question.

[43]   Augustine, *Letters*, 20*, esp. 2, 5–6 and 31 ('ex monacho pauperrimo episcopus'). See also Augustine, *Letters*, 209 for the same case.

serve God, but in order to run away from a poor and laborious life, and to be fed and clothed. Augustine repeatedly points out that these recruits too are to be taken in. However, he holds it unacceptable if they later complain and ask what the leaving of their former lives profited them if they still have to toil like common workmen.[44] Indeed, some of the sisters in Hippo sought from the monastery those things they could not have outside it, since their poverty before entering the monastery was so great that they were unable to secure even the bare necessities of life.[45]

Stories about Egyptian ascetics refer to similar kinds of situations and some interesting anecdotes are told in *Apophthegmata Patrum*: a certain Cario had left his family for the desert, but when the country was attacked by famine, his children and wife followed him into the ascetic life. The implication here is that there was more food in the 'desert' than in the villages.[46] The ascetic or monastic careers were among the only possible ways for less well-off people to exchange their earlier professions for something else and thus to enhance their previous social standing or at least to survive during difficult times. Paradoxically, the ascetic lifestyle would have ensured better life conditions for the poorest in society.

This can be seen especially in the cases of slaves and servants. Ideologically the expansion of kinship ties to include all humanity was essential for the ascetics. One of the central ways of proclaiming one's new awareness of the divine reality was to treat one's former subjects as equals. According to Gregory of Nyssa, the first sign of the new lifestyle of his mother Emmelia was that she began to regard her slaves and servants as if they were her sisters and belonged to the same rank as herself.[47] It is unclear if these servants actually adopted ascetic practices themselves. However, many writers mention that the elite ascetics took their servants with them when they retired from the world. Jerome is particularly bitter towards this luxury.[48] On the other hand, Jerome urged Eustochium to accept maidservants with her when she began her virgin life, but warned her not to behave towards them with a sense of superiority. She should be aware that there were those who simulated interest in the virginal life in order to be free of their servitude. Paula had kept her servants with her at her ascetic community

---

[44] Augustine, *On the Works of Monks*, 22 (25) and 25 (32).

[45] Augustine, *Letters*, 211.5.

[46] *Apophthegmata patrum*, Cario 2. In *Apophthegmata patrum*, Arsenius 36 we hear of an unnamed former shepherd, who had lived his life with much toil and trouble, but now has retired to a quiet *cella*. See also *History of the Monks in Egypt*, 2.12.

[47] Gregory of Nyssa, *Life of Macrina*, 7.

[48] Jerome, *Letters*, 130.19 with 108.20.

144 *Children and Asceticism in Late Antiquity*

in Rome and Jerome claims not only that they had assumed the ascetic lifestyle, but also that Paula had changed the status of the slaves and servants of her small household to that of spiritual brothers and sisters.[49]

It is difficult to assess how autonomous the decisions of those 'servants who would follow the example of their mistress' to asceticism would have been, as Augustine expects the servants of Demetrias to do. In another context Augustine indeed claimed that some slave-owners freed their slaves on condition that they would enter monasteries and would thus contribute to their former masters spiritually.[50] The *Canons of Athanasius* even decreed that if there were a rich woman of faith without a virgin daughter, she should dedicate a servant who loved virginity as a home ascetic.[51] For a slave, the decision to make the vow of chastity could seldom have been autonomous.

It was plausible for the hagiographical writers to assume that servants followed their masters in asceticism. The stories of Melania the Younger and her mother Albina include many references to their followers of servile origin. We are told, for example, that they settled into their new life with 15 eunuchs and 60 virgins, both free and enslaved. Likewise, when Olympias founded a monastery in Constantinople, it is told that she initially filled it with 50 of her own chambermaids.[52] If these texts reflect actual practices, it may be assumed that the inclination to asceticism of these recruits was not always a necessary criterion.

Taken as a whole, ascetic communities comprised some of the very few spaces in which the different strata of society were expected to interact daily with each other on a nearly equal standing. This ideal was not always met, as can be deduced from Augustine's rules for the nuns of the monastery he had founded: the elite members of the community were not to have contempt for their poor sisters, nor should the lower-status members boast of their 'associating with those whom they did not dare to approach outside'. There were, in fact, people who wanted to enter monastic life in order to be honoured by those who had formerly despised them.[53] Jerome gave Paula special praise for having sisters from all the

---

[49]   Jerome, *Letters*, 108.2 and 22.29: 'Si quae ancillae sunt comites propositi tui, ne erigaris adversus eas, ne infleris ut domina. Unum sponsum habere coepitis ... cur mensa diversa sit?'

[50]   Augustine, *Letters*, 150: 'Imitentur eam multae famulae dominam, ignobiles nobilem'; Augustine, *On the Works of Monks*, 22(25).

[51]   *Canons of Pseudo-Athanasius*, 104 (Arabic text).

[52]   Palladius, *The Lausiac History*, 61.6; Gerontius, *Life of Melania* (Latina), 22. On Olympias: *Life of Olympias*, 6. See also *History of the Monks in Egypt*, 22.2; and Theodoret of Cyrrhus, *Religious History*, 29.2–3.

[53]   Augustine, *Letters*, 211.6: 'Nec erigant cervicem quia sociantur eis, ad quas foris accedere non audebant'; Augustine, *On the Works of Monks*, 22(25).

levels of society in her monasteries in Bethlehem, praying and singing together and dressing in the same way. Moreover, Paula did not allow ascetics of noble background to have attendants who had belonged to their former households so that they would not return to their old habits, that is, to treating them as their inferiors.[54] There were members of different social backgrounds living in close contact with each other and it was necessary to prevent the women from returning to their former social roles.

At least ideologically, the former slaves were turned into ascetics and members of the spiritual family. Even if social roles were not always much altered, an ascetic community would mean at least partial freedom from servile obligations and the slaves were aware of that too. Basil's *Longer Rules* decree that bound slaves who flee to monasteries for refuge should be returned to their masters, but that the owners are to be persuaded to let the slaves continue in the ascetic life. An anonymous Eastern text of the first part of the fourth century warns the owners of slaves not to hinder those who are eager to live in chastity.[55] Actual cases are hard to find, but Theodoret of Cyrrhus mentions an unmarried girl in the service of an intemperate former officer who ran away from him and her family to enter a convent. After a series of miraculous events, she was able to remain there.[56] The last-mentioned case also shows the vague status of many of those in service. They were not in the strictest sense slaves, but were very much at the mercy of their patrons and landlords since they belonged to the large and undefined mass of *humiliores* of Late Antiquity.[57]

The overall implication is clear: by the early fifth century, at least in Rome and Northern Africa, the regions most influenced by ascetic ideals in the Western Empire, being a nun or monk was a worthwhile aspiration. Asceticism could mean not only a means of survival and enhanced living conditions for ordinary people, but also, most importantly, a rise in status. One question, however, is worth asking: how would asceticism have fitted with the lifestyle of the upper levels of society, their status and the nobility of their lineages?

---

[54] Jerome, *Letters*, 108.20. For social equality as a monastic virtue, see also John Chrysostom, *Against the Opponents of Monastic Life*, 3.11.

[55] Basil of Caesarea, *Longer Rules*, 11; *Anonymous Homily on Virginity*, 11–12.

[56] Theodoret of Cyrrhus, *Religious History*, 9.12.

[57] For the *honestiores* and *humiliores* in Late Antiquity and the difference between the latter and slaves, see e.g. C. Whittaker, 'Circe's Pigs: From Slavery to Serfdom in the Later Roman world', in M. Finley (ed.), *Classical Slavery* (London, 1987), esp. pp. 101–3, 108–14.

Chapter 7

Progeny, Reputation and Memory

Illustrious and chaste virgin Eunomia, outstanding in nobility, fertile in writings, altogether worthy of the esteem of the entire world.[1]

Better than this [i.e., to have children] is childlessness with virtue, for in the memory of virtue is immortality, because it is known both by God and by men.[2]

In what follows I shall investigate the usefulness of asceticism in acquiring social capital during one's lifetime, and in ensuring the transfer of privileges, name, memory and various family traditions to generations to come among the elites of Late Antiquity.[3] The first section shows how asceticism and chastity repeatedly come into view in connection with certain families: celibacy was, indeed, hereditary and formed an important part of the family heritage for some elite kin groups. The immaterial benefits of asceticism for individuals and the family group are analysed in the following sections; asceticism as a family tradition was a way of proclaiming family piety and a constituent of power and privileges in Christian communities. Ideas of *nobilitas* and *fama* were associated with asceticism and these were propagated and used as the superior way of attaining renown, nobility and immortal remembrance both on earth and among the members of the family of Christ. Indeed, the reputation of the ascetics spread throughout Christendom and an ascetic in the family would further contribute to the family status and to the perpetuation of the memory of the whole kin group and its members.

Family Traditions of Asceticism

As I have noted earlier, in many cases children followed or were expected to follow in their parents' footsteps into an ascetic life. Among some ascetics, this already seems to have been part of their patrimony. Of the children of Paula

---

[1] *Anthologia latina* 768, 1–4: 'Fulgens Eunomia decensque virgo / pollens nobilis et fecunda libris / et totus venerabilis per orbem.'

[2] *Wisdom of the Salomo* 4.1: 'κρείσσων ἀτεκνία μετὰ ἀρετῆς ἀθανασία γάρ ἐστιν ἐν μνήμῃ αὐτῆς ὅτι καὶ παρὰ θεῷ γινώσκεται καὶ παρὰ ἀνθρώποις' (second century BCE–first century CE).

[3] See also Figure 1, p. 41 above.

the Elder, Blesilla was a dedicated widow; Eustochium was a virgin; Paulina was married to Pammachius, who remained a chaste widower after Paulina's death; and her granddaughter and namesake, Paula the Younger, was dedicated to virginity.[4] Asella and her sister Marcella, both virgins, belonged to the ascetic community of Albina (the Elder) and her widowed daughter Marcella.[5] Moreover, the elder Albina was the great-great-aunt of Paula the Younger and the great-aunt of Albina the Younger, who was the daughter-in-law of Melania the Elder and mother of the younger Melania.[6] Thus, Marcella the widow was a relative of both Melania the Younger and Paula the Younger, who were second cousins. Melania the Younger, who is reported to have persuaded her husband Pinian to chastity, was the granddaughter of the elder Melania, who in turn persuaded Apronianus, the husband of her niece Avita, to live in chastity with his wife. Their virgin daughter, Eunomia, was a second cousin of Melania the Younger. The widowed mother of Melania the Younger, the younger Albina, also joined the community. Paulinus of Nola, in turn, was a relative of Melania the Elder.[7] Even if this family group is perhaps the largest such network of ascetics, it is not the only case in which asceticism was clearly a familial tendency. In the West, for example, Salvina, Demetrias and Geruchia were all surrounded by older ascetic relatives, and in the East it is claimed that Olympias was followed by her niece and namesake, and by three other relatives, Elisanthia, Palladia and Martyria, who were siblings.[8]

---

[4]   Blesilla: Jerome, *Letters*, 39; Eustochium: e.g. Jerome, *Letters*, 22; Paulina: Jerome, *Letters*, 66.3; Paula the Younger: Jerome, *Letters*, 107.3.

[5]   Jerome, *Letters*, 24.2 and 4; 32; 45.7: 'Saluta matrem Albinam, sororesque Marcellas'; *Letters*, 127, esp. 2 and 4–5. Thus, there were two Marcellas, one the widowed daughter of Albina, another a virgin and sister of Asella (against e.g. Krumeich, '*Hieronymus*', Stemmata 1; J. Martindale (ed.), *The Prosopography of the Later Roman Empire, Vol. 2, A.D. 395–527* (Cambridge, 1980), p. 542 (Marcella 2); Desmulliez et al., *Prosopographie chrétienne*, 2.2, pp. 1357–62 (Marcella 2)).

[6]   A. Yarborough, 'Christianization in the Fourth Century: The Example of Women', *Church History* 45 (1976), p. 150; Krumeich, '*Hieronymus*', Stemmata 1 and 2.2; Krumeich, however, presents Laeta as Marcella's daughter.

[7]   Gerontius, *Life of Melania* (Greek), esp. 1 and 6; Palladius, *The Lausiac History*, 61.2. Avita: Palladius, *The Lausiac History*, 54.4. Melania the Younger and Eunomia: Paulinus of Nola, *Poems*, 21.60–73. Albina at Nola: Paulinus of Nola, *Poems*, 21.281–5; Paulinus as a relative of Melania: Paulinus of Nola, *Letters*, 19.5.

[8]   Salvina: Jerome, *Letters*, 79.9; Demetrias: Augustine, *On the Good of Widowhood*, 14 (18) and 19 (24) and *Letters*, 188; Jerome, *Letters*, 130, esp. 1–3, 7. Geruchia: Jerome, *Letters*, 123.1 and 123.14. Olympias: *Life of Olympias*, 6. See also Augustine, *Letters*, 111.7. Jerome's sister was also an ascetic: Jerome, *Letters*, 6.2 and 7.4.

Progeny, Reputation and Memory 149

For the members of the ecclesiastical elites, highlighting family tradition and continuity had a role in establishing personal authority. The bishops aspired to being known for their own asceticism and for being surrounded by ascetics. Even if individual family traditions indubitably played an important role in this, the bishops themselves also actively contributed to it. They not only established episcopal monastic communities,[9] but also widened their sphere of sanctity by emphasizing their ascetic and martyred ancestors, and by recruiting ascetics from among their relatives. These connections, moreover, were duly referred to in their texts and preaching in appropriate contexts.

Theodoret of Cyrrhus is a prime example of these tendencies. He programmatically highlights his closeness to ascetic sainthood, depicting his life as an enterprise that continues the spiritual lineage of the local Antiochian ascetics by whom he was educated and whose heir he was. By invoking family stories of his childhood and youth, with the dominating figure of an ascetically minded and saintly mother, he assures his audience that he was acquainted early on with proper values and a certain way of life, and his character and authority are securely embedded in the family tradition.[10] Similarly, Gregory Nazianzen's rhetorical strategy was to create for himself a philosophical family of parents, siblings and spiritual children; Gregory of Nyssa was eager to highlight the spiritual nobility of his ascetic family members; and Basil of Caesarea invoked the memory of his grandmother, Macrina, to support his claim of orthodoxy, stressing that she was responsible for his religious education.[11] Continuity and the existing authentic family heritage were worth pointing out.

In the West, similar tendencies prevailed: Hilary of Arles, for example, highlighted his own nobility, both spiritual and cultural, by linking himself to the *nobilitas* of Honoratus, as his relative, friend and spiritual successor.[12] Ambrose of Milan was especially active in building a spiritual family tradition for his own support. He had a sister, Marcellina, an avowed virgin, and he made sure that this was known to his hearers. Unfortunately, the result of his propagation of sacred widowhood to his more distant relative Juliana, and of virginity to her children,

---

[9]   On the episcopal monastic communities backing the episcopal authority (by Eusebius of Vercelli, Valerian of Aquilea, Augustine of Hippo, Martin of Tours, Epiphanius of Salamis and Porphyry of Gaza), see further Rapp, *Holy Bishops*, pp. 149–52.

[10]   Theodoret of Cyrrhus, *Religious History*, 9.4, 9.9–10, 9.14–15; 13.3, 13.16, 13.18 with Vuolanto, 'A Self-made Living Saint?', pp. 49–65.

[11]   On Gregory Nazianzen, see Vuolanto, 'A Self-made Living Saint?', pp. 58–61 with Elm 'Gregory's Women', esp. pp. 189–91; Gregory of Nyssa, *Life of Macrina, passim*. Basil of Caesarea, *Letters*, 204.6, see also *Letters*, 210.1 and 223.3. 2. Tim. 1:5 seems to serve here as the prototype.

[12]   Hilarius of Arles, *Life of Honoratus*, 16, 23–4, 31–3, 36 and 38.

150 *Children and Asceticism in Late Antiquity*

is not known. On the other hand, this work of persuasion was made public in his treatise *Exhortation to Virginity* and, moreover, he highlighted his status as a relative of the virgin martyr Sotheris, attaching to her the highest nobility, both spiritual and earthly. Augustine acted in a similar way.[13] These claims and activities no doubt added to their prestige as ascetic bishops and members of families of spiritual nobility. Asceticism brought honour and authority in Christian communities and this was well exploited by the ecclesiastical leaders. The case of Glycerius serves as an extreme indication of the alleged potential of an ascetical entourage: as a deacon he gathered virgins around him and designated himself as their patriarch, thus seeking status and prestige in the local Christian community.[14]

In retrospect, the family of Basil the Elder and Emmelia would be a classic example of a family investing in ascetic values and an ecclesiastical career. Emmelia was the daughter of a martyr and Basil the Elder was the son of a Christian couple who suffered during the persecutions. Macrina, their daughter, introduced asceticism into their household, pledged herself to virginity and became a renowned leader of a female ascetic community. When Emmelia was widowed, she began to practise asceticism under the guidance of her daughter. Basil of Caesarea, a brother of Macrina, became a bishop and leader of ascetic communities; another brother, Naucratius, died in a hunting accident after he had withdrawn from the world. When their brother, Gregory of Nyssa, was made a bishop, Gregory and his wife continued to live together in chastity; their sister, Theosebeia, was a dedicated virgin; and lastly, another brother, Peter of Sebaste, became a bishop. However, on the death of Emmelia in around 370 CE, their four anonymous sisters led secular lives in 'excellent marriages' arranged by their mother, and Gregory was married (even if he had already adopted an ascetic lifestyle) and was still living a secular life. Only after Basil's need for support was he ordained and elected Bishop of Nyssa, probably in 371, and at about the same time Peter was ordained a priest. It seems that the death of their mother and the election of Basil to the see of Caesarea (370) resulted in at least a partial shift in

---

[13] Ambrose, *On Virgins*, 1–3 (Marcellina); Ambrose, *On Virgins*, 3.7.39 (Sotheris); Ambrose, *Exhortation to Virginity*, 12.82 (Juliana and Sotheris). See also Ambrose, *On the Death of His Brother Satyrus*, 53 and letters to Marcellina: Ambrose, *Letters*, 76.1 and *Letters outside the Collection*, 1. For Augustine's sister as a head of a religious community, see Augustine, *Letters*, 210 and 211, and his nephew as member of Augustine's ascetic community, see Augustine, *Sermons*, 356.3. Augustine was also ready to highlight his mother's piety in any convenient occasion. For the family traditions of ecclesiastical service, often linked with the traditions of asceticism, see also Rapp, *Holy Bishops*, pp. 195–9.

[14] Basil of Caesarea, *Letters*, 169; see also *Letters*, 170 and 171.

Progeny, Reputation and Memory   151

the familial strategies. Basil's brothers were recruited to support Basil's episcopal career as a project of the whole family, and in this way to contribute to the family traditions and honour. Unfortunately, nothing is known of any children whom the four anonymous sisters may have had, but in any case, by this date (as even the youngest child of the family was over 30 years old) the fate of the possible biological continuity of the family was known to the brothers.[15]

Another group of ascetics joining the family tradition consists of children of couples who had made vows of chastity and had withdrawn to ascetic seclusion with their progeny. In these cases the prominence of Gaul is interesting. The sons of Eucherius and Galla joined them in the ascetic community of Lérins and were eventually elected bishops. Auspiciola, daughter of Salvian and Palladia, likewise followed her parents into the ascetic life.[16] The ascetic vow of the daughter of Apronianus and Avita, Eunomia, who was dedicated to chastity and was living with her parents in the ascetic community of Paulinus of Nola, took not place in Gaul, but even here the link exists through the influence of Paulinus, who was a native of Aquitania.[17] Thus, all the cases outside hagiography in which underage children withdraw from the world together with their parents come from Gaul. All this strengthens the case put forward by Richard Bartlett that in Gaul the local aristocracy during the fifth century was much more receptive to the opportunities offered by asceticism and ecclesiastical careers than, for example, in Italy – in spite of the fact that it was especially in Gaul that we also hear of the most persistent opposition to the ascetic ideals.[18] Asceticism was seen

---

[15]   Macrina seems to have started her ascetic 'career' in the late 340s; Naucratius his seclusion around 350, dying some five years later; Emmelia after the mid-350s. Basil embraced asceticism in the early years of the 350s, became a priest in 363 and a bishop in 370; Gregory of Nyssa started his ascetic lifestyle in the late 360s and became a bishop in 371. On the problems of *ex post facto* assuming the existence of asceticism in the household of Emmelia and Basil the Elder, see also Elm, *Virgins*, pp. 81–7 with references to earlier studies. See further Rousseau, 'The Pious Household'; Van Dam, *Families and Friends*, esp. pp. 15–39, 65–73, 99–113; and A. Silvas, *Gregory of Nyssa: The Letters. Introduction, Translation, and Commentary* (Boston, 2007), pp. 21–9, 98–100 (esp. for Theosebeia).

[16]   Salvian, *Letters*, 4; Paulinus of Nola, *Letters*, 39.1–2. Paulinus hoped that the children of Aper and Amanda, who had set up an ascetic home community in Gaul, would also continue to live with their parents in chastity: Paulinus of Nola, *Letters*, 51.

[17]   Palladius, *The Historia Lausica*, 41.5; Paulinus of Nola, *Poems*, 21.66–71. See also Jerome, *Letters*, 117: the (imaginary) case of a widow and virgin living together set in Gaul.

[18]   R. Bartlett, 'Aristocracy and Asceticism: The Letters of Ennodius and the Gallic and Italian Churches', in R.W. Mathisen and D. Shanzer (eds), *Society and Culture in Late Antique Gaul: Revisiting the Sources* (Aldershot, 2001), pp. 201–6. For the resistance in Gaul, see above, pp. 59–60 with notes.

a beguiling alternative that allowed the local elites to form an aristocratic and noble lineage outside the traditional limits of the *cursus honorum*.

In the hagiographical sources there are numerous references to ascetic family traditions. In the earliest tradition connected to Pachomius in Egypt, we hear of his older ascetic brother John and also of an anonymous sister's son, who was expelled from the *koinonia*. His sister became the mother and superior of a women's community. The mother of the major Pachomian figures Theodore and his brother Paphnouti is also reported to have entered monastic life to stay close to her sons. There was also a family monastery headed by a certain Petronius who joined the Pachomian community, bringing his father, a brother, sisters and other relatives with him.[19] Antony the Great sent his sister to become a member of a community of virgins and she did not have any say in the matter.[20] In the later lives of the ascetic saints it became commonplace to surround the main protagonist with ascetic relatives. Thus, for example, the struggles of Honoratus with his father did not prevent one of his brothers from joining him freely in the ascetic life.[21] Sozomen records that Ajax of Gaza lived with his wife in chastity and dedicated two of his three sons to God, but the third he married off. In this way Ajax selected one of the children to ensure the biological succession and the others to gain spiritual fruits. Zeno, the brother of Ajax, was also an ascetic having renounced marriage in his youth.[22]

---

[19]   *Life of Pachomius* (Sahidic version), frg. 1.3 (Pachomius and John); frg. 6.24 (sister's son); *Life of Pachomius* (first Greek version), 32 (sister of Pachomius), 37 (Theodore's and Paphnuti's mother); *Life of Pachomius* (Bohairic version), 19 and 38 (brother of Pachomius), 56 (Petronius and his family). For the early Christian asceticism as a series of family affairs, see also Elm, *Virgins*, esp. pp. 291–2 with notes.

[20]   Athanasius, *Life of Antony*, 3. See also Caesarius, Bishop of Arles and his sister Caesaria: *Life of Caesarius of Arles*, 1.35.

[21]   Hilarius of Arles, *Life of Honoratus*, 9, with Pseudo-Athanasius, *Life of Syncletica*, 5 and 11 (Syncletica and one of his brothers); Palladius, *The Lausiac History*, 11.1 (Abba Ammonius had five ascetic siblings); Palladius, *The Lausiac History*, 1.4 (Abba Isidore had two virgin sisters); Theodoret of Cyrrhus, *Religious History*, 4.3 (Marianos had his two nephews in his monastery); Callinicus, *Life of Hypatius*, 53 (Hypatius' sister and her daughter were dedicated widows); *Life of Eupraxia*, 2.8 (fifth or sixth century CE: Eupraxia (Euphrasia) entered a convent with her mother).

[22]   Sozomen, *Ecclesiastical History*, 7.28. In view of this, it is curious that John Cassian, in telling a story of Patermuthius who entered a monastery with his eight-year-old son, remarks that this is contrary to custom (John Cassian, *Institutions*, 4.27.2–3). The comment of John should perhaps be interpreted in the context of the discussions of free will (see Brown, *Body and Society*, pp. 420–23 on Cassian and 'Augustinians' on concupiscence and free will).

Progeny, Reputation and Memory 153

The unpredictable turns of fate due to demographic realities could easily ruin the plans of parents, and children were needed for the secular life. Augustine was involved in the case of a widowed mother who had pledged her daughter to virginity. However, as her other children later died, the widow wanted to rescind the vow.[23] Changes in parental strategies are also reflected in the monastic rules of Basil: when parents want to dedicate their children as a *votum* to be brought up in the monastery, two precepts have to be followed. First, the children have to be received with witnesses present in order to avoid subsequent malevolent talk and, second, children who are received should not immediately be counted as full members of the community as the vow of virginity could be taken only when children were old enough for independent decision making, again in the presence of witnesses, to avoid charges of kidnapping. The implication here is that there were parents who later wanted to take their children away from the ascetic community, arguing that the children were coerced by the ascetics to stay. Such controversies were not rare in the early medieval West and a complex web of statutes, laws and canons tried to regulate the phenomenon.[24]

Later, in the legislation of Justinian, this phenomenon is recognized and parents were forbidden from removing their children from monasteries once they had adopted a monastic life. A contemporary hagiographic story by Cyril of Scythopolis offers a glimpse of the possible reasons for such behaviour, although it concerns uncles, not parents: when the parents of Sabas moved away, they left their son and property to be looked after by his maternal uncle, Hermias. As the boy was unhappy due to the evil character of Hermias' wife, the paternal uncle took the boy. However, the uncles quarrelled about his upbringing and family wealth, and put him in a monastery when he was about eight years old. Later the uncles arrived at an agreement and tried to remove him from the monastery to marry him off, but Sabas did not agree and he was able to stay.[25]

In many families in Late Antiquity the ascetic life itself formed part of the family tradition, to contribute to its renown and continuity. Parents were willing to give their children to chastity and thus to endanger the biological continuity of the family, although there were usually other siblings alive when children were dedicated to virginity. Sometimes, however, the high rates of mortality rendered these considerations void. Parents tried to reduce the possibility of such

---

[23] Augustine, *Letters*, 3*.1.

[24] Basil of Caesarea, *Longer Rules*, 15.1 and 4. Benedict's Rule refers to both drawing up a document and witnesses when oblates are to be taken in to monasteries (*Rule of Benedict*, 59). For the early medieval world, see de Jong, *In Samuel's Image*, pp. 23–55.

[25] *Novellae Iustiniani*, 123.41; Cyril of Scythopolis, *The Lives of the Monks of Palestine*, Life of Sabas 1–2.

154 Children and Asceticism in Late Antiquity

accidents by careful planning, but were not always successful. In the face of such risks, what made asceticism a tempting choice for the individuals themselves and for their offspring? How was it possible to ensure familial continuity by means of asceticism?

Familial and Spiritual *Nobilitas* in the Ascetic Discourse

The concept of *nobilitas* appears frequently in the narratives of early Christian authors attached to the very persons who posed the threat to the succession of earthly *nobilitas*, namely the ascetics, who had refused to reproduce this virtue in their offspring. Whereas *pietas* was a personal virtue, ideally guarding the proper behaviour in all familial relationships and attainable by people at all levels of society, *nobilitas* was a virtue shared and renewed by a kin group, and it was reserved for the most distinguished members of society in the Roman Empire. Although being noble implied that a person was also a cultivated individual, active in public affairs and possessing superior personal qualities, a person's claim to nobility was essentially based on the high offices held by ancestors and current family members. This idea was established as early as the end of the Roman Republic, but as late as the fourth century, a person was understood to belong to the nobility only if he or she could boast consular ancestors or belonged to the senatorial aristocracy, or at least if the family was granted the right to the title of *illustris* which was linked to a number of military and civic offices.[26]

For the nobility, it was of the greatest importance to increase personal honour and renown in connection with the family *nobilitas*. For the ecclesiastical writers, in turn, it was essential to renounce the value of earthly honour once and for all – at least when this suited the argument. The immortality due to honour and earthly glory is not for ascetic Christians, even if the ecclesiastical writers identified it as one of the most important values for the traditional elite culture. Gregory of Nyssa crystallizes this attitude when he claims that there is nothing enviable in earthly honour, even if many strive for it: 'The mortal remains mortal whether he is honoured or not.' He connects these honours to wealth: 'What good does the possessor of many acres gain?'[27] Augustine claims that even the most virtuous of Roman families, such as the *Scaevolae*, *Curtii* and *Decii*, were surpassed in virtue by the *pietas* of the martyrs. The old Romans could not but

---

[26]   Salzman, 'Competing Claims', pp. 359–61 with further references.

[27]   Gregory of Nyssa, *On Virginity*, 4.3: 'Διαμένει γὰρ θνητὸς ὁ θνητός, κἂν τιμᾶται κἂν μή. Ἤ τὸ πολλὰ πλέθρα κεκτῆσθαι γῆς.'

love earthly glory, by which they wished to live on even after death, since they sought safety and immortality not in heaven, but on earth. Thus, they placed their hopes not in eternal life, but in the succession of the mortals.[28] Earthly renown (*fama*) is attached to the striving for earthly immortality and inevitable death in the same way as the need for offspring was seen as the inevitable result of the fear of death and the urge for survival.

In the Late Antique texts concerning Christians, spiritual nobility is attached almost invariably to people with explicit links to asceticism. The epitaph of Sextus Petronius Probus is one of the exceptions: after listing the traditional honour of his career, the nobility and honour granted in 'the service of Christ' is put above the high offices held by him and his ancestors.[29] Claudius Postumus Dardanus, ex-prefect of Gaul, is another case. He had taken charge honourably of his double prefecture, but is, according to Jerome, 'still more honoured in Christ' after he had retired from public life. He is 'more illustrious in Christ's charity than in the dignity of this world' and 'the most noble of Christians and the most Christian among nobles'.[30] Earthly rank and achievements are ultimately subordinated to spiritual *nobilitas*.

This nobility was associated equally with women and men. The rhetorical strategies used are clearly visible in the funeral orations by Gregory Nazianzen for his family members, where Gregory claims the highest nobility for his family – and therefore also for himself – by superficially shunning it. Thus, according to him, the only genuine form of noble birth that his mother Nonna recognized was piety and the knowledge of the origins and goal of human life in Christ.[31] His sister Gorgonia, in turn, is claimed to have derived her reputation (δοκιμεῖν) – her piety, her good way of life and her happy death with better hopes – from her parents. According to Gregory, these qualities are not easily attained by those who are proud of their lineage (γένεια). Her nobility therefore derives not from the bloodline, but from her preservation of the image of Christ in herself.[32] Gregory further claims that his father, Gregory the Elder, was from an unrenowned family, not well suited to *pietas*. He is described

---

[28]   Augustine, *City of God*, 5.14.

[29]   *Corpus inscriptionum Latinarum*, vol. 6, 1756 with Salzman, 'Competing Claims', pp. 364–5.

[30]   Jerome, *Letters*, 129.1: 'Christianorum nobilissime, nobilium christianissime'; Jerome, *Letters*, 129.8: 'vir erudissime, in duplicis prefecturae honore transacto, nunc in Christo honoratior'; Augustine, *Letters*, 187.1: 'frater dilectissime Dardane, illustrior mihi in caritate Christi, quam in huius saeculi dignitate'.

[31]   Gregory Nazianzen, *Oration 18*, 8.

[32]   Gregory Nazianzen, *Oration 8*, 6–8, 20. Gorgonia is as near to a virgin as a widow can be. See also Van Dam, *Families and Friends*, p. 96.

156 *Children and Asceticism in Late Antiquity*

as having endured the loss of his mother and his property for the sake of the true inheritance in heaven, and to have accepted dishonours more readily than others accepted the greatest honours. However, Gregory the Elder was a wealthy local notable, a curial and later a bishop. In fact, in another oration Gregory Nazianzen mentions his parents as the 'Abraham and Sarah of these latter days', known and honoured by all.[33]

For the ascetics, the culture appreciative of family *nobilitas* and striving for personal honour is strongly present alongside the Christian ideas of humility, equality and spiritual reward. The claim to superior nobility was one of the most pervasive literary devices in ascetic discourse. A man who has learned that his citizenship is in heaven is not prey to longings for ambition or glory. According to John Chrysostom, the ascetic life is nobler than high birth and family dignity, and thus ascetics themselves are noble and glorious.[34] These ideas are found frequently in the writings of Gregory of Nyssa on his family members: Macrina and Emmelia, when they entered the ascetic life, 'had cast away all vain desires for honour and glory, all vanity, arrogance and the like. Continence was their luxury, and obscurity their glory'. They could easily dispense with all the things people eagerly pursue in this life. At the same time, however, Gregory of Nyssa has Macrina remark that her family members boast of being well born and of a noble family. The reputation (ἡ φήμη) of their father, the elder Basil, did not extend beyond Pontus, but he was satisfied with this renown in his own land. However, it is God's grace and the prayers of his parents, not his personal qualities, that have made Gregory 'renowned in cities and peoples and nations'. Gregory applies the epithet 'the common glory of the family' both for his brother Basil of Caesarea and for his sister Macrina, and the death of his 'world renowned' brother is referred to as 'the common grief of his native land and the whole world'.[35]

In the Western texts that propagate asceticism for the traditional Roman nobility, there seems at first sight to be a new interpretation of *nobilitas* as a value connected to personal achievements and not to family pedigree.

---

[33] Gregory Nazianzen, *Oration 18*, 5; Gregory Nazianzen, *Oration 8*, 4.

[34] John Chrysostom, *Letters to Theodore*, 1.14 and 2.3–5; John Chrysostom, *Against the Opponents of Monastic Life*, 2.5–7, 3.6–7, 20–21.

[35] Gregory of Nyssa, *Life of Macrina*, 11.21–7: 'ἥ τε τῶν ματαίων ἐπιθυμία, τιμῆς τε καὶ δόξης καὶ τύφου καὶ ὑπερηφανίας καὶ πάντων τῶν τοιούτων, ἐκβέβλητο· τρυφὴ δὲ ἦν ἡ ἐγκράτεια καὶ δόξα τό μὴ γινώσκεσθαι'; Renown of Basil the Elder, Gregory and Macrina: Gregory of Nyssa, *Life of Macrina*, 21.9–17: 'πόλεσι καὶ δήμοις καὶ ἔθνεσιν ὀνομαστὸς'; 14.25–26: 'τὸ κοινὸν τῆς γενεᾶς καλόν' (on Basil); 22.18–19: 'τὸ κοινὸν καύχημα τῆς γενεᾶς' (on Macrina); Death of Basil: 'ὁ κατὰ πᾶσαν τὴν οἰκουμένην ὀνομαστὸς'; 'κοινὴ πένθυς ἀφορμὴ τῇ πατρίδι καὶ οἰκουμένῃ γενόμενος'. See also Rousseau, 'The Pious Household', esp. pp. 172 and 186 with Elm, *Virgins*, pp. 93–4.

Progeny, Reputation and Memory 157

The stock claim was that ascetics who were part of the earthly nobility were still nobler if they were part of the ascetic family of Christ: Paula the Elder, for example, was 'of noble line, but much nobler in sanctity' according to Jerome, and for Augustine, the young virgin Demetrias was 'noble by birth, but nobler still by sanctity'.[36] In highlighting the great efforts of female ascetics to shun their earthly families, nobility and wealth, the ecclesiastical writers repeatedly point out their noble lineage. Paula the Elder's connection to the most distinguished Roman families and ancient heroes, such as Agamemnon, Aeneas, Scipio, Paulus, the *Julii, Gracchi* and *Toxotii* are noted; due attention is paid to the background of Demetrias with illustrious parents and ancestors in the families of the *Anicii, Probi* and *Olybrii*; the pedigrees of Melania the Elder, Furia, Marcella and Eustochium with consuls and praetorian prefects are dutifully highlighted and elaborated upon.[37]

In the case of men, the same comparison between earthly and heavenly *nobilitas* persists. However, the arguments refer less to illustrious family backgrounds and more to the earthly status of the ascetics themselves as members of the earthly nobility. Writing on the death of Publicola, son of Melania the Elder and father of Melania the Younger, Augustine regrets that he did not 'exchange the glory of earthly affairs for that of resurrection', as he continued as a senator and did not retire to become a monk. By mocking his earthly status, Augustine makes sure it is paid proper attention and, ultimately, describes him as a person who had built a house in heaven by his almsgiving and humility. He also argues that Donatus, a retired civil servant about to enter religious life, would offer fruit for Christ 'more worthy of eternal and heavenly glory than of transitory and worldly distinction'.[38] This rhetoric was also used by Paulinus of Nola. He claimed that Pammachius was made truly noble and worthy of 'the heavenly senate' (*caeli senatus*) by his extensive almsgiving after

---

[36] Paula the Elder: Jerome, *Letters*, 108.1: 'nobilis genere sed multo nobilior sanctitate'; Demetrias: Augustine, *Letters*, 150: 'nobilis genere, sed nobilior sanctitate' with Jerome, *Letters*, 130. See also Pelagius, *Letter to Demetrias*, 22; Constantius, *Life of Germanus of Auxerre*, 4.22; and Ambrose, *On Virgins*, 1.11.65.

[37] Paula the Elder: Jerome, *Letters*, 108.3–4, 33; Demetria: Jerome, *Letters*, 130.1–4; Pelagius, *Letter to Demetrias*, 1, 11, 14, 22, 30; Augustine, *Letters*, 150 with *Letters*, 130.1–2 (412 CE) on Proba; Paulinus of Nola, *Letters*, 29.6–7 on Melania the Elder; Jerome, *Letters*, 54.6 on Furia; Jerome, *Letters*, 127.1, on Marcella; Jerome, *Letters*, 66.3, on Eustochium, with Jerome, *Letters*, 79 on Nebridius and *Letters*, 107.13 on Paula the Younger.

[38] Augustine, *Letters*, 94.2: 'non ... ut de conversationis gloria transisset ad gloriam resurrectionis'; Augustine, *Letters*, 112.1: 'ut fructus ei afferas aeterna et coelesti gloria quam temporali et terreno praeconio digniores'. See also Augustine, *Letters*, 218.3.

he began his ascetic life.[39] In his letter to Crispianus, a rich young man from a distinguished family who intended to embark on a military career, Paulinus reminds him that Christ bestows on his soldiers not only the glory of eternal life, but also 'the distinction of the heavenly kingdom and the riches of His inheritance'. He admires his friend Sulpicius Severus, who left his father, his deceased wife's riches, his own consular status and his former friendships. With these arguments, Paulinus also explains his own status and choices in leaving the Senate for the ascetic life.[40]

Most conspicuously, Jerome manages to combine the high appreciation of traditional nobility with the rhetoric of shunning high birth. In playing down the importance of the old *nobilitas* on a textual level, Jerome makes its existence one of the focal points of his argumentation. He boasts that he does not deduce Fabiola's lineage 'from the nobility of the family tradition', but 'from the humility of the Church', not exalting her by stressing her noble line with ancestors such as Quintus Maximus Cunctator and the whole Fabian family.[41] Jerome argues that the consular status of Pammachius is bound to be forgotten, especially, he laments, as the office is now obtained by rustic and savage men or by merely belonging to the army. Jerome does not base his argument on rejecting aristocratic values, but on developing them: Pammachius the ascetic is more than ever 'the glory of the Funian line', 'greatest among the great and very first among the first, leader of the monks'. In rejecting earthly honours and offices, he receives more than he has given and the whole world (*orbis*) marvels at his conduct. Pammachius and Marcella are the lights of 'the Christian senate'.[42] Pammachius and his peers only gain renown and glory when they reject the outward signs of their worldly status. They do not lose or nullify their *nobilitas* and it shines forth more brightly than ever.

What the ecclesiastical writers offered to converts to asceticism was, ultimately, nothing new but glory, both earthly and heavenly. Striving for personal honour in the community was seen as a natural attitude of elite ascetics, even if these ideas were hierarchically subjugated to spiritual nobility and spiritual

---

[39]   Paulinus of Nola, *Letters*, 13.11–15.

[40]   Paulinus of Nola, *Letters*, 25.3–5: 'militantibus sibi gloriam vitae aeternae, honorem regni caelestis et divitias hereditatis suae et divinae cognitionis consortium perenne largitur'. Paulinus of Nola, *Letters*, 5.6 (to Sulpicius Severus). See also Paulinus of Nola, *Poems*, 21.836.

[41]   Jerome, *Letters*, 77.2: 'ancillam Christi non de nobilitate veteris historiae, sed de ecclesiae humilitate producam'.

[42]   Jerome, *Letters*, 66.6: 'Funiani germinis decus'; 66.4: 'magnus in magnis, primus in primis, arkhistrategos monachorum'; 97.3: 'Vos, Christiani senatus lumina'. See also *Letters*, 130.7; 118.5 ('Cur qui in saeculo primus es, non et in Christi familia primus sis?'); 3.4.

Progeny, Reputation and Memory 159

honour; spiritual *nobilitas* was ascribed to those who were already ennobled by traditional aristocratic standards.[43] The more radical claims of equality did not affect this rhetoric, even if in theory it was 'Christ's noble doctrine that ennobles men', not their rank and familial lineage, as Prudentius claimed.[44]

Turning to hagiography, which would offer a comparison to the ideological discourses of the ascetic treatises and their more practical solutions in the pastoral letters of the ecclesiastical writers, one would expect a more egalitarian approach. Since these stories do not only consider members of the highest nobility, and their audience is not confined only to the senatorial aristocracy or local elites, the highborn status should not have been the *a priori* starting point. However, it is interesting to note that in these accounts there appears no move towards attaching nobility to low birth and humble origins. The Christian athletes worth eulogizing had their share of earthly nobility, or at least they were wealthy and of good birth, and this fact was brought forth whenever possible. According to Athanasius, Antony the Great was well-born and carefully brought up. In the *Life of Pachomius*, even if it was impossible to attach highborn status to Pachomius himself, at least his successor, Theodore, was 'a son of a prominent family'. Even in cases where, for some reason, no direct association was made with the (local) nobility, the author makes reference to wealth in order to convey a sense of elite character. Thus, Jerome's fictitious hero, Paul of Thebes, was a wealthy heir at the age of 16 and the anonymous would-be ascetic mentioned by John Chrysostom was 'very rich'.[45]

The same features are present in the lives of many of the Western saints written in the late fourth and early fifth centuries. Due attention was paid to the high status of the families of Felix of Nola or Romanus. Even Martin of Tours, son of a soldier who became a military tribune, was affirmed to be 'of no mean rank as far as worldly status goes' and Martin's childhood was noble (*inlustris*).[46]

---

[43] See also Salzman, 'Competing Claims', pp. 373–4, 384; and Cloke, '*This Female Man of God*', pp. 68–9, 111–14.

[44] Prudentius, *Crowns of Martyrdom*, 10.123–5: 'Absit, ut me nobilem / sanguis parentum praestet aut lex curiae / Generosa Christi secta nobilitat viros.' See also Hilarius of Arles, *Life of Honoratus*, 4.1; Augustine, *Sermons*, 200.1 (2) with Salzman, 'Competing Claims', pp. 376–9.

[45] Athanasius, *Life of Antony* 1; *Life of Pachomius* (Bohairic version), 31; Jerome, *Life of Paul*, 4; also Jerome, *Life of Hilarius*, 2.6; John Chrysostom, *Against the Opponents of Monastic Life*, 3.12.

[46] Martin: Sulpicius Severus, *Life of Saint Martin*, 2.1–2: 'parentibus secundum saeculi dignitatem non infimis' with Salzman, 'Competing Claims', pp. 367–8 and 375–7. Felix: Paulinus of Nola, *Poems*, 15.50–52; 18.162–8; Romanus: Prudentius, *Crowns of Martyrdom*, 10.112–13 (see also 10.123–5; 10.129).

Honoratus of Arles had an aristocratic background and for Hilary, his relative and successor in the see, this offered a leading theme for a sermon on him. Hilary claims that

> the height of nobility is to be reckoned among the sons of God. Nor can the glory of our earthly birth add anything to our dignity except when we renounce it. No one in heaven is more glorious than he who has repudiated his family ancestry and chosen to be enrolled as only a descendant of Christ.[47]

Hilary, against traditional Roman thinking, separates the glory of high birth from dignity, but he still firmly connects the new *nobilitas* to membership of the family of Christ: nobility is a family virtue, a virtue of belonging. Furthermore, for Hilary, this denial serves as a starting point for his narrative, which is deeply committed to the traditional values of good reputation and honour. Although Hilary describes Honoratus as suppressing the earthly familial *pietas* in his struggle against his father, Honoratus acted as a patron and promoted the careers of his kinsmen, and Hilary himself is an example of this. Ultimately, Honoratus is 'most worthy of manifold honour', and Hilary claims that the praetorian prefect and other prefects were present on his deathbed.[48] Paradoxically, in repudiating his family ancestry, Honoratus is not only glorious in heaven, but is also depicted as having increased his own honour and his family's standing in this world.

Nobility was connected with female saints too and Ambrose mentions nobility in connection with the virgin martyrs Agnes, Thecla and Pelagia. This has been interpreted to mean that their nobility was due to their martyr status.[49] However, nobility is not attached directly to them: Ambrose stated that Agnes, Thecla and Pelagia were bringing forth 'noble offspring as they rushed to death as if to immortality' and their successors, the contemporary virgins of Ambrose, were noble in their imitation. Similarly, it is not Agnes herself who is referred to as noble by Damasus, but her renowned body, present in the church of *Sant'Agnese fuori le mura* in Rome, encouraging contemporary girls to follow Christ. However, their nobility is not only spiritual, and already in second-century stories Thecla was depicted as having a family background of high

---

[47] Hilarius of Arles, *Life of Honoratus*, 4.1; translation from Salzman, 'Competing Claims', p. 378.

[48] Hilarius of Arles, *Life of Honoratus*, 16.2: 'multiplici honore dignissimus'; 23–4 and 36–8 (as a patron); 31–3 (deathbed). See Prudentius on the true *nobilitas* of Romanus in e.g. *Crowns of Martyrdom*, 10.123–5; 10.138.

[49] Salzman, 'Competing Claims', p. 372.

Progeny, Reputation and Memory 161

status. In the case of Agnes, the fifth-century legend claims that she belonged to the Roman nobility and rejected the proposals of the wealthiest men in Rome.[50]

If the high status of the ascetics and saints is conspicuously highlighted in the first hagiographies, later in the fifth and sixth centuries, this had developed into a literary *topos*. Most of the heroes and heroines of the *Vitae* were highborn and important citizens in their native surroundings; for example, Ammon had rich parents and was of noble birth, Hypatius was from a good family, Theodosius of Antioch was from an illustrious family, Zenon was one of the richest citizens of Pontus, Marcian had an excellent aristocratic pedigree and Syncletica had an illustrious background.[51] Less surprisingly, some ascetic bishops were claimed to have come from honourable and prosperous, or even markedly aristocratic, families with boundless wealth such as Porphyry of Gaza in Greece or Germanus of Auxerre in Gaul.[52]

Even if Palladius did not stress the earthly nobility of the Egyptian ascetics as strongly as many of his contemporaries, he willingly described the nobility of his heroines. The earthly status of Melania the Elder and Olympias is pointedly brought to the attention of readers and the nobility and spectacular riches which the ex-count Verus and his wife Bosporia gave away in order to attain heavenly reward get their due attention.[53]

The various accounts of the status and riches of Melania the Younger make it possible to see the different narrative strategies available to the ecclesiastical writers with regard to earthly nobility and family continuity. In Palladius' text, Melania is not so much praised for leaving behind her nobility and family, but rather her role is that of continuing the work of her grandmother Melania the Elder.

---

[50]   Ambrose, *Letters*, 7.36: 'Quid Theclam, quid Agnen, quid Pelagian loquar, quae tamquam nobilia vitulamina pullulantes ad mortem quasi ad immortalitatem festinaverunt?' Thecla: *Acts of Paul and Thecla*, esp. 10–13 and above pp. 109–10; Agnes: *Epigrammata Damasi* 37, in *Anthologia latina*; *Life of Agnes* 1.5 with P.F. de'Cavalieri, 'Agnese nella tradizione e nella leggenda', repr. in *Scritti Agiografici*, vol. I (1893–1900) (Vatican City, 1962), pp. 328–51; Pelagia: Ambrose, *On Virgins*, 3.7.33 and John Chrysostom, *Homilies on Matteus*, 67.3.

[51]   *History of the Monks in Egypt*, 22.1 (Ammon); Callinicus, *Life of Hypatius*, 1.1; Theodoret of Cyrrhus, *Religious History*, 10.1 (Theodosius); 12.1 (Zenon); 3.2 (Marcian); Pseudo-Athanasius, *Life of Syncletica*, 1, with e.g. Theodoret of Cyrrhus, *Religious History*, 8.1 (Aphrahat) and the virgin Helia in the fifth century *Life of Saint Helia* (cited in Burrus, '"Honor the Fathers"', p. 447). See also Cyril of Scythopolis, *The Lives of the Monks of Palestine*, Life of Euthymius 2, Life of Sabas 1, Life of John the Hesychast 1, Life of Cyriacus 1, Life of Theodosius 5 with Caseau, 'Childhood', pp. 132–4, 140–43.

[52]   Mark the Deacon, *Life of Porphyry*, 4; Constantius, *Life of Germanus of Auxerre*, 1. See also *Life of Caesarius of Arles*, 1.3.

[53]   Palladius, *The Lausiac History*, 46.1; 56.1; 66.1.

162   *Children and Asceticism in Late Antiquity*

Palladius stresses the nobility of her husband Pinian ('son of Severus the ex-prefect') and shifts the focus from her earthly familial background to her spiritual qualities. The interpretation in the *Life of Melania the Younger* by Gerontius is quite different: her life is told as the story of a member of a distinguished family ridding herself of the constituent elements of the aristocratic lifestyle. Melania endangered the continuity of her family by dedicating her daughter to virginity; then she stopped bathing and enjoying the other luxuries pertaining to her status, and ultimately shunned the whole idea of familial continuity and *nobilitas* by dedicating herself to chastity with her husband. Lastly, she was able to cast off the outward signs of nobility when she gave her enormous wealth away.[54]

Whereas Palladius wants the reader to understand that Melania showed the traditional Roman elites a new way of understanding the old values of familial continuity and nobility, Gerontius highlighted the rifts and otherness of Melania's conduct: Melania was against her husband, against her parents and parents-in-law, against family continuity and against the transfer of the patrimony. Gerontius does not even mention her grandmother, Melania the Elder, as his narrative does not play with the element of continuity. In this respect the account represents a unique viewpoint among the texts concerning ascetics, not fitting into the paradigmatic storyline of his times. There are at least two possible explanations, which are not mutually exclusive. First, Gerontius depicts himself as giving direct access to the experience and ideas of Melania herself: this is not a distanced and refined approach with the traditional rhetoric of values, as exemplified by Palladius. Second, Gerontius seems to have had specific theological reasons to present a distinctive picture of the life of an ideal holy virgin.[55] The wealth of material that seemingly can be gleaned from Gerontius' account may have caused some scholars to take the account as more typical and more trustworthy in its details than it actually is.[56]

---

[54]   Palladius, *The Lausiac History*, 61.1–2; Gerontius, *Life of Melania* (Greek), 1. See also Cooper, 'The Household and the Desert', p. 15.

[55]   The heterodox nature of Gerontius is highlighted especially by Cyril of Scythopolis, himself an admirer of Melania the Younger (Cyril of Scythopolis, *The Lives of the Monks of Palestine*, Life of Euthymius, 27 and 45, Life of Sabas, 30 and Life of Theodosius, 4); See also Gorge, *Vie de sainte Mélanie*, pp. 56–62 (on Gerontius' monophysitism) and Clark, 'Piety' (on the propaganda and politics of Gerontius' *vita*. She refers to the doctrinal differences between Melania the Elder and Gerontius as the reason why she does not appear in the *Life* of her grandchild). See also Cooper, 'The Household and the Desert', p. 15; and Sivan, 'On Hymens and Holiness', p. 85.

[56]   Cf. e.g. Nathan, *The Family*, pp. 92–6, and 145, who despite his own warnings against such a use of the text seems to take Gerontius' version at face value. See also Drijvers, 'Virginity and Asceticism', p. 260; and Gorge, *Vie de sainte Mélanie*, pp. 62–6.

In hagiographic narratives, earthly status was also used as a rhetorical device to highlight spiritual nobility, especially in cases where the ascetic cannot claim *nobilitas*. The *Apophthegmata* of Abba Arsenius mentions a highborn ascetic, whose father was a 'prince'. His wealth tortured him, and after he met a former shepherd who had worked hard but now lived quietly in his *cella*, he opted for a similar way of life. Thus, there emerges a seemingly opposite view of the noble life: a humble peasant who had achieved the highest virtue.[57] In the great collections of the desert fathers' lives from the beginning of the fifth century, there is only one instance in which the low status of the hero is particularly stressed, as Palladius gives the origins of Philoromus as follows: 'His mother was a maidservant, his father a free man.' Even here, this is meant to highlight his subsequent importance as an example for the highborn: 'But he showed such nobility in the Christ-like mode of life that even those whose family record was unsurpassable revered his life and virtue.'[58] This is not praise for his humble worldly status, but an explanation of his alleged nobility in the brotherhood in Christ, the nobility which draws its justification from his fame and influence among the traditional, hereditary nobility. The focus on Philoromus' lower status is used to highlight the new spiritual nobility of the other protagonists, not to praise his humble status.

Attaching nobility and high birth to ascetic heroes and heroines was a strategy in response to the accusations that Christian ascetics posed a threat to both the reputation and continuity of biological families. Moreover, in connection with the rhetoric of scorn and hate for one's biological kinship ties, leaving behind a life dominated by hunger and need was not sufficiently virtuous to be highlighted, but rejecting nobility and wealth was a sign of spiritual strength and a source for glory in itself. Hence, the family background of the ascetic saints was important enough to be mentioned only if it was possible to link it to wealth, power and prestige.

Even if the Christian writers claimed that worldly honour and wealth had no significance in Christian communities or that these might even constitute an impediment to following Christ,[59] being of low birth did not become a source of

---

[57] *Apophthegmata patrum*, Arsenius 36. See also Cyril of Scythopolis, *The Lives of the Monks of Palestine*, Life of Theodosius, 3, which relates that a certain Acacius, a *vir illustris*, came to see Theodosius and made obeisance to him.

[58] Palladius, *The Lausiac History*, 45.1: '... ἐξ οἰκέτιδος μητρὸς ἐλθέρου δὲ πατρός· τοσαύτην δὲ εὐγένειαν εἰς τὴν κατὰ Χριστὸν ἐνεδείξατο πολιτείαν, ὡς καὶ αὐτοὺς τοὺς ἀνικήτους ἐν γένει αἰδεῖσθαι αὐτοῦ τὴν ζωὴν καὶ τὴν ἀρετήν'. Translated by W.K. Lowther Clarke.

[59] For example, Augustine notes that the disciples of Christ were of the lowest status, and Christ Himself was born *carnaliter* humble and poor (Augustine, *Tractates on the Gospel*

virtue. Consequently, *nobilitas* and high birth were attached to individuals whose real background was obscure or had faded into oblivion. Therefore, it would be easy to overestimate the elite characteristics of early Christian asceticism, especially as the ecclesiastical writers themselves had their background in the upper strata of society and were writing about their peers and acquaintances.

In general, in Christian usage, *nobilitas* retained its close association with issues of family status and lineage. This was linked to the aim of facilitating the conversion of the aristocracy 'by making Christianity appear as less of a change' and attaching old values to the new ways of life, as Michele Salzman has pointed out. However, the claim of Salzman that the Christian interpretation of *nobilitas* 'emphasized the personal nature of this virtue' needs some particularization.[60] For the Christian authors, the true and higher *nobilitas* did indeed imply contemplation and ascetic practices, but that was not enough; Christian nobility also indicated an active role within the family of Christ. The claim to *nobilitas* needed public manifestation both in Christian discourse and in its more traditional use. In this, the Christian idea corresponds to that of Seneca, according to whom *nobilitas* is derived from a life of contemplation combined with public office.[61] Now, instead, one was to hold high office in the City of God.[62] The notion of noble lineage was simultaneously anchored both in the biological family of the ascetic in question and in the spiritual nobility based on the lineage of the ascetic saints in the family of Christ.

Indeed, the notions of spiritual *nobilitas* and elite *nobilitas* were not antithetical. The traditional view of the social nobility of heroes and heroines was by no means played down, but, on the contrary, this quality is repeatedly stressed, carefully reflected upon and highly appreciated. A noble Christian was widely acclaimed to be noble. By the late fourth century, only ascetics with high status in the secular world could boast a provincial or even universal reputation following their endeavour. An essential constituent of Christian *nobilitas* was that the noble ascetics shone on the Christian *oecumene* and on the pagan disbelievers. This was possible because of their position as both members of their

---

of John, 7.17; Augustine, *The First Catechetical Instruction*, 22.40; Augustine, *Sermons*, 197.2 and 200.1(2)).

[60] First quote: Salzman, *The Making*, p. 218. Second quote: Salzman, 'Competing Claims', p. 384.

[61] Seneca, *Letters to Lucilius*, 44.5 and 66.3. For Cicero and Juvenal, see Salzman, 'Competing Claims', p. 361.

[62] Later in the fifth century, the politics of combining the episcopal office with ascetic strivings meant that the claim to *nobilitas* spread more generally to the holders of ecclesiastical offices: see Kuefler, *The Manly Eunuch*, pp. 151–60; and Salzman, 'Competing Claims', pp. 375–6 on bishops, with Jerome, *Letters*, 60.10 on the honour attached to the priesthood.

Progeny, Reputation and Memory 165

noble lineages and as noble members of the family of Christ, producing spiritual offspring by their example. Already in this world, in Christian communities, *nobilitas* implied both personally achieved honour and glory for the ascetics, and strengthened the claim of nobility for their families.

Renown, Honour and the Ascetic Practices

Salvian, writing in Gaul in the 430s, somewhat ironically comments that if a noble man converts to God, he at once loses the honour associated with his nobility (*honorem nobilitatis amittit*) and becomes contemptible, vile and wretched in the eyes of his peers.[63] This comment, however, was directed towards the pagan aristocracy, and within the Christian communities, the situation was different. Although there was resistance to asceticism when this was understood as the ultimate perfection of the Christian message,[64] in those Christian communities in which the ascetic ideals were established, the ascetics, male and female, enjoyed special recognition. In the fifth century many of the ascetic monks, renowned for their virtue, were ordained to the priesthood and the reputation of an ascetic became one of the clearest signs of competence for episcopal office.[65]

Already by the mid-fourth century, Eusebius of Emesa made the general observation that virgins were honoured in the Christian communities. In Rome, where, according to Jerome, asceticism had earlier met with reproach and was perceived as strange, ignominious and degrading, monasticism had become a source of honour and privilege among Christians by the beginning of the fifth century.[66] In the East, John Chrysostom, in a text of the 380s directed at the opponents of the monastic life, was eager to point out the universal fame and glory that were paid to asceticism. According to him, the Christian chaste widows were admired and honoured not only by the Christians themselves but also by the unbelievers.[67]

The theme of the 'others', unbelievers and uncivilized people, knowing and respecting chaste virgins and widows was repeated on many occasions. Jerome,

---

[63] Salvian, *On the Goverment of God*, 4.7.32–3.

[64] On this resistance, see above pp. 59–60.

[65] Rapp, *Holy Bishops*, pp. 137–49.

[66] Eusebius of Emesa, *Sermons*, 7.3; Jerome, *Letters*, 127.5 and 8 with Jerome, *Letters*, 60.10 and Augustine, *On Holy Virginity*, 10 (9).

[67] John Chrysostom, *Against the Opponents of Monastic Life*, 2.5–6, 2.9–10, 3.18 and 21 with John Chrysostom, *To a Young Widow*, 2; John Chrysostom, *Homilies on Ephesians*, 21.2.

166 *Children and Asceticism in Late Antiquity*

for example, mentions that Paula was admired in the barbarian lands, and Proba's sanctity and charity won her esteem even among the barbarians.[68] Augustine tells a curious story about the respect enjoyed by the ascetics: according to him, a nun, a relative of the Bishop of Sitif in Africa, was abducted from her parents by barbarians. However, when several of the sons in the barbarian household fell ill, 'their mother noticed the girl was consecrated to God, and believed that the sons would be liberated from the now imminent mortal danger through the virgin's prayers'. The brothers indeed recovered their health and the nun was most respectfully restored to her own parents.[69]

The actual reputation of virgins and ascetics in 'the outside world' could be somewhat suspect, but within the local Christian communities, their honoured position was used as a means of pointing out the outstanding benefits of asceticism, especially for aristocratic audiences. Thus, Jerome could claim that Pammachius and Paulinus of Nola had benefited from rejecting earthly honours and offices: made poor and unhonoured (*pauperes et inhonorati*), they are not only nobler and richer but also more famous and authoratitative than ever.[70] This also holds true for women. In his letter to Geruchia, a rich widow in Gaul, Jerome argues against remarriage by referring to her older relatives who live in chastity:

> Do not your grandmother, your mother and your aunt enjoy even more than their old authority and honour, looked up to as they are by the whole province and by the leaders of the churches?[71]

Similarly, Palladius relates a tale of Magna, 'a venerable woman', who won the reverence of the bishops by her ascetic way of life.[72] The context for these remarks is the discourse about the dangers and precarious position of widows. The ecclesiastical writers tried to neutralize this threat by claiming that widowhood and asceticism bring authority and renowned status in the Christian communities. The influence and respect which aristocratic widows or virgins

---

[68]   Jerome, *Letters*, 108.3 and 130.7.

[69]   Augustine, *Letters*, 111.7: 'mater animadvertit puellam Deo deditam, et credidit quod eius orationibus sui filii possent ab imminentis iam mortis periculo liberari'.

[70]   Jerome, *Letters*, 118.5.

[71]   Jerome, *Letters*, 123.14: 'Avia tua, mater et avita, nonne auctoritatis pristinae, honorisque maioris sunt, dum eas et tota provincia et ecclesiarum principes suscipiunt?', with Jerome, *Letters*, 24.2 on 'the honour of future blessedness (honore futurae beatitudinis consecratur)' due to asceticism.

[72]   Palladius, *The Lausiac History*, 67.2.

Progeny, Reputation and Memory 167

such as Proba, Paula the Elder, the two Melanias, Marcella or Demetrias held among the secular and ecclesiastical elites was indeed considerable.[73] However, the material and immaterial capital due to their lineage played a more decisive role in this authority than asceticism itself.

On the other hand, it was claimed that the reputation of prominent ascetics would spread throughout the Christian world. Wanting to persuade Paulinus and Therasia to visit his congregation in Hippo, Augustine appeals to their *fama* and claims that in them the glory of Christ is manifested. Similarly, he wants Albina, Pinian and Melania the Younger to visit his native Tagaste, since he claims they are already famous among the local people there.[74] In Rome, Fabiola's funeral is described as a triumph of a celebrated general, with all wanting to have a share in the *fama* of her penitence. She is 'the glory of the Christians, the marvel of the non-Christian peoples, the sorrow of the poor, and the consolation of the monks'.[75] The same laudatory remarks are repeated by Jerome in the case of many ascetics. When Paula the Elder died, her 'praises are sung by the whole world, she is admired by bishops, regretted by bands of virgins, and wept over by crowds of monks and paupers'. As a member of the old nobility, she was known only to Romans, but when she hid herself in Bethlehem, both Roman and barbarian lands admired her: 'by shunning glory she earned glory'.[76] When Nepotian died, all Altinum and all Italy mourned him, but this was not much compared to Jerome's account of Demetrias taking the veil: all the churches in Africa rejoiced; the glad tidings spread far and wide; even the ruined walls of Rome resumed their ancient glory; the news penetrated to the coasts of the East and was heard in all the cities around the Mediterranean. Indeed, 'the whole world' would now know Demetrias as she takes the veil,

---

[73]   See e.g. Jerome, *Letters*, 130.7 and Augustine, *Letters*, 130 on Proba; Jerome, *Letters*, 108 on Paula the Elder; Jerome, *Letters*, 127, esp. 7 and 9 on Marcella; Gerontius, *Life of Melania* (Greek); Palladius, *The Lausiac History*, 46, 54 and 61 with Augustine, *Letters*, 124.1 for the two Melanias. See also Ambrose, *On Widows*, 8.44. On the authority of Demetrias in the 440s, see Jacobs 'Writing Demetrias', pp. 745–6. Further, see also Clark, 'Ascetic Renunciation', pp. 185–93; and Sivan, 'On Hymens and Holiness', esp. p. 93.

[74]   Augustine, *Letters*, 31.5 and 124.1.

[75]   Jerome, *Letters*, 77.11; 77.2: 'Tradis mihi Fabiolam, laudem christianorum, miraculum gentilium, luctum pauperum, solacium monachorum.' See also Sulpicius Severus, *Letters*, 3, esp. 21 on the universal sorrow caused by the death of Martin of Tours, and of his funeral as a triumph.

[76]   Jerome, *Letters*, 108.2–3: 'meritis, quam totus orbis canis, sacerdotes mirantur, virginum chori desiderant, monachorum et pauperum turba deplangit'; 'Fugiendo gloriam, gloriam merebatur'. See also Jerome, *Letters*, 127.1 on Marcella.

whereas, as one man's bride, she would have been known to 'but one province'.[77] Not surprisingly, renown due to asceticism was highlighted by writers who themselves practised asceticism. Thus, for example, Ambrose, modest as always, refers to his own worldwide reputation as an ascetically minded bishop when he claims that virgins keep coming from Mauretania – that is, from the edge of the known world – to be consecrated in Milan.[78]

The *fama* of the saint reaching the whole Christian world and even transcending its borders quickly became a main *topos* in hagiographic literature. Jerome used the theme in his own hagiographic essay on Hilarius: 'It was not only through Palestine and the neighbouring cities of Egypt or Syria that his *fama* spread, but also throughout the remote provinces.'[79] In the mid-fifth century this claim was already a commonplace: Hilary of Arles claimed that the *fama* of his hero Honoratus and his companion and brother, Venantius, was carried to the whole of their *patria* and even to the remotest regions.[80] In the collection of Theodore of Cyrrhus, Macedonius is 'known to all the world ... He is known even in foreign countries'; Julianus was honoured and known to the whole world; the reputation of Simeon the Stylite reached all the inhabited world.[81] By turning to asceticism, the traditional nobility gains even more esteem already in this world.

That the enhancement of social standing through asceticism was not only empty talk is shown in the references to misappropriation of the ascetic status. Jerome felt obliged to warn Eustochium not to seem very devout or more humble than need be, lest she seek glory by shunning it, 'as many do'. He complains that there are women who seek esteem in Christian communities by making a show of their asceticism, desiring to seek praise and to excite admiration by dressing oddly, cutting their hair and appearing in public dirty and as if exhausted from fasting. There are also men who behave similarly, trying to look like ascetics in order to gain appraisal and honour.[82] In letters written a quarter of a century later in 411, Jerome accuses such pseudo-ascetics of trying to rise above others and 'acting like governors'. Augustine too warns women against boasting of their

---

[77] Jerome, *Letters*, 60.14; 130.6: 'Quam sponsam hominis una tantum provincia noverat, virginem Christi totus orbis audivit', with Pelagius, *Letter to Demetrias*, 14.

[78] Ambrose, *On Virgins*, 1.10.59.

[79] Jerome, *Life of Hilarius*, 13.1 (also 7.1, 8.9, 20.1–4 and 28.1): 'Non solum autem in Palestina et in vicinis Aegypti vel Syriae urbibus, sed etiam in longinquis provinciis fama eius percrebuerat.'

[80] Hilarius of Arles, *Life of Honoratus*, 10–11, esp. 10.1.

[81] Theodoret of Cyrrhus, *Religious History*, 13.1: ἴσασι μὲν ἅπαντες ... ἴσασι δὲ καὶ οἱ τούτων ὅμοροί τε καὶ γείτονες'; 2.13 (Julianos); 26.11 (Simeon).

[82] Jerome, *Letters*, 22.27–8.

chastity to gain reputation. The economic profits to be amassed by exploiting the new social capital due to asceticism have already been referred to above.[83] These reproaches reveal perhaps less about the actual behaviour of the ascetics than about the potential of asceticism as a vehicle for social survival or even upward mobility. For people who sought social distinction and honour among the Christian communities, asceticism opened up new possibilities.

Memory, Name and Continuity

In the Christian discourse of Late Antiquity an ideologically proper way of assessing the importance of personal remembrance was to regard the individual need to become immortalized by commemoration as natural but deplorable. Gregory of Nyssa mockingly sketched the idea, common in his contemporary culture, that a man 'must not be thought inferior to his forefathers; he must be deemed a great man by the generation to come by leaving his children records of himself'. The search for welfare, public honours, wealth, power and temporal glory lead to the attempt to leave an enduring memory of oneself.[84] The acknowledged naturalness of this aim was, however, contrary to the Christian notion of the afterlife. A Christian's duty should be to look for an everlasting reward from God and eternal life rather than everlasting renown on earth. Sulpicius Severus, for example, complained about people who sought to immortalize their reputation by writing biographies of others, seeking to prolong the memory of both themselves and their subjects: 'they have based their hope on fables and entrusted their souls to tombs ... they have commended their continuity only to human memory'.[85]

Even Sulpicius Severus, in comparing the old and new ways of achieving perpetuity, does not claim that the old means are ineffective, even if they are doomed ultimately to be unsuccessful: they do indeed prolong a person's memory, although the hope of immortality will vanish with the passing of this

---

[83]   Jerome, *Letters*, 125.16; Augustine, *City of God*, 1.28. For the economic benefits see above Chapter 6.

[84]   Gregory of Nyssa, *On Virginity*, 4.3: 'ὡς ἂν μὴ ἐλάττων δοκοίη τῶν πρὸ αὐτοῦ γεγονότων καὶ ἵνα μέγας τοῖς μετὰ ταῦτα νομίζοιτο καταλιπών τινα τοῖς ἐξ αὐτοῦ διηγήματα'. Translated by W. Moore and H.A. Wilson (Nicene and Post-Nicene Fathers, ser. II, vol. 5).

[85]   Sulpicius Severus, *Life of Saint Martin*, 1.3–4: 'spes suas fabulis, animas sepulchris dederint ... ad solam hominum memoriam se perpetuandos crediderunt'. For the earlier accounts, see esp. Tertullian, *On the Testimony of the Soul*, 4.9–10, mentioning works of literature, memory of the personal virtues, and tombs as means for achieving this memory.

world. The persistence of the traditional values and ideas is reflected in this kind of argumentation aiming at supplanting these with the new ideas.

Most contemporary Christian writers, however, took the tradition for granted, neither challenging it nor considering Christian ideas a break with ancient values. Theodoret of Cyrrhus, like many other writers of hagiography, expressly intended to keep and honour the memory and glory of the saints by his writings. He did not protest against the idea of immortalizing people who truly deserved it: the prophets and saints deserve not only a life immortal, but also immortal memory and glory. However, he wrote disapprovingly of 'transvestites' and athletes who were commemorated in statues and paintings by their admirers in order to preserve their memory even after their death. He himself aims to preserve and honour the memory and 'philosophy' of the saints by writing.[86]

Jerome is a good example of a Christian writer who underscored the importance of memory for an individual to achieve earthly renown and continuity. In his eulogy on the death of Nepotian, a nephew of his friend, he has two strategies for consolation: the Christian hope in the resurrection and eternal life, and the preservation of Nepotian's name in his own writings. Moreover, Jerome points to the necessity of holding the deceased in memory: 'if we can no longer speak with him, let us never cease to speak of him'.[87] Similarly, the shortness of the life of Blesilla, an elite ascetic, will be compensated by an everlasting remembrance through Jerome's own writings: she will live 'both with Christ in Heaven, and on the lips of men'. Later, he boasts that he has ensured the living memory of her mother, Paula the Elder, both by composing and placing an inscription on her tomb and by spreading the news and the text of the inscription in his letter.[88] It is somewhat ironic that all the ecclesiastical writers also claim immortality for themselves through these writings and, indeed, are still thus commemorated by their readers.

The central importance of the name for survival and for the continuity of reputation, *fama*, was a well-established tradition in Roman culture that continued in Late Antiquity. Salvian, for example, reproaches the contemporary practice that was intended to preserve the family name by all available means,

---

[86]   Theodoret of Cyrrhus, *Religious History*, prol. 2–4 and 31.16–18; A painted picture as a sign of vainglory also in Augustine, *Sermons*, 9.15.

[87]   Jerome, *Letters*, 60.6–7 and 19: 'cum quo loqui non possumus, de eo numquam loqui desinamus'.

[88]   Jerome, *Letters*, 39.8: 'Quae cum Christo vivit in caelis in hominum quoque ore victura est ... Numquam in meis moritura est libris'; Jerome, *Letters*, 108.33. See also Jerome, *Letters*, 75.5, which would serve as an epitaph for the dead Lucinius.

Progeny, Reputation and Memory
171

such as adopting an heir to take the name of the testator.[89] The preservation of the name was crucial for both personal and family identity. Asceticism, requiring chastity and almsgiving, was seen as endangering the succession of the good name. Ecclesiastical writers responded to this by connecting the themes of renowned name and lasting memory with the promotion of asceticism within families, emphasizing spiritual rewards and the continuity of the spiritual family tradition in children. This did not mean that the relation between memory and offspring had to disappear or was neglected; ascetics too had abundant offspring and they did not lack commemoration, as has been shown above in Chapter 2. As Ambrose claims, 'more numerous are the offspring of a pious soul, which holds all as its children, it is fecund in successors but barren in bereavements, it knows no funerals, but it has heirs'.[90]

The epigram praising the virtues of an otherwise unidentified Eunomia brings together the different attributes attached to ascetic heroes and heroines by Christian writers of Late Antiquity: the text describes a virgin, noble by both birth and spiritual achievements; her *fama* shines in the world; and her fertility lies in her writings (*libris*).[91] Far from being the end of her line, an ascetic is fruitful and famous, generating nobility and continuity for herself, her family and the Church.

Since the yearning for renown and name was considered by most ecclesiastical writers as a self-evident motivation for various strategies for *post mortem* remembrance, rather than attempting to suppress its relevance, they developed new rhetorical strategies for its maintenance, to motivate asceticism and to refer to new continuity and remembrance beyond death. John Chrysostom points out that ascetics are approved everywhere and their parents will be famous and honoured through them.[92] Similarly, Paulinus of Nola claimed that Paulina had crowned her husband Pammachius 'with glory and honour' in their chaste marriage. Now that she is dead, she in turn obtains honour through

---

[89] Salvian, *To the Church*, 3.2–5; 3.13.57–3.14.60. See also Palladius, *The Historia Lausica*, 6. Salvian refers to the Roman practice known as 'testamentary adoption', *nominis ferendi condicio*, on which see Gardner, *Family*, pp. 129–30; and Corbier, 'Divorce and Adoption', pp. 63–4, 69. For the link between *fama* and name in the earlier Roman tradition, see above pp. 36–7.

[90] Ambrose, *On Virgins*, 1.6.30–31: 'Non uteri onus notum, non dolor partus, et tamen numerosior suboles piae mentis, quae omnes pro liberis habet, fecunda successoribus, sterilis orbitatibus, nescit funera, novit heredes.'

[91] *Anthologia latina* 768, esp. 1–4: 'Fulgens Eunomia decensque virgo / pollens nobilis et fecunda libris / et totus venerabilis per orbem.'

[92] John Chrysostom, *Against the Opponents of Monastic Life*, 3.20–21; see also 2.10.

the charitable acts done in her memory by her husband.[93] On the other hand, spiritual nobility was linked to the continuity of the name. Paula the Younger, in her refusal to continue her lineage by bearing children, becomes the real heir of the family tradition, since she carries on the name and deeds of her grandmother and namesake, Paula the Elder. She is the successor (*heres*) of the holiness of both her ascetic grandmother and aunt.[94]

The choice of Demetrias to take the vow of virginity inspired similar comments: the new spiritual nobility and fame of Demetrias would contribute to the family honour, making her an example to others. Her mother's womb will be called blessed and her (deceased) father would be 'happier still in his offspring, for the nobility of his great grandmother Demetrias has become yet more distinguished, because of the perpetual chastity of his daughter Demetrias'. She is by no means a barren branch on a fertile root of his noble lineage: by dedicating herself to virginity, she is carrying on and strengthening the family tradition initiated by Demetrias the Elder, whose name she perpetuates. Through her virginity, her noble lineage will become nobler still.[95] Thus, women, too, could contribute to the family honour and further commemorate the great lineage, and their names were very much worthy of being perpetuated. In the absence of children, even the idea of a widow continuing the name of her husband was invoked: Ambrose claims that a widow is preserving her former husband's name in not marrying again and in this way he is not lost to her.[96]

This did not mean that women as perpetuators of the name were as highly regarded as men. A man dying childless would uproot one's name and memory,[97] but a surviving child, especially a son, would mean 'the uninterrupted succession of the name handed down', as Ambrose congratulates his friend Eusebius.[98] A son named after his deceased father renders void any claims of loneliness and

---

[93] Paulinus of Nola, *Letters*, 13.5 and 13.28. See also Jerome, *Letters*, 22.20 with the vocation of Eustochium bringing honour to her mother, Paula the Elder.

[94] Jerome, *Letters*, 108.26 and 107.13; see also the family tradition of Furia as something to be imitated in Jerome, *Letters*, 54.6.

[95] Augustine, *Letters*, 150; Jerome, *Letters*, 130.3 and 6: 'Demetriadis proaviae nobilitatem insigniorem reddidit Demetriadis filiae perpetua castitate.' For the high appreciation of well-born Roman daughters as 'personal and familial continuation' for their fathers during the Late Republic and Early Empire, see Judith Hallett, *Fathers and Daughters in Roman Society: Women and the Elite Family* (Princeton, 1984), pp. 338–41.

[96] Ambrose, *On the Death of his Brother Satyrus*, 2.13: 'non est viduata coniugio, quae non mutavit nomen mariti'. See also Tertullian, *To His Wife*, 1.6 and 8.

[97] Gregory of Nyssa, *On Virginity*, 3.7. See also van Dam, *Families and Friends*, p. 122 for the importance of especially sons continuing the family in the texts of Basil of Caesarea.

[98] Ambrose, *Letters*, 38.1: 'perpetuati vocabuli iugis successio'; see also *Letters*, 38.4.

Similar themes are also used in hagiography; in the *History of the Monks in Egypt*, it is no accident that John of Lycopolis is described as telling a high-ranking official to give his son, destined to be sent into the desert to be brought up, the name of John. It marked the boy as distinct from his own family, connecting him to the family of Christ or, more specifically, making him the spiritual son and successor of John of Lycopolis. According to Palladius, in turn, Melania the Younger is not so much to be celebrated for leaving behind her family nobility, patrimony and familial continuity in children as for becoming the real heir of the family tradition and continuing the name and memory of her grandmother, Melania the Elder.[100]

Indeed, in Late Antiquity the names of family members were carefully recycled generation after generation. This habit was scorned by John Chrysostom, urging parents to use the names of biblical heroes rather than those of their pagan ancestors. According to him, in the past, naming children after one's ancestors was a consolation in death, since the departed thus still seem to live through their names, but this is no longer needed in Christian contexts.[101] However, even among Christians, the continuity of the family names was held to be important. This can be seen in the female ascetic network in Rome, since in all the cases in which both the names of a grandmother and a granddaughter are known, they share the same name: Paula, Melania, Blesilla. A similar tendency can be seen in the families of Basil the Elder and Emmelia, and Gregory the Elder and Nonna, with the aim of establishing links and references to family traditions and preceding generations: both fathers had homonymous sons, and Basil's daughter was named after his mother, Macrina.[102] The names of the sons of Ruricius of Limoges in late fifth-century Gaul show this tendency for the naming of sons in West: the oldest son was named after the maternal grandfather, the second after the uncle of the mother, so the brothers thus repeated the names of the older

---

[99] Jerome, *Letters*, 123.1–2.

[100] *History of the Monks in Egypt*, 1.10; Palladius, *The Lausiac History*, 61.1–2.

[101] John Chrysostom, *An Address on Vainglory*, 49; John Chrysostom, *On Anna*, 1.6 – here Chrysostom mentions the names of father, uncle, grandfather and great-grandfather as those often chosen; John Chrysostom, *Homilies in Genesis*, 18.3.

[102] Van Dam, *Families and Friends*, pp. 122–4 on the families of Gregory Nazianzen and Gregory of Nyssa.

174 *Children and Asceticism in Late Antiquity*

brothers. The third boy was the namesake of his paternal uncle and the fourth was most probably named after his paternal grandfather.[103]

Consequently it is easy to understand why it was thought that an integral part of the eternal punishment reserved for Judas was that all (good) memory of his name was to be obliterated from the face of the earth. In this the punishment of having no posterity played a major part. In the absence of succeeding offspring, the name of the parents is doomed to fall into oblivion. Paulinus of Nola combines true preservation of the name with charity in stressing the correct use of wealth, in other words extensive almsgiving, for keeping one's name in the Book of Life. Wicked rich men are not named even in the Gospels since they are hated by God and erased from memory. The right use of riches would also ascertain enduring memory on earth.[104]

The most elaborate treatment of the continuity of the name in Christian contexts is in Augustine's *Holy Virginity*. Referring to the promises given to the law-abiding eunuchs in Isaiah, Augustine points out that virgins, both male and female, will gain a never failing, eternal name. 'What more do you seek?' he asks, indicating that this would be the ultimate reward for his audience, urging them to seek the continuity for their name in heaven rather than in marriage and in the uncertainty of progeny.[105]

As these examples show, the importance of the name as a tool for lasting memory and the symbol of continuity was well understood by the fourth- and fifth-century ecclesiastical writers.[106] The transmission of the name was certainly not considered vain: undying memory was something worth attaining. Christian writers shared the cultural values in which the (family) name was an important constituent of one's identity and its continuity came to mean the continuity of

---

[103] R. Mathisen, *Ruricius of Limoges and Friends: A Collection of Letters from Visigothic Aquitania* (Liverpool, 1999), pp. 23–4: the names are, in order of appearance, Ommatius, Eparchus, Leontius and Constantius. The source of the name of the fifth brother, Aurelianus, is unknown.

[104] Augustine, *Exposition on the Psalm 108*, 13 and 15, with Jerome, *Life of Hilarius*, 17.5 (before 392 CE). Paulinus of Nola, *Letters*, 13, esp. 19–20.

[105] Augustine, *On Holy Virginity*, 24–7, 30, esp. 25: 'Nomen aeternum dabo eis ... Quid quaeris amplius? Quid dicis amplius? Aeternum hoc nomen, quidquid illud est, spadonibus Dei, quod utique gloriam quamdam propriam excellentemque significat.' See also Augustine, *Letters*, 243.9; and Basil of Ancyra, *On True Purity of Virginity*, 60. For the passage on which Augustine comments, see Is. 56:4–5.

[106] Cf. Christophe Badel's explanation for the seemingly dropping numbers of aristocratic adoptions in Late Antiquity: according to him, the perception of how the family identity was formed had changed, and thus also the role of the continuity of the name as a part of that identity had already lost its relevance (Badel, 'L'adoption', pp. 102–3).

the self and the family. Spiritual salvation and the transmission of the name were not seen as mutually exclusive as both were understood to result from a pious life as a member of the family of Christ.

* * *

Memory as a means of achieving immortality was an important way of understanding one's continuity in Late Antiquity. The concepts of familial nobility and personal honour played a central role in elite culture in strategies for power and privileges in the context both of local communities and of the late Roman Empire at large. The Christian ideology of asceticism did not change these attitudes, even if in some cases conscious effort was made to redirect the continuity of the biological family – which depended on children – towards spiritual rewards and the continuity of the family tradition and its memory. By the early fifth century, asceticism was propagated as a source for good name, family nobility and distinction.[107] The fruitfulness of the ascetics renewed family traditions and *fama*, and ensured both their own renown and the continuing remembrance of their family in this world. Even if female virgins disrupted the biological (male) lineage, they continued and further sanctified the family tradition. Noble lines would be nobler still, their fame spreading to every corner of the world and their individual members remembered in prayers and in the life of Christian communities. It was not only the ascetics themselves but also their whole family who gained from their glory.

The same effects applied to continuity after death. As the *cursus honorum* of the traditional aristocracy brought to mind the past efforts of deceased members of the family, so too the efforts of the athletes of faith were preserved in multiple ways in the memories and writings of the Christian community. Thus, the ascetic discourse attached to asceticism features which were traditionally associated only with aristocratic *nobilitas*: the ascetics, both male and female, contributed to the nobility of the family group, and transferred the memory of its members to future generations.

This kind of continuity after death would have been beyond the reach of most people in the ancient world before the glorification of asceticism in the Christian culture of the late Roman world. For ordinary people, continuity

---

[107] See also Hunter, *Marriage, Celibacy*, pp. 77–83 for asceticism as a strategy in the aristocratic competition for honour and glory; and Cooper, *The Virgin and the Bride*, pp. 80–87 for asceticism as a means for social prestige for ascetic women.

in the commemoration based on the claim to nobility, even spiritual nobility – to say nothing of the continuity based on written records or other material monuments – was seldom possible. On the other hand, immortality in the remembrance and mere survival in one's nearest and dearest were open to all. Ambrose claimed that 'the best duties to discharge to the departed are that they live in our memories and continue in our affection'.[108] When the children of the deceased sister of Faustinus see him, 'they will think that their mother has not died', as in him they will know her again and feel her presence. In him she remains alive for them.[109] The common idea was that to ensure continuity in and by others, there was no better alternative to children.

---

[108] Ambrose, *On the Death of His Brother Satyrus*, 2.13: 'Haec bene defunctis officia penduntur, ut vivant in mentibus, in adfectibus perseverent.' Translated by H. de Romestin et al. (Nicene and Post-Nicene Fathers, ser. II, vol. 10).

[109] Ambrose, *Letters*, 8.2: 'Cum te vident matrem sibi non credant obisse, in te eam recognoscant, in te eius praesentiam teneant in te vitam eius sibi manere arbitrentur.'

Chapter 8

Children, Strategies and Continuity

Furthermore, they say, the childless man fails in the perfection which is according to nature, not having substituted his proper successor in his place. Perfect, on the other hand, is the man who had produced of himself his like ... Therefore we must by all means marry, both for our country's sake, for the succession of children, and as far as we are concerned, for the perfection of the world.[1]

The memory of individuals, familial wealth, traditions, values and accumulated social prestige were transferred to the following generations in children, ensuring a sense of continuity for their parents and ancestors. Thus, the most urgent need satisfied by married life was the need for legitimate progeny: children were the very point of getting married. The story told by Augustine about his and his father's visit to the baths is telling: as soon as the father saw signs of puberty in his son, he began to look to the future, rejoicing in the prospect of grandchildren.[2] Similarly, the resolution of Paulinus and Therasia to leave the senatorial way of life and enter into chastity was understood to have been appalling to the senatorial aristocracy above all because it signified the extinction of a prominent family line. The same ethos is present in the edict of the Emperor Majorian in 458, commenting on ascetic practices, since it urges noble women to save their noble lineage from extinction and marry. The edict also reproaches widows who refuse to renew their family by not marrying again.[3]

The ecclesiastical writers could not turn a deaf ear to this evaluation of progeny. Marriage is to the survival of kin as food is to the survival of an individual, as Augustine points out. This principle was acknowledged even by

---

[1]   Clemens of Alexandria, *Stromata*, 2.23.139.5–2.23.140.1: "Ἔτι, φασίν, ὁ ἄτεκνος τῆς κατὰ φύσιν τελειότητος ἀπολείπεται ἅτε μὴ ἀντικαταστήσας τῇ χώρᾳ τὸν οἰκεῖον διάδοχον· τέλειος γὰρ ὁ πεποιηκὼς ἐξ αὐτοῦ τὸν ὅμοιον. Γαμητέον οὖν πάντως καὶ τῆς πατρίδος ἕνεκα καὶ τῆς τῶν παίδων διαδοχῆς καὶ τῆς τοῦ κόσμου τὸ ὅσον ἐφ'ἡμῖν συντελειώσεως'. Translated by W. Wilson (Ante-Nicene Fathers, vol. 2). Clement refers positively here to the common opinion of those who approve of marriage, against both opponents of marriage and against those who accept marriage only for the sake of pleasure.

[2]   Augustine, *Confessions*, 2.3.6.

[3]   Ambrose, *Letters*, 27.3, with John Chrysostom, *Against the Opponents of Monastic Life*, 2.2; *Novellae Maioriani*, 6.3 and 5.

the most dedicated propagandists of asceticism, and the delights of children were seen to be abundant. At the same time it was pointed out that a desire for succession in children is the only honourable reason for sexual activity and marriage.[4] Many authors, however, had reservations about this, since Christians should be seeking heavenly, not earthly, continuity. The kind of immortality offered by children was unworthy.[5]

In this chapter, I shall investigate the functions of children for the individual and familial strategies for continuity.[6] First, we see how children were identified as the *leitmotif* of married life. However, the wish for progeny was a problem if the aim was to have people dedicate themselves or their children to chastity, and the ecclesiastical writers had to fight against the alleged joys of marriage – of which having children was culturally the most central. The second section deals with the interplay of asceticism and the need for children and grandchildren, and looks at the value of children. How did the assumed importance of biological continuity affect the response to the propagation of asceticism? What was the importance of children for the strategies of continuity? In the last section the functions of children, establishing their significance for the families and individual continuity, are analysed in detail. In the most concrete sense, the mere existence of children and grandchildren signified continuity for the parents. Moreover, children not only played a part in perpetuating the family wealth, fame and memory, but were also seen as irreplaceable with regard to the security and consolation of their parents, especially in their old age. Children also contributed to their parents in their death – and after it. A parallel theme here is the exploration of the argument that asceticism responded to these same needs.

---

[4]   Augustine, *On the Good of Marriage*, 16 (18): 'Quod enim est cibus ad salutem hominis, hoc est concubitus ad salutem generis'; Ambrose, *On Widows*, 2.9; Ambrose, *On Virgins*, 1.6.25–6; Gregory Nazianzen, *Oration 37*, 9; Augustine, *Letters*, 130.16.29; *On Marriage and Concupiscence*, 1.4 (5); *On the Good of Marriage*, 1; *Enchiridion*, 21.78; *Against Julian*, 6.30.

[5]   John Chrysostom, *Against the Opponents of Monastic Life*, 2.8 and 3.16; John Chrysostom, *Homilies in Genesis*, 18.4.2; John Chrysostom, *On Virginity*, 15.1; Basil of Ancyra, *On True Purity of Virginity*, 51, 54–5 (see further van Eijk, 'Marriage and Virginity', pp. 226–7) and Gregory of Nyssa, *On Virginity*, 3.10, with Tertullian, *An Exhortation to Chastity*, 9 and 12; Tertullian, *To His Wife*, 1.5.

[6]   See also Figure 1, p. 41 above.

Asceticism as Freedom – Children as Nuisance

It has been proposed that for women of the senatorial aristocracy and local elites, asceticism offered a personal independence and esteem which they could not achieve otherwise.[7] This view had been propagated by the ecclesiastical writers themselves. It became a *topos* to compare widowhood and virgin life to the difficulties and anxieties that women in particular were bound to encounter in ordinary married life.

Tertullian was one of the first, if not the very first, to claim that chaste widowhood was a form of freedom, exchanging the servitude of matrimony for liberty. In particular, children would be burdensome and cause inconvenience.[8] These points of view were eagerly adopted by the fourth-century authors who propagated asceticism. According to Ambrose, a marriage is a burden with pains and sorrows in giving birth to children, signifying subjection to the husband. A wife is under the power of her husband, but a virgin is free. Only servitude is bought by brides' dowries and their freedom of choice is lost. They are more like slaves (*mancipia*) than wives (*coniugia*), serving their men and trying to please them. Logically, Ambrose refers to the death of a husband as liberation for the widow. In remarriage, a widow with surviving children desires only the servitude from which she has already freed herself.[9]

The idea of marriage as slavery and freedom coming only with the death of the husband is a frequent theme in other contemporary texts too. Jerome rhetorically exaggerates the elder Melania's calmness on the death of her husband and two sons by claiming that she only thanked God for liberating her from the great burden of being a wife and mother. On the other hand, he claims that for some virgins and widows, this liberty would be dangerous, offering possibilities of lax living away from the eyes of others. These remarks by Jerome are rather general in nature and they depict well his rhetorical tactics in using the same

---

[7]   Patlagean, *Pauvreté économique*, esp. pp. 130 and 140; Clark, 'Ascetic Renunciation', esp. p. 193; Drijvers, 'Virginity and Asceticism', pp. 265–8; Verdon, 'Virgins and Widows', pp. 488, 502–3; Brown, *Body and Society*, pp. 266, 304; Salisbury, *Church Fathers*; see also Arjava, *Women and Law*, pp. 158–64; Kuefler, *The Manly Eunuch*, pp. 190 and 292–4 with further references.

[8]   Tertullian, *To His Wife*, 1.5 and 1.7; Tertullian, *An Exhortation to Chastity*, 12. See also *Acts of Thomas*, 12. Clement of Alexandria refers to these arguments, but does not accept them (Clemens of Alexandria, *Stromata*, 2.23.139–42).

[9]   Ambrose, *On Widows*, 1.2, 13.81, 18.88 (c. 380 CE); *Letters Outside the Collection*, 15.3; *Exhortation to Virginity*, 4.20–24; Ambrose, *On Widows*, 1.2, citing 1 Cor 7:39.

argument for both ends depending on the desired outcome.[10] However, they show that he at least held that it was commonly believed that chastity and being unmarried meant liberty. There are, moreover, other texts that use the same argument. The Council of Gangra had anathematized women who, in order to annul their subjection to their husbands, assumed ascetic habits and outlook, and an edict by the Emperor Majorian decries widows who choose chastity, not out of love of religion, but because of 'a lascivious freedom of living'.[11]

Some women are known to have tried to achieve this freedom. A certain Ecdicia persuaded her husband to take a vow of continence and afterwards, without consulting her husband, assumed the clothes of a widow, donated both her and her husband's property, and gave their son in marriage. For Ecdicia, the ascetic life meant freedom from the gender roles of marriage – a point to which Augustine did not subscribe.[12] In the case of the subdeacon Primus who had enticed two Catholic nuns to join him and the Donatists, Augustine branded him as rejoicing with vagabond crowds of women who refuse to be subjected to husbands. Here he argues against the idea of seeing asceticism as a way of escaping the earthly cares of married life, but, in other instances, he acknowledges the freedom of the ascetic lifestyle, such as when he praises Proba for freeing herself from worldly affairs.[13]

The increase of female independence and a comparatively wide degree of freedom were expected in many biographies of the ascetic saints. The intellectual freedom and influence of Paula the Elder, the two Melanias, Marcella or

---

[10]   Death of a husband as a relief: Jerome, *Letters*, 39.4; 77.4; 108.5; 123.10. Negative liberty: Jerome, *Letters*, 22.16; 54.13; 125.6; 130.19. It should be noted that Paulinus of Nola mentions Melania's grief at these deaths (see Paulinus of Nola, *Letters*, 29.8, with Wilkinson, 'The Elder Melania's Missing Decade', p. 174 on Jerome's rhetorical strategies).

[11]   *Council of Gangra, Canon* 17, and *Introductory Letter*, 1 and 7. *Novellae Maioriani*, 6.5: 'viduitatisque captantes lasciviam vivendi eligunt libertatem', with John Chrysostom, *On Virginity*, 40.1 (382–92 CE); Eusebius of Emesa, *Sermons*, 7.18; and Palladius, *Dialogue on the Life of John Chrysostom*, 17.134–47.

[12]   Augustine, *Letters*, 262, with M. Tilley, 'No Friendly Letters: Augustine's Correspondence with Women', in Martin and Miller (eds), *The Cultural Turn*, pp. 52–3; and Krawiec, 'From the Womb', pp. 292–5. See also *Pelagius, Letter to Celantia*, esp. pp. 26–8. Shaw, 'The Family', pp. 28 and 32–3, Brown, *Body and Society*, p. 404 and Kuefler, *The Manly Eunuch*, pp. 190–91 see such cases as indicating the prevalent patriarchal authority. However, men were likewise expected to take into account the needs and wishes of their wives: see e.g. Augustine, *Letters*, 127.9. Mutual consent was needed both for taking the vow and for distributing the common funds: Augustine, *On the Good of Marriage*, 6; Augustine, *Letters*, 220.12; Basil of Caesarea, *Longer Rules*, 12.

[13]   Augustine, *Letters*, 35.2 and Augustine, *On Holy Virginity*, 13 vs. Augustine, *On Holy Virginity*, 55 (54) and Augustine, *Letters*, 130.16.30 (on Proba).

Olympias indicate what this could have meant for the widows of the nobility.[14] Even more significantly, freedom is attached to persons and circumstances in which it was seen as far from desirable. In principle, therefore, the freedom from the established gender roles was within the reach of widows and other independent women.

However, the aim for freedom can hardly be seen as a universal motivation for asceticism. As I have shown above, nearer to the grassroots level, this freedom assumed less spectacular and less tolerated manifestations: for most virgins, it was their parents who made the final decisions and kept them under strict surveillance. Virgins promised to God at birth and brought up by their parents, or those following their parents to the ascetic life, were certainly not free to choose their lot, nor were those orphans or foundlings who were taken up as minors by the monastic communities.

The freedom promoted was not freedom to make decisions or freedom to act. Indeed, this freedom is not freedom for something, but rather freedom from something: from marriage, from having children, from a life branded as ordinary. There are plenty of texts promoting virginity and chaste widowhood with examples and detailed lists of what women will escape if they remain unmarried. The pains of childbirth, the death of a daughter, the illness of a son, the absence of the husband, the lack of the necessities of life, the eventual death of the husband with tears and grief, second marriage with a second mourning or the groans of widowhood, and the ultimate depression of seeing the glory of the virgins in eternity – all these await a woman who is willing to marry.

Most of these kinds of lists are shorter than the previous example which is drawn from a sermon by an anonymous Eastern author.[15] In the lists of Ambrose and Jerome, pregnancy and giving birth are mentioned first, followed by illnesses, dangers and the fear of death, and the problems of nursing, training and marrying off of children. Moreover, there were the sorrows of possible barrenness, the need to be subject to a husband's discretion, the running of the household and finally the untimely deaths of other family members.[16] For John Chrysostom, the list begins with men treating their wives as slaves and inventing different means to punish their women. Only the wife's death ends

---

[14]   See also Clark, 'Ascetic Renunciation', esp. pp. 186–8, 192–3.

[15]   *Anonymous Homily on Virginity*, 45–57.

[16]   Ambrose, *On Virgins*, 1.6.25–26; Jerome, *Letters*, 22.2; Jerome, *Letters*, 49 (48).14 and 19; see also Eusebius of Emesa, *Sermons*, 7.16; Ambrose, *On Virgins*, 1.6.30–31; Ambrose, *On the Death of his Brother Satyrus*, 1.68; Jerome, *Against Helvidius*, 20 and 22; Augustine, *On Holy Virginity*, 16; and Augustine, *Exposition on the Psalm 127*, 15 with Beaucamp, *Le statut*, vol. II, pp. 321–5. For the pains of childbirth, see also Augustine, *Letters*, 150 and 243.7.

these sufferings. The wife is to expect tears, suffering, insults, jealousy, threats and conflicts; even the household slaves despise her. If there are no actual misappropriations, there is always the fear of them. Moreover, there are fears of not having children or having too many, fears of miscarriage and the death of a child, the pains of giving birth, the fear of a child being unhealthy or not being a boy, the problems of how to bring a child up and to protect its life, questions of a child's moral character, problems in giving them in marriage and fears about the sudden death of a child or husband. Gregory of Nyssa puts even more stress on the ubiquity of sickness and death and the resulting fears and anxieties of the mother. He also adds that the old stories of crimes, such as the murder of family members, the eating of children and incest, always begin with marriage.[17] Marriage, children and death were inevitably bound together; only asceticism can set one free from this triangle of decay.[18]

It was necessary to form an image of having children as ultimately a terrible burden for the mother. The argumentation of Eusebius of Emesa summarizes the point neatly: there is blame if no children are born, but if there are children, the problem is that they are girls; the more children are born, the worse things are: one has headache, another has pain in the eyes and yet another feels sick. Children with a pernicious character cause sorrow to their parents, whereas the good children make parents afraid of being cut off from them. If there are only few children, the parents fear they will be left alone; if there are many, they are anxious about how to feed them and establish them in life. In view of all this trouble caused by children, it is not surprising that for Jerome the crying of babies is the very symbol of all the cares and inconveniences of marriage.[19]

Marriage was branded as a burden for men too. According to Eusebius of Caesarea, the patriarchs of old lived with many wives and had countless children, living an easier and freer life, whereas at present, wives, children and domestic cares would distract men from the things that please God. These themes continued in the late fourth century: for men, chastity signified freedom from earthly cares and time for prayer and for the practice of virtues.

---

[17]   John Chrysostom, *On Virginity*, 52 and 56–7; Gregory of Nyssa, *On Virginity*, 3.4–10.

[18]   Ambrose, *On Virgins*, 1.6.30; John Chrysostom, *On Virginity*, 57.6; Gregory of Nyssa, *On Virginity*, 14.1; See also Gregory of Nyssa, *On Virginity*, 3.6–10; Jerome, *Letters*, 22.2 (384 CE); Ambrose, *On Virgins*, 1.6.25–6; Augustine, *Exposition on the Psalm 127*, 15.

[19]   Eusebius of Emesa, *Sermons*, 7.16; Jerome, *Letters*, 22.2; 22.19; 49 (48).19; *Against Helvidius*, 20; *Against Vigilantius*, 2 See also Jerome, *Letters*, 50.5 and 107.13. See also the squalling of the children symbolizing the troubles of childrearing in the Life of Saint Helia, cited in Burrus, "'Honor the Fathers'", esp. 453. This probably fifth-century text also reflects Jerome's rhetorics in its way of using the fertility metaphors for ascetics (see above, p. 87).

Children, Strategies and Continuity 183

Celibates are angels among people, since they are not slaves to the flesh, to worldly thoughts or to family matters.[20] Marriage is a threat to the freedom of conscience. After all, it is easier to live in perpetual continence than to join in marriage to have sexual relations only for the sake of children.[21] A special point is that marriage and family life are a hindrance not only to the spiritual life but also to intellectual life in general. Both Jerome and John Chrysostom point out that studying is much easier for an ascetic than for one in the midst of worldly troubles and hindrances. This line of argumentation owes much to the even older intellectual traditions of Antiquity, current particularly among authors informed by the Epicurean tradition and by Cynicism: the cares and responsibilities of married life made a life devoted to wisdom and philosophy impossible.[22]

On a more general level, a wife, children and the management of the household would draw a man earthwards and impede his spiritual strivings. Only a man who lives for Christ can be free: 'He who has contracted the obligations of marriage is bound, and he who is bound is a slave.' There are no means of liberation from this servitude but death; indeed, fathers should describe the miseries of marriage to their sons as a warning and as an exhortation to chastity.[23] This liberty of the unmarried may also have negative implications: 'I do not have a wife: I do what I will.'[24]

The gendered and age-specific expectations of behaviour emerge neatly in the discussion. The women who took too many liberties were widows – in some cases even dedicated virgins or married women – but young women are never referred to in this context. However, the men accused of misusing their liberty due to their unmarried status are young men, not ascetics. There are male ascetics who misuse their status, certainly, but then the accusation is

---

[20] Eusebius of Caesarea, *Proof of the Gospel*, 1.9 with e.g. Ambrose, *Exhortation to Virginity*, 4.19; Augustine, *On Holy Virginity*, 13, 22 and 55 (54); Augustine, *Letters*, 130.16.30; Jerome, *Against Jovinian*, 1.10–13; John Chrysostom, *On Virginity*, 79; 80.2; John Chrysostom, *Against the Opponents of Monastic Life*, 3.11, 16–17.

[21] Augustine, *On the Good of Marriage*, 13 (15); Jerome, *Against Jovinian*, 1.9.

[22] John Chrysostom, *Against the Opponents of Monastic Life*, 3.13; Jerome, *Against Jovinian*, 1.24. See also Augustine, *Confessions*, 2.3.8, with e.g. Epictetus, *Encheiridion*, 3.22.67–76 and T. Brennan, 'Epicurus on Sex, Marriage, and Child-rearing', *Classical Philology* 91(4) (1996), pp. 348–52.

[23] Jerome, *Letters*, 145: 'Qui igitur servit officio coniugali, vinctus est; qui vinctus est, servus est' with Jerome, *Letters*, 118.4; Augustine, *Letters*, 243.6–7 and 12; John Chrysostom, *Letters to Theodore*, 2.5; John Chrysostom, *On Virginity*, 28.1–3 and 80.2; Paulinus of Nola, *Letters*, 25.7 and 39.2; *Anonymous Homily on Virginity*, 60 (fathers warning their sons).

[24] Augustine, *Sermons*, 9.14: 'Uxorem non habeo, facio quod volo.'

not about their increased freedom, but about their increased authority, which leads to economic misdeeds.[25] Moreover, there are seldom any specifications or lists of the inconveniences of marriage for men in the same way that the argumentation against marriage for women was presented. In cases where details are given, the points resemble those made in connection with women, but with some exceptions. For women, the emphasis is on the actual pains and dangers of childbirth, on the running of the household and on the lack of authority in view of men's dominance, but the overwhelming majority of the accounts warning men against marriage are merely short notes on the problems about concentrating on prayer and spiritual perfection.

What is common is the great emphasis on the anxiety and sorrow caused by the deeds and the potential death of children. If a man marries a poor wife, there is a risk to his wealth; if he marries a rich wife, he risks his authority. Having children means bitter bondage in the fear of losing them; having no children is a great distress and means that the marriage itself was in vain; if the child is sick, there is fear; if it dies, there is inconsolable grief. The dearer the spouse and children are, the more anxiety they cause. On the whole, children do not bring happiness: good children die, or other children behave in such a way as to make parents envy childless couples. In the list by Gregory of Nyssa, most of the problems of marriage and running a household concern women. However, when the argument turns to the constant fear of accidents, illness and the death of a child, this distress would be equally felt by the husband. Moreover, Gregory seems to assume that fathers grieve especially over the lack of heirs, either because of childlessness or the death of the sons, or because of the survival of a reprobate son. On the other hand, in the absence of means for their support, a surplus of children also causes the father sorrows.[26]

Childlessness was one of the most frequently mentioned specific cares of the married alongside the biblical theme of the pains of childbirth. Many writers used the rhetorical figure of referring both to the trouble of bringing up children and highlighting the even worse situation of not having any children at all. Counting on children to be born is dangerous, as 'it is no slight evil to be married and to be deprived of the fruit of marriage, when the sole purpose of marriage is the begetting of children' – if there are no children, how can one

---

[25] See above pp. 138–43.

[26] John Chrysostom, *Letters to Theodore*, 2.5; Paulinus of Nola, *Letters*, 25.7. Gregory of Nyssa, *On Virginity*, 3.6 and 3.10. See already Tertullian, *To His Wife*, 1.5 on the bitter pleasures of children.

write about the joys of marriage?[27] Ambrose argues that for widows who had no children, it was not wise to remarry and chance their fertility again, but that for those whose children had died, a new marriage would be nothing more than a covering-over of the death of her lost children. There was also the danger of suffering the same fate again, shrinking from the graves of her hopes, with the memories of her past grief. Lastly, a widow with children has no need of a husband.[28] John Chrysostom attacks the desire for children and grandchildren by claiming that, in fact, parents do not even have biological children and it is not begetting that makes parents properly parents, but rather the continuity of spiritual virtues; on the other hand, when it suited his argument, he could call childlessness intolerable.[29]

The authors evinced the argument of the sorrows of childlessness as part of their overall argumentation in favour of remaining unmarried, that is, of excluding even the possibility of having children. This discrepancy in the argumentation was for two reasons: on the one hand, having children was the very point of entering into marriage, according to both the classical and the ecclesiastical writers of the time. Childlessness was a highly emotional issue and was seen as a threat to every couple, and especially for women. The stress to the husband and relatives of the couple was felt much more by the wife, as she was considered *a priori* as having more responsibility for fertility or the lack thereof. On the other hand, it was important to point out the uncertainties in counting on children to be born, and marrying was not enough to ensure progeny and the continuity of the family.

The value placed on progeny was an inevitable starting point for the argumentation of the ecclesiastical writers, reflecting the importance of children for a meaningful family life and for the pursuit of continuity. However, according to them, it would be wiser to aim for continuity by different methods, namely remaining chaste and investing in Christian asceticism. When one aims for spiritual offspring, the pain and trouble due to childlessness or the death of children do not occur. Thus, what at first sight seems a weakness in the argument for asceticism – that is, how to ensure continuity – was turned into its strongest point.

---

[27] Augustine, *Letters*, 130.16.29: 'Non parvum malum videbatur, et nuptam esse, et fructu carere nuptiarum, cum sola excuset nuptias procreandorum causa filiorum', translated by Sr W. Parsons (The Fathers of the Church, vol. 18), with John Chrysostom, *On Virginity*, 57.5; Augustine, *Letters*, 3*.1.2; and John Chrysostom, *Against the Opponents of Monastic Life*, 3.16.

[28] Ambrose, *On Widows*, 15.86–8.

[29] John Chrysostom, *Against the Opponents of Monastic Life*, 3.16; *On Anna*, 1.6–2.1.

First Children, Then Chastity

In principle, a saintly Christian did not want children or grandchildren, but the ecclesiastical writers had to deal with real people, who appreciated their continuity in children in ways that could not be explained away. The feeling of regret and pain is conveyed in the story told by Theodoret of Cyrrhus about his father who, despairing at still being childless after 13 years of marriage, begged the ascetics to ask God for children.[30] Moreover, it must not be forgotten that the writers themselves were brought up to think likewise. Indeed, the final test for the ascetic calling of Evagrius of Pontus was the suggestion by a demon that he should marry and have sons.[31]

Ambrose offers us a good example of the ambivalent tendencies. He refers to the wish of fathers to have grandchildren and to be called grandfathers, and praises those virgins who have 'left their parents, and do not obey those who are accustomed to say: "daughter, you owe us grandchildren"'.[32] Nevertheless, Ambrose understood, even if he did not share, the appreciation of biological offspring and he heartily congratulated his friend Eusebius, whom God had blessed with a son and grandchildren. Indeed, writes Ambrose, numerous children and grandchildren are a great blessing, signifying the perpetuation of the name and succession. Similarly, in arguing against the wish of a certain Paternus to marry his son to his daughter's daughter, Ambrose's final and concluding remark is that this solution would be unwise since it would not propagate the family of Paternus further: 'for this our son owes you grandchildren, and your dear granddaughter great-grandchildren'.[33] In his funeral eulogy for his brother Satyrus, he claims that he and his sister Marcellina had tried to persuade their brother Satyrus to marry. As Satyrus was not married by his early death, Ambrose was able to interpret this as an indication both of his love of chastity and of his affection for his brother and sister. The actual intentions of Satyrus are beyond our knowledge, but it seems that his brother and sister thought that there should be someone to carry on the family line. Even if this would not have been the case, at least Ambrose assumed that his congregation would think this idea plausible, or even inevitable. The same thinking is evident in another letter to Eusebius

---

[30] Theodoret of Cyrrhus, *Religious History*, 13.16.

[31] Evagrius Ponticus, *Antirrheticus*, 2.49.

[32] Ambrose, *Exhortation to Virginity*, 7.45: 'quae reliquit parentes, et non facit voluntatem eorum qui solent dicere: Debes nobis, filia, nepotes'; Ambrose, *On Virgins*, 1.7.33.

[33] Ambrose, *Letters*, 38.1 and 4; Ambrose, *Letters*, 58.11, 'Debet etiam tibi filius noster nepotes, debet etiam neptis carissima pronepotes', with Augustine, *City of God*, 15.16. See e.g. Paulinus of Nola, *Letters*, 44.5–6 on the blessings that are due to children.

where Ambrose appreciates the choice of selecting one of the children to live in chastity on behalf of the other family members, while the others are expected to perpetuate the lineage of their father.[34]

Ambrose was by no means the only ascetic who did not deny the need for the biological continuity of the family line. Both Melania the Elder and Paula the Elder seem to have cherished the idea of not only the spiritual but also the biological perpetuation of themselves and of the family lineage; Melania carefully ensured that the career of her son Publicola would have a good start and he, like Paula's children Blesilla, Rufina, Paulina and Toxotius, was to be married in due time. This was also intended for Demetrias, daughter of Juliana and granddaughter of Proba, both ascetic widows. Even in the case of Albina the Elder, whose daughter Marcella (seemingly her only child) had chosen the ascetic life, the family group itself had ascertained its continuity as Albina had at least six nephews and nieces.[35] These same tendencies were also visible among family groups who were not particularly known for their ascetic sympathies; as Béatrice Caseau points out, Ausonius had one maternal uncle and two aunts, one of whom was a dedicated virgin; on the paternal side, he had two uncles and two aunts, and again, the one aunt was a virgin consecrated to God.[36] Thus, it was important that both the heavenly and earthly lineage and networks were to be continued.

In considering this matter it was important to point out that those ascetic heroines who got married had no motivation to have children for their own sake. According to Jerome, when Paulina married, she wanted children in order to give birth to virgins for Christ and because she had to give way to her husband and mother-in-law who looked for children and grandchildren. Similarly, it was not Paula's wish to have sexual relations in marriage, but she complied with her husband's longing to have male offspring. The same claim was made about

---

[34]   Ambrose, *On the Death of His Brother Satyrus*, 53; *The Consecration of a Virgin*, 1.1; *Letters*, 38.1.

[35]   Publicola: Palladius, *The Lausiac History*, 46.1 and Paulinus of Nola, *Letters*, 29.8 with Wilkinson, 'The Elder Melania's Missing Decade', pp. 179–82; Blesilla: Jerome, *Letters*, 39; Rufina: Jerome, *Letters*, 108.4 and 6; Paulina: Jerome, *Letters*, 66.3; Toxotius: Jerome, *Letters*, 107.1; Demetrias: see e.g. Jerome, *Letters*, 130 with Krumeich, *Hieronymus*, Stemmata III.1 *Anicii*. Moreover, Demetrias had a brother. For Albina, see Sivan, 'On Hymens and Holiness', p. 82. See also Apronianus and Avita, who had a daughter (Eunomia) to stay with them to live in chastity, while the boy (Asterius) continued his life in the world (Paulinus of Nola, *Poems*, 21.66–71 and 21.313–29; Palladius, *The Historia Lausica*, 41.5).

[36]   Caseau, 'Stratégies parentales', pp. 256–7.

Melania the Younger and about Theodoret's mother.[37] Similarly, Jerome had to rebut a charge by critics of asceticism that Paula the Elder cried at her daughter Blesilla's funeral because she had not been able to have grandchildren through her. He also endeavoured to point out that Melania the Elder was not sorry for the death of her husband and two sons.[38] It is unnecessary to state here that these claims are later male interpretations aimed at pro-ascetic and eulogizing argumentation, but as such, they reveal the dominant cultural expectations with regard to children and the continuity of lineage.

Widows, especially if childless, were presumed to seek remarriage in order to have children. When Marcella was widowed, it was the default option for her ascetic mother Albina to seek to marry her off again. Likewise, Jerome expected Furia to be worried that she did not have children, particularly as her father, a devout Christian, was still without grandchildren and male heirs. He ironically asks if Furia is afraid that the Furian line (*proles Furiana*) will cease to exist and that her father will not have a grandchild 'to cover his neck with excrements'.[39] Moreover, children were not enough if grandchildren were lacking: Augustine refers to a case in which a devout widow wanted to dissolve the dedication of her daughter to virginity, since her sons and grandchildren had died, and she wanted to ensure her succession.[40]

Against these considerations it is not surprising to find that the idea of clerical celibacy was not eagerly adopted. Although many members of the clergy opted for chastity and bishops deposited their wives in monasteries, the practice was not universal and it was constantly discussed during the period under scrutiny.[41] Synesius of Cyrene was seemingly still without children when he stated that he would consent to serve as bishop only on condition that he was allowed to continue his conjugal life and have 'many and most excellent children'. Likewise, Antoninus, Bishop of Ephesus, was accused of taking back his wife and having children with her after having retired from married life when he became a bishop.[42] The earthly family with continuity in children was sometimes too

---

[37] Jerome, *Letters*, 66.3 (397 CE); Jerome, *Letters*, 108.4 (404 CE); Gerontius, *Life of Melania* (Greek), 1 (c. 450 CE); Theodoret of Cyrrhus, *Religious History*, 13.16 with Vuolanto, 'A Self-made Living Saint?', pp. 52–3. See also Palladius, *The Lausiac History*, 61.3. On the *topos* of forced marriages, see above pp. 102–13.

[38] Jerome, *Letters*, 39.6–9, with Wilkinson 'The Elder Melania's Missing Decade', p. 174.

[39] Jerome, *Letters*, 127; 54.4–5: 'cervices eius stercore linat'. See also Jerome, *Letters*, 123; and Ambrose, *On Widows*, 15.86.

[40] Augustine, *Letters*, 3*.1 and 3.

[41] For the discussion, see above pp. 71–5.

[42] Synesius, *Letters*, 105: 'συχνὰ μοι πάνυ καὶ χρηστὰ γενέσθαι παιδία'; Palladius, *Dialogue on the Life of John Chrysostom*, 13.171–2.

precious a thing to be endangered by the episcopate and having only the spiritual family shared with the other members of the clergy.

Married chastity was, naturally, also possible for laypeople. According to Basil of Caesarea, couples vowing chastity were one of the groups who entered the monastic communities. For many ecclesiastical writers, this sort of chastity would carry special merit and praise compared to mere continence, and compared to marriage it would be the most excellent and sublime way for a Christian wife and husband to live together. The practice was well established by the latter half of the fifth century both in East and West.[43] In the legendary stories and hagiographical material, the standard *topos* was that the promise of chastity was made on the wedding night and thus the couple remained virgins. In particular, the story of Ammon, who was said to have persuaded his bride to preserve their virginity together in secret, gained much popularity during the fifth century.[44]

How did this practice accord with the idea of marriage being (solely) for the procreation of children? An ambivalent case is related by the church historian Sozomen:

> It is said that Ajax married a very lovely woman, and after he had known her thrice in all that time, had three sons; and that subsequently he held no further intercourse with her, but persevered in the exercises of monasticism. He brought up two of his sons to the divine life and unmarriedness, and the third to married life.[45]

The story builds up a figure of extreme ascetic virtue by referring to his lovely wife and her three sons together with the theme of chaste marriage. In its otherworldliness and paradoxicality, the figure of Ajax was almost as compelling as the idea of a virgin having a son. Here, it is especially noteworthy that the

---

[43] Basil of Caesarea, *Longer Rules*, 12; Ambrose, *On Virgins*, 22; Augustine, *On the Sermon on the Mount*, 1.15.42; Augustine, *Letters*, 31.6; 200.3 and 220.12; *Anonymous Homily on Virginity*, 116–18; Vitricius of Rouen, *The Praise of Saints*, 3.

[44] Ammon: Palladius, *The Lausiac History*, 8; *History of the Monks in Egypt*, 22.1; Socrates, *Ecclesiastical History*, 4.23; Sozomen, *Ecclesiastical History*, 1.14 with Elm, *Virgins*, pp. 325–6. Already Jerome's hero Malchus had entered into a chaste marriage: Jerome, *Life of Malchus*, 6.7–9. See also *Acts of Thomas*, 12; Palladius, *The Lausiac History*, 67.1.

[45] Sozomen, *Ecclesiastical History*, 7.28: Λέγεται δὲ Αἴαντα μὲν γῆμαι εἰδεστάτην γυναῖκα, τρίτον δὲ μόνον αὐτῇ συνελθεῖν ἐν παντὶ τῷ χρόνῳ καὶ τρεῖς παῖδας ποιῆσαι, τὸ μετὰ ταῦτα δὲ συνουσίας ἕνεκα τοιᾶσδε τῇ γαμετῇ ἀποταξάμενον μοναχικῶς πεπολιτεῦσθαι· καὶ τῶν υἱέων δύο μὲν ἐπὶ τὰ θεῖα καὶ τὴν ἀγαμίαν παιδαγωγῆσαι, τὸν ἄλλον δὲ ἐπὶ γάμον.' Translated by A.C. Zenos (Nicene and Post-Nicene Fathers, ser. II, vol. 10). See also *History of the Monks in Egypt*, 14.13.

190   *Children and Asceticism in Late Antiquity*

fact that Ajax had taken care of his succession was interpreted as furthering, not diminishing, his exemplary character.

Indeed, in historical cases the normality of marital life 'before' is taken for granted. The promise of chastity was given only after a considerable period of ordinary marriage and often when there were already children. Thus, Aper and Amanda already had sons before taking a vow of continence. Paulinus of Nola refers to the chastity of their children, hoping that they will also be consecrated, eventually becoming the successors of their father's priesthood, 'as they do not fall below [their father] in sanctity'.[46] The heritage is transferred and the family tradition is continued.

Apronianus and Avita, later members of Paulinus' monastic communities at Nola, were persuaded to marital chastity by Avita's aunt, Melania the Elder, after having had a boy and a girl. Among Paulinus' noble friends, Eucherius and Galla retired to the islands of Lérins with their still minor sons in the 420s, and Salvian with his wife Palladia also started their life of continence, probably also in Lérins, with their little daughter Auspiciola.[47] Eusebius of Emesa connects the idea of living in chastity especially with those couples who have children, giving as an example a mother who both 'converted to the religious life' and fasted in order to save her son who was suffering from a headache. As the husband agreed, and the boy was healed, the couple expressed their gratitude by 'imitating virgins'.[48]

The intention of retiring after having children to continue the family line was not always carried out. Paulinus of Nola himself and his wife Therasia are one example of this as their only child had died in early infancy. After their vow of chastity, Paulinus grieved about this, complaining that they were unworthy to rejoice in posterity.[49] Similarly Melania the Younger and Pinian committed themselves to chastity after the death of their prematurely born boy and a slightly older girl, although this was contrary to the wishes of their families, who were still hoping for continuity of the line. Jerome's speculation on the death of Paulina also refers to these contemporary values and the right order of things: if Paulina and Pammachius had had children, Paulina would have persuaded her

---

[46]   Paulinus of Nola, *Letters*, 39.1–2 and 44.5.

[47]   Palladius, *The Lausiac History*, 41.5 and 54.2; Paulinus of Nola, *Poems*, 21.313–29, 66–8 and 21.284–7; Paulinus of Nola, *Letters*, 51; Salvian, *Letters*, 4. In the unfortunate case of Ecdicia, who wanted to start a celibate life in spite of her husband's wishes, they had an adult son: Augustine, *Letters*, 262.11.

[48]   Eusebius of Emesa, *Sermons*, 7.9: 'Ita ergo et qui in nuptiis coniuncti sunt, magis imitantur virgines.'

[49]   Paulinus of Nola, *Poems*, 31.603–4 and Paulinus of Nola, *Letters*, 27.3, with Augustine, *Letters*, 31.5–6.

Children, Strategies and Continuity 191

husband to embrace chastity.[50] It is of interest that references to protests by more distant relatives or social peers are referred to only when this familial continuity has not been achieved, notably as in the cases of Therasia and Paulinus of Nola or Melania the Younger and Pinian.

In many cases it is impossible to infer the existence or non-existence of children.[51] There is only one case in which a clearly childless couple had vowed chastity in circumstances in which there are no references to already-deceased children or to a general urge to ensure progeny before the vow. Even here, in the case of Armentarius and Paulina, there seems to have been some kind of hesitation and at least Augustine suspected that there was a danger of rescinding the vow.[52] However, in no other case outside hagiography did the couple pledge themselves to chastity 'through contempt of earthly progeny' and, indeed, most did this 'after the procreation of children'. Not surprisingly, Augustine seems to consider the first option to be more praiseworthy, but the second to be the more normal situation.[53] First children, then chastity was the order of things.

Augustine claims that a different solution was adopted by the small Christian group, *Abeloitas*, or *Abeloim*. They taught that marriage was obligatory, but intercourse prohibited, and thus the couples lived with each other, adopting a son and a daughter. When the old couple died, younger ones took their place and in turn adopted the next generation to succeed them, and the continuity of the community and the household was again guaranteed. As Augustine points out, there was never a lack of adoptees for these heretics since the neighbouring people gladly gave their children for adoption in the hope of having a share of the inheritance of a foreign household.[54] Taking into consideration the importance of lineage in Late Antiquity on the one hand, and the propagation of the ascetic ideals and purity on the other, this practice makes much sense, even if this remained a curiosity.

---

[50]   Palladius, *The Lausiac History*, 61; Gerontius, *Life of Melania* (Greek), 5–6; Jerome, *Letters*, 66.3.

[51]   See Lucinus and Theodora in Jerome, *Letters*, 71; Rusticus and Artemia in Jerome, *Letters*, 122; Comes Africae Valerius and his wife in Augustine, *Letters*, 200.3; brother and sister-in-law of a certain Hilarius in Augustine, *Letters*, 226, and the chaste couples in Rouen: Paulinus of Nola, *Letters*, 18.5; and Vitricius of Rouen, *The Praise of Saints*, 3.

[52]   Augustine, *Letters*, 127, esp. 1 (status and hesitation), 6 (hesitation) and 8 (childlessness). In the case of Rusticus and Artemia, the vow was broken (Jerome, *Letters*, 122). The husband of Ecdicia also broke the vow with another woman (Augustine, *Letters*, 262).

[53]   Augustine, *On the Sermon on the Mount*, 1.14.39: 'Beatiora sane coniugia iudicanda sunt quae sive filiis procreatis sive etiam ista terrena prole contempta continentiam inter se pari consensu servare potuerint.'

[54]   Augustine, *On Heresies*, 87.

In general, the chastity of lay couples was praised by the ecclesiastical writers of the fourth and fifth centuries and was looked upon as creating honour for the couples themselves and their families. However, the vow of chastity was only taken, or intended to be taken, after the succession in earthly progeny was ensured or when the hope for such successors had failed.[55] In these latter cases, chastity with spiritual merits and otherworldly gains can be seen as a secondary strategy for continuity. On the other hand, not all children were to enter the ascetic life as the continuity of the lineage was of central importance. In practice even the most Christianized families with a positive view of asceticism tried to ensure their own and their families' succession through biological children and grandchildren.

Children as Material and Immaterial Solace

Except for the indirect functions of children in the transfer of property, and the reputation and memory of their parents, children were also counted on as sources of more direct economic and psychological assistance and continuity for their relatives. As Augustine notes, people give birth to children for their own solace and for support in their old age.[56] This social reality also features in discussions of asceticism. Clement of Alexandria had already evinced the argument for the need of support in old age in favour of marriage, to counter the extreme ascetic tendencies of his age. A child in a monastery could no longer support elderly parents. The later ecclesiastical writers who promoted chastity, while admitting the partial truth in the general opinion that asceticism endangered security in old age, were more willing to point out that a widow could and would manage well even without a husband and children. In John Chrysostom's mocking description, for example, comfort in old age and avoiding solitude are the first considerations mentioned to explain the grief of the father on hearing that his son would enter the ascetic life. At least in the imagination of the fourth- and fifth-century authors, the problem was especially poignant in the case of widowed women. Gregory Nazianzen explained this by referring to the

---

[55]   See also Cloke, 'This Female Man of God', p. 123. In addition to the couples mentioned above, see also Jerome, Letters, 118, in which Jerome urges a certain Julianus to take a vow of chastity after he had lost his wife and children except for one daughter: now he would be free to strive for the heavenly reward and would also benefit his deceased children by the donations.

[56]   See e.g. Augustine, Exposition on the Psalm 70, 2.6: 'Generant tamen homines filios, et ad solatium suum, et ad subsidium senectutis.' See also Shaw, 'The Family', pp. 19–21.

Children, Strategies and Continuity 193

legislators, who, since they were male, had placed children under the authority of the fathers and thus left the weaker sex uncared for.[57]

It was more common, however, to refer directly to the idea of the *infirmitas* of women which was the main contemporary concept to explain and justify the legal restrictions and prejudice against feminine weakness and gullibility.[58] Accordingly, the ecclesiastical writers had to respond to the idea that women who took care of the family property by themselves would endanger its survival. Jerome depicts the thoughts of a lonely widow thus: 'My little patrimony is daily perishing, the inheritance of the ancestors is being dispersed.' Naturally the ecclesiastical writers pointed out the vanity of such thoughts and stressed the administrative skills of women.[59] A widow who wanted to keep her property safe and relieve herself of the cares, fears and dangers associated with the administration of wealth could also invest her possessions in heaven; that is, instead of taking a new husband to manage the property, she should give it away in alms.[60] The theme is often taken up in connection with widows opposing their sons' will to embark on asceticism, and in reference to the duties and difficulties in the running of the household. The mother of Laetus tried to keep him involved in managing the household and would not let him enter the monastic community. According to John Chrysostom, his own mother referred to the tasks and burdens of widowhood – such as correcting the servants, thwarting the schemes of relatives, the rudeness of public officials about taxes and safeguarding the inheritance intact for John – in persuading him to stay with her until her death. Women were inherently weak, but were able to transcend their limits, if argumentation needed this kind of approach![61]

How could childless widows be persuaded to remain unmarried? Ambrose gives an example for all holy widows by referring to Naomi in the Old Testament. They should train their daughters-in-law, and other more distant relatives, so

---

[57] Clemens of Alexandria, *Stromata*, 2.23.139; John Chrysostom, *Against the Opponents of Monastic Life*, 2.2. and 3.1; Gregory Nazianzen, *Oration 37*, 6.

[58] On *infirmitas*, see Fayer, *La familia romana*, pp. 525–7; and H. Saradi-Mendelovici, 'A Contribution to the Study of Byzantine Notarial Formulas: The *infirmitas sexus* of Women and the *Sc. Velleianum*', *Byzantinisches Zeitschrift* 83 (1990), pp. 72–3.

[59] Jerome, *Letters*, 54.15: 'Patrimoniolum meum cottidie perit, maiorum hereditas dissipatur'; see already Tertullian, *An Exhortation to Chastity*, 12. For the administrative skills of the widows, see e.g. Ambrose, *On Widows*, 8.44; Jerome, *Commentary on Ephesians*, 3.5.33; and John Chrysostom, *On Monogamy*, 4 with Arjava, *Women and Law*, pp. 132–3.

[60] See especially John Chrysostom, *To a Young Widow*, 7.

[61] Augustine, *Letters*, 243.6–7; 10–12; John Chrysostom, *On the Priesthood*, 1.2 (5) with K. Zamfir, 'Men and Women in the House(hold) of God. Chrysostom's Homilies on 1 Tim 2, 8–15', *Sacra Spripta* 6(2) (2008), p. 164 on Chrysostom.

194 *Children and Asceticism in Late Antiquity*

that these would comfort them in sorrow and support them in old age: 'Though the nearest have failed, she finds those not so near akin to cherish the mother.' Even if husband or children were not available, 'a widow should be fruitful in the offspring of virtues' and she does not need to be afraid of being left on her own in her old age.[62] A chaste and good widow guarantees support for herself. Just as the apostles had asked Jesus to cure the widowed mother-in-law of Peter, so individual widows should make the apostles their sons-in-law by associating with them in devotion, practising charity and ministering to the poor. They offer protection for the widow and act as patrons and friends for their posterity: 'Cherish, then, the nearness of Peter and the affinity of Andrew.' Similarly, an individual virgin has patriarchs for brothers and Israel for a father.[63] A Christian ascetic has no reason to remarry since apostles, martyrs and the Lord himself replace blood relationships and intercede for her. Safety is assured. For the propagation of chaste widowhood, the interrelatedness of asceticism, charity and familial relations is a leading theme. Ultimately, therefore, the family of Christ can replace the biological family.

In the late fourth and early fifth centuries when ascetic communities were beginning to take shape, especially in the western part of the Empire, the vow of virginity would keep daughters at home and would therefore enable them to serve and take care of their elderly parents when the time came. This argument was also used to persuade parents: a virgin daughter would never leave her parents, nor would she cause other problems. This theme was central, for example, in Gregory of Nyssa's depiction of his sister Macrina. As a young girl her housework was worth that of many maidservants and she even prepared meals for her mother with her own hands. Macrina later helped her widowed mother in looking after her eight other children and property scattered in three different provinces. She also shared in her mother's sorrows and instructed her spiritually, becoming her guide. Thus, by her virginity, Macrina was able to take care of the physical, psychological and spiritual needs of her mother.[64] Indeed, 'the ascetic life provided women a means

---

[62]   Ambrose, *On Widows*, 6.33–4: 'fecunda sit vidua prole virtutum, meritorumque suorum sobole, quae perire non possit'; 'Etsi proximi defuerint, invenit tamen extraneos qui matrem colant'.

[63]   Ambrose, *On Widows*, 9.53–7, esp. 9.54: 'Ama ergo propinquitatem Petri, affinitatem Andreae', 'Habetis ergo, viduae auxilium'. See also Ambrose, *On the Death of His Brother Satyrus*, 2.13. On the virgin and her 'new' family, see Jerome, *Letters*, 22.25.

[64]   Gregory of Nyssa, *Life of Macrina*, 5.16–50 and 10–11 (with Hägg, *The Art of Biography*, pp. 386–7, noting Gregory's aim to create a model for the monastic life for women, but still claiming 'a considerable degree of historicity concerning the external features'); Ambrose, *On Virgins*, 1.7.32; Ambrose, *The Consecration of a Virgin*, 1.1 and 17.107; and John Chrysostom, *Against the Opponents of Monastic Life*, 2.9.

Children, Strategies and Continuity   195

to remain together as mother and daughter'.[65] Asceticism kept a child at home, taking care of aging parents, usually the mother.

Consolation, comfort and solace (*solacia*) offered by children to their parents were not restricted to material and immediate considerations alone, as they also signified the continuity of their parents beyond death. On a more general level, children were seen as giving immortality to their deceased family members by their mere existence. The very hope of the living was in children.[66] More particularly, children were often seen as extensions of their parents, both physically and mentally reproducing and continuing their presence. Indeed, it is a cause for the greatest joy if a child is 'the very image of its parent's beauty'.[67] Gregory Nazianzen notes this same cultural function for children, but, true to his mission of promoting virginity, he refers to the offspring of a dead man as 'a memorial of misfortune'.[68] 'To those who miss his father the tiny Nebridius reveals him once more', as the child's character resembles his father's so closely, claims Jerome, writing a consoling letter to Salvina on the death of her husband. In the daughter the features of both parents can be recognized and thus, in her children, Salvina can believe she still has her husband with her.[69] The same argument appears in many variants: Asterius of Amasea, for example, when reminding the reader of the immortal character of marriage, points out that the dead wife lives on in the couple's children; one of the children preserves the tones of his mother's voice; another possesses her features; another is like her in character. Chrysostom claims that his mother, as she argued against his retirement to the desert, commented that he was a living and exact image of her dead husband and was thus a great comfort to her.[70] Indeed, the desire for children and lineage is one of the most frequently mentioned excuses for not opting for asceticism.[71]

---

[65]   S. Harvey, 'Sacred Bonding: Mothers and Daughters in Early Syriac Hagiography', *Journal of Early Christian Studies* 4(1) (1996), p. 51, for Syria of the fifth and sixth centuries CE.

[66]   See especially Augustine, *Exposition on the Psalm 131*, 19: 'Ipsa spes tamquam in filiis dicta est; quia hominis in hac vita viventis spes filii sunt, fructus filii sunt', with Ambrose, *On Virgins*, 1.6.25; John Chrysostom, *Homilies in Genesis*, 18.4.2; Gregory of Nyssa, *On Virginity*, 12.4; Augustine, *Exposition on the Psalms 70*, 2.6; 127.2 and 15. See also *Life and Miracles of Thecla*, 5, with Van Eijk, 'Marriage and Virginity', esp. p. 235.

[67]   Gregory of Nyssa, *On Virginity*, 3.6: 'αὐτὸ τῆς ὥρας τῶν γεννημένων τὸ ἀπεικόνισμα'.

[68]   Gregory Nazianzen, *Oration 7*, 20: 'συμφορᾶς ὑπόμνημα'.

[69]   Jerome, *Letters*, 79.6–7: 'Nebridius pusio patrem quaerentibus exhibet.'

[70]   Asterius of Amasea, *Homilies*, 5.10.1–2; John Chrysostom, *On the Priesthood*, 1.2 (5). See also Paulinus of Nola, *Letters*, 29.8.

[71]   See e.g. Ambrose, *Exhortation to Virginity*, 7.45; Ambrose, *On Virgins*, 1.7.33; Ambrose, *Letters*, 58.11; Jerome, *Letters*, 39.6–9; 54.4–5; 66.3; 108.4; 123; Augustine,

Duties of Children on Parents' Death

Children also provided more abstract consolation for their parents. An important part of security in old age was the knowledge that one's funeral and burial would be duly cared for. It was a common idea for ordinary Christians as well as non-Christians that both a proper burial near the ancestors and commemoration by the survivors were needed for an agreeable afterlife – in this world through commemoration by the survivors and in the other world either among the *Manes* or in heaven, depending on one's beliefs. The importance of progeny in this was paramount as children were a guarantee of a proper burial. These attitudes are clearly visible in the writings of the ecclesiastical writers.

For Gregory of Nyssa, the need for posterity to look upon the tombs of their progenitors is a symbol of human mortality and the pain it causes.[72] Augustine tells how the friends of Monica asked her if she did not fear dying far from home and her answer, in which she dismisses such mundane considerations, is a way of conveying how wholeheartedly she was socialized to Christianity. Neither the monument nor the place of burial is relevant to the future bliss of the deceased – Virgil is not to be believed when he claims that the unburied are prohibited from crossing to Hades.[73]

For Augustine, however, what was wrong with caring about the burial place was not the aim of being remembered. Augustine himself claims that an important consideration when recording his own life was to produce a memento of his parents so that the reader would remember them and pray for them and, in this way, he would also fulfil Monica's last wish 'to be remembered at the altar of the Lord'. Thus, caring about funerals and subsequent commemoration was not regarded as a sign of an un-Christian mentality *per se*. Indeed, according to Augustine, the wish to be buried in the family grave and to ensure the inviolability of the burial place stems from natural love and basic human qualities and is not wrong as such; he approvingly relates the funerals of the 'just men of old', which were organized by their children with dutiful piety. The woman anointing the feet of Jesus, and Joseph of Arimathaea taking care of the burial of Jesus, are given as examples of a virtuous approach to the death of one's nearest kin. It is true that he criticizes the expense and the heavy drinking during memorial

---

Letters, 3*.1 and 3; Augustine, *Confessions*, 2.3.6; Ambrose, *On Widows*, 15.86; John Chrysostom, *Against the Opponents of Monastic Life*, 2.2.

[72] Gregory of Nyssa, *On Virginity*, 3.3; see already Tertullian, *On the Testimony of the Soul*, 4.10 and *An Exhortation to Chastity*, 12.

[73] Augustine, *Confessions*, 9.11.27–8 with Lafferty, 'Augustine', pp. 117–18 and Augustine, *On the Care of the Dead*, 2–7 (3–5).

feasts; still, he acknowledges the importance of burial and of allowing people to commemorate their dead on the tomb and by inscriptions.[74]

The same approval of the care taken over proper burial and individual commemoration is also found in other ecclesiastical writers. When the mother of John Chrysostom objects to his leaving home to become an ascetic, a major argument she uses is that she wants to ensure that she gets a proper burial beside the bones of her husband, and only one's own child can guarantee this. Even in a story in the *History of the Monks in Egypt*, the monks are depicted as anxious about being buried decently and this is not intended to shed a negative light on them. While Gregory of Nyssa seeks to highlight the otherworldly character of his sister Macrina by claiming to have been surprised when she had not taken care of her own funeral garments, we are told that she carefully ensured that Gregory would take care of her funerary preparations.[75] The burial of one's dead may not provide salvation, but it is a duty and a solace of the living.

Augustine also points out that the Church as a universal mother has taken over the role of parents and children in commemorating and making supplications for the dead. Even those who were not buried, were buried far away from their nearest kin or have no near relatives to intercede for them will be taken care of. As this general commemoration does not require the mention of particular names, all are included and nobody is forgotten. This was, however, a kind of fallback intercession and Augustine stresses the importance of individual remembrance by relatives and concedes that the dead, to a certain extent, could be given solace by their intercessory prayers, almsgiving and the celebration of the Eucharist in commemoration of the dead. John Chrysostom likewise confirms the possibility of helping the dead by individual prayers and, most importantly, by giving alms in the name of the deceased.[76]

---

[74]   Augustine, *Confessions*, 9.11.27; 9.13.37; *On the Care of the Dead*, 2–9 (3–7); 3 (5): 'Unde et antiquorum iustorum funera officiosa pietate curata sunt'; *Letters*, 22.3–6 and 29 (feasts on the tombs); *City of God*, 1.13 (on the burial of Jesus); *Exposition on the Psalm 48*, 1.15–16 and Augustine, *Sermons*, 172.2 with Rebillard, *The Care of the Dead*, esp. pp. 85–8, 122 and 145–52; and Kotila, *Memoria mortuorum*, pp. 62–72.

[75]   John Chrysostom, *On the Priesthood*, 1.2 (5); *History of the Monks in Egypt*, 10.9–11, 15 and 19; Gregory of Nyssa, *Life of Macrina*, 25 and 28–9, with Paulinus of Nola, *Letters*, 13.3–4 and Jerome, *Letters*, 22.27. For the importance for a proper burial near the ancestors, see also van Dam, *Families and Friends*, pp. 78–9 on the families of Gregory Nazianzen and Basil of Caesarea.

[76]   Augustine, *Sermons*, 172.2; Augustine, *On the Care of the Dead*, 4 (6); 7 (9) and 18 (22); John Chrysostom, *Homilies on Philippians*, 3.4 with Rebillard, *The Care of the Dead*, pp. 167–75 and Kotila, *Memoria mortuorum*, pp. 39–51; 99–105, 140.

What emerges is a picture of a community that attaches great value to the care of the dead. In particular, the rhetoric of Augustine and John Chrysostom reveals that ordinary Christians believed that the prayers of the Church would be of help to the dead. The Church commemorated its deceased members and propagated a view of the dead as participating in the community of saints. In Christian ideology this communal remembrance was within reach of a much larger part of the population than in the traditional thinking in which the ascertaining of this kind of immaterial continuity was restricted to the more private spheres of the kin group. Thus, a practice that was formerly seen mostly as a family matter would become at least partly a communal act.

However, as Éric Rebillard points out, in Late Antiquity the cult of death of ordinary people was still much outside of the sphere of the Church, and the responsibility for commemoration was left to the family and friends.[77] The duties of the kin, especially children, were of the greatest importance in ensuring security after death, in burial, in commemoration and in intercessions. The continuity of the family line is central, not only for fulfilling these duties, but also as an ancestral lineage to which individuals are joined in their death. The basic attitude that stressed the significance of a proper burial for after-death continuity and the preservation of memory prevailed in Christian piety. Indeed, in connection with actual burials there are no references to the young man in the Gospels who was not allowed to bury his father in order to follow Christ, although this scene was occasionally used as an argument in ideological contexts to demonstrate the correct attitude of a Christian towards the issues of familial lineage.[78] More traditional values and everyday ways of thinking about continuity after death existed alongside theological reflection, even among the ecclesiastical writers themselves.

Children and the Fruits of Asceticism

Why, then, give to asceticism a child who had already survived the perils of high mortality in infancy and early childhood and who was seen as protection in old age and against death? It is no surprise that the ecclesiastical writers who propagated ascetic Christianity appealed to such benefits as resurrection and eternal life. As shown above, asceticism was depicted as a way of acquiring the best place in heaven with an unparalleled intimacy with Christ for the ascetics themselves. Moreover,

---

[77] Rebillard, *The Care of the Dead*, pp. 174–5.
[78] See Matthew 8:21–2 with Jerome, *Letters*, 22.21; 38.5; 39.4; 54.2.

asceticism contributed to an exalted position in society, at least among Christians, and therefore it could be seen as a splendid way of ensuring for one's nearest and dearest family a decent future with both heavenly and earthly glory.

The ecclesiastical writers, however, also needed to highlight the benefits accruing to the parents of ascetic children. Various mechanisms for this were referred to: first, children pray for their relatives in this world and may intercede for them if they predecease their parents. Thus, for example, Jerome reminds Heliodorus that if he leaves his parents' house for the desert, he will later be able to ask for civil rights for his parents in the kingdom of God – and also be able to pray for Jerome.[79]

Second, children given to asceticism were to be seen as precious gifts to God, showing that parents preferred the heavenly continuity to safety in old age with wealth and continuity in grandchildren: 'A virgin is a gift of the parents for God, holding a priesthood of chastity. The virgin is an offering for her mother, by whose daily sacrifice the divine power is appeased. A virgin is the inseparable pledge of her parents.'[80] Virginity, like chaste widowhood to a lesser degree, ensured the relatives of the ascetics a special distinction in heaven. Parents who nourish 'angels for God' and dedicate their children to God will have precedence at the Last Judgment, and will share the crown of immortality with their children. A father who protects his daughter's virginity will become her partner in perfection, as she brings to him 'the fruit of peace'. Virgins live not only for themselves but also benefit others: 'one virgin redeems her parents, another her brothers'.[81] Indeed, 'in every Christian house it is needful that there be a virgin, for the salvation of the whole house lies in this one virgin'.[82]

The benefit of children to their parents can also be seen in the idea that children acted as substitutes for their parents. In bringing up her daughter

---

[79]   Jerome, *Letters*, 14.3 and 39.6–9.

[80]   Ambrose, *On Virgins*, 1.7.32: 'Virgo Dei donum est, munus parentum, sacerdotium castitatis. Virgo matris hostia est, cuius quotidiano sacrificio vis divina placatur. Virgo individuum pignus parentum', translated by H. de Romestin et al. (Nicene and Post-Nicene Fathers, ser. II, vol. 2), with some modification. See also Paulinus of Nola, *Letters*, 39.1 and 44.5 and Palladius, *The Lausiac History*, 57.1.

[81]   John Chrysostom, *Against the Opponents of Monastic Life*, 3.21 (ἀγγέλους τῷ Θεῷ'); Ambrose, *Letters*, 38.1: 'fructus pacis'; Ambrose, *On Virgins*, 2.2.16: 'non solis vixerunt sibi; haec parentes redimat, haec fratres', with *Anonymous Homily on Virginity*, 42; John Chrysostom, *Homilies on First Timothy*, 9.2; Ambrose, *Exhortation to Virginity*, 14.93; Gaudentius of Brescia, *Sermons*, 8; Pelagius, *Letter to Demetrias*, 11 and 14 (413–415 CE) and Augustine, *Letters*, 188.2 on Demetrias; *On the Fall of a Consecrated Virgin*, 4.16 and *Canons of Pseudo-Athanasius* 94. See also Salvian, *To the Church*, 3.3.26: through the children promised to God, the patrimony given to them returns to God, yielding spiritual rewards for the parents.

[82]   *Canons of Pseudo-Athanasius*, 98.

Paula the Younger as a virgin, for example, Laeta renders to God what she does not render in person, that is, the gift of her chastity; a virgin dedicated to chastity compensates for the loss of the virginity of the mother.[83] Many of the mothers who dedicated their children at birth or later encouraged them to make this choice were themselves described as having longed for an ascetic life in the past. Examples of mothers with such an alleged motivation include Paula, mother of Blesilla and Eustochium; Melania the Younger and her anonymous daughter; the anonymous mother of Theodoret; Emmelia, mother of Macrina, Peter, Basil and Gregory; and later Martha, mother of Simeon the Younger.[84] The ecclesiastical writers also used this logic as an argument for dedicating children to asceticism, as in the cases of the widowed Juliana and her children; Laeta, mother of Paula the Younger; and another Juliana, mother of Demetrias.[85]

The whole household could benefit from the ascetics at home for they serve as examples of the virtuous Christian life and protect the household by their mere lifestyle. Eusebius of Emesa promises rewards for parents who honour their virgin daughters as temples of God and guard them as brides of Christ. 'A virgin is a good guardian at home' and, in particular, a virgin at home ensures that 'the mother will cherish integrity and the sisters receive instructions, the slave will be corrected, the father will become more pious, the brother will be given counsel and the neighbour will gain'. When an honourable virgin fasts, both household members and neighbours are affected, and when the fellow citizens are feasting together with the saints, God is admired in them.[86] An ascetic would sanctify all household members: if a house has a virgin, it has a guardian.[87]

---

[83] Jerome, *Letters*, 107.13, with Augustine, *On the Good of Widowhood*, 14 (18) and 8 (11): 'virginitas prolis tuae compensavit dispendium virginitatis tuae'. See also Ambrose, *Exhortation to Virginity*, 4.26.

[84] Jerome, *Letters*, 39.6–9 and 22.20 for Paula with Blesilla and Eustochium; Gerontius, *Life of Melania* (Greek), 1 and 6 for Melania the Younger; Theodoret of Cyrrhus, *Religious History*, 16–17 for his unnamed mother; Gregory of Nyssa, *Life of Macrina*, 2 for Emmelia. For the two last-mentioned, see also Brown, *Body and Society*, p. 325, also referring to the *Life of Simeon the Younger* (c. 600 CE) on Simeon and his mother Martha.

[85] Ambrose, *Exhortation to Virginity*, 4.26 (on Juliana); Jerome, *Letters*, 107.13 (on Laeta); Augustine, *Letters*, 188.2 on Demetrias.

[86] Eusebius of Emesa, *Sermons*, 7.24: 'Si enim fuerit virgo in domo, honestatem et mater colebit, et soror erudietur et servus corrigietur et pater castior erit et frater suadebitur et vicinus lucrabitur'.

[87] See also Jerome, *Letters*, 107.1: 'Sancta et fidelis domus unum sanctificat infedelem'; Eusebius of Emesa, *Sermons*, 7.24.

These claims were sometimes taken quite literally, as seen in the *Canons of Athanasius*, which promise that when wrath comes to the city, it will not affect the house in which the virgin lives. In Palladius' *Lausiac History* this idea is exemplified by the story of Piamun, a virgin who lived with her mother and who saw in a vision that her village would be attacked. She warned the local priest, but he was terrified and in turn asked Piamun to go out to meet the aggressors and turn them back. She returned to her house and spent all night in prayer. Early the next morning the enemy were found near the village standing like pillars of stone, unable to move.[88] As the *History of the Monks in Egypt* claims, through the ascetic monks the world is kept in existence and human life is preserved.[89]

The benefits of virginity are seldom mentioned in the context of sons and they are not formulated in an attempt to convince the parents. When Augustine urges Laetus to enter monastic life, he argues that by doing this he is repaying the temporal favours received from his mother with spiritual and eternal ones.[90] In the case of daughters the exhortations and argumentation are most usually directed at the parents, even if the text itself is perhaps not expressly thus formulated. This is due not only to the cultural assumptions which stressed the greater independence of sons but also to demographical factors. Due to the differences in age at marriage, it was necessary to take the decision concerning the virginity of a daughter when the girl reached puberty, whereas for boys the decisive age was not until they reached their twenties. The parents (and other older relatives) of boys were also more likely to be dead than were the relatives of girls at the time of the choice. Moreover, virgin daughters usually stayed and lived with their family of origin, whereas ascetic sons left their homes and could therefore less directly contribute to the spiritual and physical well-being of their parents.[91]

In general, children are seen as bargaining goods of the highest value. Parents could instead of themselves dedicate their children to God in order to achieve spiritual gain and immortality. Virgins cause the parents personal satisfaction as they morally improve the family and local community; they spiritually benefit their nearest kin by their fasts and prayers; they spread the Christian faith in their environment; and even their contribution to the

---

[88] *Canons of Pseudo-Athanasius*, 98; Palladius, *The Lausiac History*, 31.

[89] *History of the Monks in Egypt*, prol. 9–10. For a late parallel, see Cyril of Scythopolis, *The Lives of the Monks of Palestine*, Life of Euthymius 24: 'If this saint dies, we have no further hope of salvation; for we are all protected through his intercession.'

[90] Augustine, *Letters*, 243.7 and 10.

[91] See above p. 128.

physical safety of the household is implied. As Eusebius of Emesa sums up: 'Advancement of a virgin is the defence for the whole Church.' Ascetics are indeed 'walls around the cities'.[92] Here, it seems that a change occurred in the early medieval West as the role of *oblati* was no longer highlighted in the search for immediate spiritual rewards for parents or the community, although the function of children in the context of commemoration and nearness, even partnership, between the individuals and God (or saints) was still relevant.[93]

* * *

To conclude this analysis of the importance of children for individual survival and continuity after death, I refer to the words of Augustine: 'Happy are those who leave behind children to succeed them and take over their possessions. He has children, he is not dead.'[94] Both by bringing to mind their deceased relatives and especially in the very thought that they will continue living when their parents are dead, children were indispensable for consolation in the face of death. Late Roman children, both daughters and sons, were seen as reproducing their parents mentally and biologically, preserving their parents' personal identity even beyond their death. Children were the very reason for marrying and the highest hopes of parents were invested in children, even if they were well aware that all the cares of marriage might be in vain because of the risk of death. Moreover, to have children was not enough if there were no grandchildren to carry on the family line.

On the other hand, the familial rhetoric connected to asceticism is justified on the grounds that in asceticism, Christianity and the Church offered (or at least claimed to offer) alternatives in many of the issues that were traditionally dependent only on progeny: aiding elderly widows, taking care of the dead and their burial, transmitting spiritual traditions and inheritance and, most importantly, ensuring the afterlife of ascetics and their family members, both in renown and commemoration in this world and in immortality in the next. In asceticism a bond was formed both between the ascetic and Christ, and between the family of the ascetic and the family of Christ. The fruits of this nearness and their culturally changing values are profits that are difficult to

---

[92] Eusebius of Emesa, *Sermons*, 7.27: 'Virginis autem correctio totius ecclesiae tutamentum est'; John Chrysostom, *Homilies on Matteus*, 72.4: 'τείχη ταῖς πόλεσι περικάθηνται'.

[93] See de Jong, *In Samuel's Image*, pp. 123–5, 288.

[94] Augustine, *Exposition on the Psalm 48*, 1.14: 'Ergo felices illi qui relinquunt filios in possessione sua, quibus sui succedunt. Habuit filios, non est mortuus.'

confirm in the calculations of the continuity strategies of individuals, but, at the same time, they disqualify analyses based on *a priori* views about the primacy of material, pecuniary or political gain.[95]

---

[95] Thus, to identify the attraction of asceticism merely with its function as a powerful strategy in the aristocratic competition for honour and glory, together with the possible economic gains (see Hunter, *Marriage, Celibacy*, pp. 75–83), necessarily undermines its attractiveness and the range of benefits accruing from it.

Chapter 9

Not All of Me Will Die:[1]
Conclusions

Each day we die, each day we change,
and yet we are convinced that we are eternal.[2]

In this final chapter the main findings of my study are scrutinized in four different areas. I start with the continuity and change of the family ideology and values in early Christian culture. The second theme is the impact of Christianity on late Roman family life, while the third deals with the relevance of asceticism to familial strategies. I conclude by looking back to the model of continuity strategies, presented at the end of Chapter 1, and I point out the implications of this model for further research on families in the context of the Roman culture as well as of other cultures. However, before continuing, two reminders are needed: first, most sources used in the present study concern senatorial aristocracy and local elites, and only occasionally are there references to the practices of the lower echelons of society. There is even more information about the middle levels of society (or 'sub-elites') owning more land or doing business, or about slaves and servants, than about the great majority of the population: the subsistence farmers. In what follows, unless otherwise stated, the ideology, values and social practices referred to are of those people who shared the Roman elite culture and way of thinking in Late Antiquity. Second, the results of my research are to be understood as proposals for a reconstruction of the past, particularly as the sources used deal more with the ideals and attitudes of their writers than with the actual thinking and behaviour of their audiences.

---

[1]   Horace, *Odes*, 3.30.6–7: 'Non omnis moriar multaque pars mei / vitabit Libitinam.'
[2]   Jerome, *Letters*, 60.19: 'Cotidie morimur, cotidie commutamur et tamen aeternos esse nos credimus.'

Family Discourse and Identities

In pre-modern societies the household was the basic unit in the context of which the choice and observation of values took place. Indeed, it was in and through families that the processes supporting the survival and continuance of the self and communities happened. It is not surprising, therefore, that the ecclesiastical writers of Late Antiquity, aiming to influence the traditional value hierarchy, paid extensive attention to family issues and practices, and made use of the familial language outside its traditional limits.

When ecclesiastical writers used this family language, they simultaneously revealed their ideas of the family and its functions. We have seen that they did not cast aside the old principles of the relationships within the family or old evaluations of the significance of patrimony, memory and especially of children for a meaningful life. The basic cultural values and discourses in their texts, dealing with the different ways of aspiring for continuity, were by no means specific only to this generation of late fourth- and early fifth-century ecclesiastical male intellectuals. They belonged to a culture that shared these ideas and values, and this shaped their conceptualization of the aims and needs of an individual for family life. On the other hand, in their writings and participation in the community life, they had to take into consideration the significance of these principles among their peers and in the wider culture. It would not have been rhetorically effective to negate the very values of shared and acknowledged importance.

It is clear that only in a very limited sense could there ever be any 'new' values brought forth and propagated. To promote new ideas and forms of behaviour, different strategies were required – both to convince people that the old values were compatible with the new ways of thought and required behaviour, and to demonstrate that the old values in their old context had in fact an instrumental function with regard to the actual intrinsic, real value. Here this intrinsic value was identified by the ecclesiastical writers with personal continuity and immortality. The writers claimed not only that continuity was more easily achieved using the new interpretation of the old values, but also that this intrinsic value was more truly and profoundly understood by identifying it with salvation or life in Christ. The sense of attaining such a continuity made life meaningful.

In this re-identification process there occurred not substitution, but a hierarchical subordination of the old thinking to the new Christian interpretation. The old virtues were embedded in the Christian value system, and the Stoic idea of virtues being ends in themselves, crystallized in sayings like 'virtue is its own noblest reward', were to be put aside.[3] Moreover, by asserting that salvation in fact corresponded to that 'old' intrinsic value and thus responded to the same culturally conditioned basic needs which the (literary) culture was already pursuing, the implementation of the new way of thinking and the required behaviour was both intellectually justified and emotionally and experientially meaningful. Even the old intrinsic values, as they were manifested by the ecclesiastical writers, regained their importance in the contemporary Christian ethos and thus they continued to have a profound influence on the meanings attached to individual life courses in Late Antiquity.

Instead of calling the fourth century the century that saw the rise of asceticism, it would be more to the point to use expressions such as 'reforming monasticism' and the rise of the ascetic discourse.[4] These processes have led to the illusion that asceticism was something new in the Christian culture of the fourth century. Nevertheless, the rise of the ascetic discourse had a decisive effect on the understanding of the family as the ecclesiastical writers were struggling to establish a proper place within the Christian community both for family life and for asceticism. This was pursued through two different strategies: first, to differentiate asceticism from the everyday familial sphere, leading to the struggle against the *subintroductae* (unmarried women who lived with male ascetics), to the establishment of monastic communities with fixed rules and to the discouraging of home asceticism.[5] The second strategy was to propagate asceticism by using concepts poignantly taken from the family discourse and highlighting asceticism as responding to the same needs of belonging, continuity in (spiritual) lineage, and posthumous memory and reputation that family life had previously been seen to meet.

Just as the Roman Empire was a family led by an emperor, so the Church was the bride of Christ, mother of the believers and a family led by a heavenly Father. The fruitfulness of the community was guaranteed by its family head. In the Christian context the familial language and metaphors were used to stress the identity factors, hierarchies of authority and sense of belonging, particularly in non-biological relationships. Not only had the level of abstraction taken one

---

[3] Silius Italicus, *Punica*, 13.663: 'Ipsa quidem virtus sibimet pulcherrima merces.'

[4] On this period as a reform of monasticism, see e.g. A. Louth, 'The Literature of the Monastic Movement', in F.M. Young et al. (eds), *The Cambridge History of the Early Christian Literature* (Cambridge and New York, 2004), p. 373.

[5] For the *subintroductae*, see E.A. Clark, 'John Chrysostom and the *Subintroductae*', in Clark, *Ascetic Piety*, pp. 265–90. For these phenomena, see Krause, *Witwen und Waisen*, pp. 79–92. The change away from home asceticism gradually took place during the early fifth century.

step further in terms of metaphorical expressions, but it was also ideologically directed towards new ends: Christian communities defined themselves as families consisting of brothers and sisters led by a father, abbot or pastor, and whose unity was guaranteed by a spiritual brotherhood. In particular, the paternity of the leaders cemented their leadership and authority into something natural, irrevocable and thus legitimate. This authority stemming from the naturalizing language of family also brought to the 'fathers' a means of continuity in this world; in their audiences, in their disciples and in the acts of commemoration by later generations. As Denise Buell points out, these intellectual patrilines would construct and legitimize hierarchical power structures and traditions of knowledge, while valorizing 'sameness and conformity' against diversity.[6] The very concept of 'the church fathers' is a late sign of this process.

Pietas and *nobilitas* were the main concepts in this process of adaptation. The discussion of the value of *pietas*, and of family as a whole, in Christian culture was one of the most conspicuous features of the fourth- and early fifth-century texts concerning asceticism. *Pietas* traditionally denoted an ideal relationship implying trust and a dutiful attitude, especially a reciprocal relationship between parents and children. For the Christians of Late Antiquity, *pietas* remained basically a familial virtue, directing both parental and filial behaviour. However, there was a process of rhetorical struggle to reshape its meaning: in the old Roman myths, the familial *pietas* was ideally to be subordinated to the immortal honour due to the duties accomplished towards the *res publica* and its gods,[7] and the ecclesiastical writers, too, insisted on the need to give priority to *pietas* towards God the Father and His family vis-à-vis earthly kinship ties. The construction of 'the family of God' served as a powerful mental tool in building an imagined community of belonging, and thus forming a common identity for Christians.

Traditionally, *nobilitas* had been seen as a virtue needing publicity to be realized and offspring to whom it could be passed on, and these aspects did not change in the Christian context. The reputation was still earthly reputation; the glory still contributed to the family standing and the resulting *nobilitas* still needed to be continued in the offspring, either spiritual or biological. In principle, the earthly honour and glory and family nobility were played down and they should have been actively despised. However, nobility formed the point

---

[6] Buell, *Making Christians*, pp. 5–9, 12, with her conclusions (esp. pp. 180–83) based on Clement of Alexandia's use of family language.

[7] See esp. Augustine, *City of God*, 5.18, where Augustine gives many examples of Roman mythology in which fathers sacrificed their children, thereby attaining glory for themselves and for Rome.

of departure in highlighting how ascetic strivings spread earthly reputation and glory, building up a discourse of honour and dignity, and claiming a unique prestige for the ascetics in the Christian world. Here, the writers exploited the traditional association of *nobilitas* with family traditions and lineage. The new Christian *nobilitas* was linked to the old aristocratic families; for the narratives of sanctity, an elite background was claimed, or even invented. Noble athletes of the family of God are already renowned in this world, admired by their peers and emulated; nobility shines forth to fellow citizens and fellow believers, brings honour and renown to the person himself, and adds to the glory and *nobilitas* of his family – be it the *familia Christi* or an earthly kin group. It is not hard to deduce from these narratives a desire to convince the elites that the ascetic lifestyle would contribute to the same ends as the old ways of life: honour, nobility and eternal memory.

Even if earthly marriage strategies and strengthening of the ties in kinship networks were meant to be changed to alliance with God, what did not change was the role played by children in establishing these relationships. However noble the ascetics were, the celibacy adopted by the children would endanger the family continuity. Thus, it would be difficult to retain the traditional link between the claim to nobility and the family lineage. However, as the early Christian writers were eager to point out, a noble virgin is, in fact, fertile and has noble offspring. This fertility is a result of her – or his – exemplary status in the family and in the community at large, in which the *nobilitas* is proclaimed. The spiritual nobility of the soul and the resulting honour were something to be passed on, not only to the brothers and sisters in Christ but also to possible biological offspring and relatives.

Christianity adopted the main ideas of the Roman understanding of family and progeny in spite of the anti-familial trends inherent in its dogma (individual resurrection) and praxis (the relevance of asceticism). It is a question of the rhetorical techniques, or strategies, employed to deal with the various needs to create a distinct, Christian way of life and system of values, and to ensure its compatibility with the traditional principles in achieving a virtuous life. The underlying assumption of the ecclesiastical writers was that the ideas of immortality and salvation as proposed by ascetic Christianity would be best explained by references to the benefits of family life and children. However, this rhetoric is not to be understood as a result of pure reason and calm calculation to gain supporters for their own authority and for the cause of Christianity. The identity of the authors themselves was at stake, their need both to show the distinctiveness of Christianity and to justify what they understood Christianity expected of them.

Conflict and Family Continuity: What Difference Did Asceticism Make?

The standard situation in Late Antiquity was parents dedicating their children to asceticism, just as parents were also responsible for marrying off their progeny. In some cases children were promised to the ascetic life before they were born and in many cases at least before they themselves could intervene in the matter. In the context of early asceticism, this kind of *ex voto* did not mean separation from the family unit.

The conflicts due to parents opposing their children's yearning for the ascetic life and the freedom resulting from asceticism have been exaggerated in previous scholarship. In the case of children, an alleged opposition to parents was a requirement of the Gospels and highlighting this aspect in lives of the saints stressed their holiness and exemplary character. Indeed, the actual cases of disinheritance do not seem to have anything to do with disagreements over asceticism and parental authority, but rather the parents spared the family from the dispersal of patrimony and ensured that the wealth remained in the family. Both from an economic perspective and with regard to the family continuity, money left to ascetics was wasted money. Moreover, the attitude towards the asceticism of a family member depended on the prevailing family life course situation: there were parents who first consecrated their children to virginity without asking their opinion, but later tried to revoke the vow; ascetically minded parents who married off their children despite their wishes; and dedicated widows who warned their children against hearing sermons advocating virginity. Taking an ascetic vow was, in a profound sense, a family matter.

As long as the father was alive, there was little question of any conflict becoming public. It may have been possible for a daughter to act against the wishes of her other relatives, but it was out of the question for her to oppose her father. A *filius familias* had more room to manoeuvre, but, even for him, relative freedom of action came only with the death of his father. Even then, sons were morally obliged to show familial *pietas* towards their mothers. The resulting discussions, balancing the moral obligation on the one hand and the freedom and religious obligations on the other, are apparent in the sources. For female widows of sufficient wealth, asceticism can be seen more as a result of an individual choice. It was not regarded as probable that any relative could prevent the vow of a widow, but the problem was rather the widow's own insecurity in life which would have made the vow of widowhood somewhat risky.

In the ascetic discourse of the time, there was a much more acute need to control women's religious roles than men's. One could refer here to male power over the female body in a patriarchal culture, but I would stress more down-to-earth explanations for the prevalence of daughters over sons in the ascetic literature. First of all, in the actual family context, the decision for a vow of continence had to be taken when the child was reaching marriageable age. Among the elites, the age for a first marriage for girls seems to have remained much the same as it was in the earlier Empire: the late Roman authors, sharing an elite cultural background, held it as self-evident that the discussions about entering the ascetic life would have taken place when the girls approached marriageable age in their early to mid-teens. The few actual cases for which we have information fit well into this scheme. For sons, choosing asceticism was connected to marriage only in some hagiographic stories (and in these cases no indication of the age is given) and thus there was no similar link between age, marriage and entering the ascetic life. Consequently, it is reasonable to assume that a considerable age difference between elite boys and girls still prevailed at their point of entering a first marriage. For daughters, the decision to enter the ascetic life had to be made already when they were still by any standard children, but for sons, there was more time to make a final decision to marry or remain unmarried. It is also significant that for the boys, or the young men, the variation seems to have been greater and thus also the option to defer the final decision. Moreover, the earlier the phase when the decision had to be made, the less knowledge could there be of possible grandchildren for the parents by their other children; also, parents and older relatives would be more likely to still be alive and to have greater authority over a younger daughter than, later on, over an older son. For these reasons, the discussion about daughters entering the ascetic life was much more likely to be taken up than in the case of sons. Accordingly, the idea that the ascetic movement in the West first attracted women may be more a reflection of our sources than a cultural feature of Late Antiquity.

There is another possible explanation for the over-representation of girls. At least among the traditional aristocracy and the local nobility, the patrilineal continuity of the biological line was still pursued, and there was a special value in having the bloodline continued through the males who belonged to the next generation, even if this function was not limited only to the sons. Sons were, however, preferred for administering the family wealth and for carrying on the family reputation and name to the next generation. Thus, in cases where there was any choice, sons were to play the day-to-day roles in the continuity strategies of the parents. Should this be seen as the continuity of the essentially agnatic perception of the Roman family?

212   *Children and Asceticism in Late Antiquity*

To answer this question, it is necessary to look back at the earlier Empire. A prominent feature in Roman testaments, burials, tombs and patterns of commemoration during the Roman Empire is that they are markedly family-centred. Even if property transmission, affection and a sense of duty to the deceased were interwoven, the aspects of continuity were heavily dependent and centred on the innermost circle of the household family, not on the agnatic lineage group or the wider sphere of relatives. The transmission of wealth, wills and trusts were designed for the immediate future to promote the living kin and the existing household unit rather than any more distant *posteritas* for the agnatic line. Even in the alliance strategies of the Roman aristocracy in general and adoptions in particular, the short-term and individual character of the arrangements was stressed. The action of the immediate family was seen as the best safeguard against oblivion on all levels: family members would usually be responsible not only for the burial but also for carrying on the name and taking care of active commemoration. There was a pragmatic bond between family affection and the immediate family as the continuity of the self.[8]

Indeed, the emphasis on the family who live under one roof – or on the domestic group or household – rather than on agnatic lineage in terms of economic considerations, social privileges, prestige and continuity can be detected in the late fourth- and early fifth-century material.[9] Both in the basic understanding and in the actual structuring of the elite Roman family, there seems to be little difference between the earlier Empire and Late Antiquity.[10] The family was a co-resident

---

[8]   Saller, *Patriarchy*, pp. 87–8, 97–9, 162–3, 179–80 (emphasis on the immediate descendants); Champlin, *Final Judgements*, pp. 22, 25–7; 161–8 (testaments); Treggiari, 'Roman Marriage', 503 (emotions); Andreau and Bruhns, *Introduction*, p. xx (alliance strategies); Corbier, 'Divorce and Adoption', p. 75 (adoption); Gardner, *Family*, pp. 39–42, 219–23; Pölönen, 'The Division', pp. 148–9 (legislation revoking the agnatic principles).

[9]   See also Hillner, 'Domus', esp. pp. 130–31, 144 on the importance of the *domus* for the immediate continuity of the senators in Late Antique Rome; and Shaw, 'The Family', esp. pp. 49–51, pointing out the nature of the Roman family in Late Antiquity as 'neither a true nuclear family nor an extended kin-family, much less an agnatic lineage', but rather a network of wider relations attached to a nuclear core.

[10]   In some studies of the family of Late Antiquity, there has been a tendency to see a change from 'traditional' Roman agnatic *familia* towards a family concentrating on its kin-core and conjugal relationship. This, however, takes the normative and idealizing notions of both earlier and later Roman authors too much at face value (see e.g. Krawiec, 'From the Womb', p. 285). See also Cooper, *The Fall* on the ideological shift having taking place by the sixth century; on this, see below. For the challenges to identify change in the history of family life and childhood, see also K. Bradley, 'Images of Childhood in Classical Antiquity', in P. Fass (ed.), *The Routledge History of Childhood in the Western World* (London and New York, 2013), pp. 32–4.

unit and only secondarily included other close relatives. For younger people, the primary sphere consisted of parents, brothers and sisters, and sometimes grandparents. All these are reported to have intervened authoritatively in the choice of the vocation of a young member of the household. In the case of older ascetic recruits, the possible husband or wife, parents and children are referred to. More distant relatives, like aunts and uncles, are referred to in some stories, but they usually appear only as a disturbed but powerless background chorus, who are then left behind by the would-be ascetics. The old *familia* to be abandoned also consisted of other members of the household: servants are described as either assuming the lifestyle of their superiors or as protesting against the departure of the younger generation for the ascetic life.

Not only the family members but also the household as such and the emotional attachment to the home or *domus*, the household unit, were to be despised. This, in turn, was attached to the requirements of scorning the inheritance, distributing the patrimony and divesting oneself of the landed wealth. The *domus*, the land, and ultimately the *patria* were factors that kept people attached to their family and its continuity, and thus were dangerous for the requirement of giving the first preference to the spiritual world. It was because the ecclesiastical writers themselves were attached to these values that their argumentation not only included but was even based on these same identity factors: the individual Christian ascetic was rewarded by the heavenly heritage and the noblest place in the context of the universal *familia Christi*, which lived in the heavenly Jerusalem.

However, as in most pre-modern societies, the conjugal family was the centre of both production and reproduction, and thus it is not surprising that preaching against marriage was not met with universal approval even inside the Catholic branch of the Church. For the everyday survival of Christian families, there was no better alternative to the household unit. For the old-age security and the consideration of continuity in the family wealth, and in the memories and names of the survivors, there were no better alternatives to children. Thus, the function of children for the parents far exceeded the need for the transmission of wealth and property from one generation to another.[11] Here, there is no discernible change from the earlier Roman Empire. Nor did the conflicting roles of women alter in the raising and educating of children: in the midst of actual family life, their work was acknowledged as a major factor in socializing the children and in transferring the social capital and cultural values of society to

---

[11] For an over-emphasis on the economic and material side of family life and succession, see Nathan, *The Family*, esp. p. 24; and Shaw, 'The Family', esp. pp. 36 and 43.

214   *Children and Asceticism in Late Antiquity*

the next generation, even if, ideologically, female incompetence and *infirmitas* was a dominant discourse.

Kate Cooper has claimed that the idea of subjugation of the wife to her husband's authority was increasingly stressed in Late Antiquity and that this change was clearly visible by at least the sixth century. At the same time, the marital union created a more binding social relationship between the relatives of the couple than before, and the reproductive function of the marriage itself lost its overwhelming importance: 'family' was therefore primarily seen as being formed around the marriage bond instead of being based on *pietas* between the parents and children.[12] My study tends to stress the continuity over time, while Cooper's is concentrated on change (or even 'fall'). Further studies will show whether this difference in viewpoints is due to the differences in perspective and source material (more social-historical in the present study than in Cooper's) or whether we can see here a shift in attitudes and mentality between the fifth and sixth centuries.

Reproduction in marriage and the continuity of the familial line – especially if understood as an agnatic lineage – was indeed one of the main concerns for men who belonged to the fourth- and fifth-century Roman elites; it did make a difference whether the children who were about to become ascetics were boys or girls, and whether or not their father was still alive. However, considerations of agnatic descent did not play a decisive role in the strategies aiming for the sense of immortality, since the focus of the discussions of personal and familial continuity in the fourth and fifth centuries was far from concentrated on the male descendants. Why bother about the asceticism of the daughters if their significance for the family was negligible, and what about the continuing insistence of the ecclesiastical writers that daughters, through their ascetic vows, did indeed contribute to the reputation, memory and continuity of their parents? At least for Late Antiquity, if not also for the earlier Empire, generalizations such as 'the continuity of familial line was the fundamental concern to the deceased' need specification.[13] Indeed, even for the elites, continuity of the agnatic kin group was not the ultimate end, since the concern for continuing the lineage was subordinated to the aim of perpetuating the individual. At any rate, this was identified as the fundamental concern for members of the Late Antique elites.[14]

---

[12]   Cooper, *The Fall*, esp. pp. viii–ix, 238–9.

[13]   Harlow and Laurence, *Growing Up*, p. 142, with Hellerman, *The Ancient Church*, pp. 27–37, 214–16. Cf. J. Gardner, *Being a Roman Citizen* (London and New York, 1993), pp. 82–3 and Gardner, *Family*, p. 202 on the essentially agnatic structure of Roman society (of the early Empire).

[14]   Nevertheless, here too I would be reluctant to claim that there would have occurred a change from the earlier Empire to this period even in this matter.

Family Strategies, Asceticism and Children

In dealing with questions like values, mentality and identity, the discourses are part of the reality in which people live and thus they neither precondition the actual choices that in some way reflect the mentality of the people, nor do they constitute a sphere of their own without any connection to actual family-level behaviour. For the study of family strategies, the separation of the study of rhetorical strategies from the 'real' functions of the family has often led to views of the family that attribute to it either purely materialistic and concrete functions, or else strictly individual and emotional ones. Moreover, the prevailing idea of human nature in historical research has emphasized (economic) rationalism, stressing both the conscious (economic) strategies and the experiences of modernism when considering aspects of the survival and continuity of the community and the self. This has made it difficult to see the emotionally loaded behaviour, and *a fortiori* culturally conditioned *mores*, as anything more than restrictive preconditions for the individual in the pursuit of a survival that is defined in basically rational and materialistic terms.

In the writings that propagate the ideal of virginity, the 'angelic' life was directly compared with 'Roman' family life. As Elizabeth Clark points out, the elite ascetics refused 'to act as cement holding together the familial and kinship structures of the Roman aristocracy'.[15] They refused to produce offspring for their own continuity or that of their kin and they were a danger to the family property thanks to their extensive donations to the Church and to the poor. In this respect, asceticism could be seen as the very negation of family strategies, if these were to be understood in the traditional sense as explicit decisions made by families in order to achieve economic and social power for the family.[16]

Property had a prominent place in the discourse of the ecclesiastical authors on the struggles for security and, for more wealthy people, on the strategies of power and privileges. Wealth, especially landed wealth, was an inseparable part of the status and honour of the traditional elites, and its transfer to the

---

[15]   Clark, *Ascetic Piety*, p. ix.

[16]   See e.g. Badel, 'Introduction', p. xvii, claiming that e.g. Melania the Younger 'refusa la logique des stratégies familiales'; Goody, *The European Family*, p. 42, who sees 'the new Christian norms' introduced by the Church as going 'against the best interests of families' and only contributing the Church itself financially. See also Arjava, *Women and Law*, pp. 164–7 with emphasis on the financial interests. On the effective economic irrationality of the stand taken by the Church, see Verdon, 'Virgins and Widows', pp. 495–6. See also Brown, *Body and Society*, p. 64, followed by Nathan, *The Family*, p. 37, on ascetics using 'their bodies to mock continuity'. This background assumption also leads Nathan to play down the importance of children in the Christian thought and way of life (Nathan, *The Family*, pp. 39, 45).

next generation was not only a symbol of continuity but also a concrete way in which the continuity of the lineage was manifested in the actual change of generations. The ecclesiastical writers well perceived the importance of the transfer of inheritance to one's children for the sense of continuity of their elite audiences. By shunning family wealth, an ascetic simultaneously practised charity, renounced luxury and earthly honour, and demonstrated the ability to break away from family obligations. Since patrimony was an important part of familial and personal continuity, its rejection constituted an eloquent gesture that the person in question had renounced the world.

However, when the viewpoint is widened from direct economic considerations and alliance politics to the immaterial sphere and to individual strategies, it is possible to see how asceticism would have responded to the same expectations and needs of continuity as married life in ways that would be quite rewarding in the changed ideological and political atmosphere. Indeed, being an heir was one of the main concepts in ascetic sanctity. For the Christian rhetoric, these traditional functions of the patrimony were utilized by stressing the ideas of treasures in heaven and heirship in the context of the family of Christ, thereby moving from material to immaterial forms of continuity. Even if ascetic life meant dispersal of the inheritance, and in some cases also the loss of hope of physical heirs and offspring, spiritual and immaterial posterity would not be lacking. By the act of almsgiving, the poor and, through them, Christ would become spiritual heirs, and since Christ becomes an heir for the donor, an intimate familial connection with God is established. Moreover, in times of uncertainty, weak public power and plundering troops, an argument for moving one's property to a safe yet lucrative place was enticing: a treasure in heaven cannot be plundered.

Ecclesiastical writers hold that ascetic recruits should despise any emotional attachments to the *domus*, the household unit, and keep contact even with their relatives to a minimum. Yet, in spite of this rhetoric, ascetics belonged very much to their families of origin. An ascetic as a family member meant potential renown and honour for the household and family name among Christians even in the early phase, when an ecclesiastical career did not yet constitute a major way to acquire fame, power and networks in wider society. The strategic nature of directing some children to ascetic or clerical careers is also apparent in the texts that depict how changing demographical realities, the deaths of children and the childlessness of the survivors required action to bring back offspring promised to chastity in order to continue the family line. If, traditionally, it was felt that the family and progeny would guarantee immortality for the individual, in the new Christian ethos the family of the believers guaranteed eternal life:

'We believe Jerusalem above is our city and our mother. We call God our father. We will live here wisely, in order that we might have eternal life', as we read in the *Life of Syncletica*.[17]

The ecclesiastical writers propagating asceticism were well aware of its potential. Their main message was that solace even in personal and family continuity and remembrance no longer depended on biological progeny. Continuity was secured in the context of a new family, the Christian community, in this world, and with God the Father as the ultimate guarantor of continuity in eternity. The Church assumed many of the functions formerly taken care of by the family itself: the Christian churches offered sacrifices (in the form of alms and the Eucharist) for the dead and took care of the commemoration of the dead as part of its liturgy and in burials. Not even those without close relatives were in danger of being left without a proper burial or without prayers. The Church offered the continuity that had formerly been offered only by the family group and thus the near-disappearance of adoption in early medieval Europe can be seen as a result of the understanding that the continuity of an individual was no longer as heavily dependent on the continuity of the name and family cult in the children.[18] The Church, naturally, also offered a family membership with ancestors and an imperishable patrimony with the hope of everlasting continuity with God the Father in heaven. Moreover, Christian culture and doctrine included the idea of sacraments, faith and prayer as means of achieving personal and concrete continuity, not in the context of any earthly community but also directly in connection with God – even if the emphasis was often on the community (or family) of believers more than on direct personal involvement with the Godhead. Ascetic practices, with donations, almsgiving and benevolence accomplished as *pro remedio animae*, were seen as having a strong salvific value and functioning as the means of achieving transcendental immortality. At the same time, the virtue and memory of the deceased were repristinated in donations and almsgiving.

In everyday life, religious motivations, the motivations to attain fame and leave behind a memory, and strategies to achieve material gains were combined. Christianity – and in particular ascetic Christianity – offered a new solution to the anxieties of dying and living: the heavenly family makes the believer a

---

[17]   Pseudo-Athanasius, *Life of Syncletica*, 90.

[18]   See also Badel, 'L'adoption', pp. 102–3, who, however, dates the shift already in Late Antiquity. My study does not show any change in the relevance of name taking place before the mid-fifth century. Cf. Goody, *The European Family*, pp. 34–5, who sees the opposition to adoption as a more or less conscious strategy to amass inheritances and bequests for the Church. See also Verdon, 'Virgins and Widows', pp. 497–8.

sharer in its communion, ensuring inheritance and continuity beyond death. It assumed many of the functions otherwise performed by the earthly family, but in a superior way. Asceticism was in multiple ways an efficient innovation and instrument in the strategies for continuity, and it is no wonder that the message of the ecclesiastical writers was well received.

As more alternatives to the 'biological' family emerged to achieve the different modes of continuity, it would be tempting to claim that the actual family was no longer such a significant factor, culturally speaking, in the ancient and medieval Christian contexts as it had been in the immediately preceding periods. There are also other features that point in this direction.[19] However, any possible change in family should be approached from at least three different viewpoints: first, there are the possible changes on the level of individual attitudes (the perspective of the history of mentalities); second, the possible changes on the level of the dominant ideology (the perspective of intellectual history); and, third, the possible changes in actual behaviour (the perspective of social history).[20] Even if the change in the dominant ideology is beyond doubt, the change in actual behaviour seems to have occurred only for certain individuals. Asceticism remained a minority option and continued to be criticized – or, perhaps more accurately, most Christian families were untouched by asceticism with its radical requests and new standards of life, and, after all, most married and had children.

Moreover, on the level of mentalities, not much seems to have changed. The old values and the old means for the strategies for continuity were still perceptible and affected behaviour on the family level. Immortality in children, survival in the memory of others, and personal honour and fame were still essential in late Roman Christian culture. In many ways personal immortality was still 'conceived not in terms of an afterlife but as an extension of existence by various means on this earth'.[21] Ideologically, however, the establishment of Christianity shifted the stress in continuity strategies from familial contexts to the context

---

[19] See ibid., pp. 498–500; Osiek and Balch, *Families in the New Testament*, esp. p. 214; B. Rawson, 'Death, Burial and Commemoration of Children in Roman Italy', in Balch and Osiek (eds), *Early Christian Families*, esp. pp. 296–7.

[20] 'Ideology' denotes here the ways in which the dominant institutions in society work through values, conceptions of the world, and symbol systems in order to legitimize the current order. By attitudes, in turn, I mean individuals' understanding of cultural values and their proper roles in society. Both therefore fall into the sphere of how things should be; 'ideology', however, is a view from above, while 'attitude' is a view from below. Moreover, both concepts are distinct from an 'idea', which, if it is widespread and/or gains institutional support, may become an ideology or a common attitude.

[21] See Champlin, *Final Judgements*, p. 26, for the earlier Roman Empire. Cf. Edwards, *Death*, esp. pp. 219–20, who sees a tremendous change from 'pagan' Romans to Christians:

of the communities (the Church, parishes and ascetic communities) and to the individual (direct contact with the Godhead). Accordingly, although the family was still seen as the principal vehicle for the strategies for survival and continuity during the period under scrutiny, little by little, immortality seems to have come to be understood in a more transcendental and a more concrete way.

The importance of children for the familial strategies for continuity did not change. In theory children were not needed in the Christian contexts, but the practice was different. Children were essential in the transfer of family property, for proper burial and commemoration of their parents, and they could serve as sources of spiritual benefits for their parents. The vows of children as gifts to God were investments bonding their parents with the family of Christ. By no means were children marginal in the socio-cultural discourses of the time.[22] This relationship was an anticipation of the bad days to come, in much in the same way as earthly networks between relatives, neighbours and patrons were securities against misfortunes.

There is, however, one interesting feature in the depiction of children in the ascetic family strategies: it was much more usual for children to be in their widowed mother's care than in their father's when they aspired to an ascetic career. There are also numerous instances, both in actual cases and in hagiography, in which only the death of the father, and the increased influence of the mother, sets the child free to choose an unconventional lifestyle (of not choosing family life and/or an elite public career). This seems to point not only to demographic reasons but also to the fact that (widowed) fathers were less willing to dedicate their children to asceticism, or even to allow their already adult children to make such a move. The most plausible reason would be that the value hierarchy of elite men was different from that of women.[23] I do not mean that men were more inclined than women to oppose asceticism – there is no evidence for this – but it seems that men perceived their children to be more important in building up their own family and continuing the biological family in the conservative sense,

---

for the latter, immortality meant 'the denial of death' in resurrection, whereas earlier 'the hope of an afterlife, beyond that offered by reputation, makes only rare appearances'.

[22]   'Children in the societies of Greco-Roman antiquity were never marginal beings': Bradley, 'Images of Childhood', p. 34. In comparison, Christian Laes, *Children in the Roman Empire: Outsider Within* (Cambridge, 2011) stresses the outside position of children despite their important roles in the society and culture (esp. pp. 105, 382–4). Still, both stress continuity over change: Bradley, 'Images of Childhood', p. 32–4; Laes, *Children*, pp. 285–8. See de Jong, *In Samuel's Image*, p. 225 on children as investments and bonds between the earthly and heavenly realm in the early medieval West.

[23]   See also Vuolanto, 'Family Relations', pp. 59–62, 68; Vasileiou, 'The Death of the Father', esp. pp. 81 and 86.

Strategies for Continuity

In this study the theoretical contributions by family historians, psycho-historians, sociologists and philosophers have been used as sources for ideas and innovation. The outcome was a model of the theory of strategies for continuity, linking the family strategies approach to other strategic action, as can be seen in Figure 1 (p. 41). In this model, continuity is identified as the ultimate goal of these strategies, subsuming the actions for immediate everyday survival and sustenance in old age, and the quest for a sense of continuity after death in various forms: biological (children), material (patrimony), transcendental (immortality of the soul in eternity) and different forms of personal continuity in this world (such as commemoration and values). Here the relevance of the model is shown for the understanding of strategic thought and behaviour in the context of asceticism and family in Late Antiquity: the intertwining of asceticism and family was, indeed, crucial, and even inevitable, in the discussions of the fourth and fifth centuries.

Earlier studies have often taken the preservation of patrimony as the primary driving force behind the various familial and inheritance strategies. In shifting the focus from the family (and household) strategies to the strategies for continuity, I have intended to circumvent this *a priori* economic view which perceives cultural and social factors as merely limiting the possible scope of available strategies. It would be anachronistic to impose a value hierarchy which gives more relevance to material values and considerations of the continuity of social capital than to the considerations of spiritual capital and eternal continuity.

When continuity strategies are taken as the starting point, even economic motivations bifurcate: on the one hand, the 'family property' and its transmission emerge as prerequisites for survival in the present and in one's old age, as well as for the actions taken by the next generation to ascertain the continuity of their ancestors; on the other hand, from the perspective of the dying, the family property, notably house and land, can be seen as representing (personal) continuity as such, something in which the ancestors live on and by which the individuals themselves are perpetuated. Economic strategies were a way of making an investment which was rewarding both socially and psychologically.

The argumentation of the ecclesiastical writers of the late fourth and early fifth centuries comparing the continuity offered by Christianity through salvation with continuity through lineage shows that the continuity in question was seen as individual in nature. The sense of continuity was, ultimately, a private experience, even if it was achieved in the context of some community – family, kin, religious community or participation in the family of God. The final goal was not the continuity of the family, but the continuity of the individual as part of this dynamism of succession. Indeed, from this point of view, my approach is individualistic – the family is not accepted *a priori* as an independent actor. Family strategies are strategies for families, not of families, even if this does not outweigh the possibility of common aims or discussion within the family. A family is only one of the possible environments or life spheres in which the strategic action of an individual takes place, although, in the culture of Late Antiquity, family strategies emerge as the most important constituent of the individual strategies of continuity. From this perspective, family strategies should be defined as implicit, recurrent patterns of familial behaviour resulting from individual strategies for continuity on the family level.

Strategy, as a theoretical concept, emphasizes the dynamism of families and shows families and individuals as goal-oriented actors, not passive objects of social structures and forces. This approach preserves the tension between individuals at the crossroads of external pressures and their own – culturally conditioned – intentions and choices. Indeed, the particulars of the theory of continuity strategies come close to Pierre Bourdieu's idea of social reproduction, understood as processes by which individuals aim at transmitting to the next generation the powers and privileges they themselves have inherited. Bourdieu evinces the reproduction of the *habitus* as an explanation for this transmission of social values and way of life. Indeed, the actual practices that are conceptualized together as continuity strategies can be defined in the framework of Bourdieu's theories as strategizing social practices interacting between the disposition of the *habitus* (understood as an autonomous generative principle of social practices, as a non-linguistic form of knowledge) and the constraints and options of reality.[24]

---

[24] See Levi, *Family and Kin*, pp. 567–9; Tilly, 'Beyond Family Strategies', p. 123 (goal-orientedness of the strategies); Bourdieu, 'Les stratégies', esp. pp. 1105–6, 1124 (social reproduction, practical knowledge and strategies); R. Johnson, 'Pierre Bourdieu on Art, Litrature and Culture', in P. Bourdieu, *The Field of Cultural Production: Essays on Art and Literature* (Cambridge, 1993), pp. 17–18; R. Jenkins, *Pierre Bourdieu* (London, 1992), p. 72 (for strategizing); J.-C. Kaufmann, *Ego. Pour une sociologie de l'individu*, 2nd edn (Paris, 2007), pp. 137–44; and Bourdieu, *Outline*, p. 10 (on *habitus*).

What, then, is the relationship between the continuity strategies and *habitus*? Since Bourdieu does not explain what drives the 'system' (individual or social group) to reproduce its *habitus*, his theory has been accused of determinism and circularity. Especially in his later works, he uses the word 'strategy' without any reference to intentional and individual choice.[25] The notion of continuity strategies, in turn, includes the idea of intentionality, since the goal of the strategic practices is identified with the need for a sense of individual continuity which would give the 'system' the dynamism needed for its reproduction, without determinism. This would give us two basic lines for understanding the nature of continuity strategies: either they can be seen as serving as intermediaries between *habitus* and actual practices, and therefore themselves as resulting from the interaction of the social and discursive structures and *modus vivendi* of the individual, or else they are separate but parallel principles informing the interaction between *habitus* (here approximating to 'mentalities'), social structures and actual practices. In the first alternative the origin of the continuity strategies is anchored in the social structures, and in the second alternative in the psychology and biology of *homo sapiens*. In either case the social practices anchor the actual forms that the strategies take in their cultural contexts, thus making comparative studies possible. However, to scrutinize these questions, it would be necessary to investigate whether the continuity strategies can be used to conceptualize and understand patterns of actions also found in societies and cultures that are not dependent on the cultural influences of the Greco-Roman world. How specific are the observed features to European societies? What, for example, is the importance of continuity strategies in the context of discourses and practices attached to asceticism in Indian religions?[26]

---

[25] Bourdieu, *The Logic of Practice*, pp. 53–5. See also Bourdieu, *Outline*, p. 70 and Bourdieu, 'Les stratégies', p. 1124. Thus, structures produce *habitus*, which inform practices, which in turn build up structures. For criticism, see Kaufmann, *Ego*, pp. 133–53. A useful distinction made by Kaufmann distinguishes between the (earlier) general theory of *habitus 1* (constructed by studying 'traditional' societies) and the (later) theory of *habitus 2* (used when studying contemporary societies). My interest is, naturally, directed towards *habitus 1*. Viazzo and Lynch, 'Anthropology', pp. 450–51 claim that *habitus* is a suitable concept for describing beliefs and practices below the level of consciousness (instead of 'unconscious strategies'). However, since in the system of Bourdieu the strategies take place in the field of practices, and *habitus* is the principle informing these actions, this solution would cause even more confusion. See also Emigh, 'Theorizing Strategies', p. 496; G. Hodgson, *How Economics Forgot History: The Problem of Historical Specificity in Social Science* (New York and London, 2001), p. 293; Jenkins, *Pierre Bourdieu*, pp. 77, 81–2.

[26] E.g., on asceticism in India, see J. Hawley, 'Mirabai as Wife and Yogi', and V. Narayanan, 'Renunciation and Gender Issues in the Sri Vaisnava Community', both in

The potential fruitfulness of the model of continuity strategies when studying the successors of Roman culture is, in any case, manifest. I end my book by comparing the model to the ideas presented by Zygmunt Bauman (1992) on (post)modern immortality strategies. The urge for immortality is the most obvious common point of view. Moreover, his study, like my model, aims to identify different means for achieving a sense of continuity and meaningfulness in life, and to search for the changing patterns and cultural ways of responding to that urge. There are, however, some weak points in Bauman's reasoning, mostly because of his *a priori* identification of some features of what he describes as typically belonging to modernism as antagonistic to the premodern. I point here only to some themes to illustrate my findings and to pose questions for further studies.

First, Bauman identifies the very search for the meaning for life in immortality as a modern phenomenon.[27] However, this kind of searching was clearly already a concern for individuals in the late Roman world, since the meaningfulness of life was strongly dependent, both in the traditional Roman and in the emerging Christian cultures, on the sense of continuity beyond physical death in terms of reputation, patrimony, children, commemoration and transcendental afterlife. The assumed 'tameness' of death, and the claim that in premodern societies death was not a challenge since nothing could or should be done about it, is simply wrong.[28] A world without great changes did not make individual death any less of a tragedy and a danger to the continuity of one's identity – or, at any rate, the possible change cannot be identified with the modernity–premodernity dichotomy. If there were changes, these could be more comfortably explained by referring to changing cultural values and to the loss of trust in the transcendental strategies for continuity.

Second, we must ask if it is really impossible for the modern 'masses' (those who are not capable of leaving behind intellectual or physical masterworks, or 'making history' or attaining universal celebrity) to attain individual immortality, as Bauman claims. What makes immortality in commemoration by the family – or, more abstractly, sensing continuity in progeny – less 'universal'

V.L. Wimbush and R. Valantasis (eds), *Asceticism*, 2nd edn (Oxford and New York, 2002), pp. 301–19 and 443–58 respectively. Both chapters analyse the woman's role in asceticism; the issue of continuity is only implicitly dealt with in the discussions of duties towards the husband and childbearing, and in the figure of a female ascetic as a bride of the god.

[27]   Bauman, *Mortality, Immortality*, pp. 88–160.

[28]   Cf. Bauman, *Mortality, Immortality*, esp. pp. 94–7 (and pp. 132–4), referring, naturally, to P. Ariès, *L'homme devant la mort* (Paris, 1977) and M. Vovelle, *La Mort et l'Occident: de 1300 à nos jours* (Paris, 1983), esp. p. 382.

than continuity in fighting death by reducing it to 'manageable morsels'?[29] Might it be a modernistic mistake to think of such an immortality *a priori* as universal and to play down the importance of progeny for modern individuals? In comparing Bauman's analysis to my own, one change does indeed appear to have happened: in modernity, the importance of family patrimony and land as carriers of immortality seems to have radically diminished.

The third point concerns the collectivization of immortality, which (according to Bauman) occurs in modernity. Since the lower classes had no access to individual immortality, nationalism (with 'nation' and 'race' as concepts for identification) became the primary channel for such tendencies.[30] However, the Church, for example, had already offered a similar kind of imagined community to perpetuate the immortality of an individual. In general terms these questions deserve further study based on empirical material, thus establishing comparative criteria for examining the change from pre-modern to (post)modern mentalities.

In all, the present study has shown the importance of the strategies for continuity for understanding the late Roman family ideals and practices. The applicability of the model constructed here to other cultures is yet to be tested. As we have seen, a similar emphasis on immortality and continuity strategies can be identified even in the (post)modern Western world. Accordingly, the analysis of specific features of the phenomena, with the help of the present theoretical conceptualization and of categories such as social status and class, gender and age, and geographical and cultural variation, would probably be fruitful and useful, for example, in examining the relative importance of different strategies and the variety of means at individuals' disposal. What kind of *longue durée* changes have occurred in the significance of the various functions fulfilled by the family? How has the relative importance of continuity strategies in the transcendental and immanent realm been changed in Western societies by the process of modernization? These viewpoints are central to the analysis of what were, and continue to be, experienced as the most important constituents of meaningful life.

---

[29] Cf. Bauman, *Mortality, Immortality*, esp. p. 81.
[30] Ibid., pp. 123–8.

Bibliography

Primary Sources

Acts of Paul and Thecla, in *Acta Pauli et Theclae*, ed. A. Lipsius, *Acta Apostolorum Apocrypha*, vol. 1 (Hildesheim: Georg Olms, 1990).

Acts of Thomas, in *Acta Thomae A*, ed. M. Bonnet, *Acta Apostolorum Apocrypha*, vol. 2.2 (Hildesheim; Georg Olms, 1972).

Ambrose of Milan, *Commentary on Luke*, in *Expositio evangelii secundum Lucam*, ed. J.-P. Migne, *Patrologiae cursus completus. Series Latina*, vol. 15 (Paris: J.-P. Migne, 1845).

——. *Commentary on Psalm 118*, in *In psalmum David CXVIII expositio*, ed. J.-P. Migne, *Patrologiae cursus completus. Series Latina*, vol. 15 (Paris: J.-P. Migne, 1845).

——. *The Consecration of a Virgin*, in *De institutione virginis*, ed. J.-P. Migne, *Patrologiae cursus completus. Series Latina*, vol. 16 (Paris: J.-P. Migne, 1845).

——. *Exhortation to Virginity*, in *Exhortatio virginitatis,* ed. J.-P. Migne, *Patrologiae cursus completus. Series Latina*, vol. 16 (Paris: J.-P. Migne, 1845).

——. *Letters*, in *Epistulae et acta*, 3 vol., ed. O. Faller and M. Zelzer, *Corpus Scriptorum Ecclesiasticorum Latinorum* 82.1–3 (Vindobonae: Hoelder-Pichler-Tempsky, 1968, 1982, 1990).

——. *Letters Outside the Collection*, in *Epistulae et acta*, vol. III, ed. M. Zelzer, *Corpus Scriptorum Ecclesiasticorum Latinorum* 82.3 (Vindobonae: Hoelder-Pichler-Tempsky, 1982).

——. *On Abraham*, in *De Abraham*, ed. J.-P. Migne, *Patrologiae cursus completus. Series Latina*, vol. 16 (Paris: J.-P. Migne, 1845).

——. *On the Death of His Brother Satyrus,* in *De excessu fratris sui Satyri*, ed. J.-P. Migne, *Patrologiae cursus completus. Series Latina*, vol. 16 (Paris: J.-P. Migne, 1845).

——. *On the Duties of the Clergy*, in *De officiis ministrorum*, ed. J.-P. Migne, *Patrologiae cursus completus. Series Latina*, vol. 16 (Paris: J.-P. Migne, 1845).

——. *On the Faith*, in *De fide ad Gratianum Augustum*, ed. J.-P. Migne, *Patrologiae cursus completus. Series Latina*, vol. 16 (Paris: J.-P. Migne, 1845).

———. *On the Mysteries*, in *De mysteriis*, ed. J.-P. Migne, *Patrologiae cursus completus. Series Latina*, vol. 16 (Paris: J.-P. Migne, 1845).

———. *On Paradise*, in *De Paradiso*, ed. J.-P. Migne, *Patrologiae cursus completus. Series Latina*, vol. 14 (Paris: J.-P. Migne, 1845).

———. *On Virginity*, in *De virginitate*, ed. E. Cazzaniga, *Corpus Scriptorum Latinorum Paravianum* (Aug. Taurinorum: Paravia, 1954).

———. *On Virgins*, in *De virginibus*, ed. E. Cazzaniga, *Corpus Scriptorum Latinorum Paravianum* (Aug. Taurinorum: Paravia, 1948).

———. *On Widows*, in *De viduis*, ed. J.-P. Migne, *Patrologiae cursus completus. Series Latina*, vol. 16 (Paris: J.-P. Migne, 1845).

Ammianus Marcellinus, *Rerum gestarum libri qui supersunt*, 2 vols, ed. W. Seyfarth with L. Jacob-Karau and I. Ulmann (Leipzig: Teubner, 1978).

Anonymous Homily on Virginity, in D. Amand De Mendieta, and M.-C. Moons, 'Une curieuse homélie grecque inédite sur la virginité addressée aux pères de famille', *Revue Bénédictine* 63 (1953), 18–69 and 211–38.

Anthologia latina sive poesis latina supplementum, vol. 3, ed. F. Buecheler and A. Riese (Leipzig: Teubner, 1895).

Apophthegmata patrum, ed. J.-P. Migne, *Patrologiae cursus completus. Series Graeca*, vol. 65 (Paris: J.-P. Migne, 1864).

Apostolic Constitutions, ed. F.X. Funk, in *Didascalia et constitutiones apostolorum*, 2 vols (Paderborn: Libraria Ferdinandi Schoeningh, 1905).

Aristotle, *Politics*, in *Politica*, ed. W.D. Ross (Oxford: Clarendon Press, 1957).

Asterius of Amasea, *Homilies I–XIV*, ed. C. Datema (Leiden: Brill, 1970).

Athanasius of Alexandria, *Life of Antony*, in *Vie d'Antoine*, ed. G.J.M. Bartelink, *Sources chrétiennes*, vol. 400 (Paris: Éditions du Cerf, 1994).

Athanasius of Alexandria, *The Second Apology*, in *Apologia secunda/contra Arianos*, ed. H.G. Opitz, *Athanasius Alexandrinus Werke*, vol. 2 (Berlin: Kirchenväter-Kommission des Preussischen Akademie der Wissenschaften, 1938 and 1940).

Augustine of Hippo, *Against Julian*, in *Contra secundam Iuliani responsionem, lib. 4–6*, ed. M. Zelzer, *Corpus Scriptorum Ecclesiasticorum Latinorum*, vol. 85.2 (Vindobonae: Verlag der österreichischen Akademie der Wissenschaften, 2004).

———. *Answer to Petilian*, in *Contra litteras Petiliani*, ed. M. Petschenig, *Corpus Scriptorum Ecclesiasticorum Latinorum*, vol. 52 (Vindobonae: Tempsky, 1909).

———. *City of God*, in *De civitate Dei*, ed. B. Dombart and A. Kalb, *Corpus Scriptorum Ecclesiasticorum Latinorum*, vol. 47 (Turnholt: Brepols, 1955).

——. *Confessions*, in *Confessionum Libri XIII*, ed. L. Verheijen, *Corpus Christianorum Series Latina*, vol. 27 (Turnhout: Brepols, 1981).

——. *Enchridion*, ed. M. Evans, *Corpus Christianorum Series Latina* 46 (Turnhout: Brepols, 1969).

——. *Expositions on the Psalms*, in *Enarrationes in Psalmos*, ed. E. Dekkers and J. Fraipont, *Corpus Christianorum Series Latina*, vols 38–40 (Turnhout: Brepols, 1956).

——. *The First Catechetical Instruction*, in *De catechizandis rudibus*, ed. W.Y. Fausset, 3rd edn (London: Methuen & Co., 1915).

——. *Letters 1*–29**, in *Epistulae 1*–29**, ed. J. Divjak, *Corpus Scriptorum Ecclesiasticorum Latinorum*, vol. 88 (Vindobonae: Verlag der österreichischen Akademie der Wissenschaften, 1981).

——. *Letters 1–55*, in *Epistulae I–LV*, ed. K.D. Daur, *Corpus Christianorum Series Latina*, vol. 31 (Turnhout: Brepols, 2004).

——. *Letters 56–100*, in *Epistulae LVI-C*, ed. K.D. Daur, *Corpus Christianorum Series Latina*, vol. 31a (Turnhout: Brepols, 2005).

——. *Letters 101–139*, in *Epistulae CI-CXXXIX*, ed. K.D. Daur, *Corpus Christianorum Series Latina*, vol. 31b (Turnhout: Brepols, 2009).

——. *Letters 124–184*, in *Epistulae CXXIV-CLXXXIV*, ed. A. Goldbacher, *Corpus Scriptorum Ecclesiasticorum Latinorum*, vol. 44 (Vindobonae: Tempsky, 1904).

——. *Letters 185–270*, in *Epistulae CLXXXV-CCLXX*, ed. A. Goldbacher, *Corpus Scriptorum Ecclesiasticorum Latinorum*, vol. 57 (Vindobonae: Tempsky, 1911).

——. *On the Care of the Dead*, in *De cura pro mortuis gerenda*, ed. J. Zycha, *Corpus Scriptorum Ecclesiasticorum Latinorum*, vol. 41 (Vindobonae: Tempsky, 1900).

——. *On Continence*, in *De Continentia*, ed. J. Zycha, *Corpus Scriptorum Ecclesiasticorum Latinorum*, vol. 41 (Vindobonae: Tempsky, 1900).

——. *On the Good of Marriage*, in *De bono coniugali / De sancta virginitate*, ed. P.G. Walsh (Oxford: Clarendon Press, 2001).

——. *On the Good of Widowhood*, in *De bono viduitatis*, ed. J. Zycha, *Corpus Scriptorum Ecclesiasticorum Latinorum*, vol. 41 (Vindobonae: Tempsky, 1900).

——. *On Heresies*, eds R. Vander Plaetse and C. Beukers, *Corpus Christianorum Series Latina*, vol. 46 (Turnhout: Brepols, 1969).

——. *On Holy Virginity*, in *De bono coniugali / De sancta virginitate*, ed. P.G. Walsh (Oxford: Clarendon Press, 2001).

——. *On Marriage and Concupiscence*, in *De nuptiis et concupiscentia*, ed. C.F. Urba and J. Zycha, *Corpus Scriptorum Ecclesiasticorum Latinorum*, vol. 42 (Vindobonae: Tempsky, 1902).

——. *On the Sermon on the Mount*, in *De sermone domini in monte*, ed. A. Mutzenbecher, *Corpus Christianorum Series Latina*, vol. 35 (Turnhout: Brepols, 1967).

——. *On the Works of Monks*, in *De opere monachorum*, ed. J. Zycha, *Corpus Scriptorum Ecclesiasticorum Latinorum*, vol. 41 (Vindobonae: Tempsky, 1900).

——. *Retractions*, in Augustinus, *Retractationum libri II*, ed. A. Mutzenbecher, *Corpus Christianorum Series Latina*, vol. 57 (Turnhout: Brepols, 1984).

——. *Sermons*, in Augustinus, *Sermones*, ed. J.-P. Migne, *Patrologiae cursus completus. Series Latina*, vols 38–9 (Paris: J.-P. Migne, 1863 and 1865).

——. *Tractates on the Gospel of John*, in *In Iohannis evangelium tractatus*, ed. R. Willems, *Corpus Christianorum Series Latina*, vol. 36 (Turnhout: Brepols, 1954).

Basil of Ancyra, *On True Purity of Virginity, in De vera Virginitate*, ed. J.-P. Migne, *Patrologiae cursus completus. Series Graeca*, vol. 30 (Paris: J.-P. Migne, 1857).

Basil of Caesarea, *Letters*, in *Lettres*, ed. Y. Courtonne, 3 vols, *Collection des universités de France* (Paris: Les Belles Lettres, 1957, 1961, 1966).

——. *Longer Rules*, in *Regulae fusius tractatae*, ed. J.-P. Migne, *Patrologiae cursus completus. Series Graeca*, vol. 31 (Paris: J.-P. Migne, 1857).

——. *Shorter Rules*, in *Regulae brevius tractatae*, ed. J.-P. Migne, *Patrologiae cursus completus. Series Graeca*, vol. 31 (Paris: J.-P. Migne, 1857).

Callinicus, *Life of Hypatius*, in *Vie d'Hypatios*, ed. G.J.M. Bartelink, *Sources chrétiennes*, vol. 177 (Paris: Éditions du Cerf, 1971).

Canons of Pseudo-Athanasius, in W. Riedel and W.E. Crum (eds), *The Canons of Athanasius of Alexandria: The Arabic and Coptic Versions* (London and Oxford: Text and Translation Society, 1904).

Cicero, *Cato the Elder on Old Age*, in *De re publica; De legibus; Cato maior de senectute; Laelius de amicitia*, ed. J. Powell, *Scriptorum classicorum Bibliotheca Oxoniensis* (Oxford: Clarendon Press, 2006).

——. *For Archias*, in *Pro Archia Poeta Oratio*, ed. S.M. Cerutti, 2nd edn (Wauconda (Ill.): Bolchazy-Carducci, 2007).

——. *For Rabirius*, in *Orationes de lege agraria; Oratio pro C. Rabirio perduellionis reo*, ed. V. Marek, *M. Tulli Ciceronis Scripta quae manserunt omnia*, vol. 16 (Leipzig: Teubner, 1983).

——. *Letters to Friends*, in *Epistulae ad familiares libri I–XVI*, ed. D.R. Shackleton Bailey (Stuttgart: Teubner, 1988).

———. *On His House*, in *De domo sua ad pontifices oratio*, ed. R.G. Nisbet (New York: Arno Press, 1979).

———. *On the Nature of the Gods*, in *De natura deorum*, ed. A.S. Pease, 2 vols (New York: Arno Press, 1979).

———. *Stoic Paradoxes*, in *Paradoxa Stoicorum*, ed. A.G. Lee (London, Macmillan, 1953).

———. *Tusculan Disputations*, in *Tusculanae disputationes*, ed. M. Giusta, *Corpus scriptorum Latinorum Paravianum* (Aug. Taurinorum: Paravia, 1984).

Clement of Alexandria, *Stromata*, in *Stromata*, 2 vols, ed. O. Stählin and L. Früchtel, 3rd edn, *Die griechischen christlichen Schriftsteller der ersten Jahrhunderte*, vols 15 and 17 (Berlin: Akademie-Verlag, 1960 and 1970).

Codex Justinianus, ed. P. Krueger, in *Corpus iuris civilis*, vol. 2, 11th edn (Berlin: Apud Weidmannos, 1954).

Codex Theodosianus, in *Theodosiani libri XVI cum Constitutionibus Sirmondianis*, vol. 1, ed. P. Krueger (Berlin: Apud Weidmannos, 1954).

Constantius, *Life of Germanus of Auxerre*, in *Vita Germani Episcopi Autissiodorensis*, ed. W. Levison, *Monumenta Germaniae Historica, Scriptores Rerum Merovingicarum*, vol. 7 (Hannover: Hahn, 1920).

Constitutiones Apostolorum: *Les Constitutions apostoliques*, 3 vols, ed. P.M. Metzger, *Sources chrétiennes*, vols 320, 329, 336 (Paris: Éditions du Cerf, 1985–7).

Consultations of Zacchaeus and Apollonius, in Questions d'un païen à un chrétien, 2 vols, eds J.L. Feiertag and W. Steinmann, *Sources chrétiennes*, vols 401–2 (Paris: Éditions du Cerf, 1994).

Corpus inscriptionum Latinarum, vol. 6, part 1, ed. E. Bormann and G. Henzen (Berlin: Reimer, 1876).

Council of Ancyra, ed. J.D. Mansi, in *Sacrorum Conciliorum nova et amplissima collectio*, vol. 2 (Antonius Zatta: Florentiae, 1759).

Council of Gangra, Canons, ed. J.D. Mansi, in *Sacrorum Conciliorum nova et amplissima collectio*, vol. 2 (Florence: Antonius Zatta, 1759).

Council of Neocesarea, Canons, ed. J.D. Mansi, *Sacrorum Conciliorum nova et amplissima collectio*, vol. 2 (Florence: Antonius Zatta, 1759).

Council of Nikaea I, Canons, in N. Tanner (ed.), *Decrees of the Ecumenical Councils*, vol. 1, text established by G. Alberigo (London and Washington DC: Sheed and Ward, and Georgetown University Press, 1990).

Councils of Carthage, Canons, in *Concilia Africae a. 345–525*, ed. C. Munier, *Corpus Christianorum Series Latina*, vol. 149 (Turnhout: Brepols, 1974).

Cyprian, *On the Unity of the Church*, in *De lapsis and De ecclesiae catholicae unitate*, ed. M. Bévenot (Oxford: Clarendon Press, 1971).

Cyril of Scythopolis, *The Lives of the Monks of Palestine*, in *Les moines de Palestine*, 3 vols, ed. A.J. Festugière, *Les Moines d'Orient*, vol. 3 (Paris: Éditions du Cerf, 1962–3).

Digesta, ed. T. Mommsen, in *Corpus iuris civilis*, vol. 1, 16th edn (Berlin: Apud Weidmannos, 1954).

Dio Cassius, *Roman History*, 9 vols, eds H.B. Foster and E. Cary, The Loeb Classical Library (London: Heinemann, 1914–27).

Epictetus, *Encheiridion*, ed. G.J. Boter (Berlin: Walter de Gruyter, 2007).

Epiphanius, *Panarion*, vol. 2, 34–64, ed. K. Holl and J. Dummer, in *Die griechischen christlichen Schriftsteller der ersten Jahrhunderte*, vol. 31 (Berlin: Akademie Verlag, 1980).

Eusebius of Caesarea, *Ecclesiastical History*, in *Histoire ecclésiastique*, 4 vols, ed. G. Bardy, *Sources chrétiennes*, vols 31, 41, 55 and 73 (Paris: Éditions du Cerf, 1952–60).

——. *Proof of the Gospel*, in *Demonstratio evangelica*, ed. I. Heikel, *Die griechischen christlichen Schriftsteller der ersten Jahrhunderte*, vol. 23 (Leipzig: J.C. Hinrichs'sche Buchhandlung, 1913).

Eusebius of Emesa, *Sermons*, in *Discours conservés en Latin*, ed. E. Buytaert (Spicilegium Sacrum: Louvain, 1953).

Evagrius Ponticus, *Antirrheticus*, ed. W. Frankenberg, in *Abhandlungen der Königlichen gesellschaft der wissenschaften zu Göttingen. Philologisch-historische klasse, Neue Folge* 13, no. 2 (Berlin: Weidmannsche Buchhandlung, 1912).

——. *Praktikos*, in *Évagre le Pontique, Traité pratique, ou, Le moine*, eds C. and A. Guillaumont, *Sources chrétiennes*, vol. 171 (Paris: Éditions du Cerf, 1971).

Gaudentius of Brescia, *Sermons*, in *Sermones*, ed. J.-P. Migne, *Patrologiae cursus completus. Series Latina*, vol. 20 (Paris: J.-P. Migne, 1845).

Gerontius, *Life of Melania* (Greek), in *Vie de Sainte Mélanie*, ed. D. Gorce, *Sources chrétiennes*, vol. 90 (Paris: Éditions du Cerf, 1962).

——. *Life of Melania* (Latin), in *La vie latine de sainte Mélanie*, ed. P. Laurence, *Collectio minor. Studium Biblicum Franciscarum*, 41 (Jerusalem: Franciscan Printing Press, 2002).

Gregory Nazianzen, *Oration 2*, in *Discours 6–12*, ed. J. Bernardi, *Sources chrétiennes*, vol. 247 (Paris: Éditions du Cerf, 1978).

——. *Oration 7*, in *Discours 6–12*, ed. M.-A. Calvet-Sébasti, *Sources chrétiennes*, vol. 405 (Paris: Éditions du Cerf, 1995).

——. *Oration 8*, in *Discours 6–12*, ed. M.-A. Calvet-Sébasti, *Sources chrétiennes*, vol. 405 (Paris: Éditions du Cerf, 1995).

——. *Oration 18*, in *Orationes*, ed. J.-P. Migne, *Patrologiae cursus completus. Series Graeca*, vol. 35 (Paris: J.-P. Migne, 1857).

———. *Oration 37*, in *Discours 32–37*, ed. C. Moreschini, *Sources chrétiennes*, vol. 318 (Paris: Éditions du Cerf, 1985).

———. *Poems*, in *Oeuvres poétiques, tom. 1.1, Poèmes personnels II, 1, 1–11*, eds A. Tuilier and G. Bady, *Collection des universités de France* (Paris: Les Belles Lettres, 2004).

Gregory of Nyssa, *Life of Macrina*, in *Vie de Sainte Macrine*, ed. P. Maraval, *Sources chrétiennes*, vol. 178 (Paris: Éditions du Cerf, 1971).

———. *On the Making of Man*, in *La Création de l'homme*, ed. J. Laplace, 2nd edn, *Sources chrétiennes*, vol. 6 (Paris: Éditions du Cerf, 2002).

———. *On Soul and Resurrection*, in *Sur l'âme et la résurrection*, ed. J. Terriex, *Sagesses chrétiennes* (Paris: Éditions du Cerf, 1995).

———. *On Virginity*, in *Traité de la virginité*, ed. M. Aubineau, *Sources chrétiennes*, vol. 119 (Paris: Éditions du Cerf, 1966)

Hilarius of Arles, *Life of Honoratus*, in *Vie de saint Honorat,* ed. M.-D. Valentin, *Sources chrétiennes*, vol. 235 (Paris: Éditions du Cerf, 1977).

History of the Monks in Egypt, in *Historia Monachorum in Aegypto*, ed. A.-J. Festugière, in *Subsidia Hagiographica*, vol. 34 (Brussels: Société des Bollandistes, 1961).

Horace, *Odes*, in *Opera*, ed. S. Bailey (Stuttgart: Teubneri, 1985).

Innocentius, *Letters*, in *Epistulae*, ed. J.-P. Migne, *Patrologiae cursus completus. Series Latina*, vol. 20 (Paris: J.-P. Migne, 1845).

Jacob of Serug, *Homily on Simeon the Stylite*, trans. S.A. Harvey, in V.L. Wimbush (ed.), *Ascetic Behavior in Greco-Roman Antiquity: A Sourcebook* (Minneapolis: Fortress Press, 1990), pp. 15–28.

Jerome, *Against Helvidius*, in *Adversus Helvidium*: *Liber de perpetua virginitate beatae Mariae*, ed. J.-P. Migne, *Patrologiae cursus completus. Series Latina*, vol. 23, ed. J.-P. Migne (Paris: J.-P. Migne, 1845).

———. *Against Jovinian*, in *Adversus Jovinianum,* ed. J.-P. Migne, *Patrologiae cursus completus. Series Latina*, vol. 23, ed. J.-P. Migne (Paris: J.-P. Migne, 1845).

———. *Against the Pelagians*, in *Dialogus adversus Pelagianos*, ed. C. Moreschini, *Corpus Christianorum Series Latina*, vol. 80 (Turnholt: Brepols, 1990).

———. *Against Vigilantius*, in *Contra Vigilantium*, ed. J.L. Feiertag, *Corpus Christianorum Series Latina*, vol. 79C (Turnholt: Brepols, 2005).

———. *Commentary on Ephesians*, in *Commentariorum in Epistolam ad Ephesios,* ed. J.-P. Migne, *Patrologiae cursus completus. Series Latina*, vol. 26, ed. J.-P. Migne (Paris: J.-P. Migne, 1845).

———. *Letters*, in *Lettres*, 8 vol., ed. J. Labourt, *Collection des universités de France* (Paris: Les Belles Lettres, 1949–63).

——. *Life of Hilarius*, in *Trois vies de moines. Paul, Malchus, Hilarion*, ed. E.M. Morales, *Sources chrétiennes*, vol. 508 (Paris: Éditions du Cerf, 2007).

——. *Life of Malchus*, in *Trois vies de moines. Paul, Malchus, Hilarion*, ed. E.M. Morales, *Sources chrétiennes*, vol. 508 (Paris: Éditions du Cerf, 2007).

——. *Life of Paul*, in *Trois vies de moines. Paul, Malchus, Hilarion*, ed. E.M. Morales, *Sources chrétiennes*, vol. 508 (Paris: Éditions du Cerf, 2007).

John Cassian, *Conferences*, in *Conlationes*, ed. Michael Petschenig, *Corpus Scriptorum Ecclesiasticorum Latinorum*, vol. 13 (Vindobonae: Tempsky, 1886).

——. *Institutions*, in *De institutis coenobiorum*, ed. Michael Petschenig, *Corpus Scriptorum Ecclesiasticorum Latinorum*, vol. 17 (Vindobonae: Tempsky, 1888).

John Chrysostom, *An Address on Vainglory*, in *Sur le vaine gloire et l'education des enfants*, ed. A.-M. Malingrey, *Sources chrétiennes*, vol. 188 (Paris: Éditions du Cerf, 1972).

——. *Against the Opponents of Monastic Life*, in *Adversus oppugnatores vitae monasticae*, ed. J.-P. Migne, *Patrologiae cursus completus. Series Graeca*, vol. 47 (Paris: J.-P. Migne, 1864).

——. *Homilies in Genesis*, in *Homiliae in Genesim*, ed. J.-P. Migne, *Patrologiae cursus completus. Series Graeca*, vol. 53 (Paris: J.-P. Migne, 1862).

——. *Homilies on Ephesians*, in *Homiliae in Epistolam ad Ephesios*, ed. J.-P. Migne, *Patrologiae cursus completus. Series Graeca*, vol. 62 (Paris: J.-P. Migne, 1862).

——. *Homilies on First Timothy*, in *Homiliae in Epistolam primam ad Timotheum*, ed. J.-P. Migne, *Patrologiae cursus completus. Series Graeca*, vol. 62 (Paris: J.-P. Migne, 1862).

——. *Homilies on Matteus*, in *Homiliae in Matthaeum*, ed. J.-P. Migne, *Patrologiae cursus completus. Series Graeca*, vol. 57 (Paris: J.-P. Migne, 1862).

——. *Homilies on Penitence*, in *Homiliae de poenitentia*, ed. J.-P. Migne, *Patrologiae cursus completus. Series Graeca*, vol. 49 (Paris: J.-P. Migne, 1862).

——. *Homilies on Philippians*, in *Homiliae in Epistolam ad Philippenses*, ed. J.-P. Migne, *Patrologiae cursus completus. Series Graeca*, vol. 62 (Paris: J.-P. Migne, 1862).

——. *Letters to Theodore*, in *Ad Theodorum lapsum*, ed. J.-P. Migne, *Patrologiae cursus completus. Series Graeca*, vol. 47 (Paris: J.-P. Migne, 1864).

——. *On Anna*, in *De Anna sermones*, ed. J.-P. Migne, *Patrologiae cursus completus. Series Graeca*, vol. 54 (Paris: J.-P. Migne, 1862).

——. *On Monogamy*, in *A une jeune veuve – Sur le mariage unique*, ed. B. Grillet, *Sources chrétiennes*, vol. 138 (Paris: Éditions du Cerf, 1968).

Bibliography 233

———. *On the Priesthood*, in *Sur le sacerdoce (Dialogue et Homélie)*, ed. A.-M. Malingrey, *Sources chrétiennes*, vol. 272 (Paris: Éditions du Cerf, 1980).

———. *On Virginity*, in *La Virginité*, ed. H. Musurillo, *Sources chrétiennes*, vol. 125 (Paris: Éditions du Cerf, 1966).

———. *Quales ducendae sint uxores*, ed. J.-P. Migne, *Patrologiae cursus completus. Series Graeca*, vol. 51 (Paris: J.-P. Migne, 1862).

———. *Regulares feminae*, in *regulares feminae viris cohabitare non debeant*, ed. J.-P. Migne, *Patrologiae cursus completus. Series Graeca*, vol. 47 (Paris: J.-P. Migne, 1864).

———. *To Stagirius*, in *Ad Stagirium*, ed. J.-P. Migne, *Patrologiae cursus completus. Series Graeca*, vol. 47 (Paris: J.-P. Migne, 1864).

———. *To a Young Widow*, in *A une jeune veuve – Sur le mariage unique*, ed. B. Grillet, *Sources chrétiennes*, vol. 138 (Paris: Éditions du Cerf, 1968).

Lactantius, *Divine Institutes*, in *Divinae institutiones*, ed. S. Brandt, *Corpus Scriptorum Ecclesiasticorum Latinorum*, vol. 22 (Vindobonae: Tempsky 1890).

Leo, *Letters*, in *Epistulae*, ed. J.-P. Migne, *Patrologiae cursus completus. Series Latina*, vol. 54 (Paris: J.-P. Migne, 1846).

Letter of Ammon, in *The Letter of Ammon and Pachomian Monasticism*, ed. James Goehring (New York: De Gruyter 1986).

Libanius, *Autobiography (Oration 1)*, ed. A.F. Norman (Oxford: Oxford University Press, 1965).

———. *Oration 30*, in *Libanius, Selected Orations*, vol. 2, ed. A.F. Norman, The Loeb Classical Library (London: Heinemann, *1977)*.

Life and Miracles of Thecla, in *Vie et miracles de Sainte Thècle*, ed. G. Dagron, *Subsidia Hagiographica*, vol. 62 (Brussels: Société des Bollandistes, 1978).

Life of Agnes, in *Epistolae ex Ambrosianarum numero segregatae*, 1, ed. J.-P. Migne, *Patrologiae cursus completus. Series Latina*, vol. 17 (Paris: J.-P. Migne, 1845).

Life of Caesarius of Arles, in *Vita Caesari Arelatense*, ed. B. Krusch, *Monumenta Germanicae Historica. Scriptores Rerum Merovingicarum*, vol. 3 (Hannover: Hahniani, 1896).

Life of Euphrosyne, in *Vita sanctae Euphrosynae secundum textum graecum primaevum*, ed. A. Boucherie, *Analecta Bollandiana* 2 (1883), pp. 195–205.

Life of Eupraxia, in *Vita Eupraxiae*, ed. J.-P. Migne, *Patrologiae cursus completus. Series Latina*, vol. 73 (Paris: J.-P. Migne, 1849).

Life of Olympias, in *Vie anonyme d'Olympias*, ed. A.-M. Malingrey, in *Jean Chrysostome. Lettres à Olympias*, *Sources Chrétiennes*, vol. 13 (Paris: Éditions du Cerf, 1968).

234 *Children and Asceticism in Late Antiquity*

Life of Pachomius (Bohairic version), trans. J.E. Goehring, 'Theodore's Entry in the Pachomian Movement (Selections from Life of Pachomius)', in V.L. Wimbush (ed.), *Ascetic Behavior in Greco-Roman Antiquity: A Sourcebook* (Minneapolis: Fortress Press 1990), pp. 349–56.

——. (First Greek version), trans. A. Veilleux, in *Pachomian Koinonia. Volume 1: The Llife of Saint Pachomius and His Sisciples, Cistercian Studies*, vol. 45 (Kalamazoo, MI: Cistercian Publications, 1980).

——. (Sahidic version), trans. J.E. Goehring, 'The First Sahidic *Life of Pachomius*', in R. Valantasis (ed.), *Religions of Late Antiquity in Practice* (Princeton: Princeton University Press, 2000), pp. 19–33.

Livy, *History of Rome*, in *Ab urbe condita. Libri I–V*, ed. R.M. Ogilvie (Oxford: Clarendon Press, 1974).

The London Papyri VI, in H.I. Bell and W.E Crum (eds), *Jews and Christians in Egypt. The Jewish Troubles in Alexandria and the Athanasian Controversy, Greek Papyri in the British Museum*, vol. VI (London, British Museum, 1924).

Lucian, *The Death of Peregrinus*, ed. A.M. Harmon, in *Lucian*, vol. 5, The Loeb Classical Library (Cambridge, MA: Harvard University Press and Heinemann, 1936).

——. *How to Write History*, in *Comment écrire l'histoire*, ed. A. Hurst (Paris: Les Belles Lettres, 2010).

Mark the Deacon, *Life of Porphyry*, in *Vie de Porphyre*, eds H. Grégoire and M.-A. Kugener (Paris: Belles Lettres, 1930).

Methodius of Olympus, *Symposium*, in *Le banquet*, eds H. Musurillo and V. Debidour, *Sources chrétiennes*, vol. 95 (Paris: Éditions du Cerf, 1963).

Namatianus, Rutilius Claudius, *De reditu suo*, ed. R. Helm (Heidelberg: Carl Winters, 1933).

Novellae Iustiniani, eds. R. Schoell and G. Kroll, in *Corpus iuris civilis*, vol. 3, 6th edn (Berlin: Apud Weidmannos, 1959).

Novellae Maioriani, in *Codex Theodosianus, vol. 2: Leges novellae ad Theodosianum pertinentes*, ed. T. Mommsen and P. Meyer, 2nd edn (Berlin: Apud Weidmannos, 1954).

On the Fall of a Consecrated Virgin, in *Incerti auctoris De lapsu Susannae*, ed. E. Cazzaniga, *Corpus scriptorum Latinorum Paravianum* (Turin: Paravia, 1948).

Ovid, *Letters from the Black Sea*, in *Epistulae ex Ponto*, ed. A.L. Wheeler, in *Ovid in Six Volumes*, vol. 6, The Loeb Classical Library (London: Heinemann, 1975).

Palladius, *Dialogue on the Life of John Chrysostom*, in *Dialogue sur la vie de Jean Chrysostome*, eds A.-M. Malingrey, P. Leclercq and J. Leclercq, *Sources chrétiennes*, vols 341–2 (Paris: Éditions du Cerf, 1988).

———. *The Lausiac History*, in *La Storia Lausiaca*, ed. G.J.M. Bartelink (Verona: Mondadori, 1974).

Paulinus of Nola, *Letters*, in *Epistulae*, ed. G. de Hartel, *Corpus Scriptorum Ecclesiasticorum Latinorum*, vol. 29, 2nd edn (Vienna: Verlag der österreichischen Akademie der Wissenschaften, 1999).

———. *Poems*, in *Carmina*, ed. G. de Hartel, *Corpus Scriptorum Ecclesiasticorum Latinorum*, vol. 30 (Vienna: Tempsky, 1894).

Paulinus of Pella, *Thanksgiving*, in *Poème d'action de grâces et prière*, ed. C. Moussy, *Sources Chrétiennes* 209 (Paris: Éditions du Cerf, 1974).

Pelagius, *Letter to Celantia*, in *Hieronymus, Epistula 148,* ed. J.-P. Migne, *Patrologiae cursus completus. Series Latina*, vol. 22 (Paris: J.-P. Migne, 1846).

———. *Letter to Demetrias*, in *Epistula ad Demetriadem*, ed. J.-P. Migne, *Patrologiae cursus completus. Series Latina*, vol. 30 (Paris: J.-P. Migne, 1846).

Plato, *Symposium*, ed. W.R.M. Lamb, in *Plato in Twelve Volumes*, vol. 3, The Loeb Classical Library (Cambridge, MA: Harvard University Press, 1975).

Porphyry the Philosopher, *To Marcella*, ed. K. O'Brien Wicker (Atlanta: Scholars Press, 1987).

Prudentius, *Crowns of Martyrdom*, in Prudence, *Tome 4: Le livre des couronnes (Peristephanon liber); Dittochaeon; Épilogue*, ed. M. Lavarenne, *Collection des universités de France* (Paris: Les Belles Lettres, 1951).

Pseudo-Athanasius of Alexandria, *Life of Syncletica*, in *Vita et gesta sanctae Syncleticae*, ed. J.-P. Migne, *Patrologiae cursus completus. Series Graeca*, vol. 28 (Paris: J.-P. Migne, 1857).

———. *On Virginity*, ed. D. Brakke, *Corpus Scriptorum Christianorum Orientalium*, vol. 593 (Louvain: Peeters, 2002).

Pseudo-Hilary of Poitiers, *Commentary of the Psalms*, in *Tractatus super psalmos*, ed. A. Zingerle, *Corpus Scriptorum Ecclesiasticorum Latinorum*, vol. 22 (Vindobonae: Tempsky, 1891).

Regula orientalis, ed. A. Vogüe, in *Les Règles des saints Pères*, vol. II, *Sources chrétiennes*, vol. 298 (Paris : Éditions du Cerf, 1983).

Rufinus, *Historia monachorum*, in *Historia monachorum sive de vita sanctorum patrum*, ed. E. Schulz-Flügel (Berlin: De Gruyter, 1990).

Rule of Benedict, eds T. Fry et al., in *The Rule of St Benedict in Latin and English with Notes* (Collegeville, MN: Liturgical Press, 1980).

Salvian, *Letters*, in *Ouvres, vol. I*, ed. G. Lagarrigue, *Sources chrétiennes*, vol. 176 (Paris: Éditions du Cerf, 1971).

———. *On the Goverment of God*, in *Ouvres, vol. II*, ed. G. Lagarrigue, *Sources chrétiennes*, vol. 220 (Paris: Éditions du Cerf, 1975).

———. *To the Church*, in *Ouvres, vol. I*, ed. G. Lagarrigue, *Sources chrétiennes*, vol. 176 (Paris: Éditions du Cerf, 1971).

Seneca, *Letters to Lucilius*, in *Ad Lucilium epistulae morales*, 3 vols, ed. R.M. Gummere, in *Seneca in Ten Volumes*, vols 4–6, 2nd edn, The Loeb Classical Library (London: Heinemann, 1971).

Silius Italicus, *Punica*, ed. I. Delz (Stutgardiae: B.G. Teubneri, 1987).

Siricius, *Letters*, in *Epistulae*, ed. J.-P. Migne, *Patrologiae cursus completus. Series Latina*, vol. 13 (Paris: J.-P. Migne, 1845).

Socrates, *Ecclesiastical History*, in *Histoire ecclésiastique*, 4 vols, ed. G.C. Hansen with P. Périchon and P. Maraval, *Sources chrétiennes*, vols 477, 493, 505, 506 (Paris: Éditions du Cerf, 2004–7).

Sozomen, *Ecclesiastical History*, in *Kirchengeschichte*, eds J. Bidez and G.C. Hansen, *Die griechischen christlichen Schriftsteller der ersten Jahrhunderte*, vol. 50 (Berlin: Akademie-Verlag, 1960).

Sulpicius Severus, *Dialogues*, in *Gallus: Dialogues sur les vertus de saint Martin*, ed. J. Fontaine, *Sources chrétiennes*, vol. 510 (Paris: Éditions du Cerf, 2006).

———. *Letters*, in *Epistulae*, ed. C. Halm, *Corpus Scriptorum Ecclesiasticorum Latinorum*, vol. 1 (Vindobonae: Apud G. Geroldi Filium, 1866).

———. *Life of Saint Martin*, in *Vie de Saint Martin*, 3 vols, ed. J. Fontaine, *Sources chrétiennes*, vols 133–5 (Paris: Éditions du Cerf, 1967–9).

Synesius, *Letters*, in *Correspondance*, 2 vols, eds A. Garzya and D. Roques, *Collection des universités de France* (Paris: Les Belles Lettres, 2000).

Tertullian, *An Exhortation to Chastity*, in *De exhortatione castitatis*, ed. E. Kroymann, *Corpus Christianorum Series Latina*, vol. 2 (Turnhout: Brepols, 1954).

———. *On the Testimony of the Soul*, in *De testimonio animae*, ed. R. Willems, *Corpus Christianorum Series Latina*, vol. 1 (Turnhout: Brepols, 1954).

———. *To His Wife*, in *Ad uxorem*, ed. E. Kroymann, in *Corpus Christianorum Series Latina*, vol. 1 (Turnhout: Brepols, 1954).

Theodoret of Cyrrhus, *Religious History*, in *Histoire des moines de Syrie*, 2 vol., eds P. Canivet and A. Leroy-Molinghen, *Sources Chrétiennes*, vols 234 and 257 (Paris: Éditions du Cerf, 1977 and 1979).

Vitricius of Rouen, *The Praise of Saints*, in *De laude sanctorum*, ed. J.-P. Migne, *Patrologiae cursus completus. Series Latina*, vol. 20 (Paris: J.-P. Migne, 1845).

Secondary Sources

Aasgaard, Reidar, *'My Beloved Brothers and Sisters': Christian Siblingship in Paul* (London and New York: Continuum, 2004).

Alberici, Lisa and Harlow, Mary, 'Age and Innocence: Female Transitions to Adulthood in Late Antiquity', in A. Cohen and J.B. Rutter (eds), *Constructions of Childhood in Ancient Greece and Italy* (Princeton: ASCSA Publications, 2007).

Alciati, Roberto, 'And the Villa Became a Monastery: Sulpicius Severus' Community of Primuliacum', in H. Dey and E. Fentress (eds), *Western Monasticism* Ante Litteram: *The Spaces of Monastic Observance in Late Antiquity and the Early Middle Ages* (Turnhout: Brepols, 2011).

Andreau, Jean and Bruhns, Hinnerk, 'Introduction', in J. Andreau and H. Bruhns (eds), *Parenté et stratégies familiales dans l'antiquité romaine: acts de la table ronde des 2–4 octobre 1986* (Rome: Ecole Française de Rome, 1990).

——.*Parenté et stratégies familiales dans l'antiquité romaine: acts de la table ronde des 2 – 4 octobre 1986* (Rome: Ecole Française de Rome, 1990).

Ariès, Philippe, *L'homme devant la mort* (Paris: Du Seuil, 1977).

Arjava, Antti, 'Paternal Power in Late Antiquity', *Journal of Roman Studies* 88 (1998), 147–65.

——.*Women and Law in Late Antiquity* (Oxford: Clarendon Press, 1996).

Aubin, Melissa, 'More Apparent than Real? Questioning the Difference in Marital Age between Christian and Non-Christian Women of Rome during the Third and Fourth Century', *Ancient History Bulletin* 14 (2000), 1–13.

Badel, Christophe, 'Introduction. Que sont les stratégies devenues?', in Christophe Badel and Christian Settipani (eds), *Les stratégies familiales dans l'Antiquité tardive (IIIe–VIe siècle)* (Paris: De Boccard, 2012).

——. 'L'adoption: un modèle dépassé?', in C. Badel and C. Settipani (eds), *Les stratégies familiales dans l'Antiquité tardive (IIIe–VIe siècle)* (Paris: De Boccard, 2012).

Badel, Christophe and Settipani, Christian (eds), *Les stratégies familiales dans l'Antiquité tardive (IIIe–VIe siècle)* (Paris: De Boccard, 2012).

Bagnall, Roger, *Reading Papyri, Writing Ancient History* (London and New York: Routledge, 1995).

Bagnall, Roger and Frier, Bruce, *The Demography of Roman Egypt* (Cambridge: Cambridge University Press, 1994).

Bakke, Odd Magne, *When Children Became People: The Birth of Childhood in Early Christianity* (Minneapolis: Fortress Press, 2005).

Balch, David and Osiek, Carolyn (eds), *Early Christian Families in Context: An Interdisciplinary Dialogue* (Grand Rapids: Eerdmans, 2003).

Barclay, John, 'The Family as the Bearer of Religion in Judaism and Early Christianity', in H. Moxnes (ed.), *Constructing Early Christian Families. Family as Social Reality and Metaphor* (London and New York: Routledge, 1997).

Baroin, Catherine, 'Ancestors as Models: Memory and the Construction of Gentilician Identity', in V. Dasen and T. Späth (eds), *Children, Memory, and Family Identity in Roman Culture* (Oxford: Oxford University Press, 2010).

Barthes, Roland, 'The Discourse of History', *Comparative Criticism* 3 (1981), 7–20.

Bartlett, Richard, 'Aristocracy and Asceticism: The Letters of Ennodius and the Gallic and Italian Churches', in R.W. Mathisen and D. Shanzer (eds), *Society and Culture in Late Antique Gaul: Revisiting the Sources* (Aldershot: Ashgate, 2001).

Baud, M., 'Patriarchy and Changing Family Strategies: Class and Gender in the Dominican Republic', *History of the Family* 2(4) (1997), 355–77.

Bauman, Zygmunt, *Mortality, Immortality and Other Life Strategies* (Stanford: Stanford University Press, 1992).

Beard, Mary, North, John and Price, Simon, *Religions of Rome, Vol 1. A History*, 2nd edn (Cambridge: Cambridge University Press, 1999).

Beaucamp, Joëlle, *Le statut de la femme à Byzance (4ᶜ–7ᶜ siècle), vol. I: Le droit imperial* (Paris: De Boccard, 1990).

——. *Le statut de la femme à Byzance (4ᶜ–7ᶜ siècle), vol. II: Les pratiques sociales* (Paris: De Boccard, 1992).

Behr, John, 'The Rational Animal: A Rereading of Gregory of Nyssa's *De hominis opificio*', *Journal of Early Christian Studies* 7(2) (1999), 219–47.

Bertaux, Daniel and Thompson, Paul, 'Introduction', in D. Bertaux and P. Thompson (eds), *Between Generations: Family Models, Myths, and Memories* (Oxford: Oxford University Press, 1993).

Boswell, John, '*Expositio* and *Oblatio*: The Abandonment of Children and the Ancient and Medieval Family', *American Historical Review* 89(1) (1984), 10–33.

——. *The Kindness of Strangers: The Abandonment of Children in Western Europe from Late Antiquity to the Renaissance*, 2nd edn (London: Allen Lane and Penguin, 1989).

Bourdieu, Pierre, 'Les stratégies matrimoniales dans le système de reproduction', *Annales (ESC)* 27(4–5) (1972), 1105–27.

——. *The Logic of Practice* (Cambridge: Polity Press, 1990 [orig. in French 1980]).

——. *Outline of a Theory of Practice* (Cambridge: Cambridge University Press, 1977 [orig. in French 1972]).

Bradley, Keith, 'Child Labor in the Roman World', in *Discovering the Roman Family: Studies in Roman Social History* (Oxford: Oxford University Press, 1991).

——. 'Images of Childhood in Classical Antiquity', in P. Fass (ed.), *The Routledge History of Childhood in the Western World* (London and New York: Routledge, 2013).

Brennan, Tad, 'Epicurus on Sex, Marriage, and Child-rearing', *Classical Philology* 91(4) (1996), 346–52.

Browder, Michael, 'Coptic Manichaean *Kephalaia of the Teacher*', in V. Wimbush (ed.), *Ascetic Behavior in Greco-Roman Antiquity: A Sourcebook* (Minneapolis: Fortress Press, 1990).

Brown, Peter, *Body and Society: Men, Women and Sexual Renunciation in Early Christianity* (New York: Columbia University Press, 1988).

——. 'The Study of Elites in Late Antiquity', *Arethusa* 33 (2000), 321–46.

——. *Through the Eye of a Needle. Wealth, the Fall of Rome, and the Making of Christianity in the West, 350–550 AD* (Princeton: Princeton University Press, 2012).

Brubaker, Leslie and Tougher, Shaun (eds), *Approaches to the Byzantine Family* (Aldershot: Ashgate, 2013).

Brück, T. 'Coping with Peace: Post-War Household Strategies in Northern Mozambique', D. Phil thesis, University of Oxford, 2001. Available at: http://citeseerx.ist.psu.edu/viewdoc/download?doi=10.1.1.201.4041& rep=rep1&type=pdf. Accessed 12 January 2015.

Buell, Denise K., *Making Christians: Clement of Alexandria and the Rhetoric of Legitimacy* (Princeton: Princeton University Press, 1998).

Burrus, Victoria, '"Honor the Fathers": Exegesis and Authority in the Life of Saint Helia', in H.-U. Weidemann (ed.), *Asceticism and Exegesis in Early Christianity: The Reception of New Testament Texts in Ancient Ascetic Discourses* (Göttingen: Vandenhoeck & Ruprecht, 2013).

——. *Saving Shame: Martyrs, Saints, and Other Abject Subjects* (Philadelphia: University of Pennsylvania Press, 2008).

Cabouret-Laurioux, Bernadette, 'Parenté et stratégie familiale en Syrie a l'époque tardive: l'exemple de la famille de Libanios', in C. Badel and C. Settipani (eds), *Les stratégies familiales dans l'Antiquité tardive (IIIᵉ–VIᵉ siècle)* (Paris: De Boccard, 2012).

Caseau, Béatrice, 'Childhood in Byzantine Saints' Lives', in A. Papaconstantinou and A.-M. Talbot (eds), *Becoming Byzantine: Children and Childhood in Byzantium* (Washington DC: Dumbarton Oaks Research Library and Collection, 2009).

——. 'Stratégies parentales concernant les enfants au sein de la famille: le choix de la virginité consacrée', in C. Badel and C. Settipani (eds), *Les stratégies familiales dans l'Antiquité tardive (IIIe–VIe siècle)* (Paris: De Boccard, 2012).

Castelli, Elizabeth, 'Gender, Theory, and the Rise of Christianity: A Response to Rodney Stark', *Journal of Early Christian Studies* 6(2) (1998), 227–57.

De'Cavalieri, P. Franchi, 'Agnese nella tradizione e nella leggenda', repr. in *Scritti Agiografici*, vol. I (1893–1900) (Vatican City: Biblioteca Apostolica Vaticana, 1962).

Champlin, Edward, *Final Judgments: Duty and Emotion in Roman Wills 200 B.C.–A.D. 250* (Berkeley: University of California Press, 1991).

Clark, Elizabeth A., 'Antifamilial Tendencies in Ancient Christianity', *Journal of the History of Sexuality* 5 (1995), 356–80.

——. *Ascetic Piety and Women's Faith. Essays on Late Ancient Christianity* (Leviston: Edvin Meller Press, 1986).

——. 'Ascetic Renunciation and Feminine Advancement', in *Ascetic Piety and Women's Faith. Essays on Late Ancient Christianity* (Leviston: Edvin Meller Press, 1986).

——. *History, Theory, Text: Historians and the Linguistic Turn* (Cambridge, MA: Harvard University Press, 2004).

——. 'Holy Women, Holy Words: Early Christian Women, Social History, and the "Linguistic Turn"', *Journal of Early Christian Studies* 6(3) (1998), 413–30.

——. 'John Chrysostom and the *Subintroductae*', in *Ascetic Piety and Women's Faith: Essays on Late Ancient Christianity* (Leviston: Edvin Meller Press, 1986).

——. 'Piety, Propaganda and Politics in the Life of Melania the Younger', in *Ascetic Piety and Women's Faith: Essays on Late Ancient Christianity* (Leviston: Edvin Meller Press, 1986).

——. *Reading Renunciation: Asceticism and Scripture in Early Christianity* (Princeton: Princeton University Press, 1999).

——. 'The Uses of the *Song of Songs*: Origen and the Later Latin Fathers', in *Ascetic Piety and Women's Faith: Essays on Late Ancient Christianity* (Leviston: Edvin Meller Press, 1986).

Clark, Gillian, 'The Fathers and the Children', in D. Wood (ed.), *The Church and Childhood* (Oxford: Blackwell, 1994).

———. *'This Female Man of God': Women and Spiritual Power in the Patristic Age, AD 350–450* (London and New York: Routledge, 1995).

———. *Women in Late Antiquity: Pagan and Christian Lifestyles* (Oxford: Clarendon Press, 1993).

Colot, Blandine, 'Analyse du sens et discours chrétien chez les auteurs latins du IVe siècle', in M. Baratin and C. Moussy (eds), *Conceptions latines du sens et de la signification, Actes du Colloque de Linguistique latine du Centre Alfred Ernout (CNRS/Paris IV)* (Paris: Lingua Latina, 1999).

Cooper, Kate, 'Closely Watched Households: Visibility, Exposure and Private Power in the Roman *Domus*', *Past and Present* 197 (2007), 3–33.

———. *The Fall of the Roman Household* (Cambridge: Cambridge University Press, 2007).

———. 'The Household and the Desert: Monastic and Biological Communities in the Lives of Melania the Younger', in A. Mulder-Bakker and J. Wogan-Browne (eds), *Household, Women, and Christianities* (Turnhout: Brepols, 2005).

———. *The Virgin and the Bride: Idealized Womanhood in Late Antiquity* (Cambridge, MA: Harvard University Press 1996).

Corbier, Mireille, 'Les comportements familiaux de l'aristocratie romaine (IIe siècle av. J.-C. – IIIe siècle ap. J.-C.), in J. Andreau and H. Bruhns (eds), *Parenté et stratégies familiales dans l'antiquité romaine: acts de la table ronde des 2 – 4 octobre 1986* (Rome: Ecole Française de Rome, 1990).

———. 'Divorce and Adoption as Roman Familial Strategies', in B. Rawson (ed.), *Marriage, Divorce and Children in Ancient Rome* (Oxford: Clarendon Press, 1991).

———. 'Épigraphie et parenté', in Y. Le Bohec and Y. Roman (eds), *Epigraphie et histoire: acquis et problèmes* (Lyon: De Boccard, 1998).

———. 'Introduction. Adoptés et nourris', in M. Corbier (ed.), *Adoption et fosterage* (Paris: De Boccard, 2000).

———. (ed.), *Adoption et fosterage* (Paris: De Boccard, 2000).

Cox, Cheryl A., *Household Interests: Property, Marriage Strategies and Family Dynamics in Ancient Athens* (Princeton: Princeton University Press, 1997).

Crook, John, '"His and Hers": What Degree of Financial Responsibility Did Husband and Wife Have for the Matrimonial Home and Their Life in Common, in a Roman Marriage?', in J. Andreau and H. Bruhns (eds), *Parenté et stratégies familiales dans l'antiquité romaine: acts de la table ronde des 2 – 4 octobre 1986* (Rome: Ecole Française de Rome, 1990).

Curran, J., 'Jerome and the Sham Christians of Rome', *Journal of Ecclesiastical History* 48 (1997), 213–29.

Van Dam, Raymond, *Families and Friends in Late Roman Cappadocia* (Philadelphia: University of Pennsylvania Press, 2003).

Dasen, Véronique, 'Wax and Plaster Memories: Children in Elite and Non-Elite Strategies', in V. Dasen and T. Späth (eds), *Children, Memory, and Family Identity in Roman Culture* (Oxford: Oxford University Press, 2010).

Desmulliez, Janine, Fraisse-Coué, Christiane, Paoli-Lafaye, Elisabeth and Sotinel, Claire (eds), *Prosopographie chrétienne du Bas-Empire* 2 *(PCBE)*: *Prosopographie de l'Italie chrétienne (313–604)*, 2 vols (Rome: École française de Rome, 1999 and 2000).

Dietz, Maribel, *Wandering Monks, Virgins*, and *Pilgrims*: *Ascetic Travel in the Mediterranean World, A.D. 300–800* (University Park, PA: Pennsylvania State University, 2005).

Dixon, Susan, 'The Circulation of Children in Roman Society', in M. Corbier (ed.), *Adoption et fosterage* (Paris: De Boccard, 2000).

———. *The Roman Family* (Baltimore: Johns Hopkins University Press, 1992).

Domańska, Ewa, *Encounters. Philosophy of History after Postmodernism* (Charlottesville: University Press of Virginia, 1998).

Dondin-Payre, Monique, 'La stratégie symbolique de la parenté sous la République et l'empire romains', in J. Andreau and H. Bruhns (eds), *Parenté et stratégies familiales dans l'antiquité romaine: acts de la table ronde des 2 – 4 octobre 1986* (Rome: Ecole Française de Rome, 1990).

Drijvers, Jan, 'Virginity and Asceticism in Late Roman Western Elites', in J. Blok and P. Mason (eds), *Sexual Asymmetry*: *Studies in Ancient Society* (Amsterdam: Gieben, 1987).

Dyer, Christopher, 'The Peasant Landmarket in Medieval England', in L. Feller and C. Wickham (eds), *Le marché de la terre au Moyen Âge* (Rome: École Française de Rome, 2005).

Edwards, Catharine, *Death in Ancient Rome* (New Haven: Yale University Press, 2007).

Van Eijk, Ton H.C., 'Marriage and Virginity, Death and Immortality', in J. Fontaine and C. Kannengiesser (eds), Epektasis. *Mélanges patristiques offerts au Cardinal Jean Daniélou* (Paris: Beauchesne, 1972).

Elm, Susanna, 'Gregory's Women: Creating a Philosopher's Family', in J. Børtnes and T. Hägg (eds), *Gregory Nazianzen: Images and Reflections* (Copenhagen: Museum Tusculanum Press, 2006).

———. *Virgins of God. The Making of Asceticism in Late Antiquity* (Oxford: Clarendon Press, 1994).

Emigh, Rebecca J. 'Theorizing Strategies: Households and Markets in Fifteenth-Century Tuscany', *History of the Family* 6 (2001), 495–517.

Engelen, Theo, Kok, Jan and Paping, Richard, 'The Family Strategies Concept: An Evaluation of Four Empirical Case Studies', *History of the Family* 9 (2004), 239–51.

Evans Grubbs, Judith, 'The Dynamics of Infant Abandonment: Motives, Attitudes and (Unintended) Consequences', in K. Mustakallio and C. Laes (eds), *The Dark Side of Childhood in Late Antiquity and the Middle Ages* (Oxford: Oxbow, 2011).

——. 'Hidden in Plain Sight: *Expositi* in the Community', in V. Dasen and T. Späth (eds), *Children, Memory, and Family Identity in Roman Culture* (Oxford: Oxford University Press, 2010).

——. *Law and Family in Late Antiquity. The Emperor Constantine's Marriage Legislation*, 2nd edn (Oxford: Oxford University Press, 1999).

——. 'Marrying and its Documentation in Later Roman Law' in P. Reynolds and J. Witte (eds), *To Have and to Hold: Marrying and its Documentation in Western Christendom, 400–1600* (Cambridge: Cambridge University Press, 2007).

——. '"Pagan" and "Christian" Marriage: The State of the Question', *Journal of Early Christian Studies* 2(3) (1994), 361–412.

——. 'Parent-Child Conflict in the Roman Family: The Evidence of the Code of Justinian', in M. George (ed.), *The Roman Family in the Empire: Rome, Italy, and Beyond* (Oxford: Oxford University Press, 2005).

——. 'Promoting *Pietas* through Roman Law', in B. Rawson (ed.), *A Companion to Families in the Greek and Roman Worlds* (Oxford: Blackwell, 2011).

——. 'Review of *The Age of Marriage in Ancient Rome*, by A. Lelis, W. Percy, and B. Verstraete', *Mouseion* III(7) (2007), 67.

——. 'Virgins and Widows, Show-Girls and Whores: Late Roman Legislation on Women and Christianity', in R. Mathisen (ed.), *Law, Society, and Authority in Late Antiquity* (Oxford: Oxford University Press, 2001).

Evans Grubbs, Judith and Parkin, Tim, with Bell, Roslynne (eds), *The Oxford Handbook of Childhood and Education in the Classical World* (Oxford: Oxford University Press, 2013).

Fayer, Carla, *La familia romana: Aspetti giuridici ed antiquari*, 3 vols (Rome: L'Erma di Bretschneider, 1994, 2005, 2005).

Feller, Laurent, 'Introduction. Enrichissement, accumulation et circulation des bien', in L. Feller and C. Wickham (eds), *Le marché de la terre au Moyen Âge* (Rome: École Française de Rome, 2005).

Finn, Richard, *Asceticism in the Graeco-Roman World: Key Themes in Ancient History* (Cambridge: Cambridge University Press, 2009).

Fontaine, Laurence and Jürgen Schlumbohm, 'Introduction', in L. Fontaine and J. Schlumbohm (eds), *Household Strategies for Survival, 1600–2000: Fission, Faction and Cooperation* (Cambridge: University of Cambridge Press, 2001).

Forbes, Hamish, 'Of Grandfathers and Grand Theories: The Hierarchised Ordering of Responses to Hazard in a Greek Rural Community', in P. Halstead and J. O'Shea (eds), *Bad Year Economics: Cultural Responses to Risk and Uncertainty*, 2nd edn (Cambridge: Cambridge University Press, 1995).

Freedman, Paul, 'North-American Historiography of the Peasant Land Market' in L. Feller and C. Wickham (eds), *Le marché de la terre au Moyen Âge* (Rome: École Française de Rome, 2005).

Gadamer, Hans-Georg, *Truth and Method*, 2nd edn (London: Sheed and Ward, 1985).

Gardner, Jane, *Being a Roman Citizen* (London and New York: Routledge, 1993).

——. *Family and Familia in Roman Law and Life* (Oxford: Clarendon Press, 1998).

——. 'Status, Sentiment and Strategy in Roman Adoption', in M. Corbier (ed.), *Adoption et fosterage* (Paris: De Boccard, 2000).

Garnsey, Peter, *Famine and Food Supply in the Greco-Roman World: Responses to Risk and Crisis*, 2nd edn (Cambridge: Cambridge University Press, 1989).

Garnsey, Peter and Saller, Richard, *The Roman Empire: Economy, Society and Culture*, 4th edn (London: Duckworth, 1996).

Gaventa, Beverly, *Our Mother Saint Paul* (Louisville: Westminster John Knox, 2007).

Giardina, Andrea, 'Macrina the Saint', in A. Fraschetti (ed.), *Roman Women*, 2nd edn (Chicago: University of Chicago Press, 2001).

Goody, Ester, 'Sharing and Transferring Component of Parenthood: The West African Case', in Mireille Corbier (ed.), *Adoption et fosterage* (Paris: De Boccard, 2000).

Goody, Jack, *The European Family* (Oxford: Blackwell, 2000).

——. *Production and Reproduction: A Comparative Study of the Domestic Domain* (Cambridge: Cambridge University Press, 1976).

Gorce, Denys, *Vie de sainte Mélanie. Texte grec, introduction, traduction et notes* (Paris: Éditions du Cerf, 1962).

Grant, Michael, *Greek and Roman Historians: Information and Misinformation*, 2nd edn (London and New York: Routledge, 2000).

Guerreau-Jalabert, Anita, '*Nutritus / oblatus*: parenté et circulation d'enfants au Moyen Âge', in M. Corbier (ed.), *Adoption et fosterage* (Paris: De Boccard, 2000).

Hägg, Tomas, *The Art of Biography in Antiquity* (Oxford: Oxford University Press, 2012).

Hallett, Judith, *Fathers and Daughters in Roman Society: Women and the Elite Family* (Princeton: Princeton University Press, 1984).

Halstead, Paul and O'Shea, John, 'Introduction: Cultural Responses to Risk and Uncertainty', in P. Halstead and J. O'Shea (eds), *Bad Year Economics: Cultural Responses to Risk and Uncertainty*, 2nd edn (Cambridge: Cambridge University Press, 1995).

Hareven, Tamara, *Family Time and Industrial Time: The Relationship between the Family and Work in a New England Industrial Community* (Cambridge: Cambridge University Press, 1982).

——. 'The History of the Family and the Complexity of Social Change', *American Historical Review* 96(1) (1991), 95–124.

Harlow, Mary and Laurence, Ray, *Growing Up and Growing Old in Ancient Rome: A Life Course Approach* (London and New York: Routledge, 2002).

Harlow, Mary, Laurence, Ray and Vuolanto, Ville, 'Past, Present and Future in the Study of Roman Childhood', in S. Crawford and G. Shepherd (eds), *Approaches to Childhood in the Past* (Oxford: Archaeopress, 2007).

Harrison, Carol, *Augustine: Christian Truth and Fractured Humanity* (Oxford: Oxford University Press, 2002).

Harvey, Susan, 'Sacred Bonding: Mothers and Daughters in Early Syriac Hagiography', *Journal of Early Christian Studies* 4(1) (1996), 27–56.

Hawley, John, 'Mirabai as Wife and Yogi', in V.L. Wimbush and R. Valantasis (eds), *Asceticism*, 2nd edn (Oxford: Oxford University Press, 2002).

Hedrick, Charles, Jr., *History and Silence: The Purge and Rehabilitation of Memory in Late Antiquity* (Austin: University of Texas Press, 2000).

Hellerman, Joseph, *The Ancient Church as Family* (Minneapolis: Fortress Press, 2001).

Hillner, Julia, 'Domus, Family, and Inheritance: The Senatorial Family House in Late Antique Rome', *Journal of Roman Studies* 93 (2003), 129–45.

Hodgson, Geoffrey, *How Economics Forgot History: The Problem of Historical Specificity in Social Science* (New York and London: Routledge, 2001).

Holleran, Claire, 'Migration and the Urban Economy of Rome', in C. Holleran and A. Pudsey (eds), *Demography and the Graeco-Roman World: New Insights and Approaches* (Cambridge: Cambridge University Press, 2011).

Hopkins, Keith, 'Seven Missing Papers', in J. Andreau and H. Bruhns (eds), *Parenté et stratégies familiales dans l'antiquité romaine: acts de la table ronde des 2 – 4 octobre 1986* (Rome: Ecole Française de Rome, 1990).

Horn, Cornelia, 'Children's Play as Social Ritual', in V. Burrus (ed.), *Late Ancient Christianity* (Minneapolis: Augsburg Fortress Press, 2005).

Horn, Cornelia and Martens, John, *'Let the Little Children Come to Me': Childhood and Children in Early Christianity* (Washington DC: Catholic University Press, 2009).

Horn, Cornelia and Phenix, Robert (eds), *Children in Late Ancient Christianity* (Tübingen: Mohr Siebeck, 2009).

Humphreys, Sarah, *The Family, Women and Death. Comparative Studies*, 2nd edn (Ann Arbor: University of Michigan Press, 1993).

Hunter, David, *Marriage, Celibacy, and Heresy in Ancient Christianity: The Jovinianist Controversy* (Oxford: Oxford University Press, 2007).

——. 'Rereading the Jovinianist Controversy: Asceticism and Clerical Authority in Late Ancient Christianity', *Journal of Medieval and Early Modern Studies* 33(3) (2003), 454–70.

——. 'Vigilantius of Calagurris and Victricius of Rouen: Ascetics, Relics and Clerics in Late Roman Gaul', *Journal of Early Christian Studies* 7(3) (1999), 401–30.

——. 'The Virgin, the Bride and the Church: Reading Psalm 45 in Ambrose, Jerome and Augustine', *Church History* 69(2) (2000), 281–303.

Jacobs, Andrew, 'Let Him Guard *Pietas*: Early Christian Exegesis and the Ascetic Family', *Journal of Early Christian Studies* 11(3) (2003), 265–81.

——. 'Writing Demetrias: Ascetic Logic in Ancient Christianity', *Church History* 69 (2000), 719–48.

Jacobs, Andrew and Krawiec, Rebecca, 'Fathers Know Best? Christian Families in the Age of Asceticism', *Journal of Early Christian Studies* 11(3) (2003), 257–63.

Jenkins, Richard, *Pierre Bourdieu* (London: Routledge, 1992).

Johnson, Randal, 'Pierre Bourdieu on Art, Literature and Culture', in P. Bourdieu, *The Field of Cultural Production: Essays on Art and Literature* (Cambridge: Polity Press, 1993).

Johnson, Scott Fitzgerald (ed.), *The Oxford Handbook of Late Antiquity* (Oxford: Oxford University Press, 2012).

Johnston, David, *Roman Law in Context* (Cambridge: Cambridge University Press, 1999).

De Jong, Mayke, *In Samuel's Image: Child Oblation in the Early Medieval West* (Leiden: Brill, 1996).

Joye, Sylvie, 'Filles et pères à la fin de l'Antiquité et au haut Moyen Âge. Des rapports familiaux à l'épreuve des stratégies', in C. Badel and C. Settipani (eds), *Les stratégies familiales dans l'Antiquité tardive (IIIᵉ–VIᵉ siècle)* (Paris: De Boccard, 2012).

Kalogeras, Nikos, 'The Role of Parents and Kin in the Education of Byzantine Children', in K. Mustakallio, J. Hanska, H.-L. Sainio and V. Vuolanto (eds), *Hoping for Continuity: Childhood, Education and Death in Antiquity and the Middle Ages* (Rome: Institutum Romanum Finlandiae, 2005).

Kan, Sergei, *Symbolic Immortality: The Tlingit Potlatch of the Nineteenth Century* (Washington DC: Smithsonian Institution Press, 1989).

Kaufmann, Jean-Claude, *Ego. Pour une sociologie de l'individu*, 2nd edn (Paris: Hachette, 2007).

Kelly, John, *Golden Mouth: The Story of John Chrysostom, Ascetic, Preacher, Bishop*, 2nd edn (Ithaca: Cornell University Press, 1998).

Kertzer, David and Richard Saller, 'Historical and Anthropological Perspectives on Italian Family Life', in D. Kertzer and R. Saller (eds), *The Family in Italy from Antiquity to the Present* (New Haven: Yale University Press, 1991).

Killgrove, Kristina, *Migration and Mobility in Imperial Rome* (PhD dissertation, University of North Carolina, 2010). Available at: http://www.piki. org/~kristina/Killgrove-2010-Migration-Mobility-Imperial-Rome.pdf. Accessed 12 January 2015.

Knuuttila, Simo, *Emotions in Ancient and Medieval Philosophy* (Oxford: Oxford University Press, 2004).

Kotila, Heikki, *Memoria mortuorum: Commemoration of the Departed in Augustine* (Rome: Institutum Patristicum Augustinianum, 1992).

Kotsifou, Chrysi, 'Papyrological Perspectives on Orphans in the World of Late Ancient Christianity', in C. Horn and R. Phenix (eds), *Children in Late Ancient Christianity* (Tübingen: Mohr Siebeck, 2009).

Krause, Jens-Uwe, *Witwen und Waisen im frühen Christentum. Witwen und Waisen im Römischen Reich 4* (Stuttgart: Franz Steiner, 1995).

Krawiec, Rebecca, '"From the Womb of the Church": Monastic Families', *Journal of Early Christian Studies* 11(3) (2003), 283–307.

——. *Shenoute and the Women of White Monastery: Egyptian Monasticism in Late Antiquity* (Oxford: Oxford University Press, 2002).

Krumeich, Christa, *Hieronymus und die christlichen feminae clarissimae* (Bonn: Habelt, 1993).

Kuefler, Matthew, *The Manly Eunuch: Masculinity, Gender Ambiguity, and Christian Ideology in Late Antiquity* (Chicago: University of Chicago Press, 2001).

——. 'Theodosian Code and Later Roman Marriage Law', *Journal of Family History* 32(4) (2007), 343–70.

Kyle, Donald, *Spectacles of Death in Ancient Rome* (London and New York: Routledge, 1998).

Laes, Christian, *Children in the Roman Empire: Outsiders Within* (Cambridge and New York: Cambridge University Press, 2011).

——. 'High Hopes, Bitter Grief: Children in Latin Literary Inscriptions', in G. Partoens, G. Roskam and T. Van Houdt (eds), *Virtutis Imago: Idealisation and Transformation of an Ancient Ideal* (Leuven: Peeters, 2004).

Laes, Christian, Mustakallio, Katariina and Vuolanto, Ville (eds), *Children and Family in Late Antiquity: Life, Death and Interaction* (Leuven: Peeters, 2015).

Lafferty, Maura, 'Augustine, the Aeneid, and the Roman Family', in K. Mustakallio, J. Hanska, H.-L. Sainio and V. Vuolanto (eds), *Hoping for Continuity: Childhood, Education and Death in Antiquity and the Middle Ages* (Rome: Institutum Romanum Finlandiae, 2005).

Laiou, Angeliki, 'Sex, Consent, and Coercion in Byzantium', in Angeliki Laiou (ed.), *Consent and Coercion to Sex and Marriage in Ancient and Medieval Societies* (Washington DC: Dumbarton Oaks, 1993).

——. (ed.), *Consent and Coercion to Sex and Marriage in Ancient and Medieval Societies* (Washington DC: Dumbarton Oaks, 1993).

Laurence, Patrick, *La vie latine de sainte Mélanie / Gérontius; Edition critique, traduction et commentaire* (Jerusalem: Franciscan Printing Press, 2002).

Lelis, Arnold, Percy, William and Verstraete, Beert, *The Age of Marriage in Ancient Rome* (Lewiston: Edwin Mellen Press, 2003).

Lett, Didier, 'L'enfant dans la chrétienté. Ve–XIIIe siècles', in D. Alexandre-Bidon and D. Lett, *Les Enfants au Moyen Age. Ve–XVe siècles*, revised edn (Paris: Hachette, 1997).

Levi, Giovanni, 'Family and Kin – A Few Thoughts', *Journal of Family History* 15(4) (1990): 567–78.

——. *Inheriting Power: The Story of an Exorcist* (Chicago: University of Chicago Press, 1988).

Leyerle, Blake, 'Appealing to Children', *Journal of Early Christian Studies* 5(2) (1997), 243–70.

Lifton, Robert, *The Broken Connection: On Death and the Continuity of Life*, 3rd edn (Washington DC: American Psychiatric Press, 1996).

——. 'The Sense of Immortality: On Death and the Continuity of Life', in H. Feifel (ed.), *New Meanings of Death* (New York: McGraw-Hill, 1977).

Van der Linden, Marcel, 'Introduction', in J. Kok (ed.), *Rebellious Families. Household Strategies and Collective Action in the Nineteenth and Twentieth Centuries* (Oxford and New York: Berghahn, 2002).

Van der Linden, Marcel, 'Conclusion', in J. Kok (ed.), *Rebellious Families. Household Strategies and Collective Action in the Nineteenth and Twentieth Centuries* (Oxford and New York: Berghahn, 2002).

Louth, Andrew, 'The Literature of the Monastic Movement', in F.M. Young, L. Ayres and A. Louth (eds), *The Cambridge History of the Early Christian Literature* (Cambridge: Cambridge University Press, 2004).

MacWilliam, Janette, 'Children Among the Dead: The Influence of Urban Life on the Commemoration of Children on Tombstone Inscriptions', in S. Dixon (ed.), *Childhood, Class and Kin in the Roman World* (London and New York: Routledge, 2001).

Martin, Dale, 'Introduction', in D. Martin and P.C. Miller (eds), *The Cultural Turn in Late Ancient Studies: Gender, Asceticism, and Historiography* (Durham, NC: Duke University Press, 2005).

Martin, Dale and Miller, Patricia Cox (eds), *The Cultural Turn in Late Ancient Studies: Gender, Asceticism, and Historiography* (Durham, NC: Duke University Press, 2005).

Martindale, John (ed.), *The Prosopography of the Later Roman Empire* (*PLRE*), *vol. 2, A.D. 395–527* (Cambridge: Cambridge University Press, 1980).

Mathisen, Ralph, *Ruricius of Limoges and Friends: A Collection of Letters from Visigothic Aquitania* (Liverpool: Liverpool University Press, 1999).

Mayer, Wendy and Allen, Pauline, *John Chrysostom* (London: Routledge, 2000).

McGinn, Thomas A.J., 'Roman Children and the Law', in J. Evans Grubbs and T. Parkin with R. Bell (eds), *The Oxford Handbook of Childhood and Education in the Classical World* (Oxford: Oxford University Press, 2013).

Miller, Timothy, *The Orphans of Byzantium: Child Welfare in the Christian Empire* (Washington DC: Catholic University of America Press, 2003).

Moen, Phyllis and Wethington, Elaine, 'The Concept of Family Adaptive Strategies', *Annual Review of Sociology* 18 (1992), 233–51.

Moxnes, Halvor, 'What is Family? Problems in Constructing Early Christian Families', in H. Moxnes (ed.), *Constructing Early Christian Families. Family as Social Reality and Metaphor* (London and New York: Routledge, 1997).

——. (ed.), *Constructing Early Christian Families: Family as Social Reality and Metaphor* (London and New York: Routledge, 1997).

Mustakallio, Katariina, *Death and Disgrace: Capital Penalties with Post Mortem Sanctions in Early Roman Historiography* (Helsinki: Academia Scientiarum Fennica, 1994).

Narayanan, Vasudha, 'Renunciation and Gender Issues in the Sri Vaisnava Community', in V. L. Wimbush and R. Valantasis (eds), *Asceticism*, 2nd edn (Oxford: Oxford University Press, 2002).

Nathan, Geoffrey, *The Family in Late Antiquity: The Rise of Christianity and the Endurance of Tradition* (London and New York: Routledge, 2000).

Nicosia, Salvatore, 'Altre vie per l'immortalità nella cultura greca', in S. Beta and F. Focaroli (eds), *Vecchiaia, giuventù, immortalità: fra natura e cultura; Le maschere della persona: identità e alterità di un essere sociale* (Fiesole: Cadmo, 2009).

Nielsen, Hanne S., 'Quasi-kin, Quasi-adoption and the Roman Family', in M. Corbier (ed.), *Adoption et fosterage* (Paris: De Boccard, 2000).

North, John, 'Family Strategy and Priesthood in the Late Republic', in J. Andreau and H. Bruhns (eds), *Parenté et stratégies familiales dans l'antiquité romaine: acts de la table ronde des 2 – 4 octobre 1986* (Rome: Ecole Française de Rome, 1990).

Osiek, Carolyn, 'The Family and Early Christianity: "Family Values" Revisited', *Catholic Biblical Quarterly* 58 (1996), 1–24.

Osiek, Carolyn and Balch, David, *Families in the New Testament World: Households and House Churches* (Louisville, KY: Westminster John Knox, 1997).

Papaconstantinou, Arietta and Talbot, Alice-Mary (eds), *Becoming Byzantine: Children and Childhood in Byzantium* (Washington DC: Dumbarton Oaks Research Library and Collection, 2009).

Parkin, Tim, 'Life Cycle', in M. Harlow and R. Laurence (eds), *A Cultural History of Childhood and Family in Antiquity* (Oxford: Berg, 2010).

———. *Old Age in the Roman World: A Cultural and Social History* (Baltimore: Johns Hopkins University Press, 2003).

Patlagean, Evelyne, 'L'enfant et son avenir dans la famille byzantine (IVe–XIIe siècles)', *Annales de démographie historique* (1973), 85–93.

———. *Pauvreté économique et pauvreté sociale à Byzance 4ᵉ–7ᵉ siècles* (Paris: Mouton & EHESS, 1977).

Pesthy, Monika, 'Thecla Among the Fathers of the Church', in J. Bremmer (ed.), *The Apocryphal Acts of Paul and Thecla* (Kampen: Kok Pharos, 1996).

Plumpe, Joseph, '*Ecclesia Mater*', *Transactions of the American Philological Association* 70 (1939), 536–51.

Pölönen, Janne, 'The Division of Wealth between Men and Women in Roman Succession (c.a. 50 BC–AD 250)', in P. Setälä et al., *Women, Power and Property in Roman Empire* (Rome: Institutum Romanum Finlandiae, 2002).

Rapp, Claudia, *Holy Bishops in Late Antiquity: The Nature of Christian Leadership in an Age of Transition* (Berkeley: University of California Press, 2005).

Rawson, Beryl, *Children and Childhood in Roman Italy* (Oxford: Oxford University Press, 2003).

———. 'Death, Burial and Commemoration of Children in Roman Italy', in D. Balch and C. Osiek (eds), *Early Christian Families in Context: An Interdisciplinary Dialogue* (Grand Rapids: Eerdmans, 2003).

Rebillard, Eric, *The Care of the Dead in Late Antiquity* (Ithaca: Cornell University Press, 2009).

Ricoeur, Paul, *Interpretation Theory: Discourse and the Surplus of Meaning* (Forth Worth: Texas Christian University Press, 1976).

Rousseau, Philip, 'The Historiography of Asceticism: Current Achievements and Future Opportunities', in C. Straw and R. Lim (eds), *The Past Before Us: The Challenge of Historiographies of Late Antiquity* (Turnhout: Brepols, 2005).

———. 'The Pious Household and the Virgin Chorus: Reflections on Gregory of Nyssa's Life of Macrina', *Journal of Early Christian Studies* 13 (2005), 165–86.

———. (ed.), *A Companion to Late Antiquity* (Oxford: Oxford University Press, 2009).

Rowlandson, Jane and Takahashi, Ryosuke, 'Brother-Sister Marriage and Inheritance Strategies in Greco-Roman Egypt', *Journal of Roman Studies* 99 (2009), 104–39.

Rudolph, Richard, 'The European Family and Economy: Central Themes and Issues', *Journal of Family History* 17(2) (1992), 119–38.

Salisbury, Joyce, *Church Fathers, Independent Virgins* (London and New York: Verso, 1991).

Saller, Richard, 'Men's Age at Marriage and its Consequences for the Roman Family', *Classical Philology* 82 (1987), 21–34.

———. *Patriarchy, Property and Death in the Roman Family*, 2nd edn (Cambridge: Cambridge University Press, 1997).

———. 'The Social Dynamics of Consent to Marriage and Sexual Relations: The Evidence of Roman Comedy' in A. Laiou (ed.), *Consent and Coercion to Sex and Marriage in Ancient and Medieval Societies* (Washington DC: Dumbarton Oaks, 1993).

Salomies, Olli, 'Names and Adoption in Ancient Rome', in M. Corbier (ed.), *Adoption et fosterage* (Paris: De Boccard, 2000).

Salzman, Michele, 'Competing Claims to *Nobilitas* in the Western Empire of the Fourth and Fifth Centuries', *Journal of Early Christian Studies* 9(3) (2001), 359–85.

——. 'Elite Realities and *Mentalités*: The Making of a Western Christian Aristocracy', *Arethusa* 33 (2000), 347–62.

——. *The Making of a Christian Aristocracy: Social and Religious Change in the Western Roman Empire* (Cambridge, MA: Harvard University Press, 2002).

Sandwell, Isabella, *Religious Identity in Late Antiquity: Greeks, Jews and Christians in Antioch* (Cambridge: Cambridge University Press, 2007).

Saradi-Mendelovici, Helen, 'A Contribution to the Study of Byzantine Notarial Formulas: The *Infirmitas Sexus* of Women and the *Sc. Velleianum*', *Byzantinisches Zeitschrift* 83 (1990), 72–90.

Scheffler, Samuel, *Death and the Afterlife*, ed. Niko Kolodny (Oxford: Oxford University Press, 2013).

Scheidel, Walter, 'Roman Age Structure: Evidence and Models', *Journal of Roman Studies* 91 (2001), 1–26.

——. 'Roman Funerary Commemoration and the Age at First Marriage', *Classical Philology* 102(4) (2007), 389–402.

Schroeder, Caroline, 'Child Sacrifice in Egyptian Monastic Culture: From Familial Renunciation to Jephthah's Lost Daughter', *Journal of Early Christian Studies* 20 (2012): 269–30.

——. *Monastic Bodies: Discipline and Salvation in Shenoute of Atripe* (Philadelphia: University of Pennsylvania Press, 2007).

——. 'Children in Early Egyptian Monasticism', in Cornelia Horn and Robert Phenix (eds), *Children in Late Ancient Christianity* (Tübingen: Mohr Siebeck, 2009).

——. 'Queer Eye for the Ascetic Guy? Homoeroticism, Children, and the Making of Monks in Late Antique Egypt', *Journal of the American Academy of Religion* 77 (2009), 333–47.

Shaw, Brent, 'The Age of Roman Girls at Marriage: Some Reconsiderations', *Journal of Roman Studies* 77 (1987), 30–46.

——. 'The Family in Late Antiquity: The Experience of Augustine', *Past and Present* 115 (1987), 3–51.

——. '"With Whom I Lived": Measuring Roman Marriage', *Ancient Society* 32 (2002), 195–242.

Shneidman, Edwin, 'The Postself', in J.B. Williamson and E.S. Shneidman (eds), *Death: Current Perspectives*, 4th edn (Mountain View, CA: Mayfield, 1995).

Silvas, Anna, *The Asketikon of St Basil the Great* (Oxford: Oxford University Press, 2005).

—. *Gregory of Nyssa: The Letters. Introduction, Translation, and Commentary*, Supplements to *Vigiliae Christianae*, vol. 83 (Boston: Brill, 2007).

Sivan Hagith, 'On Hymens and Holiness in Late Antiquity. Opposition to Aristocratic Female Asceticism at Rome', *Jahrbuch für Antike und Christentum* 36 (1993), 81–93.

Smith, Daniel, 'Family Strategy: More than a Metaphor?', *Historical Methods* 20(3) (1987): 118–20.

Southon, Emma, Harlow, Mary and Callow, Chris, 'The Family in the Late Antique West (AD 400–700): A Historiographical Review', in L. Brubaker and S. Tougher (eds), *Approaches to the Byzantine Family* (Aldershot: Ashgate, 2013).

Tilley, Maureen, 'No Friendly Letters: Augustine's Correspondence with Women', in D. Martin and P.C. Miller (eds), *The Cultural Turn in Late Ancient Studies: Gender, Asceticism, and Historiography* (Durham, NC: Duke University Press, 2005).

Tilly, Louise, 'Beyond Family Strategies, What?', *Historical Methods* 20(3) (1987), 123–5.

Tilly, Louise and Scott, Joan, *Women, Work, and Family*, 2nd edn (New York: Methuen, 1987).

Toynbee, Arnold, 'Traditional Attitudes Towards Death', in A. Toynbee et al., *Man's Concern with Death* (London: Hodder & Stoughton, 1968).

Treggiari, Susan, *Roman Marriage: Iusti Coniuges from the Time of Cicero to the Time of Ulpian* (Oxford: Clarendon Press, 1991).

Trout, Dennis, *Paulinus of Nola: Life, Letters, and Poems* (Berkeley: University of California Press, 1999).

Unruh, David, 'Death and Personal History: Strategies of Identity Preservation', *Social Problems* 30(3) (1983), 340–51.

Uro, Risto, 'Ascetism and Anti-familial Language in the *Gospel of Thomas*', in H. Moxnes (ed.), *Constructing Early Christian Families. Family as Social Reality and Metaphor* (London and New York: Routledge, 1997).

—. 'Explaining Early Christian Asceticism: Methodological Considerations', in A. Mustakallio, H. Leppä and H. Räisänen (eds), *Lux Humana, Lux Aeterna: Essays on Biblical and Related Themes in Honour of Lars Aejmelaeus* (Helsinki and Göttingen: Finnish Exegetical Society and Vandenhoeck & Ruprecht, 2005).

Valantasis, Richard, 'A Theory of the Social Function of Asceticism', in V.L. Wimbush and R. Valantasis (eds), *Asceticism*, 2nd edn (Oxford: Oxford University Press, 2002).

Vasileiou, Fotis, 'The Death of the Father in Late Antique Christian Literature', in L. Brubaker and S. Tougher (eds), *Approaches to the Byzantine Family* (Aldershot: Ashgate, 2013).

Verdon, Michel, 'Virgins and Widows: European Kinship and Early Christianity', *Man* 23(3) (1988), 488–505.

Viazzo, Pier and Katherine Lynch, 'Anthropology, Family History, and the Concept of Strategy', *International Review for Social History* 47 (2002), 423–52.

Vigilant, Lee and Williamson, John, 'Symbolic Immortality and Social Theory: The Relevance of an Underutilized Concept', in C. Bryant (ed.), *The Handbook of Thanatology, Vol. 1, The Presence of Death* (Thousand Oaks, CA: Sage, 2003).

Vovelle, Michel, *La Mort et l'Occident: de 1300 à nos jours* (Paris: Gallimard, 1983).

Vuolanto, Ville, 'Children and Asceticism: Strategies of Continuity in the Late Fourth and Early Fifth Centuries', in K. Mustakallio, J. Hanska, H.-L. Sainio and V. Vuolanto (eds), *Hoping for Continuity: Childhood, Education and Death in Antiquity and the Middle Ages* (Rome: Institutum Romanum Finlandiae, 2005).

———. 'Choosing Asceticism: Children and Parents, Vows and Conflicts', in C. Horn and R. Phenix (eds), *Children in Late Ancient Christianity* (Tübingen: Mohr Siebeck, 2009).

———. 'Family Relations and the Socialization of Children in the Autobiographical Narratives of Late Antiquity', in L. Brubaker and S. Tougher (eds), *Approaches to the Byzantine Family* (Aldershot: Ashgate, 2013).

———. 'Infant Abandonment and the Christianization of Medieval Europe', in K. Mustakallio and C. Laes (eds), *The Dark Side of Childhood in Late Antiquity and the Middle Ages* (Oxford: Oxbow, 2011).

———. 'Male and Female Euergetism in Late Antiquity: A Study on Italian and Adriatic Church Floor Mosaics', in P. Setälä et al., *Women, Power and Property in the Roman Empire* (Rome: Institutum Romanum Finlandiae, 2002).

———. 'A Self-made Living Saint? Authority and the Two Families of Theodoret of Cyrrhus', in J. Ott and T. Vedriš (eds), *Saintly Bishops and Bishops' Saints* (Zagreb: Hagiotheca, 2012).

———. 'Selling a Freeborn Child: Rhetoric and Social Realities in the Late Roman World', *Ancient Society* 33 (2003): 169–207.

———. 'Women and the Property of Fatherless Children in the Roman Empire', in P. Setälä et al., *Women, Power and Property in the Roman Empire* (Rome: Institutum Romanum Finlandiae, 2002).

Wallace-Hadrill, Andrew, 'Houses and Households: Sampling Pompeii and Herculaneum', in B. Rawson (ed.), *Marriage, Divorce and Children in Ancient Rome* (Oxford: Clarendon Press, 1991).

Walsh, Patrick, *Letters of Paulinus of Nola* (Westminster, MD and London: Newman and Longmans, Green & Co, 1967).

Wemple, S. 'Consent and Dissent to Sexual Intercourse in Germanic Societies', in A. Laiou (ed.), *Consent and Coercion to Sex and Marriage in Ancient and Medieval Societies* (Washington DC: Dumbarton Oaks, 1993).

Whittaker, Charles, 'Circe's Pigs: From Slavery to Serfdom in the Later Roman World', in M. Finley (ed.), *Classical Slavery* (London: Frank Cass, 1987).

Widdicombe, Peter, *The Fatherhood of God from Origen to Athanasius* (Oxford: Oxford University Press, 1994).

Wilkinson, Kevin, 'The Elder Melania's Missing Decade', *Journal of Late Antiquity* 5(1) (2012), 166–84.

Wimbush, Vincent and Valantasis, Richard, 'Introduction', in V. Wimbush and R. Valantasis (eds), *Asceticism* (Oxford: Oxford University Press, 2002).

Wipszycka, Ewa, 'L'ascétisme féminin dans l'Égypte de l'antiquité tardive: topoi littéraires et formes d'ascèse', in H. Melaerts and L. Mooren (eds), *Le rôle et le statut de la femme en Égypte hellénistique, romaine et byzantine. Actes du Colloque international, Bruxelles – Leuven 27–29 novembre 1997* (Leuven: Peeters, 2002).

Wolf, Diane, 'Daughters, Decisions and Domination: An Empirical and Conceptual Critique of Household Strategies', *Development and Change* 21 (1990), 43–71.

Woodman, Anthony, *Rhetoric in Classical Historiography: Four Studies* (London and Sydney: Croom Helm, 1988).

Yarborough, Anne, 'Christianization in the Fourth Century: The Example of Women', *Church History* 45 (1976), 149–65.

Zamfir, Korinna, 'Men and Women in the House(hold) of God. Chrysostom's Homilies on 1 Tim 2, 8–15', *Sacra Spripta* 6(2) (2008), 144–64.

Index

Note: Page numbers followed by n. refer to footnotes.

abandonment of children 125, 131–3
    see also foundlings
Abeloitae 58, 191
Abraham 45, 55, 72, 85, 156
adoption 1, 29–33, 35–6, 133, 174n.106,
    191, 212, 217
    see also testamentary adoption
afterlife, *see* immortality
Agnes, a martyr virgin 84, 160–61
Ajax of Gaza 118n.78, 152, 189–90
Albina the Elder 74, 109, 115, 134, 148,
    187–8
Albina the Younger, mother of Melania the
    Younger 106, 115, 144, 148, 167
almsgiving, *see* benefaction
Alypius of Thagaste 71, 141
Ambrose of Milan 71, 149–50, 168
Ambrosia, a young virgin 64, 114
Ammon, Abba, an ascetic 110, 118n.80,
    161, 189
Antoninus of Fussala 114–15, 142
Antony the Great 48–9, 51, 58, 119, 127,
    152, 159
Aper and Amanda, an ascetic couple 52, 86,
    151n.16, 190
Apronianus and Avita, an ascetic couple,
    see Avita
Arjava, Antti 8, 97
Armentarius and Paulina, an ascetic couple
    191
ascetic vow 77–8, 83, 99–102, 104,
    107–23, 127, 133–6, 142–5,
    151–3, 168, 172, 180, 186–94, 201,
    210–11
    see also children, vowed to God

asceticism
    opposition to 59–61, 72, 104–13, 126,
        134–7, 151, 193, 210
    as a source of honour, *see* honour, *honor*
Asella, a Roman virgin 113, 116, 148
Avita, niece of Melania the Elder, 148, 151,
    187n.35, 190
Augustine of Hippo 98, 101, 103,
    127n.109, 141, 150, 177
aunts and uncles 107, 119n.84, 134, 148,
    153, 166, 172–4, 187, 190, 213
Auspiciola, daughter of Salvian and Palladia
    151, 190
authority
    ecclesiastical 70–75, 79–80, 86, 142,
        149–50, 165–7, 207–9
    in families 70, 74, 79–80, 104–13,
        115–29, 136, 180–81, 184, 192–3,
        210–11, 214

Bartlett, Richard 151
Basil of Caesarea 120, 149–51, 156
Basil the Elder 120, 122, 150, 156, 173
Bassula, mother-in-law of Sulpicius Severus
    78
Bauman, Zygmund 27, 223–4
benefaction 29–30, 38, 40, 50–53, 70, 73,
    76, 87, 119, 127, 137–8, 141–2,
    144, 157, 161–2, 172, 174, 180,
    197, 215–17
Blesilla, daughter of Paula the Elder 47,
    112, 115, 148, 170, 173, 187–8
Bourdieu, Pierre 22, 24, 221–2
bridal metaphors 47n.8, 57, 81–4, 88, 134,
    200, 207

Brown, Peter 7, 104, 131
burial, *see* funeral

canons of the Church councils 15, 17,
    57–8, 72–3, 125, 142, 180
celibacy of the clergy 71–3, 75, 188–9
charity, *see* benefaction
childlessness 53, 81, 87, 136, 140, 147, 172,
    177, 184–6, 188, 190–93, 216
children
    as burden 179–85
    circulation of 32, 35, 73, 103, 125,
        131–3, 144
    as consolation in death 92, 173, 178,
        195–6, 202
    death of 33, 91–2, 181–2, 184–5, 190,
        216
        see also demography
    joys of having 91, 178, 184–6, 194–6,
        202
    in monasteries 102–4, 110, 114–15,
        132, 135, 142, 145, 151–3, 181,
        192
    vowed to God 46, 64, 85, 102–3,
        115–16, 122–3, 129, 132–3,
        135–6, 151–3, 173, 181, 186–7,
        199–202, 210, 216
    see also father, fatherhood; infants;
        mother, motherhood; parents,
        obedience towards
Christianization of the Roman culture 2,
    17, 44, 62, 67–8, 80, 206–9
Church as family, *see* family, the Church as
Cicero, M. Tullius 34–5
Clark, Elizabeth 7, 215
commemoration, *see* memory
conflicts between parents and children
    42, 44, 99, 104–13, 116, 123–9,
    133–7, 210–11
    see also disinheritance
consolation, *see* children, as consolation in
    death

continuity strategies 4, 12, 25–8, 31,
    33–44, 54, 57, 75, 88–93, 151–3,
    170–78, 185, 187–8, 191–2,
    195, 198, 202–3, 206–8, 210–12,
    214–24
    see also sense of continuity
Cooper, Kate 7, 214
Copres, an ascetic monk 75
councils, ecclesiastical, *see* canons of the
    Church councils

dedication of children, *see* children, vowed
    to God; *oblatio* of children
Demetrias, an aristocratic virgin 84, 98,
    108, 115, 144, 148, 157, 167–8,
    172–3, 187
Demetrias the Elder 172–3
demography 28–9, 34–5, 96–9, 101,
    127–8, 153, 198, 201, 216, 219
discourse (as a theoretical concept) 7,
    18–19, 80, 102, 206–7
disinheritance 50, 107, 133–8, 141, 210
domus 30, 53n.42, 55–6, 212–13, 216
donations, *see* benefaction
Donatism 2, 116, 180
dowry 134–6, 179

Ecdicia, an ascetic housewife 141, 180
economic rationalism, *see* household
    economy
economic strategies 11, 20, 23–6, 29, 36,
    40–41, 138–43, 145, 169, 192,
    203n.95, 210, 212, 215–16
Emmelia, mother of Macrina and her
    siblings 109, 122, 143, 150–51,
    156, 173, 200
emotions 25–6, 34–5, 46, 49, 53–6, 63–6,
    68, 185, 207, 212–13, 215–16
enculturation, *see* socialization
Eucherius (of Lyon) and Galla, an ascetic
    couple 151, 190
Eunomia, daughter of Apronianus and
    Avita 148, 151, 187n.35

Euphrosyne of Alexandria 110
Eusebius of Bologna, friend of Ambrose of
    Milan 64, 114, 172, 186–7
Eustathians 58, 125
Eustochium, daughter of Paula the Elder
    56, 82, 106–7, 110, 115, 143, 148,
    157, 168
Evagrius Ponticus 186

Fabiola, an ascetic Roman widow 158, 167
fama, good reputation 30, 37–8, 147,
    153–6, 158, 165–76, 202, 209, 214,
    216–17, 223
family, the Church as 66, 69–77, 80, 189,
    197–8, 207–8, 217–19, 220
family of Christ 50, 52, 54, 64–5, 68,
    75–81, 85, 96, 126, 145, 147, 157,
    160, 164–5, 173, 175, 194, 202,
    208–9, 213, 216, 219
family dynamics 4–5, 11–12, 25–6, 29–43,
    95–101, 125–9, 210–22
family line, propagation of, *see* lineage
family strategies 11, 19–26, 28–9, 32, 42–3,
    96, 131, 135–7, 150–53, 178, 210,
    215–21
    see also marriage strategies
family traditions 32, 34–5, 37, 41, 45, 52,
    87, 119, 127, 147–53, 171–5, 177,
    190, 209, 217
family wealth 41, 47, 50–54, 57, 65, 87,
    133–42, 154–5, 161, 163, 177, 193,
    206, 210–13, 215–16, 220, 223–4
    see also economic strategies; household
    economy
fasting 57, 168, 190, 200–201
father, fatherhood 45–7, 49, 53–4, 63–7,
    89, 99–101, 104–12, 114–22,
    125–8, 151–2, 177, 183–4, 192–3,
    210, 214, 219–20
fatherhood, symbolic 49, 62–3, 69–79, 82,
    85–9, 149, 194, 207–8, 216–17
fertility 76, 79–81, 83–8, 93, 171–2, 175,
    185, 194, 209
Florentina, a virgin 116, 122
foundlings 32, 73, 103, 181

funeral, funerary rituals 37–41, 45, 48, 54,
    65, 155, 167, 196–8, 212, 217, 219
funerary monuments 36–7, 39–40,
    169–70, 176, 196–7, 212
Furia, an elite widow 53, 157, 172n.94, 188

gender, gender roles 6–7, 44, 56, 95, 117,
    121–2, 126–9, 172–3, 180–84,
    210–11, 213–14
Gerontius, writer of the *Life of Melania the
    Younger* 106, 162
Geruchia, a young widow in Gaul 148, 166,
    173
Gorgonia, sister of Gregory Nazianzen 55,
    155
grandparents 84–5, 92, 101, 108, 114–15,
    119, 149, 161–2, 166, 172–4, 178,
    186–8, 199, 213
Gregory the Elder (father of Gregory
    Nazianzen) 55, 72, 120–21, 155–6,
    173
Gregory Nazianzen 102, 117, 120–22, 149
Gregory of Nyssa 149–51, 156, 197
guardianship, guardians (of minors) 31, 33,
    101, 103, 111, 137–9

Helia, a virgin 87, 110n.47
Heliodorus, a friend of Jerome 55, 95n.1,
    111, 199
heresy, accusations of 57–60, 67–8
Hilarius, an ascetic invented by Jerome 119,
    168
home-asceticism 5, 56, 100, 102, 104, 123,
    128, 194–5, 201, 207
Honoratus of Arles 63, 71, 88, 149, 152,
    160, 168
honour, *honor*, through asceticism 7, 30,
    34, 52, 74–5, 79, 90, 113, 124, 144,
    150–51, 154–76, 192, 200, 203
    n.95, 208–9, 216, 218
household economy 23–5, 27, 30–31, 34,
    40, 131–8, 193, 215, 220
    see also family wealth
Hymetius, uncle of Eustochium 107
Hypatius of Bithynia, a monk 111, 118, 161

Ianuarius, a presbyter in Hippo 114, 134, 141
identity 2, 25, 27 n.65, 56, 68, 70, 74, 80, 171, 174, 202, 207–9, 213, 215, 223
imagined communities 41, 43, 208, 224
immortality 25–7, 31, 35, 38–42, 46, 57, 77, 81, 84, 89–93, 154–5, 169–70, 175–6, 178, 195–6, 198–9, 201–2, 206, 208–9, 214, 216–20, 223–4
   see also symbolic immortality
Indicia, a virgin 112–13
infants, newborn children 28, 60, 74, 77, 112, 116–17, 122, 132–3, 181–2
inheritance, inheritance strategies 23–4, 30–37, 41–2, 50–54, 65, 87, 92, 106, 114, 131–42, 171, 191, 193, 213, 216, 220–21
   see also disinheritance
inheritance, symbolic 46–7, 50–55, 69, 77, 79, 87–9, 92, 156–8, 171, 213, 216–18

Jerome 72, 140
Jerusalem 51, 54–5, 69, 78, 125, 213, 217
John Cassian 58–9
John Chrysostom 111, 121n.89, 127, 193, 197
John of Lycopolis 118 n.78, 173
Jovinianist controversy 3, 59–60
Juliana, a relative of Ambrose of Milan 122, 149–50, 200
Juliana, mother of Demetrias 108, 187, 200

kin relations beyond nuclear family 20, 28–30, 33, 35–6, 39, 41, 43, 47–9, 53–6, 63–6, 77, 79–80, 105, 107, 129, 148, 153, 160, 176, 194, 196, 210, 212–13, 219

Laeta, mother of Paula the Younger 85, 200
Laetus, a young correspondent of Augustine 65–6, 77, 111, 127, 141, 193, 201

legislation, Roman 8, 15, 17, 31–3, 53, 97, 99–101, 127, 133, 136, 138–9, 153, 177, 180, 193
Lérins, a monastic community 103, 151, 190
letter-writing 7, 15–16, 44, 63, 70, 119
Levi, Giovanni 20n.47, 24, 25n.62
Libanius 87–8
Lifton, Robert J. 26–7
lineage, family line, considerations of 29, 31–5, 41–2, 53, 62, 65, 79, 85, 87–92, 101, 117, 135, 138, 152–5, 164–5, 172–7, 184–92, 195, 198, 207–16, 219, 221
Lucinus of Baetica 52

Macrina the Elder 149, 173
Macrina the Younger 73, 98, 108–10, 120, 122, 128, 150–51, 156, 173, 194, 197
Magna, an ascetic widow 110, 118, 166
Malchus, an ascetic invented by Jerome, 110, 189n.44
Manichaeism 3n.8, 57–9, 67
Marcella, a dedicated widow 109, 115, 134, 148, 157–8, 167, 180, 187–8
Marcella, a Roman virgin 148
Marcellina, sister of Ambrose of Milan 120, 149, 186
marriage
   age at 28, 34, 96–101, 117, 127–8, 201, 211
   as a burden 181–4
   chaste 51, 57–9, 72, 78–9, 86–7, 148, 150–51, 162, 171, 189–92
   Christian conceptions of 2–3, 46–7, 57–62, 66, 90–93, 126, 178, 181–5, 213–14
   forced 104, 108–10, 113, 115, 118, 119n.84, 126, 210
   spiritual 81–8
marriage strategies 11, 29–30, 132, 209
Martin of Tours 71n.11, 110–11, 159, 167n.75

Mary, mother of Jesus, *see* Virgin Mary
meaningfulness in life 27, 93, 185, 206–7, 223–4
Melania the Elder 51, 55, 112, 124–5, 137, 148, 157, 161–2, 167, 173, 179–80, 187–8, 190
Melania the Younger 51, 98, 100, 106, 110, 115, 117, 135, 137, 144, 148, 161–2, 167, 173, 180, 188, 190–91, 200
memory, commemoration 25, 31–2, 34, 36–42, 89, 91–2, 149, 169–77, 180, 185, 192, 195–8, 202, 206–9, 212–14, 217–20, 223
mentality 7, 18, 61, 95, 214–15, 218, 222, 224
methodology 18–28, 40–44, 220, 224
migration 23, 28–9
monasteries
    and children, *see* children in monasteries
    monastic lifestyle 47–50, 52, 54–6, 65–7, 73–8, 102–4, 109–10, 112, 115, 132–3, 135–6, 142–5, 151–3, 189–90, 207–8
    monastic rules 47–8, 103, 141–2, 144–5, 153
Monica, mother of Augustine 54, 76, 122, 127n.109, 196
monuments, *see* funerary monuments
mother, motherhood 33, 46–8, 65–6, 77, 84–5, 87, 102, 105–12, 114–18, 121–2, 127, 141, 149, 151–2, 194–5, 200, 210, 219–20
motherhood, symbolic 48, 71–7, 74–8, 84–5, 88, 152, 207, 216–17

name, continuity of 1, 30–32, 35–7, 39, 41–2, 92, 170–76, 186, 197, 211–13, 217
Naomi, mother of Ruth 85, 193–4
nation state, nationalism 41, 43, 224

Naucratius, brother of Macrina 120, 150–51
Nebridius, a friend of Augustine 111, 127
Nepotian, an ascetic son of Jerome's friend 95n.1, 140, 167, 170
nobilitas, nobility 7, 30, 147–50, 154–65, 168, 171–6, 199, 208–9
Nonna, mother of Gregory Nazianzen 72, 122, 155, 173

oblatio of children 102, 132–3, 153n.24, 202
    see also children, vowed to God
old age security 23, 31–4, 39–41, 85, 192–6, 198–9, 213, 220
Olympias, an elite widow 83, 119n.84, 144, 148, 161, 181
Or, Abba, an ascetic 86
orphans, orphanhood 9, 71, 73, 91, 103, 109, 119–20, 127, 139, 181

Pacatula, an infant vowed to God 116, 121
Pachomius 48, 70, 152, 159
Paesius and Isaias, ascetic brothers 51–2, 119
Palladia, wife of Salvian 151, 190
Palladius of Galatia 161–2
Pammachius, an ascetic senator 52, 60, 87, 148, 157–8, 166, 171, 190
parents, obedience towards 55–6, 61–8, 80, 123, 126–7, 134, 181, 186
Patermutus, a monk 49, 118n.78, 121
patria 54–6, 68, 168, 213
Patricius, father of Augustine 54, 76, 177
Paul of Thebes, an ascetic invented by Jerome 113n.58, 119, 159
Paula the Elder 16, 47, 52, 55, 64–5, 107, 115, 124, 136–7, 141, 144, 148, 157, 166–7, 170, 172–3, 180, 187–8, 200
Paula the Younger 85, 116, 148, 172–3, 200
Paulina, daughter of Paula the Elder 52, 87, 108, 148, 171, 187, 190

Paulinus of Nola 15, 17, 52, 54–5, 74, 78, 98, 112, 151, 158, 166–7, 177, 190–91

Paulinus of Pella 98, 126

Pelagia of Antioch, a virgin martyr 84, 160

Peter of Sebaste 120, 150

pietas 39, 46, 55, 61–8, 73, 75, 80, 142, 154–5, 160, 196, 208, 210, 214

Pinian, husband of Melania the Younger 98, 106, 115, 117, 137, 148, 162, 167, 190–91

postmodern age 27, 223–4

Proba, Anicia Faltonia 52, 67, 90, 108, 166–7, 180, 187

Publicola, Valerius, father of Melania the Younger 106, 115, 125, 135, 157, 187

Rapp, Claudia 75

reputation, renown, *see fama*

Rufina, daughter of Paula the Elder 124, 187

Ruricius of Limoges 173–4

Rusticus, friend of Jerome 55–6

Saller, Richard 10, 61

Salonius, bishop, son of Eucherius of Lyon 79, 151

Salvian 79, 151, 190

Salvina, an aristocratic widow 148, 195

Salzman, Michelle 7, 164

Satyrus, brother of Ambrose of Milan 186

sense of continuity 26, 28, 34, 40–41, 88, 177, 214–15, 220, 223–4

sex, sexuality 2–3, 46, 68, 86, 91–2, 138, 178, 183

siblings 36, 47–8, 55, 60, 64–5, 67, 107, 112–13, 120, 126–7, 134–5, 137, 140–41, 148–53, 156, 168, 173–4, 176, 186, 199, 213

siblings, symbolic 48, 65, 69–71, 74, 76–9, 82, 88, 124, 144, 163, 194, 208–9

Simeon the Stylite 71, 168

slaves, slavery 1n.3, 32, 79, 84, 100, 142–5, 179, 182–3, 200, 205, 213

social capital, *see* symbolic capital

socialization 2, 42, 100–101, 117, 122, 196, 213–14

Stagirius, friend of John Chrysostom 112, 121

stoicism 38, 164, 206–7

strategy, as a theoretical concept, 19–24, 40–43

    see also continuity strategies; economic strategies; family strategies; marriage strategies; inheritance strategies

Sulpicius Severus 15, 52, 71n.11, 78, 112, 158

survival, material 22, 24–6, 31, 33, 40–41, 142–3, 145, 155, 213, 215, 220

symbolic capital 24–5, 40–41, 167, 169, 177, 211–15, 220

symbolic immortality 12, 26–7, 40–41

Syncletica, a virgin 109, 118n.80, 119, 126–7, 161

Synesius of Cyrene 88, 188

testamentary adoption 35–6, 171

testaments 1, 31, 35–8, 139–41, 171, 212

    see also inheritance; disinheritance

Thecla, a virgin and friend of St Paul 84, 109–10, 125, 160–61

Theodore of Tabennese 48, 110, 118, 152, 159

Theodoret of Cyrrhus 17, 102, 117, 121n.89, 122, 127, 149

Theodoret of Cyrrhus, parents of 186, 188, 200

Theonas, Abba, an ascetic 58–9, 125

Therasia, wife of Paulinus of Nola 98, 112, 167, 177, 190–91

Toxotius, son of Paula the Elder 124, 187

topoi 18, 37, 53, 109–10, 113, 119, 121, 126, 161, 168, 179, 189 uncles, *see* aunts and uncles

veiling of virgins 71–2, 75–6, 167–8
Venantius, brother of Honoratus of Arles 71, 168
Verus and Bosporia, an ascetic couple 51, 161
Vigilantius, an opponent of asceticism 60
Virgin Mary 60, 76, 113

wealth, *see* family wealth; household economy
widowhood, widows 16, 47, 52–3, 59, 64, 74, 83–6, 104, 108, 111–13, 115, 120–21, 127, 129, 132, 136–8, 153, 165–7, 172–3, 177, 179–81, 183, 185, 188, 192–4, 199, 210, 219
wills, *see* testaments